Cases That Changed Our Lives

Cases That Changed Our Lives

Ian McDougall,
General Editor
with a team of specialist contributors

Members of the LexisNexis Group worldwide

United Kingdom	LexisNexis UK, a Division of Reed Elsevier (UK) Ltd, Halsbury House, 35 Chancery Lane, LONDON, WC2A 1EL, and 4 Hill Street, EDINBURGH EH2 3JZ
Argentina	LexisNexis Argentina, BUENOS AIRES
Australia	LexisNexis Butterworths, CHATSWOOD, New South Wales
Austria	LexisNexis Verlag ARD Orac GmbH & Co KG, VIENNA
Canada	LexisNexis Butterworths, MARKHAM, Ontario
Chile	LexisNexis Chile Ltda, SANTIAGO DE CHILE
Czech Republic	Nakladatelství Orac sro, PRAGUE
France	Editions du Juris-Classeur SA, PARIS
Germany	LexisNexis Deutschland GmbH, FRANKFURT, MUNSTER
Hong Kong	LexisNexis Butterworths, HONG KONG
Hungary	HVG-Orac, BUDAPEST
India	LexisNexis Butterworths, NEW DELHI
Ireland	LexisNexis, DUBLIN
Italy	Giuffrè Editore, MILAN
Malaysia	Malayan Law Journal Sdn Bhd, KUALA LUMPUR
New Zealand	LexisNexis Butterworths, WELLINGTON
Poland	Wydawnictwo Prawnicze LexisNexis, WARSAW
Singapore	LexisNexis Butterworths, SINGAPORE
South Africa	LexisNexis Butterworths, DURBAN
Switzerland	Stämpfli Verlag AG, BERNE
USA	LexisNexis, DAYTON, Ohio

This book is published by Reed Elsevier (UK) Ltd trading as LexisNexis ('LexisNexis') and copyright in this collection is owned by LexisNexis.

A CIP Catalogue record for this book is available from the British Library.

ISBN 9 781 40575 588 7

Printed and bound in Great Britain by Hobbs the Printers Ltd, Totton, Hampshire

Visit LexisNexis UK at www.lexisnexis.co.uk

Foreword

To borrow from John Adams, the second president of the United States, we live in a world governed by laws not men. Those laws shape our lives, guide our conduct and define our relationship with the State.

In the common law world, the evolution of law through precedent can change lives in profound ways. It can even shake the foundations of Constitutions, or at least try to do so. Sir Edward Coke CJ's famous attempt in *Dr Bonham's case* 8 Coke 113 (1610) to establish the common law as the supreme law of the land, superior even to Parliament, may not have taken hold in England and Wales, but its echo can clearly be heard in Chief Justice Marshall's equally famous decision in *Marbury v Madison* 5 U.S. 137 (1803) and to a lesser extent in *Associated Provincial Picture Houses Ltd v Wednesbury Corporation* [1947] 2 All ER 680. In this it shapes the lives not just of citizens, but also of states – and not always for the good, as can be seen from the US Supreme Court's shameful decision in *Plessy v Ferguson* 163 U.S. 537 (1896). This shaping and reshaping continues even now, through decisions such as *R (Factortame Ltd and others) v Secretary of State for Transport* [1989] 2 All ER 692, *Campbell v MGN Limited* [2004] 2 All ER 680, and *R (Purdy) v Director of Public Prosecutions* [2009] 4 All ER 1147: each of which is part of an ongoing development of the common law and of our relationship with European Union and European human rights law.

On a more prosaic, but more immediate, private law level, case law shapes everyone's day-to-day life – for example, through giving birth to a general duty of care in negligence, as it did in *Donoghue (or M'Alister) v Stevenson* [1932] 1 All ER 1. Where it goes too far in any direction it can correct itself, as the law of negligence ultimately did in *Caparo Industries plc v Dickman and others* [1990] 1 All ER 568. And one can move from the prosaic, to the unhappy, albeit too common, reality that is the need to ascertain the correct approach to distributing the assets of former spouses (*White v White* [2001] 2 All ER 43), and from there to the gruesome realities of the criminal law, of which *R v Dudley and Stephens* [1881–1885] All ER 61 is a prime example. Through all these cases, the common law shapes the world in which we live.

This collection of chapters on cases that changed our lives thus provides a great insight into the common law. More importantly, the essays draw out the many different ways in which the common law shapes the world in which we live, and demonstrate its great strength, namely its ability to adapt to change and experience. In a world governed by laws not men, an understanding of the common law and its legacy is of great importance, particularly in a legal system, such as ours, where it still holds sway. This collection of essays provides a truly informative and accessible contribution to that understanding and I commend it to you.

Lord Neuberger of Abbotsbury, Master of the Rolls

July 2010

Preface

I always think it interesting to start with a seemingly grand and outlandish proposition. So let me say, right at the start, that I see this book as a celebration. It celebrates nothing less than the wonder of civilisation and the intellectual settlement that civilised humankind has made to itself. The title is unashamedly bold and the narrative that underlies the work can be founded on two bold and fundamental propositions that, I believe, are worth celebrating.

The first proposition to celebrate is civilisation itself. The second is the human condition, as expressed through the stories of human relations which prompted the cases you are about to read. It is fascinating to observe the interrelation of these two propositions through the medium of important legal decisions.

So, considering the first of our propositions, the triumph of humankind is that, in most countries around the world, humans have established a way of living based on basic rules; the rule of law. We may disagree about what those rules should say, but fundamentally human societies have them in some way or another. Totalitarian dictatorships, of course, do not often adhere to the rule of law but even they sometimes pretend that they are founded on some principle that supports their legitimacy. A foundation from the rule of law, if you like. But before passing over those statements as if unimportant truisms, let's take a moment to reflect on what we have really said.

The 'law' is an abstract, intellectual concept. We cannot touch it. We cannot taste it. We can see written representations of it in books and on computer screens. But those books are mere representations of ideas; rules intended to govern the conduct of humankind. As you will see from the following sections of this book, those ideas have expanded far beyond the simple rule making of religious history or early human civilisation. The sections of this book deal with laws affecting Public or Administrative Law, Family Law, and limits on the power of the state, to name a few. I should say, at this point, that it is not the purpose of the book to discuss the philosophy of law per se. That is a great subject that needs its own treatment. This book is a reflection, and examination, of the effects of that great intellectual settlement. This book seeks to draw out the practical effects of adherence to the principles of rule by law.

Let us also wonder at the power of thought and of word. To quote Thomas Jefferson's phrase in a letter to Thomas Paine, 'Go on doing with your pen what in other times was done with the sword'. Probably the crowning consequence of the intellectual settlement I referred to earlier is that we have elevated the power of word and thought to a pre-eminent position. The ability of great and/or powerful people to change our lives, perceptions and ways of behaving by nothing more than the power of their words and ideas is surely something to be marvelled.

Many of the great moments you will read about in various parts of this book involve nothing more than the explanation by a judge of a theme or guiding principle that will govern our lives from that moment on. Again, I ask you to stop and think about the wonder of that for a moment. That a person, with little more than the expression of ideas in a judgment on a case before them, utters words and phrases so powerful (supported, of course, by society's adherence to that procedure) that they have the effect of changing our conduct and our lives. But we are human after all and that effect is sometimes for good and, as Henry Horbaczewski so powerfully points out in Chapter 7, sometimes for ill.

But that point leads me to the second important fundamental proposition underlying this work; all of these fundamental principles have their origins in the events and acts of real human beings. The great discussions that result in the grand principles began with the acts of real human beings who all have their own story and motivations. From those, sometimes small or insignificant, events we try to learn lessons and develop rules to govern our conduct.

So another theme of this book is to remind ourselves of the stories behind the headlines. Who were the people whose lives led to important decisions affecting everyone else? Who could imagine that a snail could have such an influence on the development of the law! Who would have thought that a case of mistaken identity through the eyes of mental incapacity would produce such far-reaching consequences?

The book has been divided thematically.

Part 1 deals with the separation of powers and the constitutions of nations. *Dr Bonham's case* establishes the proposition that no one may be judge in their own cause, and is still cited in that regard today. As to the separation of powers, Mr Justice Coke's (as he then was) attempt to proclaim the supremacy of the common law over legislation in *Dr Bonham's* case ultimately failed. By contrast, in the United States the Supreme Court in *Marbury v Madison* found the power to strike down what it considered to be unconstitutional legislation. An interesting counterpoint *to Dr Bonham's case* in an environment with a written constitution.

Centuries after *Dr Bonham*, a more decisive step in the English courts' relationship with other branches of government was taken. *Associated Provincial Picture Houses Ltd v Wednesbury Corpn* is a name instantly familiar to many lawyers, to the point where the full name of the case is never considered necessary by counsel, judges or legal editors. It set the limits on the courts' supervision of the executive and remains the starting point in almost every judicial review case. A notable feature about this case, to my mind, is that it represents an example of a court both holding to itself the power to review yet setting restraining limits in its ability to do so; an attempt to strike a balance between the power of the state, and the protection of the individual by court review. Of course, whether it achieves that result is not a matter for this work.

Wednesbury was decided at a time when the Dicean view of parliamentary supremacy was widely accepted in the common law and long before Britain entered the European Union. Could those involved have ever foreseen the development of multi-national law in the supremacy of European law, as established by the *Factortame* case?

A different perspective is provided by the Australian cases reviewed by Dr Lindgren QC, where the Australian High Court found, in the Australian Constitution, an implied protection for freedom of speech, despite the Constitution lacking any equivalent to the US Bill of Rights or the European Convention on Human Rights.

The *Trial of Dr Sacheverell* has significance not just as another round in the Tory v Whig battles of old, but also for being partly responsible for the Riot Act of common parlance. The central issue in the case – whether citizens always owe obedience to lawful authority – is one that still arises in any number of different contexts, be it 'whistleblowers' disclosing public scandals or soldiers objecting to serving in particular conflicts or carrying out orders in battle. The difficult question of whether orders must always be obeyed by soldiers and, if not, the parameters within which a soldier may unilaterally decide not to follow an order is one which deserves its own book. It is a question we still grapple with today.

Plessy v Ferguson is part of the narrative of race relations in the United States which forms a central part of that nation's social and political history. Much more recently the *Mabo* case assumed similar significance in Australia.

As pointed out in the respective chapters, the toxin of *Plessy* can leave its imprint on society long after the decision is overturned. Commentators better placed than I can consider whether it has quite been expunged from the bloodstream of the United States. Whilst *Mabo,* like many cases before and since, gave rise to extreme media reaction which paid little heed to the actual legal reasoning in the judgment. As I mentioned earlier, the fact that we have achieved much by respecting the rule of law cannot detract from the fact that sometimes the courts get it wrong. It can only be hoped that, when they do, it doesn't take quite so long as it did in *Plessy* to remedy the error. I am proud that this book has not shied away from recognising these issues.

Part II considers the significance of real property to people's lives. One might say that this is one of the most fundamental areas of the human condition. Since the moment that William of Normandy first set foot on English soil and declared that the Crown owned the lot. Land Law has given rise to many issues which still affect us today. The decision in *Tulk v Moxhay*, that in certain cases a restrictive covenant can run with the land, remains as relevant to house buyers in the present day as in 1848.

A century later, in an obiter statement concerning a less glamorous property, Lord Denning in *Central London Property Trust Ltd v High Trees House Ltd* suggested that, in the right circumstances, the law would hold a person to his or her promise. Denning at the time did not suggest his statement was entirely new. Afterwards he did not suggest it was entirely obiter. One way or another, however, the case has been seen as the foundation of the doctrine of promissory estoppel, nowadays an integral part of the common law.

Part III deals with criminal cases. It seems this area tends to generate more than its fair share of *cause celebres*. We have three illustrations; two ancient and one modern. It is to be hoped that most of us will never have direct involvement with the law of insanity, necessity or criminal responsibility. However, it is surely not uncontroversial to say that the means by which any society defines a criminal, and chooses to punish them, says a very great deal indeed about that society and its values. Criminal cases, therefore, may properly be said to affect all our lives. I can certainly say they generate opinions in us all.

The first case in Part III, *M'Naghten's case*, concerned the unfortunate wood-turner who shot a civil servant, allegedly having mistaken him for the Prime Minister of the day, Sir Robert Peel. His defence, funded by a very large sum of money he had on him at the time of the attack, was based on his state of mind. The ruling, and hence M'Naghten's name itself, has framed the English law of insanity in the criminal context ever since. Somewhat ironically, it has been argued that M'Naghten was a paid assassin who invented the faux-insanity defence in order to cover his tracks but, whether we will ever really know that is moot. The fact remains that it is a great example of the thematic direction of this work; that the actions of real people generate a set of principles which ultimately govern our lives.

Most have heard of the dilemma of shipwrecked sailors eating the unfortunate cabin boy; fewer would realise that the real-life case from which it is taken, *R v Dudley and Stephens*, remains good law to this day for the proposition that necessity is no defence to murder.

Train crashes, though infrequent in the modern age, always attain considerable media coverage, and cases such as *R v Morgan* constitute modern attempts to frame fault and responsibility.

Part IV deals with what is generally, but rather unhelpfully, referred to as Civil Law. Be it in professional duties, or rights as consumers, or even relations with their physical neighbours, many legal rights and responsibilities today owe something to *Donaghue v Stevenson* in many common law jurisdictions around the world. These cases, together with the raft of cases that followed, of which *Caparo* is an important example, represents a great example of the way in which the courts have dealt with the need to develop rules which try to strike a balance between the freedom to conduct oneself and the rights of others affected by those actions.

Practising lawyers know well that legal rights are one thing, actually securing and enforcing them is another. What is a right if it cannot be suitably enforced or protected? Thus the ability to prevent defendants from dissipating assets prior to trial is of the first importance. Of the mechanisms for protecting those rights, the *Mareva* injunction (or freezing injunction to use the name given in the comically 'de-jargoned' CPR world), is sometimes referred to as the 'nuclear option' for the severity of its consequences.

New causes of action evolve infrequently and never without controversy. One of the more recent involves the right to privacy, a reflection perhaps of the rather modern notion of 'celebrity' and the ever more intrusive popular press. The litigation involving the model Naomi Campbell forms one of the landmark decisions in this developing area of the law.

In Part V, two cases are placed together as raising the most fundamental question of all: the right to life. The issues concerning that right are perhaps most acute when they concern individuals at each end of the moral spectrum, such as the convicted murderer Colin Middleton on the one hand, and the terminally ill Debbie Purdy and Diane Pretty, blameless good citizens, on the other.

All three wished to end their lives. In Middleton's case it was as a result of his depression and claimed mental illness, and the first issue concerned the extent to which the state was under a duty to prevent him killing himself since, as a prisoner, he was under the state's control. The state having failed to prevent his suicide, the second issue arose as to its obligation to carry out an investigation into the circumstances of his death.

In the tragic cases of *Purdy* and *Pretty*, each wished to be able to choose to end her life at a time and in a manner of her own choosing. Suicide was, and remains, illegal under the Suicide Act 1961. No-one, however, could have anything other than the highest sympathy for Ms Pretty or Ms Purdie in their tragic circumstances. Yet it is one thing to accept (if one does) that anyone in their position should have their wishes respected, but quite another to find a legal mechanism to allow it. It is, tragically, an issue which the courts have to grapple on a regular basis.

Part VI, returns us to the starting point of our theme for this book: the interaction of the individual with society and the state.

In years past it is probably fair to assume that any lawyer in the Western world used to living in a society based on the rule of law would never have anticipated that fundamentals such as habeas corpus, the presumption of innocence and the right to liberty would all come under close scrutiny in their own countries. These issues have, however, come into focus as governments of the day have sought to deal with the threat of international terrorism.

The first chapter in Part VI, concerning *A v SSHD*, deals with the issue of liberty for suspected terrorists. If someone cannot be returned to another country (for example because of the risk of torture), and there is insufficient evidence to charge him with any crime, most lawyers would have said that he should be released unconditionally. The furthest the state could have gone would have been to subject the suspect to police surveillance.

Following the appalling terrorist attacks in the United States in 2001, however, governments had to weigh the risk of a currently innocent man committing mass murder on a scale unprecedented in peacetime against these traditional rights to liberty. *A v SSHD* shows how the courts and Parliament attempted to respond.

Another fundamental legal concept is the more general principle of the rule of law, and in particular the independence of the prosecutorial authorities and the judiciary. In the *Corner House* case, the court found the fundamental concept of independence to have been infringed. An implied threat from foreign nationals that co-operation on terrorism would be withdrawn if the UK authorities continued with an investigation into alleged fraud was not considered a valid reason for failing to prosecute. To be told by a foreign country that unless you stop investigating us we will put your nationals into increased danger is a severe test of one's adherence to the rule of law.

On appeal, the House of Lords found the authorities had correctly taken account of the UK's international relations when exercising their discretion in deciding whether to prosecute. Many would argue that the decision was a pragmatic and realistic one. But many others would also argue that it was not the House of Lords' finest hour in the field of adherence to the rule of law.

Part VII, our final section, concerns the family. It has always been an area ripe for disagreement because this field of law, probably more than any other, is directly affected by the moral norms of society that prevail at the time. However, it is interesting to note how often crusty old middle-aged men have been at the forefront of protecting (or even creating!) rights for people who are oppressed or otherwise not fully protected. Of course, there have been many occasions where those same crusty, old middle-aged men have been reactionary blocks to developments, but then perfection is still an aspiration.

Of course, one point of contention, particularly amongst readers with legal training, will be a discussion of the cases that were not included. The consideration of what to include, and what to leave out, is always very difficult and always open to criticism. It certainly consumed a good deal of consideration and effort! What about the *Carbolic Smoke Ball* case, I hear the cry. In my defence I can only say that this book is not intended to be an encyclopaedia. It is a selection of cases that are both interesting and, I hope, are illustrative of the important themes that underlie the book. I trust the book is none the less interesting for the many cases that could have been included but were not. So, at this point, I wish to pay a special word of appreciation and thanks to all of the contributors who, sometimes at very short notice, produced exactly what I hoped they would: an interesting, opinionated and lively discussion of the Cases That Changed Our Lives.

In summary, I ask that you read these cases with renewed interest. Not only in the cases themselves, many of which will be familiar to readers already, but reread them in the knowledge that, in one way or another, they contribute to humanity's finest achievement. That these issues are settled, for good or sometimes not so good, in the context of a system based upon the rule of law is an overlooked miracle of human development. We accept the process as our mutual settlement to each other. We change those decisions in a system approved in a democratic manner (in the myriad forms that it has to offer) in the search for improvement of law that we all live under. These are things we should proclaim and proudly remember that, to paraphrase Thomas Jefferson, we now do that with the pen that we previously did with the sword.

Ian McDougall

Halsbury House

July 2010

Contributors

General Editor – General Editor

Ian McDougall

Ian McDougall is Vice President and Legal Director for LexisNexis International (LNI). Ian is responsible for management of the LNI corporate legal department and provision of legal advice across all business activities in the LNI region. Previously Ian was Legal Director at Telco Global Ltd, responsible for Legal, HR and Facilities Departments, and Group Company Secretary. Ian has also been Chief European Counsel for Hughes Electronics Inc (then a subsidiary of General Motors) and Group General Counsel for PayPoint plc, the UK's largest independent bill payments service. Ian is a Barrister and has experience of handling litigation in courts in many jurisdictions around the world and has published and lectured on various EU legal and regulatory matters.

Contributors

Janet Bazley QC

Janet Bazley QC is joint head of chambers at 1 Garden Court, a dedicated family law set based in Temple, London. She holds a law degree from the University of London and was called to the Bar in 1980, before being appointed as a Recorder in 2000 and taking silk in 2006. She sits on the Law Reform Committee of the Bar Council, for whom she regularly writes responses to consultations by the Ministry of Justice, and is a member of the Family Law Bar Association. She is the joint author of the book *Money Laundering for Lawyers*, published by LexisNexis, and is a contributor to *Halsbury's Laws of England*. She is the editor and lead author of the 1 Garden Court book *Applications under Schedule 1 of the Children Act 1989* to be published in September 2010.

John Cooper QC LLB (Hons), FRSA

John Cooper QC is a leading criminal and human rights barrister practising from 25 Bedford Row. He has appeared in many of the leading cases in the last decade and was shortlisted as Human Rights Barrister of the Year in 2008. A former lawyer at Clifford Chance, John broadcasts and writes regularly, having presented a number of documentaries on the law. He can be read most weeks in *The Observer* and his books include an influential text on *Article 3, Torture*, cited recently in the Supreme Court. His fictional work has been widely produced on the BBC, ITV and at The Royal Court Theatre, London.

Jeremy Dein QC

Jeremy Dein QC is a tenant at 25 Bedford Row. He was called to the Bar in 1982. He has a criminal defence practice and has defended in all areas of crime and specialises in murder trials. He was appointed as a Recorder in 2004.

Gerard Forlin QC

Gerard Forlin QC is a barrister at 2–3 Gray's Inn Square. He acted for the drivers in the Watford, Southall and Paddington train crashes. He was also involved in the Teebay and Hatfield train disasters and acted for Mr Morgan in the 2007 successful appeal. He has acted in many of the most important related cases in recent times. www.gerardforlin.com.

Andrew Goddard QC

Andrew Goddard QC was called to the Bar in 1985. He is a tenant at Atkin Chambers and specialises in the law of commercial obligations and professional negligence, particularly in the context of disputes concerning major construction and engineering contracts and IT projects. He has had much involvement in energy, infrastructure and telecommunications disputes and has acted for main contractors, sub-contractors, professionals and employers, including national and foreign governments. He is also a member of the Attorney General's panel of Special Advocates for the Special Immigration Appeals Commission. Andrew was recently admitted on an ad hoc basis to the Bar of Hong Kong and spent a considerable period during 2009 in Trinidad and Tobago acting as counsel in a Public Enquiry and associated Judicial Review proceedings. Andrew is listed as a leading silk by The Legal 500 (Construction, Commercial Arbitration and Information Technology), Chambers Guide to the UK Legal Profession (Construction, Information Technology and International Arbitration), Chambers Guide to Asia (Arbitration) and Chambers Global Guide (Construction).

Marie-Thérèse Groarke

Marie-Thérèse Groarke graduated with a 2:1 in Law from the University of Reading in 2003 and was called to the Bar in 2006. She works at LexisNexis as a Senior Editor for the *All England Law Reporter*. She has also worked as a Senior Editor for *News and Current Awareness*. Marie-Thérèse regularly writes articles for a number of publications such as: *Current Awareness*, *Legal News Analysis*, the *Personal Injury Newsletter*, *Butterworths LawLeader* and *Criminal Law & Justice Weekly*. Marie-Thérèse has also worked with the *New Law Journal* on their Twitter blog.

Philippa Harris

Philippa Harris is a tenant at Hardwicke Buildings. She attended Bristol University where she graduated with a First Class Honours Degree in Law in 2003. She was called to the Bar in 2005. Philippa has a broad civil and commercial practice. She undertakes work in all aspects of property and private client including real property; commercial and residential landlord and tenant; property-related insolvency issues; trusts of land disputes; professional negligence; inheritance and probate and matrimonial finance.

Henry Z Horbaczewski

Henry Z Horbaczewski is Senior Vice President and General Counsel of Reed Elsevier Inc, at its headquarters in New York City. Reed Elsevier Inc is the principal US subsidiary of the Reed Elsevier group, an international publisher and provider of information services for science, technology and medicine, education, business and the legal profession. Mr Horbaczewski practices commercial, intellectual property and corporate transactional law. Prior to joining Reed Elsevier, he was a partner at Coudert Brothers in New York City. Mr Horbaczewski has written and been a speaker on the subject of intellectual property law before the American Bar Association, the Association of American Publishers, American Business Media and the International Publishers Association. He received his JD in 1975 from Harvard University, and his BA, magna cum laude, in 1972 from Harvard College, where he was Phi Beta Kappa. He is admitted to the Bars of New York and Massachusetts.

Alexander Horne

Alexander Horne is an employed barrister at the House of Commons. He was called to the Bar by Lincoln's Inn in 1999. In 2009, he completed an LLM (Distinction) at the University of London (Birkbeck) and is now undertaking a PhD, part-time, at Queen Mary, University of London. He has also acted as a consultant for the Centre for Defence Studies, King's College London, lecturing on the interaction between law and counter-terrorism policy. Alexander currently works at the Home Affairs Research Section in the House of Commons, where he has been the senior legal researcher on issues relating to public law, human rights and counter-terrorism since 2006. Previously, following a short spell at city based law firm, Kingsford, Stacey and Blackwell, he spent several years as a law reporter for the *All England Law Reports*. He was appointed as the principal legal adviser to the (then) House of Commons Select Committee on Constitutional Affairs in 2003, where he worked until 2006.

Dr Jo Hunt

Dr Jo Hunt is a Senior Lecturer at Cardiff Law School, where her teaching and research interests lie primarily in the field of EU law and governance. She is the co-author (with Jo Shaw and Chloe Wallace) of *Economic and Social Law of the European Union* (Palgrave, 2007), and numerous journal articles. Her current research looks at regionalism and decentralisation within the framework of the European Union. She has degrees from the Universities of Southampton, Keele and Leeds.

Jennifer James

Jennifer James was admitted to the Roll of Solicitors in 1992 and since 2002 has sat as a Deputy Judge in the Senior Court Costs Office. She has practised as a Costs Draftsman in Sydney, Australia, and is a Fellow of the ALCD. Jennifer was admitted to practise law in the state of New York, USA in 2007. Since 2007, Jennifer has taught on the civil side of the Bar Vocational Course at the College of Law in London Bloomsbury. She has also been the author of 'The Insider' a humorous column in the *New Law Journal*, for the past decade. Her hobbies include stand-up comedy, cartooning and book illustration.

Stephen Jarmain

Stephen Jarmain is a junior barrister at 1 Garden Court. He holds a degree in Psychology from the University of Reading, a Postgraduate Diploma in Law from City University and a Practice Diploma in International Human Rights Law and Practice from the College of Law. He was called to the Bar in 2005 and is a member of the Family Law Bar Association and the International Society for Family Law. He is a contributor to the *Family Law Journal*, writes case summaries for *FamilyLawWeek* and the book *Applications under Schedule 1 of the Children Act 1989*(to be published in September 2010).

Richard de Lacy QC

Richard de Lacy QC has been in practice at the Chancery and Commercial Bar since 1978. He has wide international experience of litigation and arbitration in relation to property, companies, insolvency, and contractual disputes. He is a Fellow of the Chartered Institute of Arbitrators and one of the Serious Fraud Office's approved leading counsel.

The Hon Kevin Edmund Lindgren QC

Kevin Edmund Lindgren QC is a recently retired Judge of the Federal Court of Australia. At the time of his appointment to the Federal Court in July 1994, he was practising as Queen's Counsel at the Sydney Bar, mainly in the commercial law area. While on the Court, Dr Lindgren was the President of the Copyright Tribunal of Australia (2000–2007) and a member of the Corporations, Patents, Tax and Competition Law Panels in the NSW District Registry of the Court. He is the author of several books and some hundreds of articles and conference papers on commercial law subjects. Since retirement at the mandatory retirement age of 70 years, Dr Lindgren currently serves temporarily as an Acting Judge of the Supreme Court of NSW and Acting Judge of Appeal in the NSW Court of Appeal. He is a Foundation Fellow of the Australian Academy of Law, Adjunct Professor of Law at the University of Sydney and the University of Technology, Sydney, and Conjoint Professor of Law at the University of Newcastle.

Paul Lowenstein QC

Paul Lowenstein QC is a barrister at 3 Verulam Buildings. He is a specialist in commercial, financial and business litigation and advisory work. In the Legal 500 directory for 2009–10, Paul is listed as a Leading New Commercial Silk and is picked out for particular mention in the London Bar Overview as being an example of 3 Verulam Buildings' ' . . . ability to deliver consistently high-quality advice on commercial disputes from a user-friendly range of counsel'. In Chambers & Partners 2010, Paul is listed as a Leading New Silk in Commercial Dispute Resolution, where he is described as being 'very useful and very sensible'; in Media and Entertainment for being 'extremely effective and user-friendly' and 'a growing authority in the computer games sector' and in Telecommunications where the editors comment that: 'the clarity of advice and decisive nature of his advocacy earn Paul Lowenstein QC wide market kudos. Clear, concise and decisive, he is particularly effective in court and handles matters of great significance'.

Robert Pearce QC

Robert Pearce QC practices at the Chancery Bar in London. His main fields of practice are property law, private client and charities. He is also a contributing editor the annual *The Civil Court Practice* (the 'Green Book') published by LexisNexis.

David Perry QC

David Perry QC is a tenant at 6 King's Bench Walk. He was called to the Bar in 1980 and specialises in criminal law, extradition and judicial review. In 2001, David was appointed as Senior Treasury Counsel. In 2003, he was appointed as a Deputy High Court Judge. During his time as Treasury Counsel he prosecuted a wide range of cases and frequently appeared in the Court of Appeal and the House of Lords. For example, he appeared on behalf of prosecution in *R v Abu Hamza* and *R v Keogh and O'Connor* (an Official Secrets Act prosecution which followed the leak of a secret memorandum relating to a meeting between President Bush and the Prime Minister Blair). David is also an advisory editor for *Blackstone's Criminal Practice* and the *Criminal Law Review*.

John Randall QC MA (Cantab)

John Randall QC tudied law at Jesus College, Cambridge before being called to the Bar in 1978. Since 1980 he has been a practising barrister on the Midland Circuit, and is a member and former head of St Philips Chambers, Birmingham. John principally specialises in commercial and chancery work, and took silk in 1995. He is a bencher of Lincoln's Inn, and sits as a Recorder and Deputy High Court Judge. He is a Visiting Fellow at the Faculty of Law of the University of New South Wales, Sydney, and has been called to the bars of New South Wales (1979) and Western Australia (2001).

Paul Reed QC

Paul Reed QC is a tenant at Hardwicke Buildings. He was called to the Bar in 1988 and specialises in commercial, construction and engineering, professional negligence and insurance. Paul is also a postgraduate tutor and occasional lecturer in construction law and arbitration at King's College and an experienced mediation advocate who also acts as a commercial arbitrator and mediator.

Heather Rogers QC

Heather Rogers QC specialises in media law, human rights and public law at Doughty Street Chambers. Recent cases include *British Chiropractic Association v Singh* (2010) (for BCA), *Michael Napier & Irwin Mitchell v Pressdram Limited* (2009) (for *Private Eye*), *Harper v Seaga* (Privy Council) (2009), and *Inner West London Assistant Deputy Coroner v Channel 4 Television Corpn* (2008). Notable libel cases include defending Penguin Books against David Irving and acting for George Galloway MP and Roman Polanski. She is a trustee of ARTICLE 19 and co-author of *Duncan & Neill on Defamation* (3rd edn, 2009, LexisNexis).

Dr Craig Rose

Dr Craig Rose is the Publisher of Reports and Statutes at LexisNexis UK. A member of the Bar of England and Wales, he was the Editor of the *All England Law Reports* from 1999–2003 and the Editor-in-Chief from 2003–2006. After graduating from Bristol University in 1985 with First Class Honours in History, he did research at Cambridge University where he was awarded a PhD in 1989 and was successively a Research Fellow of Selwyn College and Darwin College. He is the author of *England in the 1690s: Revolution, Religion and War* (1999, Blackwell, Oxford), and a number of articles on late seventeenth and early eighteenth-century English history.

Jo Sidhu

Jo Sidhu graduated from the University of Oxford in Philosophy, Politics and Economics. He subsequently obtained a masters degree in the Politics of the World Economy at the London School of Economics. Before being called to the Bar in 1993 he worked as a senior researcher for the BBC, a policy advisor for a local authority, a tutor in economics and as a voluntary caseworker for a community group in Southall where he was raised. He was an elected Councillor with the London Borough of Ealing and has served as the chair of his primary school governing body for the last fourteen years. Called to the Bar in 1993, he is a leading specialist in criminal law with particular expertise in terrorism cases, homicides, and conspiracies involving frauds, robberies and drugs trafficking. He also serves as vice-chair of the Equality and Diversity Committee of the Bar Council and is a member of the Criminal Bar Association.

Kenneth R Thompson II

Kenneth R Thompson II is Senior Vice President and Global Chief Legal Officer of the LexisNexis Group. As LexisNexis Global Chief Legal Officer, Ken Thompson has transformed the Legal Department into a global legal services organisation, trusted by leadership and deeply embedded in the company's day-to day operations. In 2001, Ken joined LexisNexis as a partner from a Cincinnati law firm. He has served as LexisNexis Group Chief Legal Officer since 2005. In his role as Global CLO, Ken continues to focus on his core areas of expertise: intellectual property, acquisitions and divestiture, anti-trust, corporate social responsibility and Internet security issues. As a member of the LexisNexis Group Management Committee, Ken leads and advises at the highest levels of the company. He also remains the principal legal advisor to the LexisNexis Global Chief Executive Officer. Ken has a BA degree from Capital University and a JD from the University of Cincinnati College of Law. His broad expertise makes him an authoritative and highly engaging public speaker on a range of issues: intellectual property, acquisitions and divestitures, anti-trust, corporate social responsibility and Internet security. Ken is also active in the IBA, the ABA, ACC and other professional organisations. Ken is also a member of the Advisory Board for Corporate Pro Bono.

Lynne Townley

Lynne Townley is a practising barrister who was called to the Bar in October 1996. She practised until March 1998, when she joined LexisNexis and became an editor on the *Law Reports of the Commonwealth*. From April 2000 to April 2003 she was a Law Reporter in the Court of Appeal (Criminal Division) for the *All England Reporter* service. Thereafter she returned to the Bar. She is the author of a number of publications including *Blackstone's Book of Moots* (co-authored with Professor Tim Kaye, 1996, OUP), and *Forensic Practice in Criminal Cases* (co-authored with District Judge Roger Ede, 2004, The Law Society). Lynne is a board member of the Transformative Justice Forum of Race on the Agenda and is a trustee of Save Your Rights, a charity promoting human rights particularly around the issue of forced marriage.

Dr Karen Widdicombe

Dr Karen Widdicombe read English at St Catherine's College, Oxford and received her doctorate from the University of Toronto. In 1991 she was admitted as a solicitor and practised as a private client lawyer. Since 2003 she has been the Editor of the *All England Law Reports*.

His Honour Judge Stephen Wildblood QC

Stephen Wildblood QC sits as a Circuit Judge in Devon and Cornwall. He has written extensively in many areas of family law. He practised at the family Bar for 27 years (of which nine of those years were as a QC).

James Wilson

James Wilson BA LLB (Hons) is the Managing Editor of *All England Reporter*, LexisNexis. He has previously worked as a commercial litigation solicitor in London and New Zealand, and is a barrister and solicitor of the High Court of New Zealand. He has written articles for the *New Law Journal* and a number of legal websites. James wrote the chapter introductions for this volume.

Contents

Foreword v

Preface vii

Contributors xiii

Table of Cases xxv

PART I PUBLIC LAW

1 Changing Perspectives on the Constitution and the Courts: Dr Bonham's Case *by Andrew Goddard QC and Marie-Thérèse Groarke* 3

2 What Breathes Life into the US Constitution? Marbury v Madison *by Kenneth R Thompson II* 13

3 Associated Provincial Picture Houses Ltd v Wednesbury Corporation *by Jennifer James* 21

4 The Factortame Litigation: Factortame Ltd v Secretary of State for Transport *by Dr Jo Hunt* 27

5 An Implied Constitutional Freedom of Speech in Australia *by The Hon Dr Kevin Lindgren QC* 37

6 A Right to Resist? The Trial of Dr Sacheverell *by Dr Craig Rose* 51

7 'The Evil That Men Do Lives After Them': Plessy v Ferguson *by Henry Horbaczewski* 59

8 Native title in Australia: Mabo v The State of Queensland *by The Hon Dr Kevin Lindgren QC* 69

PART II LAND LAW

9 Tulk v Moxhay *by Richard de Lacy QC* 81

10 A Promise is a Promise: Central London Property Trust Ltd v High Trees House Ltd *by Robert Pearce QC* 91

PART III CRIMINAL LAW

11	Legal Insanity: The Enduring Legacy of Daniel M'Naghten's Case *by Jeremy Dein QC and Jo Sidhu*	103
12	Death on the High Seas: The Cabin Boy, the Cannibals and the Criminal Law: R v Dudley and Stephens *by David Perry QC*	113
13	Red Light Spells Danger: R v Morgan *by Gerard Forlin QC*	121

PART IV CIVIL LAW

14	The Snail in the Bottle: Donoghue v Stevenson *by Paul Reed QC and Philippa Harris*	131
15	Legal Celebrity or Jurisprudential Substance? Caparo Industries plc v Dickman *by John Randall QC*	139
16	'As If By A Side-Wind . . . ': The Mareva/Freezing Order Jurisdiction in England *by Paul Lowenstein QC*	153
17	From Catwalk to Courtroom: Public Figure, Private Life: Naomi Campbell v MGN Limited *by Heather Rogers QC*	163

PART V THE RIGHT TO LIFE

18	'How . . . the deceased came by his death': R (on the application of Middleton) v West Somerset Coroner *by Dr Karen Widdicombe*	175
19	How the Law Lords Made Way for a Compassionate Clarification of the Law on Assisting Suicide: R (on the Application of Purdy) v Director of Public Prosecutions *by Lynne Townley*	183

PART VI THE STATE AND TERRORISM IN THE TWENTY-FIRST CENTURY

20	The Courts and Counter-Terrorism – Asserting the Rule of Law? A v Secretary of State for the Home Department *by Alexander Horne*	195
21	The Day We Sold the Rule of Law: R (on the Application of Corner House Research) v Director of Serious Fraud Office *by John Cooper QC*	207

PART VII FAMILY LAW

22 Is it that simple? Stack v Dowden and Buying a House Together *by His Honour Judge Stephen Wildblood QC* 219

23 An Ordinary Tale of Farming Folk? White v White and its legacy *by Janet Bazley QC and Stephen Jarmain* 227

24 Gillick and the Dwindling Right of Parental Authority: Gillick v West Norfolk and Wisbech Area Health Authority *by Janet Bazley QC and Stephen Jarmain* 235

Index 245

Table of Cases

References in bold indicate the number of the chapter wherein the case is expounded

A

A (children) (conjoined twins: surgical separation), Re [2001] Fam 147, [2000] 4 All ER 961, [2001] 2 WLR 480, [2000] 3 FCR 577, [2001] 1 FLR 1, [2001] Fam Law 18, 57 BMLR 1, 9 BHRC 261, CA 12.9

A v Secretary of State for the Home Department [2004] UKHL 56, [2005] 2 AC 68, [2005] 3 All ER 169, [2005] 2 WLR 87, [2005] NLJR 23, (2004) Times, 17 December, 149 Sol Jo LB BHRC 496, [2005] 5 LRC 34, [2004] All ER (D) 271 (Dec) .... 4.4, **Ch 20**, 20.1, 20.3, 20.4, 20.5

A v Secretary of State for the Home Department (No 2) [2005] UKHL 71, [2006] 2 AC 221, [2006] 1 All ER 575, [2005] NLJR 1924, (2005) Times, 9 December, 19 BHRC 441, [2006] 4 LRC 110, [2005] All ER (D) 124 (Dec) 20.2

A v United Kingdom (Application 3455/05) (2009) 49 EHRR 625, (2009) Times, 20 February, 26 BHRC 1, [2009] ECHR 3455/05, [2009] All ER (D) 203 (Feb), ECtHR 20.4

APESCO v EC Commission: 207/86 [1988] ECR 2151, [1989] 3 CMLR 687, ECJ 4.2

Abbott v Sullivan [1952] 1 KB 189, [1952] 1 All ER 226, [1951] 2 Lloyd's Rep 573, 96 Sol Jo 119, [1952] 1 TLR 133, CA 1.4

Ajayi (t/a Colony Carrier Co) v RT Briscoe (Nigeria) Ltd [1964] 3 All ER 556, [1964] 1 WLR 1326, 108 Sol Jo 857, PC 10.7

Algemene Transport-en Expeditie Onderneming van Gend en Loos NV v Nederlandse Belastingadministratie: 26/62 [1963] ECR 1, [1963] CMLR 105, ECJ 4.3

American Cyanamid Co v Ethicon Ltd [1975] AC 396, [1975] 1 All ER 504, [1975] 2 WLR 316, [1975] FSR 101, [1975] RPC 513, 119 Sol Jo 136, HL 4.3, 16.4

Anisminic Ltd v Foreign Compensation Commission [1969] 2 AC 147, [1969] 1 All ER 208, [1969] 2 WLR 163, 113 Sol Jo 55, HL 1.6

Anns v Merton London Borough Council [1978] AC 728, [1977] 2 All ER 492, [1977] 2 WLR 1024, 75 LGR 555, 141 JP 526, 121 Sol Jo 377, 5 BLR 1, 243 Estates Gazette 523, 591, [1977] JPL 514, HL 14.9, 15.4, 15.5, 15.7, 15.13

Ashworth Hospital Authority v MGN Ltd [2002] UKHL 29, [2002] 4 All ER 193, [2002] 1 WLR 2033, 12 BHRC 443, [2003] IP & T 601, 67 BMLR 175, (2002) Times, 1 July, [2003] 2 LRC 431, [2002] All ER (D) 234 (Jun) 16.3

Asociacion provincial de Armadores de buques de pesca de Gran Sol de Pontevedra (ARPOSOL) v EC Council: 55/86 [1988] ECR 13, [1989] 2 CMLR 508, ECJ 4.2

Associated Provincial Picture Houses Ltd v Wednesbury Corpn [1948] 1 KB 223, [1947] 2 All ER 680, 45 LGR 635, 112 JP 55, [1948] LJR 190, 92 Sol Jo 26, 177 LT 641, 63 TLR 623, CA .... **Ch 3**, 3.3, 3.5, 3.6, 21.6

Austerberry v Oldham Corpn (1885) 29 Ch D 750, 49 JP 532, 55 LJ Ch 633, 33 WR 807, 53 LT 543, 1 TLR 473, CA 9.7, 9.8

Australian Capital Television Pty Ltd v Commonwealth of Australia (1992) 177 CLR 106, 108 ALR 577, Aus HC 5.1, 5.3, 5.4, 5.6

B

Babanaft International Co SA v Bassatne [1990] Ch 13, [1989] 1 All ER 433, [1989] 2 WLR 232, [1988] 2 Lloyd's Rep 435, 11 LDAB 175, 133 Sol Jo 46, [1989] 4 LS Gaz R 43, [1988] NLJR 203, CA 16.5

Baird Textiles Holdings Ltd v Marks & Spencer plc [2001] EWCA Civ 274, [2002] 1 All ER (Comm) 737, [2001] All ER (D) 352 (Feb) 10.10
Banque Bruxelles Lambert SA v Eagle Star Insurance Co Ltd. See South Australia Asset Management Corp v York Montague Ltd
Beddow v Beddow (1878) 9 Ch D 89, 47 LJ Ch 588, 26 WR 570 .... 16.3
Berry v Berry [1929] 2 KB 316, 98 LJKB 748, [1929] All ER Rep 281, 141 LT 461, 45 TLR 524 .... 10.3
Birmingham and District Land Co v London and North Western Rly Co (1888) 40 Ch D 268, [1886–90] All ER Rep 620, 60 LT 527, CA 10.6
Bonham's (Dr) Case (1610) 8 Co Rep 113a, 77 ER 646 .... **Ch 1**, 1.1, 1.2, 1.4, 1.5
Bowman v Middleton 1 SCL (1 Bay) 93 (1792) 1.5
Brasserie du Pecheur SA v Germany: C-46/93 [1996] QB 404, [1996] ECR I-1029, [1996] All ER (EC) 301, [1996] 2 WLR 506, [1996] 1 CMLR 889, [1996] IRLR 267, ECJ 4.3
Bratty v A-G for Northern Ireland [1963] AC 386, [1961] 3 All ER 523, [1961] 3 WLR 965, 46 Cr App Rep 1, 105 Sol Jo 865, HL 11.7
Brown v Board of Education 347 U.S. 483 (1954) 7.1, 7.4, 7.6
Browne (Lord) of Madingley v Associated Newspapers Ltd [2007] EWCA Civ 295, [2008] QB 103, [2007] 3 WLR 289, [2007] NLJR 671, [2007] EMLR 538, [2007] All ER (D) 12 (May) 17.6
Bush (George W) and Cheney (Richard) v Gore (Albert), Junior 531 U.S. 98, 121 S. Ct. 525, 148 L. Ed. 2d 388, 2000 U.S. LEXIS 8430, 69 U.S.L.W. 4029, 2000 Cal. Daily Op. Service 9879, 2000 Colo. J. C.A.R. 6606, 14 Fla. L. Weekly Fed. S 26 .... 2.1, 2.4

C

Caldwell v Texas 137 U.S. 692 (1891) 7.3
Calvin's Case (1608) 7 Co Rep 1a, Jenk 306, sub nom Union of Scotland and England Case Moore KB 790, sub nom Postnati Case 2 State Tr 559, Ex Ch 1.4
Campbell v Frisbee [2002] EWCA Civ 1374, [2003] ICR 141, [2003] IP & T 86, 146 Sol Jo LB 233, [2003] EMLR 76, [2002] All ER (D) 178 (Oct) 17.1, 17.3
Campbell (Naomi) v MGN Ltd [2005] UKHL 61, [2005] 4 All ER 793, [2005] 1 WLR 3394, [2006] IP & T 54, [2005] 42 LS Gaz R 23, [2005] NLJR 1633, 21 BHRC 516, [2006] 1 Costs LR 120, [2006] EMLR 1, [2005] All ER (D) 215 (Oct) 17.7
Campbell v Mirror Group Newspapers Ltd [2002] EWHC 499 (QB), [2002] IP & T 612, (2002) Times, 29 March, [2002] EMLR 10, [2002] All ER (D) 448 (Mar); revsd [2002] EWCA Civ 1373, [2003] QB 633, [2003] 1 All ER 224, [2003] 2 WLR 80, [2002] IP & T 944, (2002) Times, 16 October, [2003] EMLR 39, [2002] All ER (D) 177 (Oct); revsd [2004] UKHL 22, [2004] 2 AC 457, [2004] 2 All ER 995, [2004] 2 WLR 1232, [2004] IP & T 764, [2004] 21 LS Gaz R 36, [2004] NLJR 733, (2004) Times, 7 May, 148 Sol Jo LB 572, 16 BHRC 500, [2005] 1 LRC 397, [2004] All ER (D) 67 (May) .... **Ch 17**, 17.1, 17.2, 17.3, 17.4, 17.5, 17.6, 17.8, 17.10
Candler v Crane Christmas & Co [1951] 2 KB 164, [1951] 1 All ER 426, 95 Sol Jo 171, [1951] 1 TLR 371, CA 15.13
Caparo Industries plc v Dickman [1988] BCLC 387; revsd [1989] QB 653, [1989] 1 All ER 798, [1989] 2 WLR 316, [1989] BCLC 154, 4 BCC 144, 133 Sol Jo 221, [1989] 11 LS Gaz R 44, [1988] NLJR 289, CA; revsd [1990] 2 AC 605, [1990] 1 All ER 568, [1990] 2 WLR 358, [1990] BCLC 273, [1990] BCC 164, 11 LDAB 563, 134 Sol Jo 494, [1990] 12 LS Gaz R 42, [1990] NLJR 248, [1991] LRC (Comm) 460, HL .. 14.9, **Ch 15**, 15.1, 15.2, 15.3, 15.5, 15.6, 15.7, 15.8, 15.9, 15.10, 15.11, 15.12, 15.13, 15.14
Cardile v LED Builders Pty Ltd (1999) 198 CLR 381 .... 16.3
Central London Property Trust Ltd v High Trees House Ltd [1947] KB 130, [1956] 1 All ER 256n, [1947] LJR 77, 175 LT 332, 62 TLR 557 ... **Ch 10**, 10.1, 10.4, 10.6, 10.7, 10.8, 10.9, 10.10, 10.11
Chahal v United Kingdom (Application 22414/93) (1996) 23 EHRR 413, (1996) Times, 28 November, 1 BHRC 405, [1996] ECHR 22414/93, ECtHR 20.1
Charman v Charman [2007] EWCA Civ 503, 9 ITELR 913, [2007] 2 FCR 217, [2007] 1 FLR 1246, [2007] Fam Law 682, [2007] NLJR 814, 151 Sol Jo LB 710, [2007] All ER (D) 425 (May) 23.5
City of London v Wood (1701) 12 Mod Rep 669 .... 1.4

Civil Rights Cases 109 U.S. 3 (1883) 7.3
Collier v P & M J Wright (Holdings) Ltd [2007] EWCA Civ 1329, [2008] 1 WLR 643, [2007] BPIR 1452, [2007] All ER (D) 233 (Dec) 10.9
Colt v Glover. See Commendam Case, Colt and Glover v Bishop of Coventry and Lichfield
Colt's Case. See Commendam Case, Colt and Glover v Bishop of Coventry and Lichfield
Combe v Combe [1951] 2 KB 215, [1951] 1 All ER 767, 95 Sol Jo 317, [1951] 1 TLR 811, CA 10.7, 10.10
Commendam Case, Colt and Glover v Bishop of Coventry and Lichfield (1617) Hob 140, Moore KB 898, sub nom Colt v Glover 1 Roll Rep 451, sub nom Colt's Case Jenk 300, Ex Ch 1.1
Cooke v Chilcott (1876) 3 Ch D 694, 34 LT 207 .... 9.4, 9.5, 9.7
Costa v ENEL: 6/64 [1964] ECR 585, [1964] CMLR 425, ECJ 4.3, 4.4
Crabb v Arun District Council [1976] Ch 179, [1975] 3 All ER 865, [1975] 3 WLR 847, 119 Sol Jo 711, CA 22.8
Cream Holdings Ltd v Banerjee [2004] UKHL 44, [2005] 1 AC 253, [2004] 4 All ER 617, [2004] 3 WLR 918, [2005] IP & T 101, [2004] NLJR 1589, (2004) Times, 15 October, 148 Sol Jo LB 1215, 17 BHRC 464, [2005] EMLR 1, [2004] All ER (D) 182 (Oct) 17.6
Customs and Excise Comrs v Barclays Bank plc [2006] UKHL 28, [2007] 1 AC 181, [2006] 4 All ER 256, [2006] 2 All ER (Comm) 831, [2006] 3 WLR 1, [2006] 2 Lloyd's Rep 327, [2006] NLJR 1060, (2006) Times, 22 June, 150 Sol Jo LB 859, [2007] 1 LRC 566, [2006] All ER (D) 215 (Jun) 15.1, 15.7, 15.12, 15.13

D

D & C Builders Ltd v Rees [1966] 2 QB 617, [1965] 3 All ER 837, [1966] 2 WLR 288, 109 Sol Jo 971, CA 10.7, 10.8, 10.9
Dadourian Group International Inc v Simms [2006] EWCA Civ 399, [2006] 3 All ER 48, [2006] 1 All ER (Comm) 709, [2006] 1 WLR 2499, [2006] 2 Lloyd's Rep 354, (2006) Times, 23 May, [2006] All ER (D) 143 (Apr) 16.5
Daniel v Stepney (1874) LR 9 Exch 185, 22 WR 662, Ex Ch 9.4
Davis v Radcliffe [1990] 2 All ER 536, [1990] 1 WLR 821, [1990] BCLC 647, 134 Sol Jo 862, 1078, [1990] 19 LS Gaz R 43, PC 15.13
Day v Savadge (1614) Hob 85, 80 ER 235 .... 1.4
Derby & Co Ltd v Weldon [1990] Ch 48, [1989] 1 All ER 469, [1989] 2 WLR 276, [1989] 1 Lloyd's Rep 122, 133 Sol Jo 83, [1989] 6 LS Gaz R 43, [1988] NLJR 236, CA 16.5
Dominion Natural Gas Co Ltd v Collins and Perkins [1909] AC 640, 79 LJPC 13, [1908–10] All ER Rep 61, 101 LT 359, 25 TLR 831, PC 14.3
Donoghue (or McAlister) v Stevenson. See M'Alister (or Donoghue) v Stevenson
Douglas v Hello! Ltd [2005] EWCA Civ 595, [2006] QB 125, [2005] 4 All ER 128, [2005] 3 WLR 881, [2005] 2 FCR 487, [2005] IP & T 1057, [2005] 28 LS Gaz R 30, [2005] NLJR 828, (2005) Times, 24 May, [2005] EMLR 609, [2005] All ER (D) 280 (May); revsd in part sub nom Douglas v Hello! Ltd (No 3) [2007] UKHL 21, [2008] 1 AC 1, [2007] 4 All ER 545, [2008] 1 All ER (Comm) 1, [2007] 2 WLR 920, [2007] Bus LR 1600, (2007) Times, 3 May, 151 Sol Jo LB 674, [2007] EMLR 325, [2008] 1 LRC 279, [2007] All ER (D) 44 (May) 17.5
Dred Scott v Sanford 60 U.S. 393 (1857) 7.1, 7.5

E

Ebner v Official Trustee in Bankruptcy [2000] HCA 63, [2001] 2 LRC 369 .... 1.4

F

Factortame Ltd v Secretary of State for the Environment, Transport and the Regions [2002] EWCA Civ 22, [2002] 2 All ER 838, [2002] 1 WLR 2438, [2002] All ER (D) 238 (Jan) 4.3

Factortame Ltd v Secretary of State for Transport. See R v Secretary of State for Transport, ex p Factortame Ltd
Factortame Ltd v Secretary of State for Transport (No 2). See R v Secretary of State for Transport, ex p Factortame Ltd
Foakes v Beer (1884) 9 App Cas 605, 54 LJQB 130, 33 WR 233, [1881–5] All ER Rep 106, 51 LT 833, HL 10.7, 10.8, 10.9
Formby v Barker [1903] 2 Ch 539, 72 LJ Ch 716, 51 WR 646, [1900–3] All ER Rep 445, 47 Sol Jo 690, 89 LT 249, CA 9.6
Francovich and Bonifaci v Italy: C-6/90 and C-9/90 [1991] ECR I-5357, [1993] 2 CMLR 66, [1995] ICR 722, [1992] IRLR 84, ECJ 4.3

G

George v Rockett [1991] LRC (Crim) 93, (1990) 170 CLR 104, Aus HC 20.1
Gideon v Wainwright 372 U.S. 335 (1963) 7.1
Gillick v West Norfolk and Wisbech Area Health Authority [1984] QB 581, [1984] 1 All ER 365, [1983] 3 WLR 859, [1984] FLR 249, [1984] Fam Law 207, 147 JP 888, 127 Sol Jo 696, [1983] LS Gaz R 2678, 133 NLJ 888; on appeal [1986] AC 112, [1985] 1 All ER 533, [1985] 2 WLR 413, [1985] FLR 736, [1985] Fam Law 165, 129 Sol Jo 47, [1985] LS Gaz R 762, [1985] NLJ Rep 81, CA; revsd [1986] AC 112, [1985] 3 All ER 402, [1985] 3 WLR 830, [1986] 1 FLR 224, [1986] Crim LR 113, 129 Sol Jo 738, 2 BMLR 11, [1985] LS Gaz R 3551, [1985] NLJ Rep 1055, HL ... **Ch 24**, 24.1, 24.2, 24.3, 24.4, 24.5, 24.6, 24.7, 24.8, 24.9
Gilmore v Harris 184 U.S. 475 (1903) 7.3
Gissing v Gissing [1971] AC 886, [1970] 2 All ER 780, [1970] 3 WLR 255, 21 P & CR 702, 114 Sol Jo 550, 216 Estates Gazette 1257, HL 22.1
Gonzalez v Williams 192 U.S. 1 (1904) 7.3
Grand Junction Canal Co v Dimes [1852] HL Cas 759, (1838) 2 Jur 1077 .... 1.4
Greene v Associated Newspapers Ltd [2004] EWCA Civ 1462, [2005] QB 972, [2005] 1 All ER 30, [2005] 3 WLR 281, (2004) Times, 10 November, 148 Sol Jo LB 1318, [2004] All ER (D) 93 (Nov) 17.6
Guinn v United States 238 U.S. 347 (1915) 7.3

H

H v H (financial provision) [2009] EWHC 494 (Fam), [2009] 2 FLR 795, [2009] Fam Law 787 .... 23.8
HRH Prince of Wales v Associated Newspapers Ltd [2006] EWCA Civ 1776, [2008] Ch 57, [2007] 2 All ER 139, [2007] 3 WLR 222, [2008] IP & T 583, (2006) Times, 28 December, [2008] EMLR 121, [2006] All ER (D) 335 (Dec) 17.6
Hadfield's Case (1800) 27 State Tr 1281, 1 Collinson on Idiots, Lunatics 480 .... 11.1
Ham v McClaws 1 SCL (1 Bay) 93 (1789) 1.5, 1.6
Harris v Wyre Forest District Council [1988] QB 835, [1988] 1 All ER 691, [1988] 2 WLR 1173, 87 LGR 19, 20 HLR 278, 132 Sol Jo 91, [1988] 1 EGLR 132, [1988] 7 LS Gaz R 40, [1988] NLJR 15, [1988] 05 EG 57, CA; sub nom Smith v Eric S Bush (a firm), Harris v Wyre Forest District Council [1990] 1 AC 831, [1989] 2 All ER 514, [1989] 2 WLR 790, 87 LGR 685, 21 HLR 424, 17 ConLR 1, 11 LDAB 412, 133 Sol Jo 597, [1989] 1 EGLR 169, [1989] NLJR 576, [1989] 17 EG 68, 18 EG 99, HL 15.9, 15.13
Haywood v Brunswick Permanent Benefit Building Society (1881) LR 8 QBD 403 . 9.5, 9.7, 9.10
Heathfield v Chilton (1767) 4 Burr 2015 .... 1.4
Heaven v Pender (1883) 11 QBD 503, 47 JP 709, 52 LJQB 702, [1881–5] All ER Rep 35, 27 Sol Jo 667, 49 LT 357, CA 14.3
Hedley Byrne & Co Ltd v Heller & Partners Ltd [1964] AC 465, [1963] 2 All ER 575, [1963] 3 WLR 101, [1963] 1 Lloyd's Rep 485, 8 LDAB 155, 107 Sol Jo 454, HL 15.5, 15.12, 15.13
Henderson v Merrett Syndicates [1995] 2 AC 145, [1994] 3 All ER 506, [1994] 3 WLR 761, [1994] NLJR 1204, [1994] 4 LRC 355, HL 15.12

Hewer v Bryant [1970] 1 QB 357, [1969] 3 All ER 578, [1969] 3 WLR 425, 113 Sol Jo 525, CA 24.8
Holbeck Hall Hotel Ltd v Scarborough Borough Council [2000] QB 836, [2000] 2 All ER 705, [2000] 2 WLR 1396, [2000] LGR 412, 69 ConLR 1, [2000] 12 LS Gaz R 36, [2000] NLJR 307, [2000] BLR 109, CA 14.10
Home Office v Dorset Yacht Co Ltd [1970] AC 1004, [1970] 2 All ER 294, [1970] 2 WLR 1140, [1970] 1 Lloyd's Rep 453, 114 Sol Jo 375, HL 14.9, 15.5
Hughes v Metropolitan Rly Co (1877) 2 App Cas 439, 42 JP 421, 46 LJQB 583, 25 WR 680, [1874–80] All ER Rep 187, 36 LT 932, HL 10.6, 10.8
Hurtado v California 100 U.S. 516 .... 7.3

I

Internationale Handelsgesellschaft mbH v Einfuhr und Vorratsstelle für Getreide und Futtermittel: 11/70 [1970] ECR 1125, [1972] CMLR 255, ECJ 4.4

J

JEB Fasteners Ltd v Marks, Bloom & Co (a firm) [1981] 3 All ER 289, [1982] Com LR 226; on appeal [1983] 1 All ER 583, [1982] Com LR 226, CA 15.4
John (Elton) v Associated Newspapers [2006] EMLR 772 .... 17.6
John v MGN Ltd [1997] QB 586, [1996] 2 All ER 35, [1996] 3 WLR 593, [1996] NLJR 13, [1996] EMLR 229, CA 17.1
John Pfeiffer Pty Ltd v Canny [1981] HCA 52, (1981) 36 ALR 466, 148 CLR 218, 55 ALJR 683, Aus HC 15.13
Johnson v Gore Wood & Co (a firm) [2002] 2 AC 1, [2001] 1 All ER 481, [2000] All ER (D) 2293, [2001] 2 WLR 72, [2001] 1 BCLC 313, [2001] BCC 820, 150 NLJ 1889, HL 10.7
Jordan's Applications for Judicial Review, Re [2004] NICA 29, [2005] NI 144; revsd in part sub nom Jordan v Lord Chancellor [2007] UKHL 14, [2007] 2 AC 226, [2007] NI 214, [2007] 2 WLR 754 .... 18.14
Jorden v Money (1854) 5 HL Cas 185, 23 LJ Ch 865, 101 RR 116, 10 ER 868, [1843–60] All ER Rep 350, 24 LTOS 160, HL 10.3
Junior Books Ltd v Veitchi Co Ltd [1983] 1 AC 520, [1982] 3 All ER 201, [1982] 3 WLR 477, [1982] Com LR 221, 126 Sol Jo 538, [1982] LS Gaz R 1413, 21 BLR 66, 1982 SLT 492, HL 14.9

K

K (a minor), Re [1990] 3 All ER 795, [1990] 1 WLR 431, [1990] FCR 553, [1990] 2 FLR 64, [1990] Fam Law 256, 134 Sol Jo 49, CA 24.5
Kaye v Robertson [1991] FSR 62, (1990) Times, 21 March, (1990) Independent, 22 March, CA 17.5

L

L (medical treatment: Gillick competency), Re [1999] 2 FCR 524, [1998] 2 FLR 810, [1998] Fam Law 591, 51 BMLR 137 .... 24.6
LNS v Persons Unknown [2010] EWHC 119 (QB), [2010] 1 FCR 659, [2010] Fam Law 453, [2010] 07 LS Gaz R 18, [2010] EMLR 400, [2010] All ER (D) 197 (Jan) .. 17.6, 17.8
Lange v Australian Broadcasting Corp (1997) 189 CLR 520, 2 BHRC 513, [1997] 4 LRC 192, Aus HC 5.1, 5.4, 5.6, 5.7, 5.8
Langridge v Levy (1837) 6 LJ Ex 137, 2 M & W 519, 150 ER 863, [1835–42] All ER Rep 586, Exch Ct; affd sub nom Levy v Langridge (1838) 7 LJ Ex 387, 1 Horn & H 325, 4 M & W 337, sub nom Langridge v Levy [1835–42] All ER Rep 586, Ex Ch 14.3

Laskar v Laskar [2008] EWCA Civ 347, [2008] 1 WLR 2695, [2008] 2 P & CR 245, [2008] 2 FLR 589, [2008] Fam Law 638, [2008] 07 EG 142 (CS), [2008] All ER (D) 104 (Feb) 22.9
Lee v Bude and Torrington Junction Rly Co (1871) LR 6 CP 576, 40 LJCP 285, 19 WR 954, 24 LT 827 .... 1.6
Levy v Langridge. See Langridge v Levy
Lexi Holdings plc v Luqman [2007] EWHC 1508 (Ch), [2007] All ER (D) 23 (Jul) 16.6
Lister & Co v Stubbs (1890) 45 Ch D 1, 59 LJ Ch 570, 38 WR 548, [1886–90] All ER Rep 797, 63 LT 75, 6 TLR 317, CA 16.2, 16.3
Liversidge v Anderson [1942] AC 206, [1941] 3 All ER 338, 110 LJKB 724, 85 Sol Jo 439, 166 LT 1, 58 TLR 35, HL 20.1
Lloyds Bank plc v Rosset [1991] 1 AC 107, [1990] 1 All ER 1111, [1990] 2 WLR 867, 60 P & CR 311, [1990] 2 FLR 155, [1990] Fam Law 395, 22 HLR 349, [1990] 16 LS Gaz R 41, [1990] NLJR 478, HL 22.1
Lochner v New York 198 U.S. 45 (1905) 7.3
Lockton Companies International v Persons Unknown and Google Inc [2009] EWHC 3423 (QB) 16.3
Loving v Virginia 388 U.S. 1 (1967) 7.4
Lumley v Wagner (1852) 1 De GM & G 604, 21 LJ Ch 898, 16 Jur 871, 42 ER 687, [1843–60] All ER Rep 368, 19 LTOS 264 .... 9.5

M

Mabo v State of Queensland (No 2) (1992) 175 CLR 1, 107 ALR 1, 66 ALJR 408, [1993] 1 LRC 194, Aus HC .... **Ch 8**, 8.1, 8.5, 8.6, 8.7
Mabon v Mabon [2005] EWCA Civ 634, [2005] Fam 366, [2005] 3 WLR 460, [2005] 2 FCR 354, [2005] 2 FLR 1011, (2005) Times, 2 June, [2005] All ER (D) 419 (May) 24.7
M'Alister (or Donoghue) v Stevenson [1932] AC 562, 101 LJPC 119, 37 Com Cas 350, 48 TLR 494, 1932 SC (HL) 31, sub nom Donoghue (or McAlister) v Stevenson [1932] All ER Rep 1, 1932 SLT 317, sub nom McAlister (or Donoghue) v Stevenson 76 Sol Jo 396, 147 LT 281, HL .... **Ch 14**, 14.1, 14.2, 14.3, 14.7, 15.5
McFarlane v McFarlane [2004] EWCA Civ 872, [2005] Fam 171, [2004] 3 All ER 921, [2004] 3 WLR 1480, [2004] 2 FCR 657, [2004] 2 FLR 893, (2004) Times, 9 July, [2004] All ER (D) 105 (Jul); affd sub nom McFarlane v McFarlane [2006] UKHL 24, [2006] 2 AC 618, [2006] 3 All ER 1, [2006] 2 WLR 1283, [2006] 2 FCR 213, [2006] 1 FLR 1186, [2006] Fam Law 629, [2006] NLJR 916, (2006) Times, 25 May, 150 Sol Jo LB 704, [2006] All ER (D) 343 (May) 23.5, 23.6, 23.7, 23.8
McKennitt v Ash [2006] EWCA Civ 1714, [2006] QB 73, [2007] 3 WLR 194, [2008] IP & T 703, (2006) Times, 20 December, [2007] EMLR 113, [2006] All ER (D) 200 (Dec) 17.5, 17.6
McLoughlin v O'Brian [1983] 1 AC 410, [1982] 2 All ER 298, [1982] 2 WLR 982, [1982] RTR 209, 126 Sol Jo 347, [1982] LS Gaz R 922, HL 14.9
M'Naghten's Case (1843) 1 Car & Kir 130n, 10 Cl & Fin 200, 4 State Tr NS 847, 8 ER 718, [1843–60] All ER Rep 229, HL .... **Ch 11**, 11.1, 11.2, 11.3, 11.7, 11.8
MacPherson v Buick Motor Company [1916] 217 NY 382 .... 14.3
Marbury (William) v Madison (James) 5 U.S. 137, 2 L. Ed. 60, 1803 U.S. LEXIS 352, 5 U.S. (1 Cranch) 137 (1803) .... 1.5, 1.6, **Ch 2**, 2.1
Mareva Cia Naviera SA v International Bulkcarriers SA, The Mareva [1980] 1 All ER 213, [1975] 2 Lloyd's Rep 509, 9 LDAB 393, 119 Sol Jo 660, CA . **Ch 16**, 16.1, 16.3, 16.4, 16.5, 16.7
Members of the Yorta Yorta Aboriginal Community v Victoria (2002) 214 CLR 422, [2002] HCA 58, [2003] 3 LRC 185, Aus HC 8.6
Metropolitan Police Comr v Caldwell [1982] AC 341, [1981] 2 WLR 509, sub nom R v Caldwell [1981] 1 All ER 961, 73 Cr App Rep 13, 145 JP 211, 125 Sol Jo 239, HL 13.5
Milirrpum v Nabalco Pty Ltd (1972) 17 FLR 141, [1972–73] ALR 65, NT SC 8.4

Miller v Miller [2006] UKHL 24, [2006] 2 AC 618, [2006] 3 All ER 1, [2006] 2 WLR 1283, [2006] 2 FCR 213, [2006] 1 FLR 1186, [2006] Fam Law 629, [2006] NLJR 916, (2006) Times, 25 May, 150 Sol Jo LB 704, [2006] All ER (D) 343 (May) . 23.5, 23.7, 23.8
Miranda v Arizonak 384 U.S. 436 (1966) 7.1
Mosley v News Group Newspapers Ltd [2008] EWHC 1777 (QB), [2008] NLJR 1112, (2008) Times, 30 July, [2008] EMLR 679, [2008] All ER (D) 322 (Jul) 17.6, 17.8
Mosley v News Group Newspapers Ltd [2008] EWHC 687 (QB), [2008] All ER (D) 135 (Apr) 17.6
Motorola Credit Corpn v Uzan [2002] EWCA Civ 989, [2002] 2 All ER (Comm) 945, (2002) Times, 10 July, [2002] All ER (D) 223 (Jun) 16.4
Mullen v AG Barr & Company Limited [1929] SC 461 .... 14.5, 14.6, 14.7
Murphy v Brentwood District Council [1991] 1 AC 398, [1990] 2 All ER 908, [1990] 3 WLR 414, 89 LGR 24, [1990] 2 Lloyd's Rep 467, 22 HLR 502, 21 ConLR 1, 134 Sol Jo 1076, [1990] NLJR 1111, 50 BLR 1, HL 14.9, 15.4
Murray v Express Newspapers plc [2007] EWHC 1908 (Ch), [2007] 3 FCR 331, [2008] 1 FLR 704, [2007] Fam Law 1073, [2007] NLJR 1199, (2007) Times, 4 October, [2007] EMLR 583, [2007] All ER (D) 39 (Aug); revsd [2008] EWCA Civ 446, [2009] Ch 481, [2008] 3 WLR 1360, [2008] NLJR 706, (2008) Times, 12 May, [2008] EMLR 399, [2008] All ER (D) 70 (May), sub nom Murray v Big Pictures (UK) Ltd [2008] 3 FCR 661, [2008] 2 FLR 599, [2008] Fam Law 732 .... 17.6

N

Nationwide News Pty Ltd v Wills (1992) 177 CLR 1, 108 ALR 681, 66 AJLR 658, Aus HC 5.1, 5.2, 5.3, 5.4, 5.6
New Jersey Steam Navigation Co v Merchants' Bank 47 U.S. 344 (1848), 6 How. 344 .... 7.4
New York Times Co v Sullivan 376 U.S. 254 (1964) 7.1
Nippon Yusen Kaisha v Karageorgis [1975] 3 All ER 282, [1975] 1 WLR 1093, [1975] 2 Lloyd's Rep 137, 119 Sol Jo 441, CA 16.2, 16.3
Norwich Pharmacal Co v Customs and Excise Comrs [1974] AC 133, [1973] 2 All ER 943, [1973] 3 WLR 164, [1973] FSR 365, [1974] RPC 101, 117 Sol Jo 567, HL 16.3, 16.7

O

Olcott v The Supervisors 83 U.S. 678 (1872), 16 Wall. 678 .... 7.5
Othman v United Kingdom (Application 8139/09) [2009] ECHR 855, ECHR 20.5

P

P v P (inherited property) [2004] EWHC 1364 (Fam), [2006] 2 FCR 579, [2005] 1 FLR 576, sub nom V, Re (financial relief: family farm) [2005] Fam Law 101 .... 23.5
Parlour v Parlour [2004] EWCA Civ 872, [2005] Fam 171, [2004] 3 All ER 921, [2004] 3 WLR 1480, [2004] 2 FCR 657, [2004] 2 FLR 893, (2004) Times, 9 July, [2004] All ER (D) 105 (Jul) 23.6
Patchett v Swimming Pool & Allied Trades Association Ltd [2009] EWCA Civ 717, [2009] All ER (D) 152 (Jul) 15.7, 15.12
Patrick Stevedores Operations No 2 Pty Ltd v Maritime Union of Australia (No 3) [1998] 153 ALR 643 .... 16.3
Peabody Donation Fund (Governors) v Sir Lindsay Parkinson & Co Ltd [1985] AC 210, [1984] 3 All ER 529, [1984] 3 WLR 953, 83 LGR 1, 128 Sol Jo 753, [1984] LS Gaz R 3179, 28 BLR 1, [1984] CILL 128, HL 15.13
Peck v United Kingdom (Application 44647/98) (2003) 36 EHRR 719, [2003] IP & T 320, (2003) Times, 3 February, [2003] EMLR 287, [2003] ECHR 44647/98, [2003] All ER (D) 255 (Jan), ECtHR 17.5
Pesca Valentia Ltd v Minister for Fisheries and Forestry and A-G: 223/86 [1988] ECR 83, [1988] 1 CMLR 888, ECJ 4.2

Pettitt v Pettitt [1970] AC 777, [1969] 2 All ER 385, [1969] 2 WLR 966, 20 P & CR 991, 113 Sol Jo 344, 211 Estates Gazette 829, HL 22.1
Piller (Anton) KG v Manufacturing Processes Ltd [1976] Ch 55, [1976] 1 All ER 779, [1976] 2 WLR 162, [1976] FSR 129, [1976] RPC 719, 120 Sol Jo 63, CA 16.3
Plessy, ex p 11 So. 948 (La. 1892) 7.2
Plessy v Ferguson 163 U.S. 537 (1896) .... **Ch 7**, 7.1, 7.2, 7.3, 7.4, 7.6
Post Chaser, The. See Société Italo-Belge pour le Commerce et l'Industrie SA v Palm and Vegetable Oils (Malaysia) Sdn Bhd, The Post Chaser
Postnati Case. See Calvin's Case
Prohibitions Del Roy (1607) 12 Co Rep 63, Mich. 5 Jacobi 1. .... 1.1

R

R (a minor), Re [1992] Fam 11, [1991] 4 All ER 177, [1991] 3 WLR 592, [1992] 2 FCR 229, [1992] Fam Law 67, [1992] 3 Med LR 342, 7 BMLR 147, [1991] NLJR 1297, sub nom R (a minor) (Wardship: Medical Treatment), Re [1992] 1 FLR 190, CA 24.6
R v Adomako [1995] 1 AC 171, [1994] 3 All ER 79, [1994] 3 WLR 288, 158 JP 653, [1994] Crim LR 757, [1994] 5 Med LR 277, 19 BMLR 56, [1994] NLJR 936, [1994] 2 LRC 800, HL 13.5
R v Bateman (1925) 19 Cr App Rep 8, 89 JP 162, 94 LJKB 791, 28 Cox CC 33, [1925] All ER Rep 45, 69 Sol Jo 622, 133 LT 730, 41 TLR 557, CCA 13.5
R v Boswell [1984] 3 All ER 353, [1984] 1 WLR 1047, [1984] RTR 315, 79 Cr App Rep 277, 6 Cr App Rep (S) 257, [1984] Crim LR 502, 128 Sol Jo 566, CA 13.5
R v Brentwood Borough Council, ex p Peck (25 November 1997, unreported), QBD; affd [1998] EMLR 697, CA 17.5
R v Burgess [1991] 2 QB 92, [1991] 2 All ER 769, [1991] 2 WLR 1206, 93 Cr App Rep 41, [1991] Crim LR 548, 135 Sol Jo 477, [1991] 19 LS Gaz R 31, [1991] NLJR 527, CA 11.7
R v Byrne [1960] 2 QB 396, [1960] 3 All ER 1, [1960] 3 WLR 440, 44 Cr App Rep 246, 104 Sol Jo 645, CCA 11.10
R v Caldwell. See Metropolitan Police Comr v Caldwell
R (on the application of Pekkelo) v Central and South East Kent Coroner [2006] EWHC 1265 (Admin), [2006] All ER (D) 20 (Jun) 18.14
R v Chargot Ltd (t/a Contract Services) [2008] UKHL 73 , [2009] 2 All ER 645, [2009] 1 WLR 1, (2008) Times, 16 December, 153 Sol Jo (no 1) 32, [2008] All ER (D) 106 (Dec) 13.6
R v Clarke [1972] 1 All ER 219, 56 Cr App Rep 225, 136 JP 184, 116 Sol Jo 56, CA 11.5
R v Connolly [2007] EWCA Crim 790, (2007) 2 Cr App R (S) 82 .... 13.6
R (on the application of P) v Coroner for the District of Avon [2009] EWCA Civ 1367, 112 BMLR 77, [2009] All ER (D) 185 (Dec) 18.14
R (on the application of Cash) v County of Northamptonshire Coroner [2007] EWHC 1354 (Admin), [2007] 4 All ER 903, [2007] NLJR 895, [2007] All ER (D) 71 (Jun) 18.14
R (on the application of Purdy) v DPP [2008] EWHC 2565 (Admin), 104 BMLR 231, (2008) Times, 17 November, 152 Sol Jo (no 43) 31, [2008] All ER (D) 284 (Oct); affd [2009] EWCA Civ 92, [2009] 1 Cr App Rep 455, 106 BMLR 170, [2009] NLJR 309, (2009) Times, 24 February, 153 Sol Jo (no 8) 27, [2009] All ER (D) 197 (Feb); revsd [2009] UKHL 45, [2010] AC 345, [2009] 4 All ER 1147, [2009] 3 WLR 403, [2010] 1 Cr App Rep 1, 109 BMLR 153, [2009] NLJR 1175, (2009) Times, 31 July, 153 Sol Jo (no 31) 28, 27 BHRC 126, [2009] All ER (D) 335 (Jul) .... **Ch 19**, 19.8
R (on the application of Pretty) v DPP (Secretary of State for the Home Dept intervening) [2001] UKHL 61, [2002] 1 AC 800, [2002] 1 All ER 1, [2001] 3 WLR 1598, [2002] 2 Cr App Rep 1, [2002] 1 FCR 1, [2002] 1 FLR 268, [2002] Fam Law 170, 11 BHRC 589, 63 BMLR 1, [2001] NLJR 1819, (2001) Times, 5 December, [2002] 3 LRC 163, [2001] All ER (D) 417 (Nov) 19.4
R v DPP, ex p Kebilene [2000] 2 AC 326, [1999] 3 WLR 972, sub nom R v DPP, ex p Kebeline [1999] 4 All ER 801, [2000] 1 Cr App Rep 275, [2000] Crim LR 486, [1999] 43 LS Gaz R 32, (1999) Times, November 2, HL 21.6

R (on the application of Corner House Research) v Director of the Serious Fraud Office (BAE Systems plc, interested party) [2008] UKHL 60, [2009] AC 756, [2008] 4 All ER 927, [2009] Crim LR 47, [2008] NLJR 1149, (2008) Times, 31 July, 152 Sol Jo (no 32) 29, [2009] 1 LRC 343, [2008] All ER (D) 399 (Jul) ..... **Ch 21**, 21.1, 21.6, 21.7, 21.8
R v Dudley and Stephens (1884) 14 QBD 273, 49 JP 69, 54 LJMC 32, 15 Cox CC 624, 33 WR 347, [1881–5] All ER Rep 61, 52 LT 107, 1 TLR 118, CCR .... **Ch 12**, 12.1, 12.9
R v F [2008] EWCA Crim 1942, [2008] All ER (D) 210 (Jul) 13.6
R (on the application of Pounder) v HM Coroner for the North and South Districts of Durham and Darlington [2009] EWHC 76 (Admin), [2009] 3 All ER 150, [2009] All ER (D) 159 (Jan) 18.13
R v Hennessy [1989] 2 All ER 9, [1989] 1 WLR 287, [1989] RTR 153, 89 Cr App Rep 10, [1989] Crim LR 356, 133 Sol Jo 263, [1989] 9 LS Gaz R 41, CA 11.7
R v Holmes (1990) 12 Cr App Rep (S) 32, CA 13.5
R v Howe [1987] AC 417, [1987] 1 All ER 771, [1987] 2 WLR 568, 85 Cr App Rep 32, 151 JP 265, [1987] Crim LR 480, 131 Sol Jo 258, [1987] LS Gaz R 900, [1987] NLJ Rep 197, HL 12.9
R v Johnson [2007] EWCA Crim 1978, [2008] Crim LR 132, 151 Sol Jo LB 1262, [2007] All ER (D) 128 (Jul) 11.5
R v Layton (1849) 4 Cox CC 149 .... 11.1
R (on the application of Wood) v Metropolitan Police Comr [2009] EWCA Civ 414, [2009] 4 All ER 951, [2010] 1 WLR 123, (2009) Times, 1 June, 153 Sol Jo (no 21) 30, [2009] All ER (D) 208 (May) 17.6
R v Ministry of Agriculture, Fisheries and Food, ex p Agegate Ltd: C-3/87 [1990] 2 QB 151, [1991] 1 All ER 6, [1989] ECR 4459, [1990] 3 WLR 226, [1990] 1 CMLR 366, ECJ 4.2
R v Ministry of Agriculture, Fisheries and Food, ex p Jaderow Ltd: C-216/87 [1990] 2 QB 193, [1991] 1 All ER 41, [1989] ECR 4509, [1990] 3 WLR 265, [1991] 2 CMLR 556, ECJ 4.2
R v Morgan [2007] EWCA Crim 3313, [2007] All ER (D) 168 (Dec) 13.4, 13.5
R v Morgan (1990) 12 Cr App Rep (S) 504, CA .... **Ch 13**, 13.6
R (on the application of Warren) v Northamptonshire Assistant Deputy Coroner [2008] EWHC 966 (Admin), [2008] All ER (D) 393 (Apr) 18.14
R v P [2007] EWCA Crim 1937, [2008] ICR 96, (2007) Times, 13 August , 151 Sol Jo LB 987, [2007] All ER (D) 173 (Jul) 13.6
R v Porter [2008] EWCA Crim 1271, [2008] ICR 1259, (2008) Times, 9 July, [2008] All ER (D) 249 (May) 13.6
R v Sanderson (1993) 98 Cr App Rep 325, [1993] Crim LR 857, CA 11.10
R (on the application of Smith) v Secretary of State for Defence (Equality and Human Rights Commission intervening) [2009] EWCA Civ 441, [2009] 4 All ER 985, [2009] 3 WLR 1099, [2009] NLJR 790, 27 BHRC 89, [2009] All ER (D) 152 (May); revsd in part sub nom R (on the application of Smith) v Secretary of State for Defence [2010] UKSC 29, [2010] 3 WLR 223, [2010] NLJR 973, (2010) Times, 08 July, 154 Sol Jo (no 26) 28, [2010] All ER (D) 261 (Jun) 18.14
R (on the application of Axon) v Secretary of State for Health (Family Planning Association intervening) [2006] EWHC 37 (Admin), [2006] QB 539, [2006] 2 WLR 1130, [2006] 1 FCR 175, [2006] 2 FLR 206, [2006] Fam Law 272, 88 BMLR 96, [2006] 08 LS Gaz R 25, (2006) Times, 26 January, [2006] All ER (D) 148 (Jan) 24.8
R (on the application of Amin) v Secretary of State for the Home Department [2003] UKHL 51, [2004] 1 AC 653, [2003] 4 All ER 1264, [2003] 3 WLR 1169, 76 BMLR 143, [2003] 44 LS Gaz R 32, [2003] NLJR 1600, (2003) Times, 17 October, 15 BHRC 362, [2004] 3 LRC 746, [2003] All ER (D) 256 (Oct) 18.14
R v Secretary of State for the Home Department, ex p Cheblak [1991] 2 All ER 319, [1991] 1 WLR 890, CA 20.1
R v Secretary of State for the Home Department, ex p Hosenball [1977] 3 All ER 452, [1977] 1 WLR 766, 141 JP 626, 121 Sol Jo 255, CA 20.1
R v Secretary of State for the Home Department, ex p Launder [1997] 3 All ER 961, [1997] 1 WLR 839, [1997] 24 LS Gaz R 33, 141 Sol Jo LB 123, [1997] 1 LRC 548, HL 21.6

R v Secretary of State for Transport, ex p Factortame Ltd [1989] 2 CMLR 353, DC; revsd [1989] 2 CMLR 353, CA; on appeal [1990] 2 AC 85, [1989] 2 WLR 997, [1989] 3 CMLR 1, 133 Sol Jo 724, [1989] 27 LS Gaz R 41, [1989] NLJR 715, sub nom Factortame Ltd v Secretary of State for Transport [1989] 2 All ER 692, HL; refd sub nom R v Secretary of State for Transport, ex p Factortame Ltd (No 2): C-213/89 [1991] 1 AC 603, [1990] ECR I-2433, [1990] 3 WLR 818, [1990] 3 CMLR 1, [1990] 2 Lloyd's Rep 351, [1990] 41 LS Gaz R 33, sub nom Factortame Ltd v Secretary of State for Transport (No 2) [1991] 1 All ER 70, [1990] NLJR 927, ECJ; apld sub nom R v Secretary of State for Transport, ex p Factortame Ltd (No 2) [1991] 1 AC 603, [1990] 3 WLR 818, [1990] 3 CMLR 375, [1990] 2 Lloyd's Rep 365n, [1991] 1 Lloyd's Rep 10, 134 Sol Jo 1189, [1990] 41 LS Gaz R 36, [1990] NLJR 1457, sub nom Factortame Ltd v Secretary of State for Transport (No 2) [1991] 1 All ER 70, HL .... 1.6, **Ch 4**, 4.1, 4.2, 4.3, 4.4
R v Secretary of State for Transport, ex p Factortame Ltd (No 3): C-221/89 [1992] QB 680, [1991] 3 All ER 769, [1991] ECR I-3905, [1992] 3 WLR 288, [1991] 3 CMLR 589, [1991] 2 Lloyd's Rep 648, [1991] NLJR 1107, ECJ 4.3
R v Secretary of State for Transport, ex p Factortame Ltd: C-48/93 [1996] QB 404, [1996] ECR I-1029, [1996] All ER (EC) 301, [1996] 2 WLR 506, [1996] 1 CMLR 889, [1996] IRLR 267, ECJ; apld sub nom R v Secretary of State for Transport, ex p Factortame Ltd [1998] 1 CMLR 1353, [1997] TLR 482, (1997) Times, 11 September, [1997] Eu LR 475, [1998] 1 All ER 736n, DC; affd [1998] 3 CMLR 192, [1998] NPC 68, [1998] TLR 261, (1998) Times, 28 April, [1998] Eu LR 456, [1999] 2 All ER 640n, CA; affd [2000] 1 AC 524, [1999] 4 All ER 906, [1999] 3 WLR 1062, [1999] 3 CMLR 597, [1999] 43 LS Gaz R 32, HL 4.3
R v Secretary of State for Transport, ex p Factortame Ltd (No 4) [2000] Eu LR 40, HL 4.3
R (on the application of Factortame) v Secretary of State for Transport, Environment and the Regions (No 2) [2002] EWCA Civ 932, [2003] QB 381, [2002] 4 All ER 97, [2002] 3 WLR 1104, [2002] 35 LS Gaz R 34, [2002] NLJR 1313, [2003] BLR 1, (2002) Times, 9 July, [2002] All ER (D) 41 (Jul) 4.3
R v Selvage [1982] QB 372, [1982] 1 All ER 96, [1981] 3 WLR 811, [1981] RTR 481, 73 Cr App Rep 333, 146 JP 115, [1982] Crim LR 47, 125 Sol Jo 708, CA 21.5
R v Sullivan [1984] AC 156, [1983] 2 All ER 673, [1983] 3 WLR 123, 77 Cr App Rep 176, 148 JP 207, 127 Sol Jo 460, HL 11.7
R v Upper Bay Ltd [2010] EWCA Crim 495, (2010) Times, 28 April, [2010] All ER (D) 270 (Mar) 13.6
R v Wacker [2002] EWCA Crim 1944, [2003] QB 1207, [2003] 4 All ER 295, [2003] 2 WLR 374, [2003] 1 Cr App Rep 329, [2003] 1 Cr App Rep (S) 487, [2003] Crim LR 108, [2002] Crim LR 839, [2002] 39 LS Gaz R 37, (2002) Times, 5 September, [2002] All ER (D) 519 (Jul) 13.6
R (on the application of Middleton) v West Somerset Coroner [2002] EWCA Civ 390, [2003] QB 581, [2002] 4 All ER 336, [2002] 3 WLR 505, 166 JP 505, 69 BMLR 35, [2002] 19 LS Gaz R 29, (2002) Times, 18 April, [2002] All ER (D) 456 (Mar); revsd in part sub nom R (on the application of Middleton) v West Somerset Coroner [2004] UKHL 10, [2004] 2 AC 182, [2004] 2 All ER 465, [2004] 2 WLR 800, 168 JP 329, 79 BMLR 51, [2004] NLJR 417, (2004) Times, 12 March, 148 Sol Jo LB 354, 16 BHRC 49, [2004] All ER (D) 218 (Mar) .... **Ch 18**, 18.1, 18.6, 18.13, 18.14
R (on the application of Sacker) v West Yorkshire Coroner [2004] UKHL 11, [2004] 2 All ER 487, [2004] 1 WLR 796, 79 BMLR 40, (2004) Times, 12 March, 148 Sol Jo LB 354, [2004] All ER (D) 225 (Mar) 18.14
R v Windle [1952] 2 QB 826, [1952] 2 All ER 1, 36 Cr App Rep 85, 116 JP 365, 96 Sol Jo 379, [1952] 1 TLR 1344, CCA 11.5
R v Winter [2010] EWCA Crim 1474, [2010] All ER (D) 48 (Jul) 13.6
RB (Algeria) and OO v Secretary of State for the Home Department [2009] UKHL 10, [2009] 4 All ER 1045, [2009] 2 WLR 512, [2009] NLJR 349, (2009) Times, 19 February, 153 Sol Jo (no 7) 32, 26 BHRC 90, [2009] All ER (D) 200 (Feb) 20.5
Rasu Maritima SA v Perusahaan Pertambangan Minyak Dan Gas Bumi Negara and Government of the Republic of Indonesia (as interveners) [1978] QB 644, [1977] 3 All ER 324, [1977] 3 WLR 518, [1977] 2 CMLR 470, [1977] 2 Lloyd's Rep 397, 121 Sol Jo 706, CA 16.6
Republic of Haiti v Duvalier [1990] 1 QB 202, [1989] 1 All ER 456, [1989] 2 WLR 261, [1989] 1 Lloyd's Rep 111, [1989] 2 LS Gaz R 38, [1988] NLJR 234, CA 16.5

Rhone v Stephens [1994] 2 AC 310, [1994] 2 All ER 65, [1994] 2 WLR 429, [1994] 2 EGLR 181, [1994] NLJR 460, [1994] 37 EG 151, 138 Sol Jo LB 77, HL 9.9
Roberts v City of Boston 5 Cush. 198 .... 7.4
Robin v Hardaway (1772) 1 Va (Jeff) 109 .... 1.4
Rogers v Hosegood [1900] 2 Ch 388, 69 LJ Ch 652, 46 WR 659, [1900–3] All ER Rep 915, 44 Sol Jo 607, 83 LT 186, 16 TLR 489, CA 9.6
Rossi v Rossi [2006] EWHC 1482 (Fam), [2006] 3 FCR 271, [2007] 1 FLR 790 ...... 23.8

S

S (a minor), Re [1995] 3 FCR 225, [1995] Fam Law 596, sub nom S (Parental Responsibility), Re [1995] 2 FLR 648, CA 24.5
S (a child) (identification: restriction on publication), Re [2004] UKHL 47, [2005] 1 AC 593, [2004] 4 All ER 683, [2004] 3 WLR 1129, [2004] 3 FCR 407, [2005] 1 FLR 591, [2005] Fam Law 113, [2005] Crim LR 310, [2004] NLJR 1654, (2004) Times, 29 October, 148 Sol Jo LB 1285, [2005] EMLR 11, [2004] All ER (D) 402 (Oct) 17.5
S v S (ancillary relief after lengthy separation) [2006] EWHC 2339 (Fam), [2007] 2 FCR 762, [2007] 1 FLR 2120, [2007] Fam Law 482, [2006] All ER (D) 118 (Oct) 23.8
Saadi v Italy (Application No 37201/06) (2008) 49 EHRR 730, [2008] Crim LR 898, 24 BHRC 123, [2008] ECHR 37201/06, [2008] All ER (D) 432 (Feb), ECtHR 20.1
Sacheverell's Case (1710) 15 State Tr 1, HL .... **Ch 6**
Salisbury v Gilmore [1942] 2 KB 38, [1942] 1 All ER 457, 111 LJKB 593, 86 Sol Jo 251, 166 LT 329, 58 TLR 226, CA 10.6
Scott Group Ltd v McFarlane [1978] 1 NZLR 553, NZ CA 15.4
Secretary of State for the Home Department v AF [2009] UKHL 28, [2009] 3 All ER 643, [2009] 3 WLR 74, (2009) Times, 11 June, 26 BHRC 738, [2009] All ER (D) 84 (Jun) 20.4
Secretary of State for the Home Dept v Rehman [2001] UKHL 47, [2003] 1 AC 153, [2002] 1 All ER 122, [2001] 3 WLR 877, [2002] Imm AR 98, [2001] 42 LS Gaz R 37, 145 Sol Jo LB 238, 11 BHRC 413, [2002] 2 LRC 650, [2001] All ER (D) 155 (Oct) 20.1, 20.3
Sellars v Coleman [2001] 2 Qd R 565 .... 5.7
Short v Poole Corpn [1926] Ch 66, 24 LGR 14, 90 JP 25, 95 LJ Ch 110, [1925] All ER Rep 74, 70 Sol Jo 245, 134 LT 110, 42 TLR 107, CA 3.5
Siskina (Cargo Owners) v Distos Cia Naviera SA, The Siskina [1979] AC 210, [1977] 3 All ER 803, [1977] 3 WLR 818, [1978] 1 CMLR 190, [1978] 1 Lloyd's Rep 1, 121 Sol Jo 744, HL 16.5
Smith v Eric S Bush (a firm), Harris v Wyre Forest District Council. See Harris v Wyre Forest District Council
Société Italo-Belge pour le Commerce et l'Industrie SA v Palm and Vegetable Oils (Malaysia) Sdn Bhd, The Post Chaser [1982] 1 All ER 19, [1981] 2 Lloyd's Rep 695, [1981] Com LR 249 .... 10.7
Soering v United Kingdom (Application 14038/88) (1989) 11 EHRR 439, ECtHR 20.1
South Australia Asset Management Corp v York Montague Ltd (sub nom Banque Bruxelles Lambert SA v Eagle Star Insurance Co Ltd) [1997] AC 191, [1996] 3 All ER 365, [1996] 3 WLR 87, 13 LDAB 14, [1996] 2 EGLR 93, [1996] 32 LS Gaz R 33, [1996] NLJR 956, 80 BLR 1, [1996] 27 EG 125, 140 Sol Jo LB 156, [1996] 4 LRC 289, HL 15.10
Spencer's Case (1583) 5 Co Rep 16a, 77 ER 72, [1558–1774] All ER Rep 68 ...... 9.2, 9.3
Stack v Dowden [2007] UKHL 17, [2007] 2 AC 432, [2007] 2 All ER 929, [2008] 2 P & CR 56, 9 ITELR 815, [2007] 2 FCR 280, [2007] 1 FLR 1858, [2007] Fam Law 593, [2007] NLJR 634, (2007) Times, 26 April, 151 Sol Jo LB 575, [2007] 2 P & CR D28, [2007] All ER (D) 208 (Apr) .... **Ch 22**, 22.1, 22.4, 22.8, 22.9, 22.10, 22.11
Stapleton v R (1952) 86 CLR 358, Aus HC 11.5
State v Gibson 163 U.S. 537 (1896), 36 Indiana, 389 [1871] 7.4, 7.5
Stauder v West Virginia 100 U.S. 303 (1879) 7.3
Stephens v West Australian Newspapers Ltd (1994) 182 CLR 211, 124 ALR 80, [1994] 3 LRC 446, Aus HC 5.1, 5.4, 5.5, 5.6

Stovin v Wise (Norfolk County Council, third party) [1996] AC 923, [1996] 3 All ER 801, [1996] 3 WLR 388, 95 LGR 260, [1996] RTR 354, [1996] 35 LS Gaz R 33, [1996] NLJR 1185, 140 Sol Jo LB 201, [1996] 3 LRC 361, HL 15.7
Sutherland Shire Council v Heyman [1985] HCA 51, (1985) 157 CLR 424, 60 ALR 1, 59 ALJR 564, 2 Const LJ 150, Aus HC 15.13

T

Theophanous v Herald & Weekly Times Ltd (1994) 182 CLR 104, 124 ALR 1, [1994] 3 LRC 369, Aus HC .... **Ch 5**, 5.1, 5.4, 5.5, 5.6
Thoburn v Sunderland City Council [2002] EWHC 195 (Admin), [2003] QB 151, [2002] 4 All ER 156, [2002] 3 WLR 247, 166 JP 257, [2002] 15 LS Gaz R 35, [2002] NLJR 312, (2002) Times, 22 February, [2002] All ER (D) 223 (Feb) 4.4
Thomas v Sorrell (or Sorrel) (1673) 2 Keb 372, 791, 3 Keb 184, 223, 233, 264, 1 Lev 217, Vaugh 330, [1558–1774] All ER Rep 107, Freem KB 85, 137, sub nom Thomas v Saltmarsh 124 ER 1098, Freem KB 115, Ex Ch 1.4
Thorner v Major [2009] UKHL 18, [2009] 3 All ER 945, [2009] 1 WLR 776, 12 ITELR 62, [2009] 3 FCR 123, [2009] 2 FLR 405, [2009] Fam Law 583, [2009] NLJR 514, [2009] 13 EG 142 (CS), (2009) Times, 26 March, 153 Sol Jo (no 12) 30, [2009] 2 P & CR D5, [2009] All ER (D) 257 (Mar), sub nom Thorner v Curtis [2009] 2 P & CR 269 .... 10.10
Tietosuojavaltuutettu v Satakunnan Markkinaporssi Oy: C-73/07 [2010] All ER (EC) 213, [2010] IP & T 262, [2008] All ER (D) 249 (Dec), ECJ 17.8
Tophams Ltd v Earl of Sefton [1967] 1 AC 50, [1966] 1 All ER 1039, [1966] 2 WLR 814, 110 Sol Jo 271, HL 9.8
Trent Strategic Health Authority v Jain [2009] UKHL 4, [2009] AC 853, [2009] 1 All ER 957, [2009] 2 WLR 248, [2009] PTSR 382, 106 BMLR 88, (2009) Times, 22 January, 153 Sol Jo (no 4) 27, [2009] All ER (D) 148 (Jan) 15.1
Trevett v Weeden (1786), unreported 1.5
Tulk v Metropolitan Board of Works (1868) LR 3 QB 682; affd (1868) LR 3 QB 682, 32 JP 548, 8 B & S 777, 37 LJQB 272, 16 WR 985, 19 LT 18, Ex Ch 9.2
Tulk v Moxhay (1848) 2 Ph 774, 18 LJ Ch 83, 1 H & Tw 105, 13 Jur 89, 41 ER 1143, [1843–60] All ER Rep 9, 13 LTOS 21 .... **Ch 9**, 9.1, 9.2, 9.5, 9.7, 9.8, 9.9
Tumey v Ohio 273 US 510 (1927) 1.5
Twomax Ltd v Dickson, McFarlane and Robinson [1982] SC 113, 1983 SLT 98, Ct of Sess; revsd 1984 SLT 424n, Ct of Sess 15.4

U

Union of Scotland and England Case. See Calvin's Case
United States v Holmes (1842) 26 Fed Cas 360 .... 12.7
United States v Nixon, President of the United States 418 U.S. 683, 94 S. Ct. 3090, 41 L. Ed. 2d 1039, 1974 U.S. LEXIS 93 .... 2.1, 2.4
United States of America v Ferras [2006] 2 SCR 77 .... 1.4

V

V, Re (financial relief: family farm). See P v P (inherited property)
Vaughan v Vaughan [2007] EWCA Civ 1085, [2007] 3 FCR 533, [2008] 1 FLR 1108, [2007] Fam Law 1126, 151 Sol Jo LB 1435, [2007] All ER (D) 43 (Nov) 23.8
Von Hannover v Germany (Application 59320/00) (2004) 43 EHRR 139, 40 EHRR 1, 16 BHRC 545, [2004] EMLR 379, [2004] ECHR 59320/00, ECtHR 17.6

W

W (a minor) (medical treatment), Re [1993] Fam 64, [1992] 4 All ER 627, [1992] 3 WLR 758, [1992] 2 FCR 785, [1993] 1 FLR 1, [1992] Fam Law 541, 9 BMLR 22, [1992] NLJR 1124, CA 24.4
Wachtel v Wachtel [1973] Fam 72, [1973] 1 All ER 113, [1973] 2 WLR 84, 116 Sol Jo 762, CA; varied [1973] Fam 72, [1973] 1 All ER 829, [1973] 2 WLR 366, 117 Sol Jo 124, CA 23.1
Wainwright v Home Office [2003] UKHL 53, [2004] 2 AC 406, [2003] 4 All ER 969, [2003] 3 WLR 1137, [2004] IP & T 78, [2003] 45 LS Gaz R 30, (2003) Times, 20 October, 147 Sol Jo LB 1208, 15 BHRC 387, [2004] 4 LRC 154, [2003] All ER (D) 279 (Oct) 17.5
Wainwright v United Kingdom (Application No 12350/04) (2006) 44 EHRR 809, [2006] NLJR 1524, (2006) Times, 3 October, 22 BHRC 287, [2006] ECHR 12350/04, [2006] All ER (D) 125 (Sep), ECtHR 17.5
Waltons Stores (Interstate) Ltd v Maher (1988) 164 CLR 387, 76 ALR 513, 62 ALJR 110, Aus HC 10.10
Western Australia v The Commonwealth (1995) 183 CLR 373 .... 8.6
White v White [2001] 1 AC 596, [2001] 1 All ER 1, [2000] 3 WLR 1571, [2000] 3 FCR 555, [2000] 2 FLR 981, [2001] Fam Law 12, [2000] 43 LS Gaz R 38, [2000] NLJR 1716, 144 Sol Jo LB 266, HL .... **Ch 23**, 23.1, 23.2, 23.5, 23.6, 23.7, 23.8, 23.9
Wik Peoples v State of Queensland (1996) 187 CLR 1, (1997) 141 ALR 129, [1997] 3 LRC 513, Aus HC 8.5, 8.6
Wongatha People v State of Western Australia (No 9) (2007) 238 ALR 1 .... 8.6
Wood v The Mayor and Commonalty of London (1701) 90 ER 1118, Holt KB 396 .... 1.4
Woodhouse AC Israel Cocoa Ltd SA v Nigerian Produce Marketing Co Ltd [1972] AC 741, [1972] 2 All ER 271, [1972] 2 WLR 1090, [1972] 1 Lloyd's Rep 439, 116 Sol Jo 392, HL 10.7, 10.11
Worcester v Georgia 31 U.S. 515 (1832) 2.4

Y

Yeoman's Row Management Ltd v Cobbe [2008] UKHL 55, [2008] 4 All ER 713, [2009] 1 All ER (Comm) 205, [2008] 1 WLR 1752, 11 ITELR 530, [2008] 35 EG 142, [2008] 36 EG 142, (2008) Times, 8 September, 152 Sol Jo (no 31) 31, [2008] All ER (D) 419 (Jul) 10.10
Yousef v Netherlands (Application 33711/96) (2002) 36 EHRR 345, [2002] 3 FCR 577, [2003] 1 FLR 210, [2003] Fam Law 89, [2002] ECHR 33711/96, ECtHR 24.8
Yuen Kun-yeu v A-G of Hong Kong [1988] AC 175, [1987] 2 All ER 705, [1987] 3 WLR 776, 131 Sol Jo 1185, [1987] LS Gaz R 2049, [1987] NLJ Rep 566, [1988] LRC (Comm) 763, PC 15.13

Decisions of the European Court of Justice are listed below numerically. These decisions are also included in the preceding alphabetical list.

26/62: Algemene Transport-en Expeditie Onderneming van Gend en Loos NV v Nederlandse Belastingadministratie [1963] ECR 1, [1963] CMLR 105, ECJ 4.3
6/64: Costa v ENEL [1964] ECR 585, [1964] CMLR 425, ECJ 4.3, 4.4
11/70: Internationale Handelsgesellschaft mbH v Einfuhr und Vorratsstelle für Getreide und Futtermittel [1970] ECR 1125, [1972] CMLR 255, ECJ 4.4
55/86: Asociacion provincial de Armadores de buques de pesca de Gran Sol de Pontevedra (ARPOSOL) v EC Council [1988] ECR 13, [1989] 2 CMLR 508, ECJ 4.2
207/86: APESCO v EC Commission [1988] ECR 2151, [1989] 3 CMLR 687, ECJ 4.2

223/86: Pesca Valentia Ltd v Minister for Fisheries and Forestry and A-G [1988] ECR 83, [1988] 1 CMLR 888, ECJ 4.2
C-3/87: R v Ministry of Agriculture, Fisheries and Food, ex p Agegate Ltd [1990] 2 QB 151, [1991] 1 All ER 6, [1989] ECR 4459, [1990] 3 WLR 226, [1990] 1 CMLR 366, ECJ 4.2
C-216/87: R v Ministry of Agriculture, Fisheries and Food, ex p Jaderow Ltd [1990] 2 QB 193, [1991] 1 All ER 41, [1989] ECR 4509, [1990] 3 WLR 265, [1991] 2 CMLR 556, ECJ 4.2
C-213/89: R v Secretary of State for Transport, ex p Factortame Ltd (No 2) [1991] 1 AC 603, [1990] ECR I-2433, [1990] 3 WLR 818, [1990] 3 CMLR 1, [1990] 2 Lloyd's Rep 351, [1990] 41 LS Gaz R 33, sub nom Factortame Ltd v Secretary of State for Transport (No 2) [1991] 1 All ER 70, [1990] NLJR 927, ECJ; apld sub nom R v Secretary of State for Transport, ex p Factortame Ltd (No 2) [1991] 1 AC 603, [1990] 3 WLR 818, [1990] 3 CMLR 375, [1990] 2 Lloyd's Rep 365n, [1991] 1 Lloyd's Rep 10, 134 Sol Jo 1189, [1990] 41 LS Gaz R 36, [1990] NLJR 1457, sub nom Factortame Ltd v Secretary of State for Transport (No 2) [1991] 1 All ER 70, HL .... 1.6, **Ch 4**, 4.1, 4.2, 4.3, 4.4
C-221/89: R v Secretary of State for Transport, ex p Factortame Ltd (No 3) [1992] QB 680, [1991] 3 All ER 769, [1991] ECR I-3905, [1992] 3 WLR 288, [1991] 3 CMLR 589, [1991] 2 Lloyd's Rep 648, [1991] NLJR 1107, ECJ 4.3
C-6/90 and C-9/90: Francovich and Bonifaci v Italy [1991] ECR I-5357, [1993] 2 CMLR 66, [1995] ICR 722, [1992] IRLR 84, ECJ 4.3
C-46/93: Brasserie du Pecheur SA v Germany [1996] QB 404, [1996] ECR I-1029, [1996] All ER (EC) 301, [1996] 2 WLR 506, [1996] 1 CMLR 889, [1996] IRLR 267, ECJ 4.3
C-48/93: R v Secretary of State for Transport, ex p Factortame Ltd [1996] QB 404, [1996] ECR I-1029, [1996] All ER (EC) 301, [1996] 2 WLR 506, [1996] 1 CMLR 889, [1996] IRLR 267, ECJ; apld sub nom R v Secretary of State for Transport, ex p Factortame Ltd [1998] 1 CMLR 1353, [1997] TLR 482, (1997) Times, 11 September, [1997] Eu LR 475, [1998] 1 All ER 736n, DC; affd [1998] 3 CMLR 192, [1998] NPC 68, [1998] TLR 261, (1998) Times, 28 April, [1998] Eu LR 456, [1999] 2 All ER 640n, CA; affd [2000] 1 AC 524, [1999] 4 All ER 906, [1999] 3 WLR 1062, [1999] 3 CMLR 597, [1999] 43 LS Gaz R 32, HL 4.3
C-73/07: Tietosuojavaltuutettu v Satakunnan Markkinaporssi Oy [2010] All ER (EC) 213, [2010] IP & T 262, [2008] All ER (D) 249 (Dec), ECJ 17.8

I

PUBLIC LAW

The cases in the first five chapters in this Part fall broadly within the category of separation of powers. That was not a phrase which would have been employed by those in Dr Bonham's time, although they were certainly familiar with territorial disputes between Parliament, the Monarchy and the courts, and within half a century would take those disputes to the ultimate extreme of civil war. In the United States of America and Australia, the presence of a written constitution gave rise to different outcomes, reflected in *Marbury v Madison* and the five Australian cases respectively.

In the years following the Second World War the landmark case of *Wednesbury* became the leading authority on one issue – the power of the courts to review executive action. It remains the leading authority on that point today, although since it was decided the role of the courts has been considerably altered by the United Kingdom's accession to the European Union. Aside from the additional complexity of another legislative layer to consider, a fundamental shift in the constitutional balance was effected by Britain's EU membership in the form of the supremacy of European law, as established by *Factortame*. The influence of European law will be seen again in several other chapters.

The trial of Dr Sacheverell concerns another key question in constitutional law, the relationship between the citizen and the state. This is an issue as old as the state itself and, unsurprisingly, as the chapters on the right to life in Part V and on the state and terrorism in Part VI demonstrate, remains one of the central legal questions of the present day. As to the people involved, there was more than a touch of irony in the champion of non-resistance becoming the icon of the mob, with Parliament eventually responding by way of 'An act for preventing tumults and riotous assemblies, and for the more speedy and effectual punishing the rioters'.

The final two chapters in this Part discuss race relations in the American and Australian contexts. It should not be too trite to observe that the United Kingdom played a key role in the development of both countries and that the ensuing legal issues should accordingly be of interest to British lawyers as well. No one in the present day would defend *Plessy* – a transparent and iniquitous attempt to justify inequality by little more than calling it something else – although the essay expresses the view that its ghost has not been entirely exorcised. *Mabo* has been a decision in the other direction: recognition of native title, which was controversial at the time but has become settled law since. As with many of the chapters, the lives of the people actually involved contain some interesting turns. As Dr Lindgren QC observes, Eddie Mabo himself was derided by some in his own community as a trouble maker and never lived to see the full effect of the legal proceedings for which his surname is now common shorthand.

1

CHANGING PERSPECTIVES ON THE CONSTITUTION AND THE COURTS

Dr Bonham's Case

Andrew Goddard QC and
Marie-Thérèse Groarke

INTRODUCTION

1.1

> 'And it appearth in our Books, that in many Cases, the Common Law doth control Acts of Parliament, and sometimes adjudge them to be void: for when an Act of Parliament is against common right and reason, or repugnant, or impossible to be performed, the common law will control it, and adjudge such Acts to be void.'

These are the audacious words of Sir Edward Coke in the famous case of Dr Bonham.[1] The case is most famous for the proposition that courts might declare Acts of Parliament void, but it also articulates fundamental principles of English justice, including the principle that no man should act as a judge in his own cause (*nemo iudex in causa sua*) and the principle that no person should be punished twice for his crime (*nemo debet bis puniri pro uno delicto*). The influence of *Dr Bonham's case* does not stop at the shores of England, but crosses over the Atlantic Ocean to the United States of America where some would argue its influence was more significantly felt.

In reviewing *Dr Bonham's case* it is helpful to bear in mind the character and age of the time in which it was heard. Parliament's function at the time was very different to Parliament's function today. It did not sit permanently and its primary purpose was to raise taxes and pass legislation for the Monarch. Parliament and the monarch co-existed together and in that regard an attack on Parliament's sovereignty might have been viewed as an attack on the sovereignty of the monarch himself.

Coke's judgment did not sit well with the prevailing schools of thought at the time, which saw Parliament as the sovereign law marker. For example, Sir

1.1 *Changing Perspectives on the Constitution & Courts*

Thomas Smith in his *Commonwealth of England*, written near the middle of Elizabeth I's reign stated:

> 'The most high and absolute power of the realme of Englande, consistheth in the Parliament . . . That which is done by this consent is called firme, stable, and sanctum, and is taken for lawe. The Parliament abrogateth olde laws, maketh newe . . . and hath the power of the whole realme, both the head and the body. For everie Englishman is entended to bee there present, either in person or by procuration and attornies.'

According to King James I he was the supreme judge and:

> ' . . . inferior judges his shadows and ministers . . . and the King may, if he please, sit and judge in Westminster Hall in any Court there, and call their judgments in question. The King beinge the author of the Lawe is the interpreter of the Lawe.'[2]

This was a view which Coke would later challenge in *Prohibitions del Roy*.[3]

James therefore did not react kindly to Coke's judgment in *Bonham's case* and ordered him to 'correct' his decision. Coke refused. Such checks to his pretensions were highly displeasing to King James. Coke steadily declined in his favour, while the obsequious Bacon increased his influence on the royal ear. Bacon, a rival of Coke at the time, had his sights set on the position of Attorney General. Bacon was instrumental in getting Coke ostensibly promoted to the King's Bench, a role which actually meant a large pay cut. Such a move meant that Hobart would be moved to the Chief Justice of Common Pleas opening up the position of Attorney General. Coke was dismissed as Chief Justice of the King's Bench three years later following the *Case of Commendams* in which Coke (along with other judges) had refused a request from the King to discuss the case with him prior to issuing their judgment.[4]

1 (1610) 8 Co Rep 113b at 118a.

2 Ceasar's notes in Landsdowne MS, 160ff 426, 427, 428, cited by Usher, EHR xviii 673.

3 (1607) 12 Co Rep 63, Mich. 5 Jacobi 1.

4 (1616) King's Bench. Coke declared such a request to be contrary to law and refused to retreat from this position when the judges were summoned to explain themselves before the King in the Privy Council. Again, together with Lord Chancellor Ellesmere, Bacon appears to have been influential in persuading the King to censure Coke and the other judges.

COKE'S CAREER AND CHARACTER

1.2 In order to understand *Dr Bonham's case* fully it is helpful to understand Coke as a judge and person.

Edward Coke was born on 1 February 1552. He studied law at Trinity College, Cambridge. He was called to the Bar in April 1578 and went on to have very successful career. He had various judicial appointments and was, for a short time, speaker of the House of Commons.

He gained notoriety for his prosecution of Sir Walter Raleigh in 1603, having been recently appointed as Attorney General. The trial was held at Winchester, to which place the court had been adjourned on account of the plague in

London. Coke was said to have conducted the trial in a ferocious manner and upon what many came to view as being upon weak evidence.

Coke's beliefs seemingly varied at different stages of his life. In the reign of Elizabeth I he was a dutiful and reverent servant of the Crown. In the later years of Elizabeth's reign he acted as Solicitor-General and Attorney General. During this time he supported acts which, in his later years, he denounced as illegal, [1] however, that may have been due to the restraining influence of Elizabeth I. One belief which was consistent throughout Coke's career was the authority of the common law. The common law had emerged in the twelfth century and, in Coke's view, it was this longevity which conferred its authority. His passion for the common law was irrepressible. The common law, wrote Coke, was 'an artificial perfection of reason'.[2] The perfection was the refinement achieved by judges over the generations, 'an infinite series of grave and learned men'.[3] Coke's definition of reason is found in his Commentary upon Littleton where he wrote:

> 'Reason is the life of the law, nay the common law itselfe is nothing else but reason, which is to be understood of an artificiall perfection of reason, gotten long study, observation, and experience, and not of every man's natural reason, for Nemo nascitur artifex. This legal reason est summa ratio. And therefore if all the reason that is dispersed into so many severall heads were united into one, yet could he not make such a law as the law of England is; because by many successions of ages it hath been fined and refined by an infinite number of grave and learned men, and by long experience growne to such a perfection, for the government of this realme, as the old rule may be justly verified of it: Neminem oportet esse sapientiorem legibus: no man out of his own private reason ought to be wiser than the law, which is the perfection of reason.'

In 1606, Coke's appointment as Chief Justice of the Common Pleas gave him the perfect position from which to fortify the common law. This was at a time where there were various courts and councils which often attacked one another's jurisdiction; for the struggle between the Common Law courts and Equity courts was still rife.

1 For example, the discretionary power of the Crown to authorise acts of torture. See *A History of English Law* by Sir William Holdsworth (1924) Vol V, p 428.

2 Coke's first institute – commentary upon Littleton.

3 Ibid.

FACTS OF *DR BONHAM'S CASE*

1.3 After completing an eleven-year course of study at Cambridge University, Thomas Bonham became a 'doctor of physic'. He had about ten-and-a-half years more education than most practitioners of the healing arts in England at that time. In the early 1600s Dr Thomas Bonham set up his medical practice in London. The Royal College of Physicians of London, established in 1518, was a licensing board. Candidates were examined by leading physicians on the board to ascertain that they were 'grave and learned' in the practice of medicine.

By letters Patent of King Henry VIII, later confirmed by an Act of Parliament (14 & 15 Hen VIII, c 5), no person could practice medicine within seven miles of the City of London without a licence. The Royal College was authorised to search, examine, correct, and punish offenders and transgressors. The Act also provided that the Royal College could retain a proportion of any fines that it imposed.

Dr Bonham did not have a licence from the College and was fined 100 shillings and ordered not to practise medicine. Bonham did not heed his warning and was arrested again and fined a further ten pounds. Bonham was then brought before the College censors (or Board of Governors). The Board imposed an increased fine and committed Bonham to prison.

Following a letter from the Archbishop of Canterbury advising the Royal College that it had made a mistake given Bonham's education, and the Archbishop's subtle threat that if the College did not rectify the error he would consult with the House of Lords concerning its charter, Bonham was released. Bonham then brought a claim against the Royal College for false imprisonment, contending that the College had had no authority to imprison him.

Coke held that the two clauses of the Act which conferred the College's power to punish for incompetent and unlicensed practice were separate. The Act only conferred power to fine and imprison for incompetent practice. In respect of unlicensed practice, the Royal College's powers were confined to imposing a fixed fine of five pounds. One of the five reasons Coke gave for this conclusion was that a clause authorising the College to fine or imprison for unlicensed practice would be adjudged void on the grounds that it permitted the College to be a judge and party in the same case[1] and was consequently contrary to 'common right and reason'. It was in this context that Coke uttered his famous words cited at **1.1** above.

1 A party in the sense that the College was interested in the proceedings because of its entitlement to retain a portion of any of the fines that it imposed.

BONHAM'S CASE IN ENGLAND AND THE COMMONWEALTH

1.4 At the time when *Dr Bonham's case* was decided the balance of power between the King, Parliament and the courts was in a state of flux. Whilst by no means universally accepted,[1] Coke's doctrine, that the courts could declare void Acts of Parliament, was nevertheless applied by courts in England up to and beyond the Glorious Revolution of 1688–89.

Thus, in *Day v Savadge*,[2] Coke's successor, Sir Henry Hobart CJ, declared that 'an act of parliament made against natural equity, as to make a man judge in his own cause, is void in itself, for jura naturae sunt immutablilia'. Such limits on the scope of Parliamentary sovereignty are confirmed by other judicial dicta of the period. In the well known case of *Thomas v Saltmarsh*,[3] which provides the classical definition of a licence in English land law, Vaughan CJ declared that 'no human authority can make lawful what divine authority hath made unlawful'.

Coke's dictum from *Dr Bonham's case* is generally considered to have been superseded in England by the Glorious Revolution. However, it is clear that it actually survived somewhat beyond 1688. In the case of *Wood v The Mayor and Commonalty of London*[4] it was argued that the Lord Mayor could not be party to a suit brought in a court over which he presided. Relying on the authority of *Dr Bonham's case* Chief Justice Holt stated as follows:

> 'What my Lord Coke says in Bonham's case, in his 8 Co., is far from any extravagancy, for it is a very reasonable and true saying that if an act of parliament should ordain that the same person should be party and judge, or which is the same thing, judge in his own cause, it would be a void act of parliament; for it is impossible that one should be judge and party, for the judge is to determine between party and party, or between the government and the party.'

The Chief Justice went on to say that:

> ' . . . an act of parliament may not make adultery lawful, that is, it cannot make it lawful for A. to lie with the wife of B: but it may make the wife of A. to be the wife of B., and dissolve her marriage with A.'

The common thread running through the judgments of Coke, Hobart, Vaughan and Holt is an appeal to a higher, more fundamental form of authority, beyond the reach of legislative power. The origins of this concept of fundamental law (or the law of nature as it was sometimes termed) can be traced to Roman law. Unsurprisingly, however, given the deeply held religious views of the time, the law of nature was often inextricably associated with religious morals. As Coke himself said in *Calvin's Case*[5] 'The law of nature is that which God at the time of creation of the nature of man infused into his heart, for his preservation and direction'. Coke's dictum in *Bonham's case* would often later be combined with appeals to 'the laws of nature' and/or 'the laws of God' by lawyers seeking to argue for the nullification of statutes.[6]

The emergence of a settled doctrine of parliamentary sovereignty in England can be traced to the publication of *Blackstone's Commentaries* in 1765 in which Blackstone disassociated himself from Coke's doctrine by his tenth rule for construing statutes.[7] The last echo of Coke's doctrine in England can, perhaps, be found in the case of *Heathfield v Chilton*[8] in which Lord Mansfield held that international law formed part of the law of England but added that an Act of Parliament could not alter the law of nations.

Following publication of Dicey's *Introduction to the Study of the Law of the Constitution* in 1885, the doctrine of parliamentary sovereignty has become firmly entrenched as a principle of the unwritten British constitution.

Accordingly, the concept that a court might declare Acts of Parliament to be void no longer finds any place in English law. Nevertheless, three aspects of *Dr Bonham's case* remain of lasting significance in England and the Commonwealth.

First and foremost, the case provides one of the earliest and clearest statements of the important public law principle that no man should act as judge in his own cause. The modern decision generally cited as authority for this proposition is the judgment of the House of Lords in *Grand Junction Canal Co v Dimes*.[9] Yet the report of the submissions made by counsel for the appellant in *Dimes* reveals that Coke's judgment in *Bonham's case*, together with the judgments of Hobart CJ in *Day v Savadge* and Holt CJ in *City of London v Wood*,[10] were all cited to their Lordships and that these cases formed the foundation of the appellant's arguments.

Dr Bonham's case continues to be cited in the context of bias and judicial independence in cases across the Commonwealth. Recent examples include the judgments of the High Court of Australia in *Ebner v Official Trustee in*

Bankruptcy[11] and the Supreme Court of Canada in *United States of America v Ferras.*[12]

The second aspect of the case which survives in Commonwealth jurisdictions is the proposition that members of a statutory tribunal who imprison a man without any jurisdiction are liable in trespass for false imprisonment: see *Abbott v Sullivan.*[13]

The final aspect of the case which remains of lasting significance across the common law world is Coke's articulation of one of the most fundamental and cherished principles of the English justice system: *Nemo debet bis puniri pro uno delicto* (no person may be punished twice for the same crime). It is highly significant that Coke of all people should have invoked this principle as a reason for not accepting the Royal College's interpretation of the statute. Coke is widely recognised as having first articulated the modern law of double jeopardy in his *Second Institutes* published some 30 years after *Dr Bonham's case* was decided.

1 Following his dismissal in 1616, Coke's decision in a number of cases, including *Dr Bonham's case*, was criticised by both Lord Chancellor Ellesmere and Sir Francis Bacon and Coke was ordered to 'correct' his reports. However, he failed to do this to the satisfaction of the King.

2 (1614) 80 ER 235.

3 (1674) 124 ER 1098.

4 (1701) 90 ER 1118.

5 (1608) 7 Co Rep 1a.

6 See, for example, *Robin v Hardaway* (1772) 1 Va (Jeff) 109, where such arguments were invoked in an attempt to nullify a statute which had reduced the plaintiffs to slavery.

7 See Commentaries, i. 91. Notwithstanding Blackstone's tenth rule his writings are not altogether consistent on this point. For example, there are passages in his Commentaries which deny that human laws can take away the natural rights of men (Comm. i. 51) and which assert that human law is of no validity if contrary to the law of nature dictated by God (Comm. i. 41).

8 (1767) 4 Burr 2015.

9 [1852] 3 HL Cas 759.

10 (1701) 12 Mod Rep 669.

11 [2001] 2 LRC 369.

12 [2006] 2 SCR 77.

13 [1952] 1 All ER 226.

THE INFLUENCE OF *BONHAM'S CASE* IN THE UNITED STATES

1.5 *Dr Bonham's case* has particular historical and constitutional significance in the United States. Just when its influence was declining in England during the eighteenth century, it was gaining prominence across the Atlantic in the American colonies. Coke was widely read among lawyers of the day. Indeed, one of the principal textbooks used by law students at the time was *Coke's Commentary upon Littleton.*

During the years leading up to the War of Independence, relations between the American colonists and the imperial Parliament in London were becoming increasingly strained. It is perhaps unsurprising therefore that a principle which appeared to contemplate that Acts of Parliament could be adjudged void by the courts would appeal to those who wished to question the authority of the British Parliament.

In 1761, a number of Boston merchants petitioned the Massachusetts Superior Court challenging the legality of writs of assistance. The writs, authorised by an Act of the British Parliament passed in 1696, were in the nature of general search warrants that empowered customs officials to carry out indiscriminate searches for contraband in private homes and businesses without obtaining a specific warrant. Moreover, once issued, the writs did not expire and could be assigned to others by the holder. James Otis, one of the lawyers for the merchants, cited *Bonham's case* and argued that:

> 'An act against the Constitution is void: an Act against natural Equity is void: and if an Act of Parliament should be made, in the very words of the petition, it would be void.'

Although the validity of the writs was upheld by the court against the merchant's arguments, many years later, John Adams (later to become the second President of the United States), who was present in court during the proceedings, remarked: 'Then and there the child Independence was born'.

Fuel was added to the growing revolutionary spirit in the colonies by the Stamp Act passed by the British Parliament in 1765. The Act imposed a tax on the colonies by requiring most formal legal documents to be issued on stamped paper, which had to be purchased in valid British currency. The Act was deeply unpopular and led to popular demonstrations. The colonists resented the fact that it was the British Parliament, as opposed to their own local assemblies, that could dictate the manner and form of the taxes they were required to pay. Indeed, they believed that this was unconstitutional according to the principles of Magna Carta because there should be no taxation without consent and the peoples of the colonies had no direct representation in the British Parliament.[1] The issue became a rallying cry for groups such as the Sons of Liberty who were advocating greater autonomy from the British Empire.

By the time of its repeal in May 1766, the courts in a number of the colonies[2] had already refused to recognise the Stamp Act 1765 and allowed proceedings in their court to continue without stamps. This move was prompted partly by necessity. Stamps were not freely available as many of the officials who had authority to sell them had been hounded out of office. Summarising a resolution debated by the Massachusetts Assembly on the issue, Massachusetts Lieutenant-Governor Thomas Hutchinson explained that the prevailing argument adopted in support of the continued operation of the courts was that: 'the Act of Parliament is against Magna Charta and the natural rights of Englishmen, and therefore according to Lord Coke null and void'.[3]

One of the most influential speeches of the Stamp Act episode was made by Patrick Henry[4] to the Virginia House of Burgesses in May 1766. Henry had risen from humble beginnings and had been admitted to the local Bar a few years earlier after only six weeks' study of *Coke on Littleton* and Virginia's legislation. He swayed members of the House with his eloquent speech which persuaded the House to vote in favour of resolutions Henry had drafted condemning the imposition of taxes by the British Parliament as unconstitutional. Henry's resolutions were reportedly drafted on the back of a blank page from his own copy of *Coke on Littleton.*

Bonham's case continued to be cited in American courts after independence. In 1786, the case of *Trevett v Weeden*[5] came before the Superior Court of Rhode

Island. The state's General Assembly had passed a statute declaring that it was an offence for any person to refuse to receive paper money in exchange for goods and a further statute provided for the offence to be tried by a special court without a jury. The defendant, Weeden, was tried for this offence but his counsel, Major-General Varnum argued that the statute was void as being contrary to fundamental principles of the unwritten constitution of Rhode Island.

There having been no annulment of Rhode Island's colonial constitution following independence, Varnum submitted that the constitutional limitations derived from the English common law and Magna Carta continued to apply to the new General Assembly. Varnum relied on the authority of *Dr Bonham's case* in support of his argument that any statute commanding trial without jury was 'repugnant and impossible'.

Although judgment in the case was given purely on the narrow question of the court's jurisdiction, Judge Howell nevertheless declared the statute to be 'repugnant and unconstitutional'.[6] Two of the four remaining judges are reported to have expressed similar opinions.[7] The case is of particular interest to scholars because it provides an example of judicial review of statutes in the absence of a written constitution and thus supports the concept of common law limitations on sovereignty.

The authority of *Dr Bonham's case* was invoked in numerous other cases in the period immediately following independence to support the nullification of statutes considered to be contrary to the principles of Magna Carta or common right and reason. Examples include the South Carolina cases of *Ham v McClaws*[8] and *Bowman v Middleton*.[9]

It was the case law identified above that formed the legal backdrop for what is widely regarded as the most significant decision in United States constitutional law – *Marbury v Madison*.[10] The case established the concept of judicial review whereby the Supreme Court can declare legislative Acts of Congress to be invalid and unconstitutional. The court did not refer to *Dr Bonham's case* directly but, in a clear echo of the language used by Coke in *Dr Bonham's case*, Chief Justice Marshall declared that 'an act of the Legislature repugnant to the Constitution is void'.

In one sense the decision in *Marbury* was far less radical than the cases which had explored the limits of parliamentary sovereignty in the 30 years leading up to the decision. As Chief Justice Marshall points out, it is inherent in the very concept of a written constitution that it holds special status above ordinary legislative acts. Although not explicitly spelt out in the Constitution, the power of the Supreme Court to review the constitutional propriety of legislation was clearly necessary to give effect to that special status. Nevertheless, it may be doubted whether the justices in *Marbury* could have dismissed the concept of legislative supremacy, as they did, in the space of a few paragraphs if it had not already been fundamentally weakened by the cases and events described above.

From the foregoing it can be seen that *Dr Bonham's case* has played a powerful role in the constitutional and historical development of the United States. Having been appropriated to legitimise the rebellion against taxes and other measures imposed by the British Parliament in the years leading up to independence, Coke's dictum in *Dr Bonham's case* became infused into the legal philosophy of the post-independence era. In common with authorities in England and the Commonwealth, *Dr Bonham's case* has, in addition, been cited by the United States Supreme Court as the origin of the principle that no man should act as judge in his own cause.[11]

1 Article 12 of Magna Carta prevented the King from raising tax except by 'common consent of our kingdom'. The position was further inflamed by the fact that breach of the Stamp Act was subject to jurisdiction of the Admiralty Courts as opposed to the Colonial Courts, thereby excluding a right to trial by jury. This was also considered to be contrary to Magna Carta.

2 The Northampton County Court in Virginia formally declared the Stamp Act to be unconstitutional in February 1766. Courts in New Jersey, South Carolina and New Hampshire followed suit. The courts in Rhode Island also continued to operate backed by an indemnity from the legislature for all officials who ignored the Act.

3 Quincy Reports (Mass) 527.

4 Regarded as one of the founding fathers of the United States.

5 (1786), unreported.

6 The only known report of the judgment is an unofficial report in a local newspaper, the *Providence Gazette.*

7 The judges were subsequently summoned before the legislature to explain their actions whereupon they maintained the unconstitutionality of the statute. The following year, the General Assembly replaced four of the five judges who had decided the case.

8 1 SCL (1 Bay) 93 (1789).

9 1 SCL (1 Bay) 252 (1792).

10 5 U.S. (1 Cranch) 137 (1803). See Chapter 2.

11 See *Tumey v Ohio* 273 US 510 (1927).

THE FUTURE OF *BONHAM'S CASE* IN ENGLAND

1.6 Is the time perhaps ripe for the reassertion of common law restrictions on the supremacy of Parliament? It appears that some eminent members of the judiciary in England believe so. Writing extra-judicially Lord Woolf of Barnes has, for example, suggested that if Parliament expressly legislated to abolish the court's power of judicial review or undermine the democratic nature of our governmental institutions, the courts may refuse to accept the validity of such laws.[1]

Even more radically, Sir John Laws postulates that fundamental rights and freedoms, such as the right to freedom of expression, form part of a higher order law which cannot be abrogated by the passage of legislation in Parliament.[2] According to Sir John 'the democratic credentials of an elected government cannot justify its enjoyment of a right to abolish fundamental freedoms'. The influence of natural law jurisprudence on the approach propounded by Sir John Laws is unmistakeable.

However, it is submitted that the dangers of adopting the position taken by Sir John Laws are all too readily apparent. In the absence of a written constitution or sovereign text, the precise boundaries of any higher order law remain elusive. Whilst it may be true that there is near-universal acceptance regarding the broad nature of certain fundamental rights, the precise scope and content of these rights and freedoms is far from settled. It is an inevitable, and undesirable, feature of the approach advocated by Sir John Laws that unelected judges become the final authority on the content of these rights.

The dangers inherent in a system where the content of higher order law remains entirely undefined can, perhaps, be illustrated no better than by reference to the American case of *Ham v McClaw*[3] where Coke's doctrine of 'common right and reason' was invoked to invalidate a statute prohibiting the importation of slaves. The court was, apparently, more concerned to recognise the slave owner's fundamental right to property than the rights and concerns of the imported slaves.

The argument against recognition of some form of higher order law is captured in the following statement of Mr Justice Willies' in *Lee v Bude and Torrington Junction Railway Co*:[4]

> 'We sit here as servants of the Queen and the legislature. Are we to act as regents over what is done by Parliament with the consent of the Queen, lords, and commons? I deny that any such authority exists. If an Act of Parliament has been obtained improperly, it is for the legislature to correct it by repealing it: but, so long as it exists as law, the Courts are bound to obey it. The proceedings here are judicial, not autocratic, which they would be if we could make laws instead of administering them.'

Whilst instances can be found where British courts have come close to refusing to apply Acts of Parliament,[5] it is widely accepted that the doctrine of parliamentary sovereignty still applies in the United Kingdom.[6] It is submitted that the only satisfactory (legitimate?) way of ensuring the entrenchment of fundamental rights and freedoms is by the incorporation of a sovereign legal text or written constitution. Unless and until this occurs[7] the British courts would be wise to continue to accept that they do not have power to invalidate Acts of Parliament.

1 'Droit Public – English Style', Lord Woolf of Barnes [1995] Public Law 57.

2 'Law and Democracy', Sir John Laws [1995] Public Law 72.

3 1 SCL (1 Bay) 93 (1789).

4 (1871) LR 6 CP 576.

5 See, for example, *Anisminic Ltd v Foreign Compensation Fund* [1969] 2 AC 147 where a statutory ouster clause was construed so narrowly as to have virtually no effect.

6 Save, perhaps, in the case of a direct conflict with provisions of European Community law: *R v Secretary of State for Transport, ex parte Factortame* [1991] 1 AC 603 (as to which, see Chapter 4). But, even then, many argue that the courts would, in all likelihood, give effect to an Act of Parliament that was expressly stated to override EC law.

7 The legitimacy of such a written constitution could, perhaps, be conferred by way of referendum. However, as illustrated by *Marbury v Madison*, it is only the courts that can ultimately decide whether to acknowledge the paramount status of any constitutional text.

2

WHAT BREATHES LIFE INTO THE US CONSTITUTION?

Marbury v Madison

Kenneth R Thompson II

'The King is under the Law for it is the Law that maketh him a King'
Henry de Bracton on the Laws and Customs of England.

INTRODUCTION

2.1 Some see the brilliance of the American system of rule of law to be captured in a Constitution that ensures checks and balances between three equal branches of government. What is forgotten is that until Chief Justice John Marshall rendered the decision of *William Marbury v James Madison, Secretary of State of the United States*,[1] this uniquely American legal system could have just as easily served as a recipe for chaos and the collapse of the country. The new republic was putting into practice many truly revolutionary theories which had never before been applied in the context of an independent, evolving society, and it was unfolding in an environment where a likely outcome for the young republic could have been another revolutionary conflict. With a persuasive stroke of a pen, Justice Marshall defined what 'checks and balances' meant in practice and he clarified the role of the Supreme Court of the United States in shaping our culture. Marshall confirmed that the US Constitution was the supreme law of the land and the Supreme Court was the final arbiter of all legal disputes regardless of the parties involved – in this instance a part of a co-equal branch of the US government. Marshall, starts with a critical premise with which no one, other than those who would champion revolution, could argue – the Constitution is the supreme law of the land and, as such, the Constitution explicitly provides that the judicial power of the United States culminates in the Supreme Court whose power is expressly extended to *all* cases arising under the laws of the United States.

Even with this rather inarguable statement of black letter law, Marshall realised that he would leave the country exposed to political turmoil if he did not take into account the political environment of the time and if he did set boundaries around those topics which were not in the purview of the

Supreme Court. Further, he knew in order to fend off complaints that this case was not a legal dispute at all he needed to establish some principles which would inarguably separate this matter from political debate. How did Marshall navigate this thorny issue? First, he acknowledged that the President 'is invested with certain important political powers, in the exercise of which he is to use his own discretion, and is accountable only to his country in his political character, and to his own conscience'. In acknowledging even this, Marshall clearly establishes by what or whom the President is so invested – the Constitution of the United States. Next, Marshall clearly established that the issue before him was a legal issue not a political matter. He pointed out that this was an appointment to office authorised under the Constitution, and once that appointment was made it created an individual legal right. If the law means anything it means that an individual injured has a right to resort to the laws of his country for a remedy.

Marshall thus reduced the entire matter to a very simple legal construct, but put in the context of when it was written, it was anything but simple. This dispute came before the court at a time when any less artful articulation could have had disastrous consequences for rule of law in the young republic, yet Marshall's persuasive opinion as to why the US Supreme Court should decide this decision, and all legal disputes, became a key underpinning to the long-term success of the American political experiment. This decision set in place an independent judiciary which has been able to survive many political threats over the years including *United States v Nixon, President of the United States et al*[2] and most recently have its decision in *George W Bush and Richard Cheney, Petitioners v Albert Gore, Junior et al*[3] accepted as the law of the land, notwithstanding the case was decided by a severely split court which granted the Presidency to the candidate who did not receive the majority of the popular vote.

1 5 U.S. 137; 2 L. Ed. 60; 1803 U.S. LEXIS 352; 1 Cranch 137 (24 February 1803).

2 418 U.S. 683; 94 S. Ct. 3090; 41 L. Ed. 2d 1039; 1974 U.S. LEXIS 93 (24 July 1974).

3 531 U.S. 98; 121 S. Ct. 525; 148 L. Ed. 2d 388; 2000 U.S. LEXIS 8430; 69 U.S.L.W. 4029; 2000 Cal. Daily Op. Service 9879; 2000 Colo. J. C.A.R. 6606; 14 Fla. L. Weekly Fed. S 26 (12 December 2000).

BACKGROUND OF THE CASE

2.2 Just prior to leaving office in 1801, John Adams, the lame duck President of the United States, appointed several people, including William Marbury, as justices of the peace for the District of Columbia. These appointments were made under the Judiciary Act of 1801, an Act passed by the lame duck Federalist-controlled Congress in an attempt to hinder changes which the Federalists knew would be forthcoming when Thomas Jefferson and the Democratic-Republicans took control of both the Presidency and the Congress. The commissions were signed by President Adams and sealed by acting Secretary of State John Marshall – the same John Marshall who Adams appointed Chief Justice of the Supreme Court and who authored this opinion. Given the hour that the commissions were signed and sealed, it was impossible to deliver all of the commissions prior to the expiration of President Adams's term of office. President Jefferson refused to honour the commissions, claiming that they were invalid because they had not been delivered by the end of Adams's term, and he instructed his Secretary of State, James Madison (who also later became President of the United States), not to deliver the commissions. Marbury sought a writ of mandamus to compel Madison to deliver the commissions pursuant to the Judiciary Act of 1789 whereby Congress had granted the Supreme Court original jurisdiction to issue writs of mandamus '. . . to any courts appointed, or persons holding office, under the authority of the United States'. One of the most intriguing things about the case is that Marshall's hands were all over all sides of this and notwithstanding that point, his decision here was accepted. He is the Secretary of State who sealed the commission and he is now the author of the decision that would decide the fate of his Executive Branch actions. Undoubtedly Mr Marbury and the Federalists believed that they could count on the fact that the man who sealed the commissions would deliver a decision affirming Marbury's right to the commission and compelling Madison to deliver it. Of course, it is not what they got. Ironically, Madison and Jefferson were not required to deliver the commission, so in that sense they won, yet Jefferson did not like the basis for Marshall's decision and made that point known in letters to his own Supreme Court appointees years after he left office. The very facts that Marshall was on both sides of this case, did not recuse himself from deciding it, issued a ruling that did not award the commission to one of his Federalist brethren and upheld Jefferson's order not to deliver the commission but on grounds which upset Jefferson and the Democratic-Republicans illustrates in very ironic ways the independence of the American judiciary.

The historical facts set up a series of questions, but the one not immediately obvious is the one for which the decision is remembered. Marshall first poses whether Marbury has a right to the commission and does the law grant Marbury a remedy? He concluded that the Judiciary Act of 1789 expanded the scope of the Supreme Court's original jurisdiction beyond what is specified in Article III of the Constitution, which grants the Supreme Court original jurisdiction to issue writs of mandamus. He then finds a conflict between Article III of the US Constitution and the Judiciary Act of 1789 causing him to ask the question of whether the Supreme Court has the authority to review acts of Congress and determine whether they are unconstitutional.

THE COURT

2.3 Chief Justice John Marshall wrote the opinion and was joined by Associate Justices Paterson, Chase and Washington. Associate Justices Cushing and Moore did not participate in the decision. Washington and Moore were both Adams appointees and Cushing, Paterson and Chase were all Washington appointees. All the remaining members of the court, other than Marshall, largely served without distinction. In fact, Chase was impeached at the behest of Thomas Jefferson but the Senate failed to convict him. Moore resigned from the court and by many is considered the worst Justice in the history of the court. One remaining item of interest is that Washington was a nephew of George Washington.

THE OPINION

2.4 Certainly, Marbury and his majority must have thought they had won as they commenced reading the decision because Marshall answers affirmatively that Marbury has a right to the commission. His rationale being that the commission was effective when the President's constitutional power of appointment has been exercised, which he decided, and the power has been exercised when the last act required from the person possessing the power has been performed. He found that the grant of the commission to Marbury became effective when signed by President Adams. Marshall proceeds to say that not only does Marbury have a right but he should also have a remedy:

> '[W]here the heads of departments are the political or confidential agents of the executive, merely to execute the will of the President, or rather to act in cases in which the executive possesses a constitutional or legal discretion, nothing can be more perfectly clear than that their acts are only politically examinable. But where a specific duty is assigned by law, and individual rights depend upon the performance of that duty, it seems equally clear that the individual who considers himself injured, has a right to resort to the laws of his country for a remedy . . . One of the first duties of government is to afford that protection.'

Having determined that Marbury has a right to the commission and should be afforded a remedy under the law, Marshall now gets to the meat of why this case has become the bedrock of the American judiciary as well as the tool which allows for the Supreme Court to be the final arbiter of whether an action of the legislative branch or the executive branch violates the United States Constitution. Marshall finds that the Supreme Court has the authority to review acts of Congress and determine whether they are unconstitutional and, if found by the court to be unconstitutional, therefore rendered void:

> 'It is emphatically the duty of the Judicial Department to say what the law is. Those who apply the rule to particular cases must, of necessity, expound and interpret the rule. If two laws conflict with each other, the Court must decide on the operation of each. If courts are to regard the Constitution, and the Constitution is superior to any ordinary act of the legislature, the Constitution, and not such ordinary act, must govern the case to which they both apply.'

Was Marshall's reading the intent of the draftsman of the Constitution on this issue? What was the original intent? Who could say? While Marshall was heavily involved in having the document ratified in Virginia, he was not a significant player in the drafting of the document so it does not seem probable that he was an authority (prior to the rendering of this decision) on the original intent of the draftsmen. Clearly Jefferson did not agree with Marshall that the Supreme Court is the final arbiter of what is and is not constitutional. A further irony of the case is that the defendant, James Madison, was the principal draftsman of the Constitution and author of a substantial part of the Federalist Papers. The Federalist Papers seem that they should offer the most authoritative original interpretation. The papers did not really provide depth on this issue. Likely the answer is that it was not an issue which was given great thought and no one really knew the original intent. In this vacuum, Marshall had the power of his pen so his interpretation was the victor over that of two of those most intimately involved in the drafting of the constitution, Madison and Jefferson.

While after two hundred years of experience this concept of judicial review and the Supreme Court decreeing the acts of Congress or the Executive Branch to be void and unconstitutional does not seem foreign to Americans, it is a concept that, if not found exclusively in the United States, certainly is a concept which has its strongest history in the United States. In most of the world's other great democracies, the concept that an appointed court will overturn a duly enacted law passed by the elected leadership of its legislative arm is still quite a radical concept. Marshall states '[t]he government of the United States has been emphatically termed a government of laws, and not of men'. It is on this premise that he finds that it is the exclusive duty of the Supreme Court to hold the Constitution the Supreme Law of the Land and not allow Congress to enact laws which conflict with the Constitution unless they go through the process of officially amending the Constitution itself.

After establishing that this review is within the exclusive province of the Supreme Court, he finds that Congress cannot expand the scope of the Supreme Court's original jurisdiction beyond what is specified in Article III of the Constitution.

The Constitution states that 'the Supreme Court shall have original jurisdiction in all cases affecting ambassadors, other public ministers and consuls, and those in which a state shall be a party. In all other cases, the Supreme Court shall have appellate jurisdiction'.

As a consequence, Marshall holds the Judiciary Act of 1789 is unconstitutional as in conflicting with Article III of the Constitution and consequently the Supreme Court does not have original jurisdiction to issue writs of mandamus because Congress cannot expand the court's original jurisdiction, only the court's appellate jurisdiction. He opines:

> '[i]f it had been intended to leave it in the discretion of the Legislature to apportion the judicial power between the Supreme and inferior courts according to the will of that body, this section is mere surplusage and is entirely without meaning. If Congress remains at liberty to give this court appellate jurisdiction where the Constitution has declared their jurisdiction shall be original, and original jurisdiction where the Constitution has declared it shall be appellate, the distribution of jurisdiction made in the Constitution, is form without substance.'

Marshall states the grant of mandamus in the Judiciary Act of 1789 cannot be considered an exercise of the court's appellate jurisdiction because:

> '[i]t is the essential criterion of appellate jurisdiction that it revises and corrects the proceedings in a cause already instituted, and does not create that case. Although, therefore, a mandamus may be directed to courts, yet to issue such a writ to an officer for the delivery of a paper is, in effect, the same as to sustain an original action for that paper, and is therefore a matter of original jurisdiction.'

From an optics standpoint, Marshall's series of decisions had to be incredibly frustrating to all involved and at the same time were brilliant in their execution. He used a holding whereby he rendered void a law which would have expanded the original jurisdiction of the Supreme Court – which on its face would have expanded the reach of he and his colleagues to establish a construct of American jurisprudence which establishes the judicial branch as the final arbiter of the constitutionality of all matters even if the other branches of government are the parties involved. Despite his being part of the executive branch and intimately involved in the dispute before the court, he does not recuse himself and given the nature of his ruling he blunts any question that he has a conflict of interest. He finds in favour of Mr Marbury and then refuses to grant the Mandamus ordering delivery of his commission. Jefferson and his administration are not ordered to deliver the commission, yet they are dealing with a Federalist appointee who has now established the Supreme Court with broader powers vis-à-vis the other two branches of government.

The role of the Supreme Court as the final authority on the Constitution is not clear from the four corners of the document. Moreover, it is a construct that Jefferson vehemently opposed. Jefferson had a very low view of the role of judges in the political pecking order, and he was riding high on the electoral sweep of 1800. As a result, Marshall had to be careful not to provoke a confrontation with a very popular President that could well have consigned the court to impotence and irrelevance. Fortunately, he saved that type of mistake for a later President. In *Worcester v Georgia*,[1] a case dealing with finding an act of the State of Georgia redrawing boundaries of Indian lands as unconstitutional for violating treaties between the US Government and the Indian tribes, Marshall overplayed his hand with Andrew Jackson. Jackson is famously attributed with saying 'John Marshall has made his decision, now let him enforce it'. As a result, the court was severely weakened by the ensuing standoff. Such a confrontation with Jefferson over this decision surely would have resulted in a much different type of judiciary, certainly one much less independent.

If one combines the political stage at the time, Marshall's ability to establish a dispute at issue as a question of law rather than a purely political question, while still recognising that some questions can be purely political, his decision is almost Solomon like in its delivery. A decision which although none of the sides were particularly happy with the outcome, they really were not in a position to object without plunging the country back into revolution. Destabilising the young republic was in no one's best interest.

Marshall's eloquence and effective advocacy is best summed up by the Justice himself in the opinion:

> 'The question, whether an act, repugnant to the constitution, can become the law of the land, is a question deeply interesting to the United States; but, happily, not of an intricacy proportioned to its interest. It seems only necessary to recognize certain principles, supposed to have been long and well established, to decide it.
>
> That the people have an original right to establish, for their future government, such principles as, in their opinion, shall most conduce to their own happiness, is the basis, on which the whole American fabric has been erected. The exercise of this original right is a very great exertion; nor can it, nor ought it to be frequently repeated. The principles, therefore, so established, are deemed fundamental. And as the authority, from which they proceed, is supreme, and can seldom act, they are designed to be permanent.
>
> This original and supreme will organizes the government, and assigns, to different departments, their respective powers. It may either stop here; or establish certain limits not to be transcended by those departments.

> The government of the United States is of the latter description. The powers of the legislature are defined, and limited; and that those limits may not be mistaken, or forgotten, the constitution is written. To what purpose are powers limited, and to what purpose is that limitation committed to writing, if these limits may, at any time, be passed by those intended to be restrained? The distinction, between a government with limited and unlimited powers, is abolished, if those limits do not confine the persons on whom they are imposed, and if acts prohibited and acts allowed, are of equal obligation. It is a proposition too plain to be contested, that the constitution controls any legislative act repugnant to it; or, that the legislature may alter the constitution by an ordinary act.
>
> Between these alternatives there is no middle ground. The constitution is either a superior, paramount law, unchangeable by ordinary means, or it is on a level with ordinary legislative acts, and like other acts, is alterable when the legislature shall please to alter it.
>
> If the former part of the alternative be true, then a legislative act contrary to the constitution is not law: if the latter part be true, then written constitutions are absurd attempts, on the part of the people, to limit a power, in its own nature illimitable.'

Clearly, Marshall's decision is at a minimum a breathtaking assertion of judicial power under the guise of judicial restraint as the court nobly refused an ultra vires grant of original jurisdiction by Congress. For Jefferson, nothing less than a wolf in sheep's clothing. No wonder Jefferson was crazed by the decision. Fortunately, Marshall managed to go up to the line and yet did not overstep to the point of a showdown with Jefferson, allowing his logic to carry the day. 201 years later we see its impact. The court has ordered a President to turn over tapes and papers in which he claimed Executive Privilege (*United States v Nixon, President Of The United States, et al*[2]) and ordered the confirmation of the election of a President who did not win the popular vote where it was asked to weigh into the actual legitimacy of the election process itself (*George W Bush And Richard Cheney, Petitioners v Albert Gore Jnr et al*[3]). The greatest importance of these decisions is not who won or lost, but who was making that decision – the United States Supreme Court.

1 31 U.S. 515 (1832).

2 418 U.S. 683; 94 S. Ct. 3090; 41 L. Ed. 2d 1039; 1974 U.S. LEXIS 93 (24 July 1974).

3 531 U.S. 98; 121 S. Ct. 525; 148 L. Ed. 2d 388; 2000 U.S. LEXIS 8430; 69 U.S.L.W. 4029; 2000 Cal. Daily Op. Service 9879; 2000 Colo. J. C.A.R. 6606; 14 Fla. L. Weekly Fed. S 26 (12 December 2000).

3

ASSOCIATED PROVINCIAL PICTURE HOUSES V WEDNESBURY CORPORATION

Jennifer James

INTRODUCTION

3.1 Entertainment in Britain in the years just after World War II was unrecognisable compared to what we know and enjoy, or at times endure, today. It was far less permissive and, in fact, was censored to a massive degree, both on grounds of 'good taste' and, in the aftermath of World War II and the very early stirrings of the Cold War, on grounds of National Security.

Swearing, depictions of sexual acts, and any reference to recreational drugs or to homosexuality (which was illegal until 1967) were simply not the done thing. Abortion was still illegal and even when it was being reported in the press, the actual term 'abortion', was not used. Doctors or back-street practitioners caught in the act were instead reported as having been prosecuted for conducting 'an illegal operation'.

As late as 1965, when the playwright, Joe Orton, wanted to depict the character of Inspector Truscott in *Loot* saying the electrifying phrase, 'You're f***ing nicked, me old beauty!' he was forbidden to do so and officers stood in the wings every night ready to stop the show and arrest the actors if the offending phrase was spoken. It had, in fact, been spoken in real life two years previously by Harold Challenor, a former SAS war hero and police officer who was suffering from either paranoid schizophrenia or possibly post traumatic stress disorder, and who planted evidence (a half-brick 'offensive weapon') upon Civil Liberties campaigner Donald Rooum. Luckily for Rooum, he had some knowledge of forensic science and was able to prove the brick had never been in his possession. Challenor was ruled too ill to stand trial for corruption and eventually (after psychiatric treatment) ended up working for the firm of solicitors who had defended him!

The phrase 'You're f***ing nicked, me old beauty!' cropped up many years later in *Monty Python's Life of Brian*, spoken by John Cleese's Roman centurion arresting Brian, not the Messiah, just a very naughty boy. It is telling that, even as late as 1979, that film raised huge issues, being banned outright by 39 local authorities and not shown in many others after disputes as to its certification (the film's distributors insisted upon it being shown uncut and with a 14 Certificate, therefore if local authorities X-rated it, it was not shown). The furore about *Life of Brian*, however, had more to do with its supposed mocking of Jesus Christ than for its swearing and nudity which, by 1979, were fairly unremarkable.

3.2 Back in 1947, very few people owned television sets as these were prohibitively expensive to buy and to run; early cathode ray tubes tended to 'go' without warning and cost a fortune to replace. In any event, since television had barely taken off by the outbreak of World War II, and since broadcasts had been suspended throughout the war, people had never really got used to having television in their lives. In fact, television did not really become popular until 1952 when the forthcoming Coronation of Queen Elizabeth II caused a surge in the ownership of sets.

Instead, people listened to the radio with shows like *It's That Man Again* and *Much-Binding-In-The-Marsh* holding the nation transfixed. Such shows, whilst hugely funny and very well-crafted, were also all fairly cosy; it was unheard-of to criticise Royalty or politicians on the radio, for example. That did not become a widespread practice until the satire boom in the 1960s. Spike Milligan always lamented that the *Goons*, who included the unparalleled mimic Peter Sellers, were not permitted by the BBC to incorporate any humorous or other portrayal of political and public figures in their shows – he felt very strongly that the *Goons* could have pre-empted the satire boom by a decade if the BBC had only allowed them to do so.

Major sporting and public events were also broadcast on the radio, and for those who wished to see them as well as hear them, they were filmed by Pathe or Gaumont British News and shown in cinemas before the main feature.

In 1947, there were three dominant cinema chains in the UK: Associated British Cinemas (ABC – not to be confused with the Aerated Bread Company's ABC tearooms); Gaumont; and the only one still well known today, the Odeon chain. Cinema was still hugely popular; it was said that one-third of the entire UK population had seen Disney's *Snow White and the Seven Dwarfs* ten years before and popular films in 1947 would regularly cause lengthy queues as patrons vied to be the first to see them.

Cinemas represented luxury in a nation that had seen privation and tragedy during World War II; in poorer areas, a visit to the cinema was often the first time that patrons had ever walked on carpet. Cinemas were not expensive, and in times of unemployment it was not uncommon for people to take refuge from their sorrows and from the elements in them. As they tended to show two films (an 'A' picture and a 'B' picture) preceded by a newsreel and perhaps a cartoon, and to start the whole programme over again once the last item had finished, it was possible to stay in the warm and be occupied, if not entertained, all day long for a few pence.

British cinema was enjoying a golden age in 1947 with David Lean's *Great Expectations* and Michael Powell and Emeric Pressbuger's *Black Narcissus* released that year; both films are now acknowledged as classics and regularly shown at film festivals and on specialist film channels. Another film to appear in 1947 was *Miracle on 34th Street*, still shown every Christmas and starring

Edmund Gwenn as Kris Kringle, the department store Santa, who might just be the real McCoy.

Some of the films released in 1947 were darker in content; Charles Chaplin departed from his beloved 'little tramp' character to portray a serial killer in *Monsieur Verdoux*, Ronald Colman became possessed by the spirit of Othello and committed murder in *A Double Life* and Richard Widmark as a psychotic gangster in *Kiss of Death* kicked a disabled person down a flight of stairs. However, entry to such films was strictly controlled and nobody under 15 years of age could have gained admittance to them.

THE WEDNESBURY CORPORATION

3.3 Sunday opening was almost unheard of in Scotland, and in England and Wales, generally there had to be a local vote before cinemas could be opened at all on a Sunday. Closing times were usually set at the early hour of 4:30 pm; a donation to charity was frequently required as a condition of attendance and cinemas traditionally showed a re-run of an old feature, rather than enticing patrons on the Lord's Day with anything new.

The owners and licensees of the Gaumont Cinema in Wednesbury, Staffordshire, had been granted a licence by the Wednesbury Corporation, the licensing authority under the Cinematograph Act of 1909, to give performances on a Sunday. However, the licence was restricted such that 'no children under the age of fifteen years shall be admitted to any entertainment whether accompanied by an adult or not'. Therefore, under the terms of the licence, the Gaumont could not show family films, or at least could not expect a family audience, on a Sunday, which might otherwise have been one of their busiest days.

It may seem that such a restriction by the Wednesbury Corporation was impossibly parochial, but the legal system in 1947 was still coming to terms with the idea of cinemas per se and with the even more radical idea that families might wish to spend their Sunday afternoons, not in religious worship, but at the pictures watching Sabu romancing Jean Simmons in *Black Narcissus*. This was a relationship given added frisson by the fact that Miss Simmons was a white British actress, portraying a native girl in a very sensual relationship with Sabu, an Indian actor, which in 1947 was pretty cataclysmic stuff.

Showing films on a Sunday had only been legal for some 15 years, since the Sunday Entertainments Act of 1932; whilst some authorities had purported to allow Sunday opening prior to the Act, that was not strictly legal. Under the 1932 Act, a local authority could poll the electors in its borough to see whether a majority wished to have cinemas open on a Sunday and, if the majority did, Sunday opening could be allowed. During the war, Defence Regulation 42B enabled a competent naval, military or air force authority to certify that Sunday opening was desirable and the local authority to permit opening in accordance with such certificate. That Regulation remained in force until the end of 1947 and was principally designed so that, even if the local government electors in a particular borough did not want (or had not been asked to vote for) cinemas to be open on Sundays, an application could be made for the benefit of forces stationed in the neighbourhood at the relevant time.

3.3 *Wednesbury Corporation*

Thus at the time of the *Wednesbury* case[1] there existed three separate scenarios; ordinary weekday opening under the 1909 Act, Sunday opening under the 1932 Act and Sunday opening under Regulation 42B.

The Wednesbury Corporation was not concerned with the Defence Regulation but with the 1932 Act; it had in fact asked its constituents for their views, receiving a result in favour of Sunday opening, 'subject to such regulations as the Authority think fit to impose'. The Corporation imposed the condition referred to above, barring children under 15 years of age from attending Sunday showings and after the Gaumont's owners had challenged their right to do so, the age restriction had been upheld at first instance by Mr Justice Henn Collins.

Mr Gallop, King's Counsel for the Gaumont Cinema, sought to persuade the Court of Appeal that the learned judge's decision was wrong and that no reasonable authority could have gone on as Wednesbury did to impose a condition preventing people who had voted to have cinemas open on a Sunday from taking their children under 15 years of age with them.

In fact, the Court of Appeal was not persuaded by Mr Gallop's learned submissions. Given the scope of the 1932 Act, they held that it was clearly within the Wednesbury Corporation's powers to impose a condition forbidding children under the age of 15 from attending Sunday performances. The Master of the Rolls, Lord Greene, stated that, 'Nobody . . . could say that the well-being and the physical and moral health of children is not a matter which a Local Authority, in exercising their powers, can properly have in mind . . . '.

1 *Associated Provincial Picture Houses v Wednesbury Corporation* [1948] 1 KB 223.

3.4 Quite why the well-being, physical and moral health of children would have been at risk from attending a Sunday showing of *Miracle on 34th Street*, the learned Lord Greene MR did not state. A child who was 14 years old by 1947 would have been born in 1933 and would certainly have been old enough to appreciate and suffer the privations of World War II first hand. Stoke-on-Trent was a strategic high-priority target for the Luftwaffe and Staffordshire suffered heavy bombing during the war, due to the presence of important industrial targets and to the existence of mainline railways in the county. It might therefore be thought that an afternoon at the pictures was just what the doctor ordered; it is certainly highly likely that many adolescents in Staffordshire, and specifically in Wednesbury, had seen a lot worse in real life than they would ever be permitted to see at a matinee at the Gaumont Cinema, but as far as the Court of Appeal was concerned, that matinee could not be on a Sunday in any event.

It should also be remembered that in the years of reconstruction that followed the war, working six days a week was far from uncommon, and for those in industries such as coal mining at pits like the Chatterley Whitfield coalmine in Staffordshire, Sunday was not only the one day of the week that they had to spend any time with their families, in the winter months it was probably the only day on which they saw natural daylight. Nevertheless, they were not to be permitted to spend dark winter evenings in a cinema with their children for years to come.

So much for the Gaumont Cinema, Wednesbury; they had to live with the Corporation's ruling and indeed across the UK it would take many years for Sunday opening of cinemas to become commonplace. Even in the Cinemas Act of 1985, whilst it is not an offence under the Sunday Observance Act of 1780 to show films on a Sunday, it is not permissible to employ somebody who has worked on each of the preceding six days, although that rule may have more to do with employee protection, enshrining the right to have at least one day off per week, than it does with religious observance.

It should also be stated that in an increasingly diverse community, the importance of Sunday as a day of worship has necessarily diminished, as Jews, Muslims and those of other faiths having their holy days on other days of the week than Sunday and at other times of the year than Christmas and Easter, participate in British society in growing numbers. Indeed, an increasing section of the population is entirely secular and sets no store by any Sabbath day; they would likely resent being precluded from enjoying their Sunday however they saw fit. As such, almost inevitably, the Wednesbury Corporation's views on Sunday opening of cinemas for the under-15s have come to seem archaic and parochial.

THE NATURE OF UNREASONABLENESS

3.5 The Court of Appeal's decision is still cited daily and given that the Wednesbury Corporation's ruling against teenagers attending the cinema on Sunday was upheld, why is that so? Why has the case come to be seen as such a beacon of hope for those beset by unreasonable exercises of power?

The simple answer is that it is because of the Master of the Rolls' learned comments upon the nature of unreasonableness itself and upon how the courts should address this issue. Lord Greene MR stated that discretion must be exercised reasonably and went on to explain what that phrase meant. A person in authority, who is exercising discretion in order to make a decision, must direct himself properly in law. He must call his attention to the matters which he is bound to consider and must put away from him any matters which are irrelevant. If he does not do so, he may be said to have acted unreasonably.

If in fact a person in authority makes a decision which is so absurd that no sensible person could ever dream that it came within the powers of the authority, that decision will clearly also be unreasonable. The Master of the Rolls gave a specific example, cited from Lord Justice Warrington in *Short v Poole Corporation*[1] of a red-haired schoolteacher dismissed because she had red hair. That would clearly be an absurd and hence unreasonable decision. Being more scientific about it, Lord Greene MR went on to assert that such a decision would be unreasonable in any event because it was reached after taking into account entirely extraneous matters, the colour of a teacher's hair having no relationship whatever to the quality of her teaching.

Therefore, the test propounded by Lord Greene MR (with assent from Lord Justice Somervell) and which is still largely effective today, is as follows. In order to be able to intervene in a decision by an administrative authority, a court must conclude that:

(1) either the authority reaching the decision took into account factors which it should not have taken into account (eg red hair); *or*

(2) the authority failed to take into account factors which it should have taken into account (eg the well-being, physical and moral health of children); *or*

(3) the decision was so unreasonable that no reasonable authority would ever have considered taking it (again, sacking someone for having red hair is patently unreasonable under this third limb).

The above three limbs constitute the *Wednesbury* test, and when something is spoken of as being *Wednesbury* unreasonable, it generally means that it is so unreasonable that no reasonable authority could possibly have taken such a decision or step, in other words, it fails under the third limb. This designation may seem somewhat ironic given that in the particular case in which the test was laid down, the Wednesbury Corporation was held to have acted entirely reasonably and intra vires, but their name has now become synonymous with unreasonable and ultra vires behaviour.

[1] [1926] Ch 66.

CONCLUSION

3.6 As time has passed, and particularly after the introduction of various human rights protections by statute and case law, the courts have become more prepared to intervene in the decisions of local authorities and other administrative law bodies. That does not in any way mean that the *Wednesbury* test has ceased to be relevant or effective, it is simply the case that if a human rights provision (and particularly the Human Rights Act 1998) is invoked, it may well 'trump' the *Wednesbury* test, giving even greater protection than the Court of Appeal set out in that case.

However, given that the very existence of such human rights legislation, and the ceding of the final power of decision making to the European Court of Human Rights, would have been unthinkable in 1947, it is impressive to say the least that the *Wednesbury* test laid down over six decades ago, still survives even these radical changes.

By way of a final irony, according to Wikipedia, in 2001, 390,127 people described their religion on the Census as 'Jedi Knight'. That would allegedly make the Jedi Knights a more popular or populous religious group than Sikhs or Buddhists in the UK, although that proud boast is undermined by the fact that a significant proportion of these people probably certified themselves as Jedi Knights in protest at being asked about their religious beliefs, or else as a joke. One nevertheless wonders what on earth Lord Greene MR would have made of that; one cannot help but think that the owners of the Gaumont Cinema, Wednesbury, would have loved it.

4

THE *FACTORTAME* LITIGATION

Factortame Ltd v Secretary of State for Transport

Dr Jo Hunt

INTRODUCTION

4.1 No student leaving law school today can hope to escape without repeated exposure to the line of cases known as the *Factortame* litigation. Early in their studies, in their public law courses, students will meet the case which stands as a signal testament to the impact of European Union (EU) law within the national legal order, and of a considerable, if not terminal, blow to the traditional concept of parliamentary sovereignty. Further, they will locate the case within a line of cases which could be seen as contributing to a shift in balance between the courts and legislature, of a move from deference from the courts, to a more robust defence of rights and the rule of law within the UK constitutional order. In students' EU law courses meanwhile, the *Factortame* jurisprudence also forms part of the constitutional fundamentals of the subject, making key contributions to our understandings of the dimensions of the principle of supremacy, the Union's system of remedies, and substantive principles of non-discrimination and free movement. Few institutions, however, would have the opportunities available to enable students to engage with the substantive policy field which lay at the heart of the dispute, that of the Common Fisheries Policy (CFP).

As with its older sibling, the Common Agricultural Policy (CAP), these are policy areas which attract the headlines in the popular press, and garner considerable public notoriety, though whose details are lost in a mist of arcane technicalities, little helped by the fact that such subjects are simply not covered by the vast majority of law school syllabi. The CFP is, however, a fascinating area of law and policy, albeit one which has salutary lessons to teach about the triumph of politics over law in the annual wrangling over the fixing of allowable catches and quota, with short-term political imperatives hastening chronic stock depletion. As with the CAP, the CFP has given rise to a significant body of case law before the European Court of Justice in Luxembourg, through which key principles of the EU's legal operating framework have emerged. Again, as with agriculture, fisheries can be seen as having a distinctly localised, regional and territorial nature, an embeddedness within place which confronts in very uncomfortable ways the imperatives of market integration.[1]

[1] See further, Lequesne, C, 'Quota Hopping: The Common Fisheries Policy Between States and Markets', *Journal of Common Market Studies*, Vol 38, No 5 (2000).

BACKGROUND: THE COMMON FISHERIES POLICY

4.2 The European Union's CFP was developed incrementally from 1970 onwards. Having no separate basis in the 1957 Treaty of Rome, the fisheries regime would be founded on the provisions on Agriculture.[1] Common elements with the CAP are seen amongst the first set of measures introduced in 1970[2] which included a Common Organisation of the Market for Fisheries, which brought with it elements of price stability and guaranteed markets for producers. A system of structural aid was also established, which earmarked part of the EU budget for support payments to the fisheries industry. Finally, with the accession of a number of States on the horizon, all of which potentially laying claim to valuable fishing waters (the UK, Ireland, Denmark and Norway), the existing Member States, and France in particular, saw it as important to introduce principle of free and equal access to EU Member States waters. This would guarantee access to waters that would otherwise be within other State's Exclusive Economic Zones (EEZ), enabling the EU seas to be fished as a common resource.

This guarantee of access to other State's EEZ was particularly crucial to establish at this time, for, over the course of the 1970s, a general, worldwide, extension in the outer limits of a State's EEZ was taking place. Waters that had previously not fallen under a State's EEZ could soon be exclusively fished by that State as lines were redrawn. This would have implications for the European States which had traditionally fished the valuable waters of the Irish and the North Seas, much of which could soon be reserved exclusively for States such as the UK and Ireland should the zone be extended. The UK itself had notoriously seen the implications of unilateral extensions of a State's EEZ when (non-EU Member State) Iceland progressively extended its own EEZ by first fifty, then 200 nautical miles, stretching into an area of the North Atlantic which has previously been fished by UK fleet. Famously, the Icelandic enforcement of its new zone led to net-cutting, retaliatory ramming of vessels, and the deployment of warships, in the 'Cod Wars' which lasted until 1976.

As Iceland had extended its own EEZ, so the existing, and new Member States[3] were keen to see an extension of their own 'European' EEZ to 200 nautical miles, and this was fixed in 1976. In addition, the principle of equal access for fishing fleets was reiterated, although it was also recognised that this could be subject to 'certain specific conditions concerning the flag or the registration of their ships'.[4]

It would not be until reforms of 1983[5] however, that an ongoing stated commitment to conservation of fish stocks would translate into measures limiting the total allowable catch (TAC) of various species, with the level set annually, in Council. In determining the level of TAC, and the amount to be held by each state, consideration would be given to historical levels of catch (as fished over the period 1973–1978), as well as to a 'fair distribution of catches having regard, most particularly, to traditional fishing activities, to the special needs of regions where the local populations are particularly dependent upon fishing' and related industries. Each State would be allocated a quota to be fished against. It was by this time already clear that stocks were being depleted at a troubling rate, though the response in terms of the TAC set was insufficient to respond to the problem.

The years immediately following the introduction of the system of quotas and limits saw the accession to the EU of Portugal and Spain, the latter in particular having significant fishing interests, indeed, their arrival would, at a stroke, double the number of those employed in the EU's fishing fleets. Already, pre-accession, the extension of the EU's EEZ saw restrictions introduced on the right to fish in areas which had previously been part of Spain's traditional fishing grounds, particularly in the North and Irish Sea. Accession did not bring immediate and free access to these waters on equal terms for them however, as the accession negotiations resulted in a package that imposed stringent transitional measures, stretching long into the future.[6] Tight restrictions were placed on the rights of Spanish and Portuguese vessels to fish for species in the existing EU waters. Only certain zones could be fished, and the number of boats which could be operated in these waters was severely limited. The Spanish 'non-specialised' fleet was drastically limited to 300 vessels, only half of which could fish simultaneously. A set of challenges to aspects of this legal regime was launched, including a challenge to the legality of the Commission's approval of the list of boats permitted to fish,[7] and a challenge to the Regulation which lay down the measures to be taken in cases of non-compliance with the Act of Accession's transitional measures.[8] Both were unsuccessful.

Faced with such obstacles, alternative routes to survival were being sought by the Spanish fleet as a means of gaining access to the fishing grounds in the North Sea. These included either buying up vessels registered in, and carrying the flag of, another EU Member States or by reflagging existing vessels under flag of another State. The UK proved a fruitful target. Decline in stocks was already affecting the financial viability of the fishing fleets, and there was a ready market in boats, sold by those leaving the industry. Further, for a vessel to be deemed 'British' under the applicable law (the Merchant Shipping Act 1894), all that was required was for it to be owned by a company incorporated in the UK. Finally, it also appears that, initially at least, the moves towards British registration by Spanish fishing vessels met little resistance, as, during the late 1970s, their catch could be counted towards the overall British level that would be used to set the TAC.

Any welcoming of the arrival of an 'Anglo-Spanish' fleet was, however, short lived. Along with the depleted stocks, the TAC allocated to the UK in 1983 was perceived by many to have been a disadvantageous settlement. Growing opposition to the practice which was to become known as 'quota-hopping' led eventually to target states, including UK and Ireland, introducing restrictions on the registration of vessels so as to ensure a genuine link between the vessel and the UK. Initial attempts included fixing in the British Fishing Boats Act and Order of 1983, a requirement that the crew of 'British' boats had to comprise at least 75% EU nationals. This would exclude the Spanish, as they had not yet acceded to the EU. Ireland subsequently introduced its own legislation mirroring this requirement. These measures were tightened further in the UK in 1986, following Iberian accession, with the introduction of:

(a) a residence requirement for the crew;
(b) an obligation for the skipper and crew to contribute to the UK social security system; and
(c) finally a requirement for 'British' vessels to fish from, and regularly land their catch in UK ports.

More legal challenges were launched by Spanish fishing interests, before both the UK and Irish courts, which led to references before the European Court of Justice.

The first of these cases to be heard by the European Court of Justice was an Irish reference, which concerned the 75% EU nationality rule. This was found to be acceptable under EU law, and it was noted that the definition of being 'registered' and 'flying the flag' of a State was a matter for the legislation of Member States.[9] There then followed two actions from UK courts, dealing with the 1986 requirements. One was brought by Agegate, a company incorporated in the UK, which was 95% owned by Spanish interests. Agegate operated a fishing vessel, the crew composed entirely of Spanish nationals. The European Court of Justice considered two aspects of the 1986 measures in this action, the requirement that skipper and crew pay social security contributions in the UK, which was deemed lawful under EU law; and the residence requirement for crew. This was deemed unlawful, an indirectly discriminatory measure that could not be justified as it was 'irrelevant' to the aim of fishing quotas, which the court ruled was to assure to each Member State a share of the Community's total allowable catch.[10] The requirement for vessels to operate from, and land catch in UK ports was challenged in *Jaderow*.[11] Here, the court was more sympathetic to the UK rules, and found nothing precluded the laying down of rules designed to ensure a 'real economic link' between the State of registration and the fishing vessel. The requirement for vessels to operate from national ports was acceptable as long as 'that condition does not involve an obligation for the vessel to depart from a national port on all its fishing trips'. The landing of a proportion of the catch in national ports was also deemed an acceptable means of confirming that the vessel was operating from national ports.

Whilst *Jaderow* and *Agegate* were still pending before the European Court of Justice, the UK Government decided to tighten up the restrictions once more, this time with the introduction of the Merchant Shipping Act 1988. This brought in new conditions for qualification as a 'British fishing vessel', the key provision being section 14 requiring that the vessel be 'British' owned, either by resident and domiciled British citizens, or by a British company. A 'British' company for these purposes was one with at least 75% of its shareholders and directors resident and domiciled British citizens. In addition, the vessel needed to be managed, directed and controlled from UK, and its operator had to be resident and domiciled in the UK. Failure to meet requirements would mean there would be no access onto the register, and boats would not able to fish against the UK quotas. These were the measures which fell to be challenged in the *Factortame* litigation.

1 See now Article 38 of the Treaty on the Functioning of the European Union.
2 Council Regulations 2141/70 and 2142/70/EEC, OJ 1970 L236/1 and 5.

3 Norway did not accede in 1972, following a negative referendum. Potential damage to Norway's agricultural and fisheries interests through membership was seen to be a contributing factor to the No vote.

4 Council Regulations 100/76 and 101/76/EEC, OJ 1976 L20/1 and 19.

5 Council Regulations 170/83 and 171/83/EEC, OJ 1983 L24/1 and 14.

6 Iberian Act of Accession 1985, OJ 1985 L302/23.

7 *APESCO v EC Commission* [1988] ECR 2151 (207/86.

8 *Arposol v Council* [1988] ECR 13 (C-55/86).

9 Pesca Valentina Ltd v Ministry for Fisheries and Forestry [1988] ECR 83, ECJ (223/86) .

10 *R v Ministry of Agriculture, Fisheries and Food, ex parte Agegate* [1989] ECR 4459 (C-3/87).

11 *R v Ministry of Agriculture, Fisheries and Food, ex parte Jaderow* [1989] ECR 4509 (C-216/87).

THE *FACTORTAME* LITIGATION

4.3 Incorporated in the UK in 1986, Factortame was one of a number of 'Anglo-Spanish' companies which between them owned nearly 100 vessels registered as British under the Merchant Shipping Act 1894. A little over half of these vessels had originally been Spanish, and then re-flagged, whilst the rest were formerly 'British' boats, which had been sold on to Spanish interests. The directors and shareholders of the companies were almost exclusively Spanish, and Spanish residents, and the boats registered to a variety of ports in Wales and the South West, including Milford Haven, Brixham and Plymouth. The exceptions included John Couceiro, a UK national and resident in Milford Haven who ran companies, including Factortame, that managed vessels operating out of Spain, but were registered to Milford Haven, and Rawlings Trawlings distinguishable on the grounds that whilst the two directors of that company were both resident in Milford Haven, albeit one, Ramon Yllera, had Spanish nationality. This precluded Rawlings's, as well as all other vessels from re-registering under the new Merchant Shipping Act rules of 1988, as the necessary 75% nationality qualification for directors and shareholders was not met. Their challenge to the legal regime which precluded their re-registration, which began before the Divisional Court in 1989, would take over a decade to reach a resolution, and would take in multiple visits to both the House of Lords and the European Court of Justice.

The *Factortame* litigation can be broken down into distinct instalments. The first, and most famed, *Factortame I*, concerned the issue of whether a national court could suspend the operation of a piece of primary legislation. Beginning with an action before the (then) Divisional Court, the claimants in *Factortame I* sought an injunction suspending the application to them of the Merchant Shipping Act 1988, and an order prohibiting the Secretary of State from removing them from the register. The substantive basis for these claims lay in EU law, and the combined operation of the principle of supremacy of directly effective EU law[1] taken alongside the basic principle of non-discrimination on the grounds of Member State nationality,[2] as well as provisions guaranteeing the right of establishment in another Member State,[3] and the free movement of capital.[4] The Divisional Court granted the injunction on 10 March 1989, and sent the substantive question to the European Court of Justice as to whether the Merchant Shipping Act was in fact contrary to EU law, and this question would become *Factortame II* before the Luxembourg court, the answer not being seen as conclusive, the judgments in *Agegate* and *Jaderow* having not yet been handed down at this point.

The reference in *Factortame II* was expected to take two years to complete. Before it could be heard, however, the Divisional Court's order for the suspension of the Act was swiftly reversed by the Court of Appeal on 22 March 1989.[5] Whilst declaring that if the EU law was clear in its meaning, and clearly in conflict with the UK statute, the latter would have to be disapplied. The court ruled that in the absence of such clarity, putative EU law rights should not be upheld against an Act of Parliament, national courts having no jurisdiction to order an interim injunction against an Act of Parliament under these conditions. Two months later, the House of Lords upheld this decision of the Court of Appeal, Lord Bridge declaring that an order granting interim relief under such circumstances would be 'unlike any form of order for interim relief known to the law'.[6] The House of Lords sought a preliminary ruling from the ECJ on the issue of the availability of interim relief when EU law rights are in issue, which was heard more swiftly than would usually be the case, with an answer coming from Luxembourg in a little over 12 months.[7] The European Court articulated the question before it as being:

> 'whether a national court, which in a case before it concerning Community law, considers that the sole obstacle which precludes it from granting interim relief is a rule of national law, must disapply that rule?'

The European Court took a few short pages to answer that question in the affirmative, drawing on its existing case law on the obligations inherent on national courts to ensure the effectiveness of EU law.

The case was thus remitted to the House of Lords, and in July 1990, the court handed down the historic judgment granting interim relief against the Crown, enabling the claimants to continue to fish against the British quota. Its reasons were later handed down in the judgment of 11 October 1990.[8] Lord Bridge took the opportunity then to attempt to deflate the claims that the action signified 'a novel and dangerous invasion by a Community institution of the sovereignty of the United Kingdom Parliament'. Sovereignty, he said, had been limited from the start of the UK's membership of the EU, and voluntarily so. The UK acceded to membership of the EU clear in the knowledge of its relevant constitutional principles, and, under the terms of the European Communities Act 1972:

> 'it has always been clear that it was the duty of the United Kingdom court, when delivering final judgment, to override any rule of national law found to be in conflict with any directly enforceable rule of Community law'.

The grant of interim relief was not automatic however, the court's earlier decision in *American Cyanamid*[9] having set out some general guidelines, including the claimant needing to show a serious case to be tried, before it could be considered whether it is just or convenient to grant the injunction. For Lord Bridge, the crucial principle in a case such as this, involving putative rights, was to ensure that the course chosen was the one which offers the best prospect that eventual injustice is avoided or minimised. As Lord Goff outlined in his leading judgment, whilst some of the companies involved in the action had managed to re-register vessels successfully, having transferred the shares in the companies to 'British' interests, the majority had not, and many had not fished at all since their registration lapsed.

The judgment in *Factortame I* thus opened the way for vessels to return to the register and be able to start fishing once more, however, by this time, some boats had been laid up for between 18 months and three years and, ultimately, few were to return to the water. The issue of damages remained to be addressed. The stages which eventually led to the companies receiving financial compensation from the Government were to draw out over ten years. In *Factortame II*,[10] the ECJ finally dealt with the question referred from the Divisional Court in March 1989, as to whether the Merchant Shipping Act 1988 was compatible with EU law. The court acknowledged that whilst Member States had the authority to set conditions in order for a vessel to be registered as belonging to that State and permitted to fly that State's flag, however, in the exercise of that authority, Member States had to comply with the rules of EU law. Both the nationality and residence requirements of the Member State Authority were seen not to comply with EU law. Back before the Divisional Court, the issue turned to whether the State could be held liable for the damage caused to the claimants through its breaches of EU law. This then gave rise to a third reference to the ECJ, *Factortame III*,[11] which filled out some of the consequences of the newly-introduced principle of the obligation of the State to make reparation to individuals for damages caused by its breach of EU law, as introduced by the ECJ case of *Francovich*.[12]

Armed with a set of criteria to apply in determining what amounted to a 'sufficiently serious breach' that would lead to liability on the part of the State, the Divisional Court made a ruling in July 1997 that the UK Government had indeed been at fault, and should compensate Factortame and the other companies.[13] This fourth stage included a number of unsuccessful appeals, ultimately, in October 1999, before the House of Lords,[14] though no further references to the ECJ were deemed necessary. The task of setting the level of the award was to have been undertaken by the Technology and Construction Court, however, in the event, an out of court settlement was reached, Factortame receiving some £584,705 in compensation out of a total pot of around £55 million, against an original claim of around £285 million.

Further, final stages included actions on limitations (the Technology and Construction Court ruling that, as an action founded in tort, claims were only admissible if brought within six years from the point the House of Lords granted interim relief),[15] and on costs.[16] Factortame itself was dissolved and removed from the Companies register in 2003.

1 As established by the ECJ in the cases of *Algemene Transport-en Expeditie Onderneming van Gend en Loos NV v Nederlandse Belastingadministratie* [1963] ECR 1 (26/62) and *Costa v ENEL* [1964] ECR 585 (C-6/64), and latterly finding a rather limited expression in the Treaty framework in a Declaration appended to the Treaty of Lisbon, Declaration 17, concerning Primacy OJ 2010 (C-83/344). 'Directly effective' rights are those found in EU law (both in the Treaties and secondary legislation) which can be relied on directly before national courts, without the need to first incorporate them into national legislation.

2 Now Article 18 of the Treaty on the Functioning of the European Union (TFEU).

3 Article 49 of the TFEU.

4 Article 63 of the TFEU.

5 [1989] 2 CMLR 353.

6 [1990] 2 AC 85.

7 *R v Secretary of State for Transport, ex parte Factortame* [1999] ECR I-2433 (C-213/89).

8 *Factortame (No 2)* [1991] 1 AC 603.

9 *American Cyanamid v Ethicon* [1975] AC 396.

4.3 *The Factortame Litigation*

[10] R v Secretary of State for Transport, ex p Factortame Ltd (No 3)I [1991] ECR I-3905 (C-221/89).

[11] Joined Cases C-46/93 and C-48/96, *Brasserie du Pêcheur and Factortame III* [1996] ECR 1-1029.

[12] *Francovich and Bonifaci v Italy* [1991] ECR I-5357 (C-6/90 and C-9/90).

[13] [1997] EULR 475.

[14] *R v Secretary of State for Transport, ex p Factortame Ltd and ors (No 4)*[1998] EULR 456 (CA), [2000] EULR 40 (HL).

[15] [2001] 1 CMLR 47 (QBD).

[16] [2002] EWCA Civ 22, EWCA Civ 932.

THE LEGACY

4.4 Twenty years on from the decision of the House of Lords in *Factortame I*, the case's place in the canon of UK constitutional judgments is assured. It has become, according to Loveland, 'an obviously comfortable part of the constitutional furniture'.[1] For some, the case is seen as simply introducing a new 'rule of interpretation to the effect that Parliament is presumed not to intend statutes to override' EU law.[2] For others though, such as Wade, the case amounts to a 'judicial revolution',[3] the doctrine of parliamentary sovereignty, the 'ultimate political fact upon which the whole system of legislation hangs' having been altered fundamentally through the actions of the judiciary when they chose to disapply the will of Parliament as expressed in the Merchant Shipping Act 1988 as a consequence of the commitments made in an earlier Act of Parliament, the European Communities Act 1972. Through the intervention of the judiciary, the Parliament of 1972 was able to bind its successor in 1988, and will continue do to do for as long as the UK remains part of the EU. The European Communities Act has thus been described as being a piece of super-legislation, a statute of 'constitutional status', immune from implied repeal.[4] Whilst Laws, in his judgment in *Thoburn*, would seem to accept that the express will of Parliament legislating clearly and explicitly in contradiction with EU law would nevertheless need to be followed, the automatic compliance with Parliament's will by our highest courts should not be necessarily presumed.

Certainly, it is possible to place the *Factortame* litigation within a trend which has seen an increasing willingness of the courts to uphold the protection of individual rights and respect for the rule of law against the stated will of Parliament. Other cases in this line would undoubtedly include *A v Secretary of State for the Home Department*,[5] which saw declarations of incompatibility made as between provisions of the Anti-terrorism Crime and Security Act 2001 and the European Convention of Human Rights, as provided for under the Human Rights Act 1998. Domestically, the legacy of the *Factortame* litigation could be seen as a contribution to the construction of an effective bulwark against any incursion into the effective guarantee of the rule of law.

What then of the legacy for European Union legal order? Whilst the ECJ started handing down radical readings of the relationship between the national and the EU legal order in the very earliest years of its existence, in cases such as *Costa*[6] and later in *Internationale Handelgesellschaft*[7] (in which the European Court clearly stated that in the event of a conflict between the principles of a national constitutional structure, and a measure of EU law, the latter would prevail), the view of this court is only one dimension of the EU legal order. The responses of national courts, including where relevant their supreme or constitutional courts, must also be factored into our understandings of the shape and nature of the EU legal order. Far from being the 'awkward partner' depicted in political accounts of UK membership,[8] the House of Lords' judgment in *Factortame* demonstrates the UK judiciary as being effective and engaged participants in the creation and maintenance of this order, supporting the Union's key constitutional doctrines. However, the UK court's acceptance of the supremacy of EU law and its attendant consequences is generally traced back to the national act of ratification, to the constitutional statute that is the European Communities Act 1972, rather than to any autonomous authority of EU law. Whilst the ECJ may depict EU law as having such autonomous authority, this view is simply not shared by the highest courts of the Member States. This has been seen especially clearly with pronouncements from the highest courts from certain of the new Member States, none more clear than that of the Polish Constitutional Court, which stated that in the event of an irreconcilable inconsistency between a constitutional norm and an EU norm 'it may not lead to the situation whereby a constitutional norm loses its binding force and is substituted by an EU norm'.[9] The statement from the Polish Court stands at one extreme of the views on the relationship between national and EU law, that of the ECJ stands at the other. From within the academic literature, a more variegated, balanced view now holds sway, which presents the EU legal order as one of constitutional pluralism, or one of constitutional tolerance, in which there is a co-existence of orders, and no automatic precedence of either one over the other. Instead, all courts should share, in cases of conflict, a commitment to find the 'right' solution, following certain tenets of constitutionalism, including commitment to the rule of law and fundamental rights.[10] This would tie with the shifts towards greater constitutional protection of such principles recently demonstrated in the House of Lords.

Finally, what of the legacy of the fishing communities in Spain and in the UK that were caught up in the litigation and sometimes very ugly wrangling, in what was seen as a fight for survival? Ongoing reforms of the CFP in 1992, and most recently 2002, have failed to provide a sustainable sector. Of course, the resource is not finite, and we are facing a worldwide collapse in stock, however, it is widely agreed that the management approach adopted by the Union has simply not been sensitive to the needs of the *communities* most affected by fisheries policy.[11] Despite its early commitment to reflect the 'special needs of regions where local populations are particularly dependent on fishing', the social implications of fisheries management have been woefully handled. In *Factortame*, the economic imperative of free movement and non-discrimination, and the Union's 'non-territorial logic',[12] triumphed over the territorially grounded interests of the local fishing communities in Wales and the South West, protecting the interests of economic operators from other States. Whilst their communities may have been thereby supported, such consequences were simply a by-product of an overriding economic policy. For a Union committed to 'unity in diversity' arguably, greater recognition and protection for the interests of regional communities is demanded.

1 Loveland, I, *Constitutional Law, Administrative Law, and Human Rights* (2006) Oxford University Press, p 483.

2 Craig, PP, 'Sovereignty of the United Kingdom Parliament after Factortame' (1991) 11 Yearbook of European Law 221.

3 Wade, HWR, 'Sovereignty – revolution or evolution?' 112 (1996) *Law Quarterly Review*, 568–575.

4 *Thoburn v Sunderland City Council* [2003] QB 151.

5 [2004] UKHL 56.

6 See n 1 at **4.3** above.

7 [1970] ECR 1125 (C-11/70).

8 George, S, *An Awkward Partner: Britain in the European Union* (1998) Oxford University Press.

9 Judgment K18/04, 11 May 2005.

10 Kumm, K, 'The Jurisprudence of Constitutional Conflict: Constitutional Supremacy in Europe Before and After the Constitutional Treaty' (2005) 11 *European Law Journal* 262.

11 Wakefield, J, 'Fisheries: A Failure of Values' (2009) 46 *Common Market Law Review* 431–470.

12 See n 1 at **4.1** above.

5

AN IMPLIED CONSTITUTIONAL FREEDOM OF SPEECH IN AUSTRALIA

*The Hon Kevin Lindgren QC**

INTRODUCTION

5.1 In five decisions in the 1990s the High Court of Australia discovered in the Australian Constitution an implied freedom of political discourse. It had lain dormant since 1 January 1901 when the Constitution established the Commonwealth of Australia. This newly discovered constitutional freedom has led to legislation inconsistent with it being struck down; to a new defence to actions for defamation; and to an expansion of the defence of qualified privilege to such actions.

Australia does not have a constitutional bill of rights or a statutory bill of rights. That is to say, neither the Commonwealth Constitution nor any Act of the national Parliament professes to be or to contain a code of rights that individuals are to enjoy. Indeed, the Constitutional Convention of 1898 rejected a proposal to include in the Constitution a guarantee of individual rights based on the Fourteenth Amendment to the Constitution of the United States including a right to due process of law and the equal protection of the law.[1] The position in Australia may be contrasted with that in the United States. Relevantly for present purposes, the Australian Constitution contains no provision comparable to the First Amendment to the Constitution of the United States, which provides: 'Congress shall make no law . . . abridging the freedom of speech, or of the press'.

There is ongoing debate as to whether Australia should have a national Human Rights Act. On 10 December 2008, the Commonwealth Attorney-General announced a National Human Rights Consultation. That date was the 60th anniversary of the Universal Declaration of Human Rights. A committee chaired by Father Frank Brennan conducted a public inquiry and released its report on 8 October 2009. The Committee recommended the introduction of a national Human Rights Act. The recommendation was controversial and the government did not endorse it. However, the government introduced a 'Human Rights Framework'. This featured changes to the way in which legislation is scrutinised by reference to human rights standards in the Commonwealth parliamentary committee system; increased funding for human rights education and training; and a National Action Plan aimed at improving public service understanding of human rights. The question of a Human Rights Act is to be reconsidered in 2014.

It is not the concern of this chapter to consider human rights in Australia in general or these developments in particular, but a series of recent cases that, to some extent, changed the human rights landscape and the law of defamation in Australia.

An individual who claims that his or her 'human rights' have been infringed in Australia may or may not have a remedy available. First, the unwritten law, the common law of the States and Territories, that is recognised and enforced in State and Territory courts and, in appropriate cases, in the federal courts, offers protections to the individual through the law of tort. For example, the freedom of movement and of assembly is recognised by the availability of remedies for the torts of trespass to the person and false imprisonment.

Second, certain statutes of the Commonwealth and State Parliaments address particular issues that might be seen as 'human rights' issues. Examples are the Racial Discrimination Act 1975 and the Racial Hatred Act 1995 of the Commonwealth Parliament and the Anti-Discrimination Act 1977 of the New South Wales Parliament.[2]

Third, the Victorian Parliament and the Australian Capital Territory Legislative Assembly have passed the Charter of Human Rights and Responsibilities Act 2006 (Vic), and the Human Rights Act 2004 (ACT) respectively. These Acts set out human rights. They require courts, so far as possible, to interpret the Acts of the same legislature so that they are compatible with the relevant Act. These Acts give the courts jurisdiction to make declarations of incompatibility, that is to say, declarations that another Act of the same legislature is incompatible with the Act. Discussion of these two Acts is beyond the scope of this chapter. Two points, however, are noteworthy. First, both Acts include as a human right the right of freedom of speech.[3] Second, being no more than an Act of the particular legislature, they can be repealed, or indeed overridden by a later inconsistent Act of that legislature. Unlike the Commonwealth Constitution, the Acts neither give nor limit legislative power with consequential power to invalidate. The question whether Australia should have a bill of rights at the national level, whether constitutional or statutory, is the subject of ongoing debate in the country.

The present chapter is concerned with something different: the finding of a freedom of political communication or discourse implied by the Australian Constitution. Since all laws of all Parliaments in Australia, Commonwealth, State and Territory, are subject to that Constitution, the possibility emerges of legislation being held invalid because of inconsistency with such an implied right.

On 30 September 1992, the High Court of Australia gave judgment in two cases in which a freedom of speech and communication on certain political subject matter was held to be implied in the Constitution. The cases were *Nationwide News Pty Ltd v Wills*[4] ('*Nationwide*') and *Australian Capital Television Pty Ltd v The Commonwealth (No 2)*[5] ('*Australian Capital Television*'). The legal principles that were recognised in these two cases were applied and explained in three further landmark cases decided shortly afterwards: *Theophanous v The Herald Weekly Times Ltd*[6] *('Theophanous')*; *Stephens v Western Australian Newspapers Ltd*[7] *('Stephens')* and *Lange v Australian Broadcasting Corporation*[8] *('Lange')*. *Theophanous* and *Stephens* were both decided on 12 October 1994.

All five cases concerned media undertakings that relied on the implied freedom as a defence to proceedings brought against them arising out of things they had published. The first two cases, *Nationwide* and *Australian Capital Television*, concerned challenges to the validity of Commonwealth legislation. The remaining three, *Theophanous, Stephens* and *Lange*, concerned claims for damages for defamation.

1 See the Official Record of the Debates of Australasian Federal Convention, Melbourne, 8 February 1898, pp 664–691 at p 673.

2 Other examples are: Age Discrimination Act 2004 (Cth); Disability Discrimination Act 1992 (Cth); Disability Discrimination and Other Human Rights Legislation Amendment Act 2009 (Cth); Racial Discrimination Act 1975 (Cth); Sex Discrimination Act 1984 (Cth); Human Rights (Sexual Conduct) Act 1994 (Cth); Discrimination Act 1991 (ACT); Anti-Discrimination Act 1992 (NT); Anti-Discrimination Act 1991 (Qld); Equal Opportunity Act 1984 (SA); Anti-Discrimination Act 1998 (Tas); Equal Opportunity Act 1995 (Vic); Equal Opportunity Act 2010 (Vic); Equal Opportunity Act 1984 (WA).

3 Charter of Human Rights and Responsibilities Act 2006 (Vic), s 15 and Human Rights Act 2004 (ACT), s 16.

4 (1992) 177 CLR 1.

5 (1992) 177 CLR 106.

6 (1994) 182 CLR 104.

7 (1994) 182 CLR 211.

8 (1997) 189 CLR 520.

NATIONWIDE NEWS PTY LTD V WILLS

5.2 In *Nationwide*[1] the newspaper proprietor and publisher, Nationwide News Pty Ltd (Nationwide), published an article in its subsidiary's newspaper, *The Australian*, of 14 November 1989, which attacked the integrity and independence of the Australian Industrial Relations Commission. The article was written by Maxwell Newton and was published under the banner 'Advance Australia Fascist'.

The Commission was established by the Industrial Relations Act 1988 (Cth). Section 299(1)(d)(ii) of that Act made it an offence by writing or speech to use words 'calculated . . . to bring a member of the Commission or the Commission into disrepute'. It will be noted immediately that it did not matter that the criticism of the Commission might be fair and reasonable.

An officer of the Australian Federal Police laid information before the Federal Court of Australia alleging that Nationwide was guilty of an offence against section 299(1)(d)(ii). One of Nationwide's defences was that section 299(1)(d)(ii) was invalid because it was beyond the legislative power given to the Commonwealth Parliament by the Constitution.

The High Court held unanimously that section 299(1)(d)(ii) was invalid. Six sets of reasons for judgment were delivered by the seven members of the court (Deane and Toohey JJ gave joint reasons). The legislative powers in question were those in section 51(xxxv) and (xxxix) of the Constitution. Placitum

(xxxv) refers to a power to make laws with respect to '[c]onciliation and arbitration for the prevention and settlement of industrial disputes beyond the limits of any one State'. Placitum (xxxix) is the incidental power – a power to make laws with respect to matters incidental to the execution of any other legislative power vested by the Constitution in the Commonwealth Parliament.

Only four of the seven members of the Court, Brennan, Deane, Toohey and Gaudron JJ, spoke in terms of an implied constitutional freedom, but Mason CJ, Dawson and McHugh JJ were influenced by the importance of, and the respect shown by the common law itself for, the freedom to criticise public institutions.

Brennan J concluded that there was a 'sufficient substantive connection' between section 299(1)(d)(ii) and section 51(xxxv) of the Constitution (at 39), but thought that an implication arose from the express terms of the Constitution with which section 299(1)(d)(ii) was inconsistent.

What was the basis and nature of this implication? His Honour found its basis in the representative democracy and responsible government for which the Constitution provides in sections 1, 2, 7, 24, 61, 64 and 71. Brennan J said (at 47 – footnotes omitted):

> 'To sustain a representative democracy embodying the principles prescribed by the Constitution, freedom of public discussion of political and economic matters is essential: it would be a parody of democracy to confer on the people a power to choose their Parliament but to deny the freedom of public discussion from which the people derive their political judgments.'

At pp 48–49, his Honour continued (footnotes omitted):

> 'However, at common law there is no right to free discussion of government. Freedoms or immunities recognised by the common law are, generally speaking, liable to impairment or abrogation by legislation. Hence, to quote A V Dicey, it is "essentially false" to say that "the right to the free expression of opinion, and especially that form of it which is known as the 'liberty of the press', are fundamental doctrines of the law of England . . . and . . . that our courts recognise the right of every man to say and write what he pleases, especially on social, political, or religious topics without fear of legal penalties". But the fragility of the common law "right" to the free expression of opinion is in part due to the absence of a constitutional entrenchment of the form of government which the public discussion of political and economic matters is required to sustain. In legal theory, it may be possible – it is not for this court to say – for the Parliament at Westminster to abolish freedom of speech in the United Kingdom and thereby destroy the representative democracy which has been so entrenched in practice. But where a representative democracy is constitutionally entrenched, it carries with it those legal incidents which are essential to the effective maintenance of that form of government. Once it is recognised that a representative democracy is constitutionally prescribed, the freedom of discussion which is essential to sustain it is as firmly entrenched in the Constitution as the system of government which the Constitution expressly ordains.'

At pp 50–51, his Honour stated the nature of the implication in these terms:

> '[T]he Constitution prohibits any legislative or executive infringement of the freedom to discuss governments and governmental institutions and political matters except to the extent necessary to protect other legitimate interests and, in

> any event, not to an extent which substantially impairs the capacity of, or opportunity for, the Australian people to form the political judgments required for the exercise of their constitutional functions.'

Brennan J concluded that although section 51(xxxv) empowered the Parliament to enact a law protecting the Commission's capacity to perform its functions, that power does not extend to authorising a law prohibiting justifiable, fair and reasonable criticism of the Commission as an important instrument of government. Yet section 299(1)(d)(ii), properly construed, purportedly went so far.

In their joint judgment, Deane and Toohey JJ identified three general doctrines of government that underlie and are implemented by the Constitution: the doctrine or concept of a federal system; the doctrine of the separation of powers; and the doctrine of representative government, that is, of 'government by representatives directly or indirectly appointed by, and ultimately responsible to, the people of the Commonwealth' (p 70). In implementing the third doctrine the Constitution provides for the people to elect the members of the legislature and to amend the Constitution. Yet these powers cannot be exercised without communication among the people of information and opinions about matters relating to the government of the Commonwealth.

Their Honours said that the primary function of the implication is to limit, as a matter of construction, the scope of the legislative powers conferred on the Commonwealth Parliament by section 51 of the Constitution. They thought it 'strongly arguable' that the implication also confined the legislative powers of the State legislatures, although this did not need to be decided.

The scope of section 299(1)(d)(ii) went far beyond protecting against unfounded and illegitimate attack: it would catch criticism that was well founded and relevant, provided only that it brought the Commission or a member into disrepute. Yet to bring an instrumentality of government into deserved disrepute would be an incident of the ordinary working of representative government.

The remaining member of the court, Gaudron J, also concluded that section 299(1)(d)(ii) was not authorised because the heads of power given by section 51 must be construed in conformity with the principles of representative parliamentary democracy. While a law might validly curtail discussion of matters relating to governmental institutions, it could do so only if its purpose is not to impair freedom, but to secure some end within power in a manner 'reasonably and appropriately adapted to that end' (at p 95).

As noted earlier, the approach of each of the remaining three members of the court was different. Mason CJ noted that in deciding whether the particular provision was 'disproportionate' to the Commission's need for protection, the court must take into account not only the importance of the Commission's reputation for integrity, objectiveness and fairness, but also the public interest in ensuring that the Commission and its activities are open to public scrutiny and criticism (at 33). The Chief Justice said (at 34) that in deciding an issue of proportionality in the context of the incidental power:

> 'The Court must take account of and scrutinise with great anxiety the adverse impact, if any, of the impugned law on such a fundamental freedom as freedom of expression, particularly when that impact impairs freedom of expression in relation to public affairs and freedom to criticise public institutions.'

Mason CJ went on to speak of 'the paramount importance of freedom of expression and of criticism of public institutions' as having strongly influenced the development of the principles of the law of contempt of court.

The Chief Justice did not find it necessary to deal with the argument that there is an implied guarantee of freedom of communication on matters of public affairs to be found in the Constitution.

In agreeing that section 229(1)(d)(ii) was invalid, Dawson J said that the test was one of sufficiency of connection between a law and the subject matter of the constitutional head of power. His Honour rejected any test expressed in terms of 'proportionality' or 'reasonableness' or 'appropriateness' on the basis that they were concerned with the merits of the legislative provision – a matter for Parliament. Like Mason CJ, his Honour did not address the implied freedom argument.

McHugh J:

- considered that, properly construed, section 299(1)(d)(ii) went beyond what was reasonably and appropriately adapted to the protection of the Commission, its members, and their functions;
- did not deal with the implied freedom argument; and
- was influenced in assessing sufficiency of connection by his assessment that the provision constituted 'a far reaching interference with the common law right of members of the public to make fair comments on matters of public interest'.

The reasons for judgment of Brennan, Deane, Toohey and Gaudron JJ lay the basis for the development in the later cases to be discussed in this chapter of an implied freedom of political discourse.

[1] (1992) 177 CLR 1.

AUSTRALIAN CAPITAL TELEVISION PTY LTD V THE COMMONWEALTH

5.3 *Australian Capital Television*[1] also concerned a challenge to the validity of Commonwealth legislation, namely Part IIID of the Broadcasting Act 1942 (Cth). Part IIID was introduced into that Act by the Political Broadcasts and Political Disclosures Act 1993 (Cth). Generally speaking, Part IIID prohibited the broadcasting of material relating to an election or referendum (for convenience, referred to as an 'election') during a certain period preceding the election ('election period') for or on behalf of the government or a government authority of the Commonwealth. There was exempted matter having no significant connection with political advertisements or political information. Part IIID contained similar prohibitions in relation to State and Territory elections.

A provision within Part IIID required broadcasters to make available free of charge units of time for election broadcasts to political parties, persons or groups identified by the Australian Broadcasting Tribunal. The Tribunal was required to identify each political party that was represented by one or more members of the relevant Parliament or legislature as at the time immediately before its last sittings, provided his, her or their party was contesting the forthcoming election with at least the prescribed number of candidates. There was a formula for the calculation of the amount of free advertising time.

It will be recalled that in *Nationwide*,[2] Mason CJ, Dawson and McHugh JJ had expressed no view on the question of an implied freedom of political speech and communication. Now, Mason CJ joined Deane, Toohey and Gaudron JJ in holding that Part IIID was wholly invalid because it infringed the freedom of political discussion that was implied in the system of representative government for which the Constitution provided.

McHugh J held that there was an implication in the Constitution's embodiment of a system of representative government, of 'freedom of participation, association and communication in respect of the election of the representatives of the people', which, under the Constitution, 'have been elevated to the status of constitutional rights' (at p 233). His Honour concluded that Part IIID was invalid, except (for reasons that do not presently matter) in its application to the Territories.

Contrasting the Australian Constitution with that of the United States, Dawson J rejected the constitutional implication of the freedoms or rights favoured by the other members of the court.

Brennan J, who had supported the existence of implied freedom in *Nationwide*, held that with the exception of two particular provisions (not necessary to discuss) the implied freedom did not have the effect of invalidating Part IIID.

The position attained, then, in *Nationwide* and *Australian Capital Television* decided on 30 September 1992, is that the implication of an implied constitutional freedom of communication of a limited kind based in the Constitution's provisions relating to the system of representative government found favour with all seven members of the High Court with the exception of Dawson J.

1 (1992) 177 CLR 106.
2 See **5.2**.

THEOPHANOUS V THE HERALD AND WEEKLY TIMES LIMITED

5.4 *Theophanous*[1] was the first case in which the implied freedom of political communication was relied upon as a defence to an action in defamation. In the cases of *Theophanous, Stephens* and *Lange*, the plaintiffs were all politicians. There was bipartisan opposition to the decisions, or at least to the first two – *Lange* was seen as representing a retreat to some extent. There was media criticism of the stance taken by the politicians as based on self-interest – a reference to sizeable tax-free awards of damages for defamation of which the beneficiaries were often politicians. It cannot be overlooked, however, that the media were the payers of these awards.

Dr Andrew Theophanous was a member of the House of Representatives. He was the Chair of the Joint Parliamentary Standing Committee on Migration Regulations and Chair of the Australian Labor Party's Federal Caucus Immigration Committee. He had been prominent in public discussion of migration issues.

Dr Theophanous has led a colourful life. In 1998 he came under suspicion for being involved in migration fraud and the National Crime Authority launched an investigation. He was charged with defrauding the Commonwealth by making false representations in relation to an immigration matter, taking an unlawful inducement and soliciting an unlawful inducement. He resigned from the Australian Labor Party on 18 April 2000 and served out the rest of his term as an independent Member of Parliament. Dr Theophanous contested the 2001 election as an independent but the seat was won by the Labor Party candidate. He was gaoled in 2002, having been sentenced to six years in prison, but successfully appealed one of the convictions, that of conspiracy to defraud. He served two years in gaol.

Bruce Ruxton was the President of the Victorian branch of the Returned Services League. Mr Ruxton wrote a letter to the editor of the *Herald Sun*, a newspaper published by the defendant. The general tone of the letter may be gauged from the title under which it was published: 'Give Theophanous the shove'. Mr Ruxton wrote that it was high time Dr Theophanous was 'thrown off Parliament's immigration committee', and 'I have read reports that he stands for most things Australians are against'. Mr Ruxton asserted that Dr Theophanous showed a bias in favour of Greek immigrants and that he wanted to dilute the British base of Australian society so that English would cease to be the country's major language.

The letter was published on 8 November 1992. An election for the Commonwealth Parliament was expected to take place in December 1992.

In his action for damages for defamation in the County Court of Victoria against the newspaper publisher and Mr Ruxton, Dr Theophanous pleaded the following defamatory imputations:

- that he showed a bias towards Greek migrants;
- that he stood for things that Australians were against;
- that he was an idiot and that his actions were the antics of an idiotic man.

Two of the defences raised were as follows:

'(a) the words were published pursuant to a freedom guaranteed by the Commonwealth Constitution to publish material:
 (i) in the course of discussion of government and political matters;
 (ii) of and concerning members of the Parliament of the Commonwealth of Australia which relates to the performance by such members of their duties as members of the Parliament or parliamentary committees;
 (iii) in relation to the suitability of persons for office as members of the Parliament.

(b) The publication of the words was:
 (i) in the course of discussion of government and political matters;
 (ii) of and concerning the plaintiff as a member of the House of Representatives and as Chairperson of the Joint Parliamentary Standing Committee on Migration Regulation and the Australian Labor Party's Federal Caucus Immigration Committee;
 (iii) in respect of the plaintiff's performance of his duties as a member and as Chairperson as aforesaid;
 (iv) in relation to the plaintiff's suitability for office as a member of Parliament;
 (v) without malice;
 (vi) reasonable in the circumstances;

(vii) not made without an honest belief in the truth of the words or made with reckless disregard for the truth or untruth of the words;
(viii) made at a time when it was publicly anticipated that a federal election was about to be called.

(c) By reason of each of the matters aforesaid the said publication is not actionable.

12. Further and alternatively, by reason of the freedom guaranteed by the Commonwealth Constitution as aforesaid, the words were published on an occasion of qualified privilege.'

Generally, 'qualified privilege' is a defence to an action for defamation that is available where a publisher, acting reasonably, publishes matter to a recipient who has an interest in receiving it.

A summons was filed to strike out paragraphs 11 and 12 of the defence. The court ordered that the proceeding be removed to the High Court.

In the High Court certain questions were reserved for the consideration of the Full Court. The court held that the defences in paragraphs 11 and 12 were not bad in law. The court also held as follows:

'(1) There is implied in the Commonwealth Constitution a freedom to publish material:
(a) discussing government and political matters;
(b) of and concerning members of the Parliament of the Commonwealth of Australia which relates to the performance by such members of their duties as members of the Parliament or parliamentary committees;
(c) in relation to the suitability of persons for office as members of the Parliament.

(2) In the light of the freedom implied in the Commonwealth Constitution, the publication will not be actionable under the law relating to defamation if the defendant establishes that:
(a) it was unaware of the falsity of the material published;
(b) it did not publish the material recklessly, that is, not caring whether the material was true or false; and
(c) the publication was reasonable in the circumstances.

(3) A publication that attracts the freedom implied in the Commonwealth Constitution can also be described as a publication on an occasion of qualified privilege. Whether a federal election is about to be called is not a relevant consideration.'

Mason CJ, Toohey and Gaudron JJ delivered joint reasons for judgment. They referred (at p 121) to the various ways in which the constitutionally implied freedom had been described in *Nationwide* and *Australian Capital Television*. Their Honours noted that the narrowest version of it was that of McHugh J – 'freedom of participation, association and communication *in relation to federal elections*' (*Australian Capital Television* at 227 – emphasis added). That formulation was based on McHugh J's view that the implication was founded on sections 7 and 24 of the Constitution.

Their Honours saw no substantial difference in the formulations adopted by Mason CJ in *Australian Capital Television* at pp 138, 142; Brennan J in *Nationwide* at p 50; Deane and Toohey JJ in *Australian Capital Television* at p 169; and Gaudron J in *Australian Capital Television* at p 214. It followed, their Honours said, that there was, as the defendant contended in paragraph 11(a)(i) of its defence, an implied freedom of communication with respect to 'discussion of government and political matters'.

Their Honours said (at p 124) that this concept included 'discussion of the conduct, policies or fitness for office of government, political parties, public bodies, public officers and those working in public office', and 'discussion of the political views and public conduct of persons who are engaged in activities that have become the subject of political debate, eg trade union leaders, Aboriginal political leaders, political and economic commentators'. Their Honours expressly accepted that the concept was not limited to political publications and addresses that were intended to influence choices.

Mason CJ, Toohey and Gaudron JJ considered the question whether the implied freedom of political discussion was a defence to a defamation claim. Dr Theophanous put several arguments to the contrary. For example, he argued that the framers of the Constitution must have accepted that the common law, including the common law as to qualified privilege, struck a satisfactory balance between the defamer and the defamed. Their Honours rejected his arguments and emphasised that the implied freedom of political discussion was not only a matter for the defamer and the defamed, but also an aspect of the public interest in the proper functioning of representative government. In any event, they said, the Constitution must prevail over the common law and ordinary statute law.

Deane J would have gone further than Mason CJ, and Toohey and Gaudron JJ. His Honour would not have insisted on three conditions which their Honours required a defendant to establish:

(a) unawareness of the falsity of material published;
(b) absence of recklessness; and
(c) reasonableness in the circumstances.

However, his Honour joined with their Honours since their narrower formulation provided an answer to Dr Theophanous's claim. In the result, there was a majority of four of the seven judges supporting their Honours' formulation.

Brennan J dissented. His Honour's reason was that the freedom of political discussion implied by the Constitution was a limitation on legislative and executive power, not a personal freedom (it will be recalled that *Nationwide* and *Australian Capital Television*[2] both concerned the validity of legislation). His Honour said (at p 153) that there was no inconsistency between the Constitution and the rules of the common law that deal with rights and liabilities of individuals inter se because the Constitution does not deal with the latter: it deals with the structure and powers of organs of government, including the powers to make laws dealing with private rights and liabilities. The common law of defamation, on the other hand, was concerned with the adjustment of private rights and freedoms. Brennan J thought that that law was not inconsistent with any implication that could be drawn from the text or structure of the Constitution.

Dawson J also dissented, consistently with his Honour's dissent in *Nationwide* and *Australian Capital Television*. He remarked that representative government had been thought to co-exist with defamation laws for over 90 years, even though those laws curtailed freedom of speech (at p 192). His Honour said (at p 193):

> 'Whilst it may disappoint some to find that the Australian Constitution provides no guarantee, express or implied, of freedom of speech, that is because those who

> framed the Constitution considered it to be one of the virtues of representative government that no such guarantee was needed.
>
> . . .
>
> They took the view that constitutional guarantees operate as a fetter upon the democratic process and did not consider it necessary to restrict the power of Parliament to regulate those liberties which the common law recognises and nurtures.'

His Honour would have answered question 1 'No' and found it unnecessary to answer the remaining questions.

McHugh J also dissented. His Honour's dissent is explained by the more limited form of implication that he was prepared to find contained in the Constitution. According to his Honour, the only basis for the relevant implication was sections 7 and 21 of the Constitution which provided for persons to be elected to the House of Representatives and the Senate. McHugh J could see no ground for any implication of a general right of political discussion when no federal election was pending. Of representative government, his Honour said that although the Constitution implemented that form of government, this was different from saying that representative government was part of the Constitution and therefore a basis for the implication of constitutional rights or freedoms.

Theophanous stands for the high watermark in the development of implied constitutional freedoms in Australia. Four of the seven members of the High Court (Mason CJ, Toohey, Gaudron and Deane JJ) supported the implication of a broad freedom of political discussion; Brennan J drew a boundary which excluded the laws of the States and Territories governing private rights and liabilities; McHugh J supported a narrow implication by reference to the conduct of federal elections; and Dawson J rejected the process of finding rights or freedoms implied in the Constitution.

1 (1994) 182 CLR 104.

2 See **5.2** and **5.3**.

STEPHENS V WEST AUSTRALIAN NEWSPAPERS LTD

5.5 In *Stephens*[1] the court unanimously held that the newspaper's defence to an action for defamation based on the newly exposed implied freedom of political communication was bad in law.

Six members of the Legislative Council of Western Australia went overseas on a trip. The newspaper reported assertions made by another member of the Legislative Council that they had gone without the knowledge of Parliament and that the trip was a 'junket of mammoth proportions'. The newspaper's first defence was a freedom allegedly supported by the Commonwealth Constitution and the Constitution Act 1889 (WA).

A second defence was that the articles were published on occasions of qualified privilege. The substance of the first defence was given as particulars of the second defence.

All members of the court held that the first defence was bad in law.

Mason CJ, Deane, Toohey and Gaudron JJ held, however, that the first defence would have afforded a defence if it had alleged that:

(a) the defendant was unaware of the falsity of the material published;
(b) the defendant did not publish the material recklessly; and
(c) publication was reasonable in the circumstances,

yet the first defence did not allege satisfaction of the first and second of those conditions. It will be recalled that these three conditions had received the endorsement of a majority in *Theophanous* – Mason CJ, Deane, Toohey and Gaudron JJ.

Brennan J held the first defence deficient on two grounds. First, the freedom implied by the Commonwealth Constitution did not extend to discussion of political matters exclusively concerned with a State. Second, although a comparable freedom could be implied from the Constitution Act 1889 of the State of Western Australia, that freedom did not affect the common law of defamation or the provisions of the Western Australian Criminal Code relating to defamation.

Consistently with the approach that they had taken in *Theophanous*, Dawson and McHugh JJ ruled against the first defence on the ground that the law recognised no freedom of the kind relied on by the defendants.

Notwithstanding the failure of the first defence, Mason CJ, Deane, Toohey and Gaudron JJ gave some encouragement to the implied freedom concept. Their Honours held that a freedom of communication about political matters was implied in the State Constitution of Western Australia and extended to criticism of the performance, conduct and fitness for office of a member of the Western Australian Parliament.

Those four judges also held (Brennan, Dawson and McHugh JJ dissenting) that the second defence pleaded (that of qualified privilege) was good in law.

1 (1994) 182 CLR 211.

LANGE V AUSTRALIAN BROADCASTING CORPORATION

5.6 By the time *Lange*[1] was decided on 8 July 1997 there had been a change in the composition of the High Court. Mason CJ and Deane J had retired – two Justices who, it might be said, had favoured a broad implied freedom of political discussion. The two new members of the court were Gummow and Kirby JJ.

The Rt Hon David Russell Lange was Prime Minister of New Zealand. On 20 April 1989 the defendant (Australian Broadcasting Corporation (ABC)) broadcast a 'Four Corners' program throughout Australia. Mr Lange claimed that the program had defamed him. He said that it gave rise to the imputation that he was guilty of abuse of public office and unfit to hold public office.

In Mr Lange's action for damages for defamation in the Supreme Court of New South Wales the ABC pleaded in paragraph 10 of its defence an implied freedom of political discussion. It relied on *Theophanous* and *Stephens*[2]. The ABC also pleaded qualified privilege in paragraph 6 of its defence.

The action was removed to the High Court where questions were stated for the consideration of the Full Court, namely, whether the two defences were bad in law.

Happily, the seven members of the court delivered a single judgment. They held that the defence pleaded in paragraph 10 was bad in law, and that the defence pleaded in paragraph 6 was not bad, in respect of the publication complained of in New South Wales, but that the particulars given did not bring the publication within that defence.

The court identified the principal questions raised by the case as being whether the court should reconsider its decisions on the implied constitutional freedom, and if so, whether those decisions were correct.

The court reviewed *Nationwide, Australian Capital Television, Theophanous* and *Stephens*. At p 560 their Honours held that sections 7 and 24 and related sections of the Commonwealth Constitution necessarily protected 'that freedom of communication between the people of Australia concerning political or government matters which enables the people to exercise a free and informed choice as electors'.

Their Honours also held (at p 561) that the freedom is not confined so as to be exercisable only during an election period. They found analogous freedoms based on section 128 of the Constitution which involves electors in voting on proposed amendments to the Constitution and on the provisions that prescribe the system of responsible government. The material complained of in the 'Four Corners' television program, relating as it did to New Zealand's Prime Minister, did not fall within any of the implied freedoms.

Finally, their Honours held that the freedom does not invalidate a law the object of which is compatible with the maintenance of Australia's constitutionally prescribed system of representative and responsible government or with the procedure of submitting a proposed amendment to the Constitution to a referendum of the people, so long as the law is reasonably appropriate and adapted to achieving that object.

Significantly for the law of defamation in particular, the court also explained that the law relating to the defence of qualified privilege, referred to above, had developed to mirror the implied freedom of political communication, so that the common law rules of qualified privilege properly reflect the requirements of sections 7, 24, 64, 128 and related sections of the Constitution. Accordingly, the court declared (at p 571) 'that each member of the Australian community has an interest in disseminating and receiving information, opinions and arguments concerning government and political matters that affect the people of Australia'. Their Honours said that the duty to disseminate such information was simply the correlative of the interest in receiving it. They said expressly that the extended category of qualified privilege embraced discussion of government or politics at State and Territory level and even at local government level, whether or not bearing on matters at the Federal level.

1 (1997) 189 CLR 520.

2 See **5.4** and **5.5**.

SUBSEQUENT CASES

5.7 There have been many subsequent cases in defendants in actions for defamation that have relied on the implied constitutional freedom as discussed above. In most of them, the material complained of has been held to fall outside the scope of the implied freedom. The cases are too numerous to be reviewed here. They have been discussed by Adrienne Stone[1] and Paul Heywood-Smith QC.[2] Professor Stone has drawn attention to the 'narrowing effect' of the decision in *Lange*[3] and to the difficulty of the distinction between the public and institutional focus of the implication of the freedom (the operation of representative and responsible government) and private and personal 'rights'. Mr Heywood-Smith suggests that it would be timely for the High Court to have the opportunity of clarifying for the benefit of lower courts the scope of *Lange*'s concept of 'that freedom of communication between the people concerning government and political matters which enables the people to exercise a free and informed choice as electors'.

A non-defamation case of some interest was *Sellars v Coleman*.[4] In December 1998, Mr Coleman made a political speech in the Flinders Mall in Townsville, Queensland without having obtained a permit from the local council as requested by a council by-law. He was fined by the local magistrate. His challenge to the validity of the by-law on the *Lange* ground failed (2:1) before the Queensland Court of Appeal and he was refused special leave to appeal to the High Court. However, the United Nations Human Rights Committee found that Australia had unduly circumscribed Mr Coleman's ability to engage in free speech and had therefore contravened the International Covenant on Civil and Political Rights.

1 Adrienne Stone, 'Rights, Personal Rights and Freedoms: The Nature of the Freedom of Political Communication' (2001) 25 *Melbourne University Law Review* 374.

2 Paul Heywood-Smith QC, 'Government and Political Matters: *Lange* Seven Years on' (2006) 80 *ALJ* 22.

3 See **5.6**.

4 [2001] 2 Qd R 565.

CONCLUSION

5.8 The five High Court cases discussed above culminating in *Lange* re quite remarkable. The importance of the cases lies in the fact that Australia lacks a bill of rights, either constitutional or statutory. By a process of implication from the express terms of the Constitution, the High Court was able to discover a constitutionally entrenched freedom of communication of information, comment and opinion on governmental and political issues. Being constitutionally entrenched, that freedom was capable of invalidating otherwise valid legislation and providing a defence to defamation claims. The cases have also given rise to a commensurately expanded common law defence of qualified privilege to actions for defamation. Although *Lange* limited the scope of the implication somewhat, the five cases have marked an important development in Australian constitutional and tort law.

* *Formerly a Judge of the Federal Court of Australia. The author acknowledges with thanks the research assistance of Lindsay Ash BA, MA in the writing of this chapter.*

6

A RIGHT TO RESIST?

The Trial of Dr Sacheverell

Craig Rose

CHURCH AND CROWN

6.1 The trial of Dr Sacheverell in 1710 is one of the most famous state trials in English history. It marked the beginning of the final, feverish phase of the conflict between Whig and Tory parties which dominated English politics in the quarter of a century after the revolution of 1688–89. It raised a great question of principle – do the people always owe obedience to lawful authority or do they have the right to resist a tyrant? It sparked one of the worst outbreaks of mob violence that London has ever witnessed. And it brought down a government which had presided over an unprecedented sequence of military victories on the Continent.

Henry Sacheverell, a 36-year-old Oxford don, was the epitome of the Oxford men of the day – 'high' in his Anglicanism, Tory in his politics and truculent in everything. Men of his ilk looked back wistfully to the last four years of Charles II's reign, in 1681–85, as a lost golden age during which the Church of England had been kept safe from 'phanatick' Protestant nonconformists and 'roundhead' Whigs because the Crown had kept its foot planted firmly on their necks.

It had all gone downhill since then. King Charles's brother and successor, the Catholic James II, had turned on the Church in his attempts to secure toleration and civil liberty for his co-religionists. He had thereby pitted the two halves of the Tory ideology – Church and Crown – against each other. From a Tory perspective, the consequences had been disastrous all round. King James had been thwarted, but only by means of a revolution that had brought to the throne King William III, a Dutch Calvinist with no sympathy for the narrow and persecuting Church state which the Tories had fashioned in the last years of King Charles's reign. In the Toleration Act of 1689, King William had given nonconformists their liberty, and over the next few years their meeting houses began sprouting up alarmingly all over the country. True, the Corporation Act of 1662 and the Test Act of 1673, which restricted public office to those who took the Anglican sacrament, remained in force, but nonconformists with political ambitions could satisfy the requirements of that test by taking the sacrament just once a year – the so-called practice of occasional conformity. In 1697, for example, the Lord Mayor of London scandalised Tories by attending a service at St Paul's Cathedral in the morning before proceeding, in full regalia, to a nonconformist meeting house for an afternoon sermon.

To make matters worse, Dutch William had immediately dragged England into a war against Holland's mortal enemy, Louis XIV of France – a ruinously expensive affair that seemed to profit only a new class of (largely Whig) 'monied men' who had grown fat on the interest paid on loans to finance the war. All this had been at the expense of the (largely Tory) country gentlemen whose taxes funded the new National Debt.

PASSIVE OBEDIENCE

6.2 Whigs and Tories were not only divided over the consequences of the revolution – they were also at loggerheads over its very nature. Whigs generally had few qualms in saying that the events of 1688–89 had been an act of legitimate resistance against a tyrannical King who had been seeking to destroy the nation's civil and religious liberties. Such a view made Tories distinctly queasy. Self-proclaimed heirs to the traditions of the Civil War royalists, they had spent the first half of the 1680s preaching damnation against all those who, in the words of the satirical verse, 'The Vicar of Bray', 'dare resist or touch the Lord's anointed'. Even when King James had turned against them, they had responded not with violent resistance, but with 'passive obedience' – what we would term a campaign of passive resistance to the King's policies.

As for King James's deposition, that could be treated not as an act of force, but as an abdication by a monarch who had abandoned his realm. True, this was a notion that required them to forget the 21,000-strong Dutch army whose landing in England had prompted the King to flee. But such absent-mindedness posed few problems for a party which also forced itself to believe that King James's baby son, the Prince of Wales, who should have succeeded him in the event of an abdication, was a suppositious babe, smuggled into the royal bedroom in a warming pan.

So, through a combination of amnesia and fantasy, the Tories had reconciled themselves to the revolution. Even then, their acceptance of the new regime of King William and his wife Queen Mary (King's James's Protestant eldest child) was hedged about with qualifications. They could regard the new monarchs as King and Queen de facto without accepting them as monarchs de jure – a stance made possible by the deliberate omission of the usual 'rightful and lawful' formula from the Oath of Allegiance.

These intellectual contortions enabled most Tories to swear allegiance to William and Mary with a reasonably clear conscience. But to Whigs, it was evidence that the Tories were at best lukewarm supporters of the new regime and, at worst, downright disloyal, secretly longing for the return of the rightful King and Prince of Wales from their refuge over the water in France – a view reinforced by the continued hostility of Tories to a united Protestant front in the war against Catholic France. In Whig eyes, nothing illustrated this better than the antics of Tory parliamentarians in the early years of the reign of King William's successor, Queen Anne, when they showed themselves willing to jeopardise the war effort while attempting, unsuccessfully, to secure legislation penalising occasional conformity.

A MIDDLE PATH

6.3 Queen Anne's accession in 1702 had aroused in Tory breasts hopes of a return to the golden days of the early 1680s. Another Protestant daughter of King James, who had died the previous year, Tories could happily swear allegiance to her as de jure monarch – provided, of course, that they continued to ignore the claims of King James's 'suppositious' and very Catholic son, whom Louis XIV had recognised as King James III on his father's death. What's more, it was well known that the Queen's political sympathies lay with the Tories.

But the high hopes of 1702 had come to nothing. A natural Tory though she was, the Queen's primary political objective was to win the war. She therefore took a dim view of any partisanship which undermined the war effort marshalled by the three leading members of her administration – the Duke of Marlborough, generalissimo of the allied armies, Sidney Godolphin, the Lord Treasurer, and Robert Harley, a wily political fixer.

For six years, during which Marlborough won a series of great victories against France, the Queen's administration sought to steer a middle path between the parties. But by 1708 parliamentary politics had become so divisive that it was clear the administration would have to rely on one or other of the two parties. Although he had started his career as a Whig, Harley was loathed by the Whig leaders, known as the Junto, for leading attacks against them during King William's reign. He therefore urged the Queen to choose the Tories. Marlborough and Godolphin, on the other hand, insisted that she should plump for the Whigs because only they could be relied upon to support the war effort wholeheartedly. Feeling herself unable to dispense with Marlborough and Godolphin, she reluctantly bowed to their wishes. Out went Harley. In came the Junto.

ILLEGALITY OF RESISTANCE

6.4 The Tories were now faced with their worst nightmare – a 'phanatick' Whig administration which would seek to demolish the Church of England. Rumours abounded that the Whigs would repeal the sacramental test and thereby completely open public office to nonconformists. Tory anger was further inflamed by the war. After rejecting a peace offer from the French, Marlborough won another victory against them, but this time at terrible cost. Word went around that Marlborough and the Whig ministers were prolonging the war for their own personal gain and that of their friends among the 'monied interest', not least the men at the top of the Bank of England which had been strongly associated with the Whigs ever since its foundation in 1694.

It was into this combustible mix that Dr Sacheverell threw a firebrand on 5 November 1709. Since the beginning of Queen Anne's reign, Sacheverell had built up a reputation as a preacher of venomously anti-nonconformist sermons. This won him an invitation from a Tory Lord Mayor to deliver a sermon at St Paul's Cathedral to the dignitaries of the City of London, marking the anniversary of the Gunpowder Plot of 1605. Never before had Sacheverell been given such a stage, and he was determined to make the most of it.

Most of the sermon consisted of the now familiar tirade against nonconformists and the 'false brethren' within the Church who supported them – namely, the Whigs and the current administration. But Sacheverell did not stop there. 'The grand security of our government', he declared, 'and the very pillar upon which it stands, is founded upon the steady belief of the subject's obligation to an absolute and unconditional obedience to the supreme power in all things lawful, and the utter illegality of resistance upon any pretence whatsoever.'

Here, Sacheverell overreached himself. By preaching the doctrine of non-resistance in such crude terms, he seemed to be questioning the legitimacy of the revolution itself. Nor was this a mere academic issue. The Tories had no problem with Queen Anne's claim to the throne, but she had no surviving children. By the Act of Settlement of 1701, Parliament had vested the succession after her death in her nearest Protestant relatives – the electoral House of Hanover. Not only were the Hanoverians over 50 steps removed from the succession, they were also German Lutherans who were unlikely to look kindly on High Church Toryism. When it came to the crunch, would the Tories really accept the Hanoverians? Or would they be tempted to turn to the King over the Water in France? Tricky, perhaps, while James III (known in England as 'the Pretender') remained resolute in his Catholicism, but tempting indeed if he ever came to the conclusion that London was worth the Anglican sacrament.

These were the thoughts that Whigs had long sought to put into the public mind. Now, at long last, Sacheverell's crassness – compounded by his decision to have the sermon printed – had given them the opportunity to prove the charge that Jacobitism and Toryism were synonymous terms. The legal device they chose to press home the charge was impeachment – the process, much used in the seventeenth century to attack unpopular royal favourites, by which the House of Commons brought a prosecution for 'high crimes and misdemeanours' against an accused who would be tried by the House of Lords. A simple vote of their Lordships' House would determine guilt or innocence. Since the administration enjoyed an unassailable majority in the Lords, the outcome, it was thought, would never be in doubt. This, then, was never intended to be an exercise in the impartial administration of justice. It would be a show trial. And the critical charge would be the one contained in the first of four articles of impeachment – that Sacheverell had impugned the right and justice of the revolution of 1688.

UGLY MOOD

6.5 There was one flaw in the Whigs' plan. It failed to take account of the possibility of a Tory counter-attack. Initially appalled by the hole that Sacheverell had landed them in, the Tory leaders soon realised that the trial gave them an opportunity. Just as the Whigs intended to use the trial to prove that the Tories were Jacobites, so the Tories would use it to establish that the Whigs were 'roundheads' and 'phanaticks', persecuting a poor, loyal clergyman in their wicked contrivance to destroy the Church England and, by extension, the Crown. For how could the Whigs be truly loyal to Queen Anne when they hated the Church to which she was devoted?

When the trial opened on 27 February 1710, with the Queen in attendance, there was an ugly mood on the streets as pro-Sacheverell crowds thronged menacingly around Westminster Hall. Undeterred, the Whig MPs managing the prosecution for the Commons, including the future Prime Minister, Robert Walpole, made no secret of their ultimate objective. A conviction, explained Walpole, 'will convince the world that every seditious, discontented, hot-headed, ungifted, unedifying preacher . . . who had no hopes of distinguishing himself in the world but by a matchless indiscretion, may not advance with impunity, doctrines destructive of the peace and quiet of her Majesty's government'.

One such doctrine was non-resistance. By demolishing it, said another prosecutor, 'we hope the record of this proceeding will remain a lasting monument to deter a successor that may inherit [Queen Anne's] crowns but not her virtues from attempting to invade the laws or the people's rights; and if not, that it will be a noble precedent to excite our posterity to wrestle and tug for liberty, as we have done'.

THE ORIGINAL CONTRACT

6.6 Nicholas Lechmere, one of the Whigs' top lawyers, explained the origin of the right of resistance:

> 'The nature of our constitution is that of a limited monarchy, wherein the supreme power was – by mutual consent and not by accident – limited and lodged in more hands than one; and the uniform preservation of such a constitution for so many ages, without any fundamental change, demonstrates . . . the continuance of the same contract. The consequences of such a form of government are obvious; that the laws are the rule to both, the common measure of the power of the Crown and of the obedience of the subject; and if the executive part endeavours the subversion and total destruction of the government the Original Contract is thereby broke, and the right of allegiance ceases, and that part of the government thus fundamentally injured hath a right to save or recover that constitution in which it had an original interest.'

Whatever the origins of the right of resistance, a denial of its existence was tantamount to rejecting the legitimacy of the revolution and all that flowed from it. 'If resistance at the Revolution was illegal', averred the Solicitor-General, Robert Eyre, 'the Revolution [was] settled in usurpation'. The point was rammed home by another prosecutor, the military man, James Stanhope. If there were no right of resistance, he asked:

> '[W]hat are the consequences? The Queen is not Queen; your lordships are not a House of Lords, for you are not duly summoned by legal writ; we are no House of Commons, for the same reason; all the taxes which have been raised for these twenty years have been arbitrary and illegal extortions; all the blood of so many brave men who have died (as they thought) in the service of their country, have been spilt in defence of a usurpation, and they were only so many rebels and traitors.'

Sacheverell was a small-minded man, but his case had given rise to great issues – and, as events were about to show, great tensions too.

RIOT AND RUSE

6.7 On the night of 1 and 2 March, the threat of violence that had hung over the trial since the start became reality. Tory mobs rampaged through the City of London, attacking carefully selected Whig and nonconformist targets. One such, the Bank of England, long the symbol of Whig war profiteering, was saved only by the intervention of the Guards regiments. Less fortunate was Burgess's nonconformist meeting house in Lincoln's Inn Fields in the heart of the legal quarter. One of the grandest meeting houses in the capital, it was razed to the ground. Four other meeting houses shared its fate that night.

It was 3 March before the situation had calmed sufficiently for the defence to open its case. It was led by Sir Simon Harcourt, a former Attorney General and the most gifted Tory lawyer of the day. A fortnight earlier, Harcourt had been elected to the Commons in a by-election. This should have disqualified him from acting for Sacheverell because, as an MP, he could not defend charges brought by the House of which he was a member. But in that age of far from instantaneous communications, his success at the polls had, deliberately, not yet been formally notified to Parliament. This ruse left him free to act.

MOVED TO TEARS

6.8 Harcourt's speech on 3 March was reckoned to be one of the finest of his career. 'His reputation as a speaker is fixed for ever', gushed one observer. But the enthusiastic reception given to Harcourt's speech surely owed more to the mellifluousness of its delivery than the consistency of its argument. On the one hand, Harcourt defused the explosive charge that Tories were closet Jacobites by accepting that the revolution had indeed involved an act of resistance – albeit one carried out only as a matter of dire necessity. 'We are hearty well-wishers to the Revolution, and to the happiness of England that is in a great measure built upon it', he said:

> 'We agree that the law of the land is the measure of the prince's authority and the people's rights; that in the case of the Revolution, when the laws were overturned, when popery was coming in upon us, and property signified nothing, the people of England being invited by his late Majesty [William III] did resort to the last remedy, that of necessity, and that necessity did induce resistance, and justify them in it, and upon that fact the Revolution succeeded.'

On the other hand, Harcourt sought to get his client off the hook by arguing that the revolution had not, in fact, involved any resistance – at least, not in the sense that Sacheverell had meant. The 'supreme power' was the legislative power. Since Parliament had concurred in the revolution and assisted it, the events of 1688–89 had not involved any resistance at all. The good doctor, no doubt, could have expressed himself more felicitously, 'but a subject of England was not to be made criminal by a laboured construction of doubtful words' – particularly not in an age when, as the other defence counsel would subsequently demonstrate, the most blood-curdling libels against the Church and its clergy were going unpunished.

When the time came for Sacheverell to speak in his own defence, he eagerly grasped the 'get out of jail card' that Harcourt had given him. In declaring 'the utter illegality of resistance upon any pretence whatsoever', he had been speaking merely in generalities. 'I neither expressly applied my doctrine of non-resistance to the case of the Revolution', he claimed, 'nor had the least thoughts of including the Revolution under my general assertion.' Far from spreading sedition, he was a martyr, suffering persecution for daring to preach the Church's traditional doctrine of loyalty and obedience:

> 'the avowed design of my impeachment is, by the means of it, to procure an eternal and indelible brand of infamy to be fixed in a parliamentary way on all those who maintain the doctrine of non-resistance, and to have the clergy directed what doctrines they are to preach, and what not.'

He had done nothing to merit the ordeal he was now suffering, but if that was the price to be paid for upholding the Church's doctrines, then so be it. By the time Sacheverell had finished, his supporters in the public gallery – specially built for the trial by Sir Christopher Wren – had been reduced to tears. It was open to question, noted one wry observer, 'whether ever the Doctor did such a feat in his pulpit'.

VERDICT AND SENTENCE

6.9 In a case that was all about politics rather than justice, the skilful presentation of the defence case, coupled with the 'Church in danger' frenzy gripping the capital, hit the spot. Sacheverell was convicted by the Lords, but only by an unexpectedly small majority of 17 – a sure sign that some of the administration's more faint-hearted supporters in the Lords were starting to waver in their allegiance. The administration's majority evaporated altogether when it came to the sentence. The ministers pressed for imprisonment. All they got was the public burning of the offending sermon and an order banning Sacheverell from preaching for three years – a reflection of the Queen's view that the punishment should be mild. The ministers had secured their conviction, but they had plainly lost the political battle. 'So all this bustle and fatigue ends in no more', sighed Godolphin.

Robert Harley's moment had come. Sensing that the Queen would happily rid herself of Godolphin and the Junto if there were a viable alternative, Harley sought to persuade her that he could form an administration which would have a Tory bias, but would still have room for moderate Whigs. He was pushing at an open door. Over the next few months, Godolphin and the Whig minsters were replaced by an administration led by Harley. At a subsequent general election, the Whigs were routed. The following year, Marlborough – too big a beast to be dispensed with initially, but now widely stigmatised as a potential second Cromwell – went the way of Godolphin and the Junto, thereby paving the way for protracted but ultimately successful peace negotiations with France. The world, it seemed, was about to be made safe for the Tory party.

Once again, however, the highest hopes of the Tories were dashed – this time by their leader, Robert Harley. Never a Tory at heart, he had no stomach for the type of red-blooded attack on nonconformists demanded by the Tory true-believers who, to his distress, had been elected in large numbers in 1710. True, legislation to penalise occasional conformity was at last enacted in 1711, but only as a result of a rebellion within Tory ranks. The only other significant piece of anti-nonconformist legislation was the Schism Act of 1714 – a measure designed to destroy nonconformist education that was pushed through Parliament by radical Tories after Harley had finally lost control of the party.

DARLING OF THE MOB

6.10 The Tory counter-revolution was brought to a grinding halt on 1 August 1714 by an event which spelt ruin for the party – the death of Queen Anne and the accession of the Elector of Hanover as King George I. Unable to persuade the Pretender to forsake his religion, and crippled by in-fighting, the Tory leaders had no choice but to acquiesce in the succession of King George – who promptly proceeded to kick them out of office and replace them with the Whigs. Within a few years, the Occasional Conformity and Schism Acts had been repealed. Altogether more enduring was the Riot Act of 1715 – enacted by the Whigs to curb the Tory mobs which had terrorised them in 1710 and had done so again in the first year of George I's reign. One of the few Acts of Parliament to become a figure of speech, the Riot Act would prove a cornerstone of the Whig Supremacy – the period of unbroken Whig rule that would last for almost 50 years.

And what of Dr Sacheverell himself? Never one to hide his light under a bushel, he had celebrated his derisory sentence with a triumphal procession through the Midlands and the West Country. He later became rector of St Andrew Holborn, a plum London living, just a stone's throw away from the focal point of the riots that his trial had provoked. He remained the darling of the Tory mob, but his ambitions for promotion to the episcopal bench were frustrated by Queen Anne who despised him for his extremism and demagoguery. Under the Whigs after 1714, there was, of course, no hope of preferment. By the time of Sacheverell's death in 1724, both Church and state were firmly under the thumb of the Whig 'false brethren' whom he had denounced in his famous sermon 15 years earlier.

Further Reading

6.11 Bennett, GV, *The Tory Crisis in Church and State 1688–1730: The Career of Francis Atterbury, Bishop of Rochester* (Oxford, 1975)

Holmes, Geoffrey, *The Trial of Dr Sacheverell* (1973)

Kenyon, JP, *Revolution Principles: The Politics of Party 1689–1720* (Cambridge, 1977)

Rose, Craig, *England in the 1690s: Revolution, Religion and War* (Blackwell, Oxford, 1999)

Speck, WA, *The Birth of Britain: A New Nation 1700–1710* (Blackwell, Oxford, 1994)

7

'THE EVIL THAT MEN DO LIVES AFTER THEM'*

* Julius Caesar, Act 3, Scene II

Plessy v Ferguson

Henry Horbaczewski

INTRODUCTION

7.1 The US Supreme Court plays a unique role in our society as the guardian of our civil liberties. More so than with other nations, the landmark decisions, such as *Brown v Board of Education*[1] ('*Brown*'), *Gideon v Wainwright*,[2] *New York Times Co v Sullivan*[3] and *Miranda v Arizona*,[4] are part of the fabric of our popular, not just our legal, culture many years after they were decided.

It is important to remember that other Supreme Court decisions were not so beneficent. *Dred Scott v Sanford*[5] has a unique place in our national hall of shame, but slavery was hardly the invention of the Taney Court, and the decision was effectively reversed within ten years with an assist from the Grand Army of the Republic. My medal of dishonour goes to *Plessy v Ferguson*[6] ('*Plessy*'), a 7:1 decision upholding legalised racial segregation that is both exceptionally pernicious and exceptionally long-lived. *Plessy* espoused the infamous doctrine of 'separate but equal'.[7] Fifty eight very long years passed between *Plessy* and *Brown*, and while the latter decision repudiated the former and represents one of the highest peaks of the Supreme Court's jurisprudence, it would take exceptional naiveté to believe that the bitterness, resentments and societal damage from the practices that *Plessy* condoned and perpetuated were fully undone by *Brown*, or in the 56 years that have followed *Brown*. This decision is a toxin that still poisons American society more than a century after it was rendered. 18 May 1896 is a day that deserves to live in infamy as much as any other.

1 347 U.S. 483 (1954).
2 372 U.S. 335 (1963).
3 376 U.S. 254 (1964).
4 384 U.S. 436 (1966).
5 60 U.S. 393 (1857).
6 163 U.S. 537 (1896).

7 Interestingly, the phrase comes from the dissenting opinion by Harlan J (at 552); the phrase used in the majority opinion, as in the underlying statute, is 'equal but separate' (at 540).

BACKGROUND OF THE CASE

7.2 In 1890, the State of Louisiana passed a statute (Acts 1890, No 111) requiring that:

> 'all railway companies carrying passengers in their coaches in this State, shall provide equal but separate accommodations for the white, and colored races, by providing two or more passenger coaches for each passenger train, or by dividing the passenger coaches by a partition so as to secure separate accommodations . . . No person or persons, shall be admitted to occupy seats in coaches, other than, the ones, assigned, to them on account of the race they belong to.'[1]

By then, reconstruction was over: the corrupt election of 1876 was a distant memory, the troops had been withdrawn, the former Confederate states had ratified the Thirteenth, Fourteenth and Fifteenth Amendments and been re-admitted to the polity, and the new governments of these rehabilitated states were busily trying to impose legal separation by race, re-imposition of slavery not being an option.

Plessy was an arranged test case. In 1892, the Citizens' Committee to Test the Separate Car Act retained a prominent (Yankee) lawyer, Albion Tourgée, and arranged with Homer Plessy, who was one-eighth African American and able to board the 'whites only' car without challenge, to board a train, then declare his race and refuse to leave the car until he had been arrested. Plessy's challenge to the law was rejected, first by the Orleans Parish criminal court, then by the Louisiana Supreme Court.[2] In what appears in retrospect to have been a spectacular misreading of the temper of the times, the case was then appealed to the US Supreme Court.

1 163 U.S. 537 (1896) at 540.
2 *Ex parte Plessy* 11 So. 948 (La. 1892).

THE COURT

7.3 Justice John Marshall Harlan is rightly remembered for his eloquent dissent, but the members of the majority should not be able to hide in obscurity, except for Justice David Brewer, who took no part in the decision.

Justice Henry Billings Brown wrote the majority opinion. A graduate of Yale and an admiralty lawyer from Michigan, he served on the court without distinction from 1890 to 1906.

Joining in the opinion were Chief Justice Melville Fuller, a Bowdoin graduate from Chicago;[1] Justice Stephen Johnson Field, a Williams College graduate from California;[2] Justice Horace Gray, a Harvard graduate from Massachusetts who preceded Oliver Wendell Holmes Jr; Justice George Shiras Jr, from Yale and Pennsylvania; Justice Edward Douglass White Jr from Tulane and Louisiana;[3] and Justice Rufus Peckham, a New Yorker who read the law in his father's law office.[4]

In solitary dissent was Justice John Marshall Harlan, from Kentucky, graduate of Centre College and Transylvania University, son of a slave owner, and Union officer during the Civil War.[5] On the subject of civil rights, Harlan J was both prescient[6] and frequently in the minority.[7]

1 Fuller CJ wrote the majority opinions in *Caldwell v Texas* 137 U.S. 692 (1891) ('By the Fourteenth Amendment the powers of the States in dealing with crime within their borders are not limited, but no State can deprive particular persons or classes of persons of equal and impartial justice under the law', Id. att 697), and *Gonzalez v Williams* 192 U.S. 1 (1904), which ruled that residents of Puerto Rico were neither citizens nor aliens.

2 Field J may be excused on the grounds of senility. See Garrow, David J, *Mental Decrepitude on the U.S. Supreme Court: the Historical Case for a 28th Amendment*, 67 U. Chi. L. Rev. 995, 1008 (2000). However, in *Stauder v West Virginia* 100 U.S. 303 (1879), Field J dissented from an opinion that struck down the exclusion of African Americans from Juries (id. at 312).

3 White J wrote the decision in *Guinn v United States* 238 U.S.347 (1915), striking down an Oklahoma and Maryland grandfather clauses as unconstitutional under the Fifteenth Amendment. Grandfather clauses were exceptions to a literacy requirement for voting for any 'person who was, on 1 January 1866, or at any time prior thereto, entitled to vote under any form of government, or who at that time resided in some foreign nation, and no lineal descendant of such person', Id. at 357.

4 Peckham J wrote the opinion in *Lochner v New York* (198 U.S. 45 (1905) ('*Lochner*'). One may wonder how state action regulating work hours offends freedom of contract, but state action prohibiting citizens from associating with fellow citizens of a human race on a common carrier does not, but history has spared us the need for such analysis.

5 Thompson, Charles, Plessy v Ferguson: Harlan's Great Dissent, http://www.law.louisville.edu/library/collections/harlan/dissent (visited 17 May 2010).

6 Harlan J believed that the Fourteenth Amendment authorised laws directed at private acts of discrimination at least as to public accommodation (Dissenting opinion in The Civil Rights Cases, 109 U.S. 3, 26 (1883) (the 'Civil Rights Cases'), and that the Fourteenth Amendment created due process rights as against states that incorporated the Bill of Rights (dissenting opinion in *Hurtado v California* 100 U.S. 516, 529 (1884) ('*Hurtado*')). Both interpretations ultimately prevailed.

7 In addition to his dissenting opinions in The Civil Rights Cases and *Hurtado* (see n 6 above), Harlan J issued dissenting opinions *Gilmore v Harris*, 184 U.S. 475, 493 (1903), contending that Federal courts had jurisdiction to hear a state-wide challenge to the refusal of state voting officials in Alabama to enrol African-American voters. Brewer J, who did not participate in *Plessy*, also dissented at 488, joined in dissent by Brown J, who wrote the majority opinion in *Plessy*. Harlan J also dissented in *Lochner*.

THE MAJORITY OPINION

7.4 *Plessy's* challenge was based on the Thirteenth and Fourteenth Amendments. The court first summarily disposed of the Thirteenth Amendment claim:[1]

> 'A statute which implies merely a legal distinction between the white and colored races – a distinction which is founded in the color of the two races, and which must always exist so long as white men are distinguished from the other race by color – has no tendency to destroy the legal equality of the two races, or re-establish a state of involuntary servitude. Indeed, we do not understand that the *Thirteenth Amendment* is strenuously relied upon by the plaintiff in error.'

As to the Fourteenth Amendment:[2]

> 'The object of the [Fourteenth A]mendment was undoubtedly to enforce the absolute equality of the two races before the law, but in the nature of things it could not have been intended to abolish distinctions based upon color, or to enforce social, as distinguished from political equality, or a commingling of the two races upon terms unsatisfactory to either. Laws permitting, and even requiring,

their separation in places where they are liable to be brought into contact do not necessarily imply the inferiority of either race to the other . . . '

In other words, the court assumed away the essence of the case, then, revealingly, reached beyond the facts of the case to justify segregated education, as well as prohibitions against mixed-race marriage.[3]

> 'The most common instance of this is connected with the establishment of separate schools for white and colored children, which has been held to be a valid exercise of the legislative power even by courts of States where the political rights of the colored race have been longest and most earnestly enforced. One of the earliest of these cases is that of *Roberts v City of Boston*, 5 Cush. 198 [1849 – ie before the passage of the Fourteenth Amendment], in which the Supreme Judicial Court of Massachusetts held that the general school committee of Boston had power to make provision for the instruction of colored children in separate schools established exclusively for them, and to prohibit their attendance upon the other schools . . . Laws forbidding the intermarriage of the two races may be said in a technical sense to interfere with the freedom of contract, and yet have been universally recognized as within the police power of the State. *State v Gibson* 36 Indiana, 389 [1871].'[4]

It is interesting, especially in lieu of *Brown*, that in its defence of segregation the court segued so quickly from railroad carriages to schools.

'Positive rights and privileges', the court went on, 'are undoubtedly secured by the *Fourteenth Amendment*; but they are secured by way of prohibition against state laws and state proceedings affecting *those rights and privileges* [emphasis supplied]', at 547.

> '[W]e think the enforced separation of the races, as applied to the internal commerce of the State, neither abridges the privileges or immunities of the colored man, deprives him of his property without due process of law, nor denies him the equal protection of the laws, within the meaning of the *Fourteenth Amendment*.'
>
> [at 548]

> 'It is claimed by the plaintiff in error that, in any mixed community, the reputation of belonging to the dominant race, in this instance the white race, is property, in the same sense that a right of action, or of inheritance, is property. Conceding this to be so, for the purposes of this case, we are unable to see how this statute deprives him of, or in any way affects his right to, such property. If he be a white man and assigned to a colored coach, he may have his action for damages against the company for being deprived of his so called property. Upon the other hand, if he be a colored man and be so assigned, he has been deprived of no property, since he is not lawfully entitled to the reputation of being a white man.'
>
> [at 549]

> 'So far, then, as a conflict with the *Fourteenth Amendment* is concerned, the case reduces itself to the question whether the statute of Louisiana is a reasonable regulation, and with respect to this there must necessarily be a large discretion on the part of the legislature. In determining the question of reasonableness it is at liberty to act with reference to the established usages, customs and traditions of the people, and with a view to the promotion of their comfort, and the preservation of the public peace and good order. Gauged by this standard, we cannot say that a law which authorizes or even requires the separation of the two races in public conveyances is unreasonable, or more obnoxious to the *Fourteenth Amendment* than the acts of Congress requiring separate schools for colored children in the

District of Columbia, the constitutionality of which does not seem to have been questioned, or the corresponding acts of state legislatures.'

[at 550–551]

'We consider the underlying fallacy of the plaintiff's argument to consist in the assumption that the enforced separation of the two races stamps the colored race with a badge of inferiority. If this be so, it is not by reason of anything found in the act, but solely because the colored race chooses to put that construction upon it. The argument necessarily assumes that if, as has been more than once the case, and is not unlikely to be so again, the colored race should become the dominant power in the state legislature, and should enact a law in precisely similar terms, it would thereby relegate the white race to an inferior position. We imagine that the white race, at least, would not acquiesce in this assumption. The argument also assumes that social prejudices may be overcome by legislation, and that equal rights cannot be secured to the negro except by an enforced commingling of the two races. We cannot accept this proposition. If the two races are to meet upon terms of social equality, it must be the result of natural affinities, a mutual appreciation of each other's merits and a voluntary consent of individuals.'

[at 551]

To summarise, equality cannot be legislated. If the former slaves saw being forcibly segregated from white people as a 'badge of inferiority', that was their subjective interpretation, and their problem, and some day, the tables might turn. Besides, if segregated schools were permissible – and they must be permissible – where could one draw the line?

1 163 U.S. 537 (1896) at 543.

2 At 544.

3 Finally repudiated in *Loving v Virginia* 388 U.S. 1 (1967).

4 163 U.S. 537 (1896) at 544–545.

THE HARLAN DISSENT

7.5 Justice Harlan was having none of the majority's reasoning, and his outrage at the casuistry of the majority opinion is palpable:[1]

'While there may be in Louisiana persons of different races who are not citizens of the United States, the words in the act, "white and colored races", necessarily include all citizens of the United States of both races residing in that State. So that we have before us a state enactment that compels, under penalties, the separation of the two races in railroad passenger coaches, and makes it a crime for a citizen of either race to enter a coach that has been assigned to citizens of the other race. Thus the State regulates the use of a public highway by citizens of the United States solely upon the basis of race.'

The segregation mandated by the Louisiana statute was not 'private':[2]

'That a railroad is a public highway, and that the corporation which owns or operates it is in the exercise of public functions, is not, at this day, to be disputed. Mr Justice Nelson, speaking for this court in *New Jersey Steam Navigation Co v Merchants' Bank* 6 How. 344, 382, said that a common carrier was in the exercise "of a sort of public office, and has public duties to perform, from which he should not be permitted to exonerate himself without the assent of the parties concerned". Mr Justice Strong, delivering the judgment of this court in *Olcott v The Supervisors* 16 Wall. 678, 694, said: "That railroads, though constructed by private corporations and owned by them, are public highways, has been the doctrine of nearly all the courts ever since such conveniences for passage and transportation have had any existence. Very early the question arose whether a State's right of eminent domain could be exercised by a private corporation created for the purpose of constructing a railroad. Clearly it could not, unless taking land for such a purpose by such an agency is taking land for public use. The right of eminent domain nowhere justifies taking property for a private use. Yet it is a doctrine universally accepted that a state legislature may authorize a private corporation to take land for the construction of such a road, making compensation to the owner. What else does this doctrine mean if not that building a railroad, though it be built by a private corporation, is an act done for a public use?".'

But, more fundamentally:[3]

'In respect of civil rights, common to all citizens, the Constitution of the United States does not, I think, permit any public authority to know the race of those entitled to be protected in the enjoyment of such rights. Every true man has pride of race, and under appropriate circumstances when the rights of others, his equals before the law, are not to be affected, it is his privilege to express such pride and to take such action based upon it as to him seems proper. But I deny that any legislative body or judicial tribunal may have regard to the race of citizens when the civil rights of those citizens are involved. Indeed, such legislation, as that here in question, is inconsistent not only with that equality of rights which pertains to citizenship, National and State, but with the personal liberty enjoyed by everyone within the United States. The *Thirteenth Amendment* does not permit the withholding or the deprivation of any right necessarily inhering in freedom. It not only struck down the institution of slavery as previously existing in the United States, but it prevents the imposition of any burdens or disabilities that constitute badges of slavery or servitude. It decreed universal civil freedom in this country. This court has so adjudged. But that amendment having been found inadequate to the protection of the rights of those who had been in slavery, it was followed by the *Fourteenth Amendment*, which added greatly to the dignity and glory of American citizenship, and to the security of personal liberty, by declaring that "all persons born or naturalized in the United States, and subject to the jurisdiction thereof, are citizens of the United States and of the State wherein they reside", and that "no State shall make or enforce any law which shall abridge the privileges or immunities of citizens of the United States; nor shall any State deprive any person of life, liberty or property without due process of law, nor deny to any person within its jurisdiction the equal protection of the laws". These two amendments, if enforced according to their true intent and meaning, will protect all the civil rights that pertain to freedom and citizenship. Finally, and to the end that no citizen should be denied, on account of his race, the privilege of participating in the political control of his country, it was declared by the *Fifteenth Amendment* that "the right of citizens of the United States to vote shall not be denied or abridged by the United States or by any State on account of race, color or previous condition of servitude". These notable additions to the fundamental law were welcomed by the friends of liberty throughout the world. They removed the race line from our governmental systems. They had, as this court has said, a common purpose, namely, to secure "to a race recently emancipated, a race that through many generations have been held in slavery, all the civil rights that the superior race enjoy". They declared, in legal effect, this court has further said, "that the law in the States shall be the same for the black as for the white; that all persons, whether colored or white, shall stand equal before the laws of the States, and, in regard to the colored race, for whose protection the amendment was primarily designed, that no discrimination shall be made against them by law because of their color". We also said: "The words of the amendment, it is true, are

> prohibitory, but they contain a necessary implication of a positive immunity, or right, most valuable to the colored race – the right to exemption from unfriendly legislation against them distinctively as colored – exemption from legal discriminations, implying inferiority in civil society, lessening the security of their enjoyment of the rights which others enjoy, and discriminations which are steps towards reducing them to the condition of a subject race".'

The veneer of neutrality to which the majority decision pretended was stripped away:[4]

> 'Everyone knows that the statute in question had its origin in the purpose, not so much to exclude white persons from railroad cars occupied by blacks, as to exclude colored people from coaches occupied by or assigned to white persons. Railroad corporations of Louisiana did not make discrimination among whites in the matter of accommodation for travelers. The thing to accomplish was, under the guise of giving equal accommodation for whites and blacks, to compel the latter to keep to themselves while travelling in railroad passenger coaches. No one would be so wanting in candor as to assert the contrary. The fundamental objection, therefore, to the statute is that it interferes with the personal freedom of citizens. "Personal liberty", it has been well said, "consists in the power of locomotion, of changing situation, or removing one's person to whatsoever places one's own inclination may direct, without imprisonment or restraint, unless by due course of law".'
>
> 'The white race deems itself to be the dominant race in this country. And so it is, in prestige, in achievements, in education, in wealth and in power . . . But in view of the Constitution, in the eye of the law, there is in this country no superior, dominant, ruling class of citizens. There is no caste here. Our Constitution is color blind, and neither knows nor tolerates classes among citizens. In respect of civil rights, all citizens are equal before the law.'
>
> [at 559]

And finally, the ruthlessly accurate prophecy:[5]

> 'In my opinion, the judgment this day rendered will, in time, prove to be quite as pernicious as the decision made by this tribunal in the *Dred Scott* case. The present decision . . . will not only stimulate aggressions, more or less brutal and irritating, upon the admitted rights of colored citizens, but will encourage the belief that it is possible, by means of state enactments, to defeat the beneficent purposes which the people of the United States had in view when they adopted the recent amendments of the Constitution, by one of which the blacks of this country were made citizens of the United States and of the States in which they respectively reside, and whose privileges and immunities, as citizens, the States are forbidden to abridge. . . . The destinies of the two races, in this country, are indissolubly linked together, and the interests of both require that the common government of all shall not permit the seeds of race hate to be planted under the sanction of law. What can more certainly arouse race hate, what more certainly create and perpetuate a feeling of distrust between these races, than state enactments, which, in fact, proceed on the ground that colored citizens are so inferior and degraded that they cannot be allowed to sit in public coaches occupied by white citizens? . . . State enactments, regulating the enjoyment of civil rights, upon the basis of race, and cunningly devised to defeat legitimate results of the war, under the pretence of recognizing equality of rights, can have no other result than to render permanent peace impossible, and to keep alive a conflict of races, the continuance of which must do harm to all concerned.'

It is important to remember, however, that as inspirational and as prophetic as the Harlan dissent was, it was a solitary defence. Not one of the other Justices was persuaded to join it, and it aroused no public protest against the decision, which continued to spread its toxin through American Society for another 60 years. It was not until *Brown* that the Harlan dissent found fertile ground.

1 163 U.S. 537 (1896) at 553.
2 At 553–554.
3 At 554–556.
4 At 557.
5 At 559–561.

EPILOGUE: *BROWN V BOARD OF EDUCATION*

7.6 The next half century, vindicated Justice Harlan's prediction, oppression under the sanction of law, together with race hate and violence directed against African-Americans. The abolition of slavery had been followed by a political flowering among the former slaves;[1] this was crushed: no African-American served in the US Senate between 1881 and 1967.

By 1951, when the *Brown* case was filed in the District Court, however, change was apparent. Scientific opinion was turning as evidenced by the publication of the UNESCO declaration, 'The Race Question' in 1950 and Gunner Myrdal's *An American Dilemma: The Negro Problem and Modern Democracy* in 1944. In 1948, President Harry Truman ordered the integration of the US armed forces.[2] In the end, however, as the *Plessy* majority had rightly divined, it came down to schools.

Brown was a consolidation of several cases, the suit in Topeka filed by the eponymous plaintiff. The three-judge panel of the District Court dismissed the suit, citing *Plessy*.[3]

The original appeal to the Supreme Court sought the reversal of *Plessy*, but the court could not reach a decision and put the case over for re-argument in the following term. By then that question was not whether 'separate but equal' would be overturned, but on what grounds, and whether by a unanimous court. The decision in *Brown* finally came down in 1954, and was unanimous. However, while *Plessy* was undone in principle, the court did not squarely repudiate the 1896 decision:[4]

> '[W]e cannot turn the clock back to 1868 when the Amendment was adopted, or even to 1896 when *Plessy v Ferguson* was written. We must consider public education in the light of its full development and its present place in American life throughout the Nation. Only in this way can it be determined if segregation in public schools deprives these plaintiffs of the equal protection of the laws.'

Rather, the court based its finding on the progress in education and social science since 1896. Fortunately, however, the court found its way back to the Equal Protection Clause:

> 'Whatever may have been the extent of psychological knowledge at the time of *Plessy v Ferguson*, this finding is amply supported by modern authority. Any language in *Plessy v Ferguson* contrary to this finding is rejected. We conclude that in the field of public education the doctrine of "separate but equal" has no place. Separate educational facilities are inherently unequal. Therefore, we hold that the

> plaintiffs and others similarly situated for whom the actions have been brought are, by reason of the segregation complained of, deprived of the equal protection of the laws guaranteed by the Fourteenth Amendment. This disposition makes unnecessary any discussion whether such segregation also violates the Due Process Clause of the Fourteenth Amendment.'[5]

Brown did not issue in an era of enlightened reconciliation. The immediate aftermath was troops in Little Rock, and it took a generation before the major efforts by the Department of Justice and the courts to desegregate schools in the face of acrimony and sometimes violence (including in Boston, whose segregated schools provided a rationalisation for *Plessy*) achieved substantial success. The residues of other forms of racial segregation under colour of law proved equally recalcitrant.

In April 2009, '[f]or the first time in CBS News polling history, a majority of blacks are casting race relations in the United States in a positive light. 59 per cent of African-Americans – along with 65 per cent of whites – now characterize[d] the relationship between blacks and whites in America as "good," according to a new CBS News/New York Times survey. Less than a year [before], just 29 per cent of blacks said race relations were good'.[6]

One wonders if a more forthright repudiation of *Plessy* based on the Harlan dissent and forthrightly recognising that segregation was wrong, and immoral, not just in the enlightened age of 1954, but in 1896, when the first Jim Crow law was enacted and at all points in between would have done more to undo the harm, and perhaps, whether absolution is possible without contrition. While a great deal of progress has been made in the 56 years since *Brown*, the bloodstream of the nation is not yet clear of the toxin of *Plessy*.

1 Two US Senators, 16 members of the House of Representatives, one Governor, four Superintendents of Education, and more than 600 State Legislators, four of whom were Speakers of the lower chamber, who were African-American elected during the period. Foner, Eric, *Reconstruction: America's unfinished revolution, 1863–1877* (Harper & Row, 1988), pp 352–355.

2 Culturally or not legally significant was the breaking of the colour barrier in professional baseball in 1947. By 1954 there were 18 African-American players on major league teams, including the legendary Jackie Robinson, Hank Aaron, Willie Mays, Ernie Banks, Don Newcombe and Roy Campanella.

3 98 F. Supp 297 (1951).

4 *Brown v Board of Education* 347 U.S. 483 (1954) at 492–493.

5 At 494–495.

6 At http://www.cbsnews.com/stories/2009/04/27/opinion/polls/main4972532.shtml. Visited 20 May 2010.

8

NATIVE TITLE IN AUSTRALIA

Mabo v The State of Queensland

*The Hon Kevin Lindgren QC**

WHITE SETTLEMENT OF THE 'GREAT SOUTH LAND'

8.1 In 1786 the British Government decided to establish a colony in what European explorers had designated the 'Great South Land', a land on the other side of the world where Aboriginal people lived. The plan was to populate the colony with convicts who had been sentenced in England to transportation.

The background to the decision was to be found in North America. From 1717 to 1776 the British Government had sold convicts to shipping contractors who had transported them to the southern colonies in North America where they had been sold to the plantations as workers. In 1776 the American colonies revolted and by 1783 the independence of the United States of America was acknowledged by the British. A new destination for convicts sentenced to transportation had to be found.

The site chosen was Botany Bay, just south of present day Sydney. The decision was announced by Lord Sydney who held the seals at the Home Office in London. Botany Bay had been 'discovered' and named by an English naval explorer, Captain James Cook. He had landed there in April 1770 and taken possession of the country for King George III under the name of 'New South Wales' – a much larger area than the present Australian State of that name. The British Government appointed a retired naval officer, Captain Arthur Phillip, as Captain General and Governor-in-Chief of New South Wales.

The first fleet, which included 750 convicts, departed from Portsmouth in England on 13 May 1787 and was anchored at Botany Bay on 20 January 1788. Captain Phillip and a small party of officers sailed north in a small boat and found 'the finest harbour in the world'. He named it Port Jackson and one of its inlets Sydney Cove, at which he decided to locate the penal settlement. The convict ships moved their cargo there on the 26 January 1788.

The conflict which forms the background to *Mabo v The State of Queensland (No 2)*[1] ('*Mabo*') then began. The noted Australian historian, Professor Manning Clark, has written of the arrival of the convict transports at Sydney Cove:[2]

> 'a handful of Aborigines on the shore set up a horrid howl and indicated by gestures with sticks and stones that the white man was not wanted'.

That night, after the convicts were landed, the British flag was unfurled, shots were fired, toasts were drunk and the first of annual 'Australia Days' marked the arrival of European civilisation in the Great South Land.

1 (1992) 175 CLR 1.

2 Manning Clark, *A Short History of Australia* (4th edn, 1995), Penguin Books Australia, at p 16.

QUEENSLAND, THE MURRAY ISLANDS AND THE MERIAM PEOPLE

8.2 Other colonies were progressively established by the British in Van Diemen's Land (the present State of Tasmania) and on the Australian continent. These colonies included Queensland. A penal settlement was established in 1824, at Redcliffe in Moreton Bay, about 28 kilometres from present day Brisbane. The colony shifted to what is now Brisbane a year or two later.

Queensland was separated from New South Wales in 1859 by Letters Patent and an Order in Council, both dated 6 June 1859, under the New South Wales Constitution Act 1855 (Imp).

Mabo concerned not the Queensland mainland, but the Murray Islands to the north of it. The three islands constituting the Murray Islands, Mer, Dauar and Waier, are located in the Torres Strait, which is to the north of the northern tip of Queensland, between Australia and New Guinea. The Islands have an area of only some nine square miles. The largest is Mer (also known as Murray Island). It is oval in shape and about 2.79 kilometres long and 1.65 kilometres across. The occupants of the Murray Islands are descended from the Meriam people who occupied them long before European contact.

In 1878 the Colonial Office in London decided to extend the maritime boundaries of Queensland to include the Murray Islands. This decision was implemented by a series of steps. On 10 October 1878, Queen Victoria issued Letters Patent authorising the Governor of Queensland by proclamation to declare the annexation; the Queensland legislature passed the Queensland Coast Islands Act 1879; and, on 21 July 1879, the Governor of Queensland by proclamation declared that from 1 August 1879 the Murray Islands were to be annexed to, and become part of, the Colony of Queensland and subject to its laws. That was some 91 years after the establishment of the penal settlement at Sydney Cove, and some 65 years after the establishment of the penal settlement at Redcliffe in Moreton Bay. The inhabitants of the Murray Islands were unaware that the annexation was taking place.

MABO – THE FACTS

8.3 Eddie Mabo, David Passi and James Rice were members of the Meriam people who occupied the Murray Islands. They were the plaintiffs in *Mabo*.

In 1982 they commenced a proceeding in Australia's highest court, the

High Court of Australia, seeking a series of declarations designed to establish that they held native title in their respective lands.

In response, in 1985 the Parliament of the State of Queensland passed the Queensland Coast Islands Declaratory Act 1985. This Act declared that upon their annexation, the Murray Islands vested in the Crown in right of Queensland freed from all other rights, interests and claims of any kind whatsoever and became waste lands of the Crown. The High Court held, however, that on the assumption that the plaintiffs could otherwise establish the land rights that they claimed, the Queensland Act did not defeat them. The reason was that the State Act was inconsistent with an Act that the Commonwealth Parliament had passed some ten years earlier, the Racial Discrimination Act 1975, and was therefore invalid (section 109 of the Constitution of the Commonwealth of Australia provides that where a law of a State is inconsistent with a law of the Commonwealth, the latter prevails and the former is, to the extent of the inconsistency, invalid).

The High Court remitted the task of hearing and determining all issues of fact in the *Mabo* proceeding to the Supreme Court of Queensland. Moynihan J of that court made several findings of fact. He found that the Meriam people had occupied the Murray Islands for generations before the first contact between the Meriam people and Europeans. The number of occupants of the Murray Islands was probably no more than 1,000 and no less than 400. Contacts with Europeans had been few and sporadic. Mainly they were attributable to passing ships in the nineteenth century, although the London Missionary Society moved its Torres Strait headquarters to Mer in 1877.

Gardening was of the most profound importance to Meriam life. There was a system of title to garden land. Garden land was identified by reference to a named locality coupled with the name of an individual. Boundaries were identified in terms of known landmarks.

MABO – THE REASONING

8.4 In *Mabo*, the High Court held by a 6 to 1 majority that the plaintiffs had established that there was a system of native title recognised by the Meriam people in 1879 when the Crown first exercised sovereignty over the Islands, and that that exercise of sovereignty did not automatically extinguish native title. The court held that putting to one side:

(a) the Islands of Dauar and Waier;
(b) certain land leased to the Board of Missions; and
(c) any land appropriated for administrative purposes the use of which was inconsistent with the continued enjoyment of the rights and privileges of the Meriam people under native title,

the Meriam people were entitled, as against the whole world, to possession, occupation, use and enjoyment of the lands of the Murray Islands.

The main judgment was delivered by Brennan J, on which the following account of the reasoning is based. His Honour said (at p 32) that international law recognised three effective ways by which sovereignty might be acquired: conquest, cession and occupation of territory that was *terra nullius* ('settlement'). As among themselves, the European nations had extended this third category to include territory occupied by 'backward' or 'barbarous' peoples. In effect, such peoples did not 'count' in terms of preventing a territory from being classified by the European powers as *terra nullius.*

There were two provisos (at p 32):

(1) the local inhabitants must not have been organised as a society that was 'united permanently for political action'; and
(2) the discovery of the territory must have been 'confirmed by occupation' by the new sovereign power.

It was accepted that this enlarged *terra nullius* doctrine applied to the colony of New South Wales, from which, it will be recalled, the colony of Queensland was excised.

The expanded concept of *terra nullius* had prevailed in *Milirrpum v Nabalco Pty Ltd.*[1] In that case, Blackburn J of the Supreme Court of the Northern Territory held that the doctrine of communal native title did not form part, and never had formed part, of the law of any part of Australia. There was no appeal from his Honour's decision. However, Commonwealth, State and Territory legislation established various regimes under which areas of land could be granted to Aboriginal peoples and Torres Strait Islanders. These regimes were not, however, systems for the recognition of 'native title'. They were the creations of the new British sovereign legal system that had arrived in Australia in 1788 and had not existed in the country previously.

A similar tripartite classification was made in relation to the reception of English law in a territory outside England. Again, conquest, cession and settlement fell to be considered. In the absence of a treaty provision, in the cases of conquest and cession, the existing law of the country continued until altered by the new sovereign power. In the case of settlement, however, the English settlers or colonists were treated as having brought with them so much of the law of England as was applicable to their new situation and to 'desert uninhabited countries' – again *terra nullius*.

But what was the position where British colonists settled in parts of the globe inhabited by 'barbarous' or 'backward' peoples? In accordance with the extended notion of *terra nullius*, it was taken that there was no local law to compete with English law, and so the settled colony 'received' the law of England. The colony of New South Wales, and therefore later the colony of Queensland, were treated as falling within this third category. The English law that the settlers brought with them could not be altered by the Royal Prerogative: it could be altered only by the Imperial Parliament at Westminster or by a local legislature.

In *Mabo*, Brennan J observed that the facts as now known did not fit the 'absence of law' or 'barbarous' theory underlying the colonial reception of the English common law, and that it was no longer supportable to apply the rules of English common law that were the product of that theory (at 39). His Honour said that the High Court was faced with a choice:

(a) to apply the existing authorities but inquire whether the Meriam people were higher 'in the scale of social organisation' than the Australian Aborigines whose claims had already been 'totally disregarded' according to the existing case law; or

(b) overrule the existing case law.

The court chose the latter course.

The court distinguished between sovereignty consisting of the power of government and the Crown's title to a colony as a whole on the one hand, and the *ownership* of the land within the colony on the other. It was only if land was truly and literally *terra nullius* that the Crown would necessarily become the owner of it. Otherwise, so the court held, the common law recognised any existing native title, and the Crown's *ownership* (but not the Crown's sovereignty) was subject to that existing native title. This was subject to any special features of the particular settlement that displaced this prima facie position.

The position as just described does not detract from the following propositions. The common law attributed to the Crown a 'radical' title over all land with the territory over which it assumed sovereignty. This enabled the Crown, in the exercise of its sovereign power, to grant an interest in land to be held of the Crown or to acquire land for the Crown's demesne (at p 48). The notion of radical title qualified the Crown as 'Paramount Lord' of all who hold a tenure granted by the Crown, and as absolute beneficial owner of unalienated land required for the Crown's purposes (at p 48). 'But it is not a corollary of the Crown's acquisition of a radical title to land in an occupied territory that that Crown acquired absolute beneficial ownership of that land to the exclusion of the indigenous inhabitants' (at p 48). It was different if the land was desert and uninhabited, a true *terra nullius*. In that case the Crown would take absolute beneficial ownership.

Brennan J referred to several cases in which courts had held that the English common law recognised usufructuary rights of the existing inhabitants of land over which sovereignty was acquired. It was not to the point that the indigenous 'rights' did not contemplate 'property' as understood in the English legal system.

The court rejected an argument that native title was recognised in the common law only if there was an act of recognition of it by the new sovereign. Brennan J concluded (at p 57) that the preferable rule supported by the authorities is that a mere change in sovereignty does not extinguish native title to land. His Honour said, in a passage that was to be the basis for the definition of 'native title' or 'native title rights and interests' in section 223 of the Native Title Act 1993 (Cth) (see below), that the expression 'native title' describes:

> '[T]he interests and rights of indigenous inhabitants in land, whether communal, group or individual, possessed under the traditional laws acknowledged by and the traditional customs observed by the indigenous inhabitants.'

Brennan J said that the preferable rule equates the indigenous inhabitants of a settled colony with the inhabitants of a conquered colony in respect of the survival of their rights and interests in land (at p 57).

His Honour acknowledged (at p 58) that to state the common law as he had done involved overruling cases in which it had been held that native title could not survive the acquisition of sovereignty and was necessarily extinguished by it. In an important passage (at p 58) he said:

> 'To maintain the authority of those cases would destroy the equality of all Australian citizens before the law. The common law of this country would perpetuate injustice if it were to continue to embrace the enlarged notion of terra nullius and to persist in characterising the indigenous inhabitants of the Australian colonies as people too low in the scale of social organisation to be acknowledged as possessing rights and interests in land. Moreover, to reject the theory that the Crown acquired absolute beneficial ownership of land is to bring the law into conformity with Australian history. The dispossession of the indigenous inhabitants of Australia was not worked by a transfer of beneficial ownership when sovereignty was acquired by the Crown, but by the recurrent exercise of a paramount power to exclude the indigenous inhabitants from their traditional lands as colonial settlement expanded and land was granted to the colonists. Dispossession is attributable not to a failure of native title to survive the acquisition of sovereignty, but to its subsequent extinction by a paramount power.'

The native title that *Mabo* recognised is not an institution of the common law. It lies outside it, but is recognised by it. If we must use the term 'institution', native title is an institution of traditional laws and customs. In this fact lie the seeds of difficulties that have been experienced in proving the existence of native title at sovereignty and its survival into modern times. But they were inherent in observations that Brennan J made in *Mabo* at p 60:

- native title can be possessed only by the indigenous inhabitants and their descendants;
- the native title claimed must be shown to have existed 'at sovereignty' (1788 for New South Wales, 1879 for the Murray Islands);
- the present day claimants must be descendants of those who were native title holders at sovereignty;
- native title can be held today only by persons who acknowledge the laws and observe the customs of the indigenous people;
- acquisition of native title must be by a clan, group or member of the indigenous people that is consistent with the laws and customs of that people;
- the tide of history must not have 'washed away any real acknowledgement of traditional law and any real observance of traditional customs';
- a native title that has ceased because of abandonment of acknowledgment of traditional laws and observance of traditional customs 'cannot be revived for contemporary recognition';
- '[o]nce traditional native title expires, the Crown's radical title expands to a full beneficial title, for there is no other proprietor than the Crown' (at p 60).

Some of the special features of the relationship between the Meriam people and the Murray Islands have been mentioned above. Others to which Brennan J referred to are as follows. Strangers were not allowed to settle on the Islands. Even after annexation in 1879, strangers living there were deported. The Meriam people asserted an exclusive right to occupy the Islands. They have maintained their identity as a people and have continued to observe traditional customs. Land was traditionally occupied by individuals or family groups and their rights and interests were capable of being established with sufficient precision to attract declaratory or other relief (at p 62). It is possible to determine, according to Meriam laws and customs, disputes among the Meriam people relating to the holding of rights and interests in particular parcels of land (at p 63). The only exception to their native title over the whole of the Islands relates to a parcel of two acres that was lost to the Meriam people by the grant of a lease by the Crown to the London Missionary Society in 1882, or by the subsequent renewal of that lease.

In his reasons for judgment, Brennan J went on to consider whether the Meriam native title had been extinguished by any post-1879 exercise of sovereign power, ie by the new sovereign, the Crown in right of Queensland. According to United States, Canadian and New Zealand cases, the intention to extinguish native title must be 'clear and plain'. After examining the history of the relevant Acts of Queensland legislature and governmental steps taken under them, his Honour concluded that there had been no extinguishment.

Mason CJ and McHugh J agreed with Brennan J. Deane and Gaudron JJ gave joint reasons for arriving at the same conclusion. Dawson J dissented.

1 (1971) 17 FLR 141.

MABO – CONTEMPORANEOUS REACTIONS TO THE DECISION

8.5 Reaction to *Mabo* was mixed. The decision was given on 3 June 1992. The Federal Minister for Aboriginal Affairs stated '[h]istory was made in the High Court today. The highest court in the land has taken the position that *terra nullius* is to be rejected and relegated to the dustbin of history'. The chairman of the Northern Land Council, Mr Galarrwuy Yunupingu, said: 'the pathetic excuse of *terra nullius* is now dead', and he called on the federal government to negotiate a treaty and implement comprehensive land rights legislation or face a barrage of litigation by indigenous people to enforce recognition of their native title. On Murray Island itself, Jillian Passi, the first to hear the news, cried 'Thank God, thank God', and the Islanders began preparing a victory feast. George Mye, of neighbouring Darnley Island, who was the Aboriginal and Torres Strait Islander Commission representative for the region, said that all islanders would now move for recognition of their traditional ownership of their lands. He said, 'I'm overjoyed . . . we want to be part of Australia, but we want autonomy'.

On the other hand, there were dire warnings that the title to white people's homes in the cities and towns of Australia was at risk. The Premier of Queensland, Mr Wayne Goss, demanded federal legislation validating all land title in Australia since 1788 – a demand that was rejected by the Australian Prime Minister, Mr Paul Keating. Opponents of native title asserted that a pending claim by the Wik people,[1] if successful, would threaten the implementation of mining projects that were important to the economy.

No doubt most people making comments about *Mabo* immediately following the decision had not read the lengthy reasons for judgment. Extreme reactions, both positive and negative, proved to be unfounded. A journalist, Cameron Forbes, gave a more measured assessment:[2]

> 'A full High Court judgment in a legal battle of tiny Murray Island is being hailed as being of sweeping significance for Australia's indigenous people and the death of the concept of terra nullius – that Australia was no one's land when Europeans arrived. In a 6–1 majority decision on what has become known as the *Mabo* case, the full High Court found that Australian common law recognised a form of native title and declared that 'the Meriam people are entitled as against the whole world to possession, occupation, use and enjoyment of the lands of the Murray Islands'.

8.5 *Native Title in Australia*

1 Later leading to *Wik Peoples v The State of Queensland* (1996) 187 CLR 1.
2 Cameron Forbes, 'Key Ruling Boosts Blacks' Land Claims', *The Age*, 4 June 1992.

MABO – SUBSEQUENT DEVELOPMENTS

8.6 It would have been possible for Aboriginal individuals or groups to have their claims to hold native title determined in the ordinary Australian courts that have jurisdiction to enforce property rights. However, the federal Parliament passed the Native Title Act 1993, the operative provisions of which commenced to operate on 1 January 1994. That Act established a National Native Title Tribunal (NNTT) before which claims were to be made. The function of determining native title claims was unsatisfactorily divided between the NNTT and the Federal Court of Australia. The Act was amended substantially by the Native Title Amendment Act 1998 to provide for applications for native title to be made and determined in the Federal Court, although the NNTT has continued to have an important ancillary role, including in connection with mediation of native title disputes.

In *Western Australia v The Commonwealth*[1] ('the *Native Title Act Case*') decided on 16 March 1995, the High Court held, in effect, that its decision in *Mabo* applied to the Australian mainland. More precisely, the court decided that the history of the establishment of the Colony of Western Australia (it was established in 1829) did not show an intention of the Crown to extinguish any native title that might exist over land within the boundaries of the Colony. Accordingly, so it was held, the presumption that a power acquiring sovereignty does not intend to extinguish native title was not rebutted.

As well, in the *Native Title Act Case*, the High Court rejected a challenge by the State of Western Australia to the validity of the Native Title Act 1993. Like the State of Queensland before it, the State of Western Australia had attempted by Act of Parliament to extinguish native title. The Act in question was the Land (Titles and Traditional Usages) Act 1993 which came into operation on 2 December 1993. Unlike the Queensland Act, the Western Australian one purported to replace native title with statutory rights of traditional usage within a regime prescribed by the Act. However, like its Queensland predecessor, this Act was also held to be inconsistent with the Racial Discrimination Act 1975 (Cth).

Two further important High Court cases that have resolved certain questions concerning the effect of *Mabo* are *Wik Peoples v The State of Queensland*[2] ('*Wik*') decided on 23 December 1996, and *Members of the Yorta Yorta Aboriginal Community v Victoria*[3] ('*Yorta Yorta*') decided on 12 December 2002.

In *Wik*, the High Court held that the granting of a pastoral lease by the Crown in right of the State of Queensland was not, without more, necessarily inconsistent with the continued subsistence of any native title that might exist over the land the subject of the lease. This meant that the holders of pastoral leases could not, by reason of nothing more than that status, deny holders of native title access. The *Wik* decision was significant because pastoral lease tenure in the various Australian States covers vast areas of land on which, at sovereignty, the Aboriginal people roamed, hunted, camped and performed ceremonies. The decision disappointed the National Farmers Federation and was the subject of partisan political controversy in Australia. Again, however, the effect of the decision was exaggerated by many commentators. The case certainly did not make it any easier for today's indigenous people to establish that they hold native title.

In *Yorta Yorta*, the High Court made clear many of the limitations that were always inherent in *Mabo*. In particular, the case shows that native title claimants in respect of an area of land must prove that native title existed in relation to that area of land immediately before the time of the acquisition of sovereignty, and that by reason of an unbroken connection of acknowledgment of traditional laws and observance of traditional customs from then down to the present day by the claimants and their ancestors, the native title which depends for its existence on that acknowledgment and observance, has never ceased to exist. The High Court emphasised that once native title has ceased to exist after sovereignty, it cannot be revived because after sovereignty only the sovereign power can create title.

Many applications by native title claimants have failed to satisfy the *Yorta Yorta* requirements: see, for example, the eight overlapping claims brought on behalf of various groups of indigenous people in *Wongatha People v State of Western Australia (No 9)*.[4] Although *Yorta Yorta* is unpopular with those who wish to see greater success in native title claims, in substance, the case emphasised limitations that were always inherent in *Mabo* itself.

1 (1995) 183 CLR 373.
2 (1996) 187 CLR 1.
3 (2002) 214 CLR 422.
4 (2007) 238 ALR 1.

CONCLUSION

8.7 Many native title claims have been resolved consensually between the indigenous claimants on the one hand and the relevant State government and pastoral, mining and other interests on the other hand. *Mabo* has proved to be more beneficial to Aboriginal claimants in this way than through litigated outcomes. Moreover, The High Court's rejection of the expanded *terra nullius* doctrine has been of great symbolic importance to the first Australians.

Eddie Mabo died on 21 January 1992, just months before the decision in *Mabo* was handed down. He was buried in Townsville in a grave bearing a simple identification. On 3 June 1995, the third anniversary of the decision in *Mabo*, this was replaced with a more elaborate tombstone. Within a day after its ceremonial unveiling, it was vandalised and a racist inscription written on it. The act was universally condemned by public figures. Eddie Mabo's remains were reburied on the Island of Mer four months later. A memorial to him was erected at Townsville on 3 June 2007 on the 15th anniversary of the decision.

The decision in *Mabo* was the culmination of a ten-year struggle by the plaintiff. It is said that Eddie Mabo's personal resolve took on life after he moved from Mer to the Australian mainland. He was shocked when he was refused permission to return home to see his dying father because, so it was said, local authorities thought him to be a troublemaker! *Mabo* was to prove them right. One can only wonder what he would have thought of the results of the case that bears his name.

8.7 *Native Title in Australia*

* *Formerly a Judge of the Federal Court of Australia. The author acknowledges with thanks the research assistance of Lindsay Ash BA, MA in the writing of this chapter.*

II

LAND LAW

The United Kingdom has one of the highest rates of private home ownership in the world, and the importance of land law to its citizens corresponds. That said, it is probably fair to assume that the majority of late-night revellers in Leicester Square remain unaware of the case of *Tulk v Moxhay* in 1848, which preserved that famous piece of land as a public square in perpetuity. Still less would they associate it with a key legal development regarding restrictive covenants.

Lord Denning became one of England's most famous judges, partly through his desire to achieve justice notwithstanding apparently hide-bound legal rules, though he did not often admit to it openly. *High Trees*, decided when he was still a first instance judge, remains one of his best known decisions due to his fashioning a legal answer which provided justice as he saw it. Unlike some of his other attempts, however, rather than being distinguished in later cases, it became the bedrock authority for the now-commonplace doctrine of promissory estoppel.

9

TULK V MOXHAY

Richard de Lacy QC

INTRODUCTION

'Goodbye, Piccadilly!

Farewell, Leicester Square!

It's a long, long way to Tipperary,

But my heart's right there.'

9.1 So in his famous song Jack Judge (of Irish descent) tipped his hat in 1912 to Leicester Square in London: one of the favourite resorts of 'Paddy' (so named in the song) who has gone 'up West' on a night out. Who would suppose that the layout of this famous place would be the starting point of a development in the property law of England and Wales which remained controversial over more than a century?[1]

1 *Tulk v Moxhay* (1848) 1 H & Tw 105, 2 Ph 774, 41 ER 1143. Bailii reference [1848] EWHC J34.

THE FACTS

9.2 The facts are minimally stated in the report of the decision. As in many leading cases, a fuller statement of the facts illuminates the legal context.

The Square had been the forecourt of Leicester House, mansion of the Earls of Leicester, which stood on the north side. By the time of the covenant, there were rows of houses on its four sides with a railed garden in the centre. The owners in the late 1780s were two families, Tulk and Perry. The immediately previous owner was Elizabeth Perry (d. 1783), heiress of the seventh Earl of Leicester, who was also the freehold owner of Leicester House, which was demolished in 1791–92. The Court of Chancery had made a decree of partition of the Square on 28 January 1789 which gave the east and south rows of houses and the garden to the then tenant for life of the Tulk family. The commissioners who inquired into the partition recommended that Tulk covenant with Perry that he would preserve and keep the garden as 'an enclosed ornamental garden', but this did not appear in the deed of partition. When a later Tulk sold the garden in 1808, the purchaser gave a covenant that:

> '[he,] his heirs, and assigns should, and would from time to time, and at all times thereafter at his and their own costs and charges, keep and maintain the said piece of ground and square garden, and the iron railing round the same in its then form, and in sufficient and proper repair as a square garden and pleasure ground, in an open state, uncovered with any buildings, in neat and ornamental order; and that it should be lawful for the inhabitants of Leicester Square, tenants of the plaintiff, on payment of a reasonable rent for the same, to have keys at their own expense and the privilege of admission therewith at any time or times into the said square garden and pleasure ground.'

Moxhay acquired the garden in due course, and evidently threatened to put the garden to some use and to build on it. He was restrained by an order of the Master of the Rolls at the suit of the contemporary Tulk, and on 22 December 1848 Moxhay's appeal came before Lord Cottenham LC on appeal from the Rolls Court.

Moxhay was represented by Roundell Palmer (later Lord Selborne LC but then a 36-year-old junior, MP for Plymouth since the 1847 election). Palmer had a starry reputation (he was elected a bencher of Lincoln's Inn the following year), but Cottenham dismissed the appeal without calling on counsel for Tulk. His seminal judgment will be considered later, but it is of interest to consider what subsequently happened to the Leicester Square garden.

It may be questioned in light of events whether the Tulk family had any real interest in enforcing the negative covenant for the benefit of the residents of Leicester Square. It seems likely that they had other irons in the fire. James Wyld the younger (since 1847 MP for Bodmin, like Plymouth in the South West of England) was a cartographer and map publisher in a large way of business who made great profit from the maps and plans which railway companies needed to attach to the parliamentary bills for authorisation of their works. The railway boom of the 1830s turned into a slump in the 1840s and Wyld undertook several schemes to restore his fortunes. Some time before 1851 (and therefore within two years of Lord Cottenham's decision) he acquired the garden from Moxhay. According to the Oxford Dictionary of National Biography:

> 'Wyld's most spectacular enterprise was his 'great globe', exhibited in Leicester Square between 1851 and 1861 to coincide with the Great Exhibition. It was 60 feet high and 40 feet in diameter and lit by gas. On its inside painted plaster of Paris reliefs illustrated the physical features of the earth at a horizontal scale of one inch to ten miles and a vertical scale of three inches to ten miles. The object of some ridicule, it was none the less extremely popular. It was surrounded by a large spherical building entered from four loggias opening into each side of the square. In the building maps, atlases, and other globes (inevitably mostly Wyld's own) were displayed.'

The buildings which had housed the great globe were in fact placed there by reason of a licence granted to Wyld by the current Tulk owner of the houses. This licence included an option to Tulk to purchase an undivided half share in the garden from Wyld at the end of the 10-year licence, which Tulk in fact exercised. The facts are to be found in the headnote to *Tulk v Metropolitan*

Board of Works,[1] where the Court of Exchequer Chamber rejected on appeal the Board's attempt to take the garden under its control under an Act of 1863 for the 'Protection of Garden or Ornamental Grounds in Cities and Boroughs'.

The Square was by this time occupied by the remains of the buildings of the Wyld great globe and filled with rubbish. The Tulks erected a hoarding around the garden in 1873 (thereby rendering impossible any access by the neighbouring occupiers, though the houses had disappeared or been converted into commercial premises by this time). In 1874 the colourful company promoter and MP Albert Grant (Abraham Gottenheimer), of Dublin (1831–1899), as one of several acts of public bounty, purchased the gardens from the Tulks and presented them to the Board. Thence they passed to the Westminster City Council as a public open space (once more to be filled with uncollected refuse sacks during the strikes of the 'winter of discontent' of 1978/79).

Certain covenants undoubtedly 'ran with the land' at common law. The benefit of the covenants in a lease passed to the assignee of the reversion under the rule derived from the early cases debated and analysed in *Spencer's Case*.[2] The perfection of the transfer of all the rights and obligations under a lease had been effected by the Grantees of Reversions Act 1540 (a very necessary reform where reversions owned by monasteries and other religious houses which would otherwise have perpetual succession were being transferred to lay owners by Henry VIII's commissioners). The Chancery judge of Lord Cottenham's time was constrained to reason why the rule at common law either did not apply at all, or was superfluous. In *Tulk v Moxhay*, Lord Cottenham's very short judgment includes a paragraph which begins as follows:

> 'That the question does not depend upon whether the covenant runs with the land is evident from this, that if there was a mere agreement and no covenant, this Court would enforce it against a party purchasing with notice of it; for if an equity is attached to the property by the owner, no one purchasing with notice of that equity can stand in a different situation from the party from whom he purchased.'

This sentence is a rich seam for interpretation. First, the issue is whether law or equity should prevail, for the question does not depend, according to Lord Cottenham, on whether the covenant 'runs with the land'. But surely, that was the point which the case decides? No, because an obligation would run with the land at common law only if it amounted to a covenant. But even if the obligation is a 'mere agreement', the Court of Chancery ('this Court') would enforce it because it is an equity attached to the property, and enforce it against a purchaser of the legal estate if he has notice of its existence.

This decision, so apparently lapidary, really leaves more questions than it answers. Tulk owned the freehold of the houses, and the covenant had clearly been taken for the benefit of the tenants. Was this essential to the decision? If not, would a purchaser's conscience be affected by notice of a covenant of which only the covenantee had the benefit, irrespective of his land holding? What was the significance of the positive parts of the covenant benefiting the houses?

1 (1868) LR 3 QB 682.
2 (1583) 5 Co Rep 16a.

STARTING POINT FOR A DEVELOPMENT OF PRINCIPLE

9.3 So far as English law is concerned, Lord Cottenham's judgment proved to be only a starting point for an elaborate development of principle which was really rendered necessary by the wholesale urbanisation of England during the later industrial revolution (the Leicester Square houses, on the forecourt of a former nobleman's palace, were an early example of this). Although Lord Cottenham's judgment does not expressly rule out the possibility of a positive obligation which could bind a purchaser in equity, the later decisions in England assumed that the principle should have its narrowest scope, because positive obligations which required action by the covenantor could not be imposed on his assignee at common law unless the action touched and concerned land demised to the covenantor (*Spencer's Case*[1] – the second resolution of the judges).

1 (1583) 5 Co Rep 16a.

COOKE V CHILCOTT

9.4 By 1881, there had been 15 decisions on this topic, of which all but one had concerned exclusively obligations restrictive of the use of the land. The exception, *Cooke v Chilcott*,[1] involved an exposition which appears on its face to be consistent with a much wider view of the rule stated by Lord Cottenham. The defendant's predecessor had covenanted with his vendor to erect a pump and reservoir connected to a well on the defendant's land and to permit the occupiers of the vendor's neighbouring cottages to receive water from the well through pipes on the defendant's land. The defendant ceased to maintain the supply, and the plaintiff, successor to the vendor, sought an injunction. The immediate obstacle to the grant of an injunction compelling the reinstatement of the supply was that it would require supervision, but Malins V-C thought that he could grant an injunction restraining the defendant from 'allowing the work to remain unperformed'. That difficulty being out of the way, the Vice-Chancellor decided that, even though the covenant was not of the kind enforceable at law under the second resolution in *Spencer's Case*, the rule in equity was that an obligation could be enforced against a purchaser with notice of the obligation. He cited *Daniel v Stepney*,[2] where the defendant sought to justify a distress on mining materials and equipment by reference to a rent charge which he asserted extended to any land of the plaintiff subsequently connected to the mine which was expressly subject to the rent charge. The Court of Exchequer held that a rent charge of that kind could not exist at law, even if the plaintiff might be bound by the covenant in question as a covenant. On appeal, the Court of Exchequer Chamber had no hesitation in accepting the defendant's argument that the plaintiff as assignee was bound by the terms of the covenant because he took the lease in question with notice of the covenant.

1 (1876) 3 Ch D 694.

2 (1874) LR 9 Exch 185.

HAYWOOD V BRUNSWICK PERMANENT BENEFIT BUILDING SOCIETY

9.5 In this state of the authorities, *Haywood v Brunswick Permanent Benefit Building Society*[1] came before the Court of Appeal. The building society was (as mortgagee) the assignee of a purchaser of land subject to a rent charge and a covenant to build on the land and to keep the buildings in good repair (if necessary by rebuilding). Stephen J at first instance thought that the plaintiff was clearly right in his contention that a covenant bound an assignee with notice of the covenant, whether the covenant related to the use of the land or to an obligation to build and to repair. He relied on *Cooke v Chilcott*.[2] On the appeal, the building society's counsel were, it seems, the first to argue directly that the rule in *Tulk v Moxhay* did not extend to a covenant which was not essentially restrictive. *Cooke v Chilcott*, according to them, should have been analysed as a case of the grant by the defendant's predecessor of an easement over his land for the passage of water from the well on his land, through pipes leading to the respective houses. Their argument continued by pointing out that the court of Chancery had refused to enforce positive obligations by injunction (for example, in *Lumley v Wagner*,[3] the case of the singer contracted exclusively to an impresario). This next step in the argument tends to confuse (1) whether in principle *Tulk v Moxhay* was so restricted and (2) whether the court should grant an injunction to compel a positive act, a question which also arises far outside the field of covenants given in relation to land (as shown by *Lumley v Wagner* itself).

Brett LJ thought it clear that the principle laid down in *Tulk v Moxhay* related to one class of covenant only, those restricting the use of the land. He also thought that a covenant which imposed a burden on the land which was enforceable against the land itself (ie without involving an act on the part of the assignee of the land) might be enforced against the assignee with notice. As a covenant to build was outside either class, the plaintiff could not rely on *Tulk v Moxhay* to carry the burden of the covenant to the building society as assignee. Cotton LJ thought that the case of the plaintiff required an extension of the doctrine of equity that the assignee was bound merely by notice of the covenant, without regard to its content, and *Tulk v Moxhay* was treated by him as merely the first in a series of cases concerning only covenants restrictive of user. Lindley LJ said that the cases since *Tulk v Moxhay* had never included a covenant under which the assignee was obliged to spend money; a user covenant had been enforced against a yearly tenant of the land on the ground of notice, but it was absurd to suppose that a covenant to repair could ever be enforced against a yearly tenant of the successor in title of the covenantor.

Curiously, the Court of Appeal did not expressly overrule *Cooke v Chilcott*, Lindley LJ saying that he would be 'sorry to overrule that case' and that it should be reconsidered on another occasion. There can be no doubt of the overall justice of the decision in *Cooke v Chilcott*. But it must be remembered that only a few years later municipal water supplies provided homes with water and the Conveyancing Act 1881 provided for the transfer of rights in the nature of easements and quasi-easements to purchasers of land, so that this problem would have been solved by reason of the advance of public law and the reform of conveyancing. Lindley LJ (with Cotton LJ and Fry LJ) had his chance in 1885.

9.5 *Tulk v Moxhay*

1 (1881) LR 8 QBD 403.
2 (1876) 3 Ch D 694.
3 (1852) 1 De GM & G 604.

FORMBY V BARKER

9.6 *Haywood* did not answer the question whether the person seeking to enforce the covenant must have land affected by it. That question was considered by the Court of Appeal in *Formby v Barker*.[1] This was not a decision on the point, as unfortunately the plaintiff failed on the question of whether the covenant prohibited what the defendant intended to do with the land. The action had, however, raised the further question whether the plaintiff as executor of the covenantee could enforce the covenant against a purchaser from the covenantor even though the executor had no land which was benefited by the covenant. Even the deceased covenantee had no such land: he had parted with all his estate in the neighbourhood when the covenant was taken. In *Rogers v Hosegood*[2] the Court of Appeal had established the principle that the benefit of a covenant could be annexed to the land which it was intended to benefit, and that such annexed benefit would pass on a conveyance of the land benefited, so that (as Collins LJ said in that case, p 407) the benefit of the covenant 'may be said to run with [the land], in contemplation as well of equity as of law without proof of special bargain or representation on the assignment'.

So the Court of Appeal decided in *Formby v Barker* that equity would not enforce a negative covenant against a purchaser with notice unless the assignee of the benefit of the covenant could show that he owned land intended to be benefited, or to which the benefit was annexed either expressly or as a matter of law.

1 [1903] 2 Ch 539.
2 [1900] 2 Ch 388.

POSITIVE OBLIGATIONS – *AUSTERBERRY V OLDHAM CORPORATION*

9.7 What of the common law relating to positive obligations? It is surprising to find that there was no decision truly focused on this issue until *Austerberry v Oldham Corporation*.[1] This case concerned a covenant given in connection with the creation of a new road in 1837. The local landowners conceived the idea that they could provide a short connecting road in place of an inconvenient ancient highway between villages in the vicinity of Oldham. A vendor (one of many along the route) conveyed land to trustees on trust for a proposed joint stock company which would eventually be the proprietor and maintainer of the road. The trustees covenanted with the vendor to make the road, and to keep it in repair, and, subject to the payment of tolls, to make it available to the public. The trustees made the road, which was called Shaw Road. The report of the case describes how municipal legislation took over this public-spirited form of private enterprise:

> 'After the completion of Shaw Road, Elliott and other owners of land adjoining the road from time to time erected houses on their land at irregular intervals along the

> line of and abutting on the road, the property in its vicinity thus gradually losing its agricultural character and becoming absorbed into the town of Oldham. The Plaintiff, who had subsequently purchased Elliott's land, alleged that the expenditure in the erection of these houses was made upon the faith of the covenants in the above-mentioned conveyances and the provisions of the trust deed, and with the full knowledge and acquiescence of the persons for the time being entitled to Shaw Road, such persons being in fact the predecessors in title of the Defendants, the Corporation of Oldham; also that the access afforded by Shaw Road was essential to the proper use and enjoyment of the houses.
>
> In the year 1865 the Oldham Borough Improvement Act 1865, was passed. Section 27 of that Act contained the following provisions as to the "road or street called Shaw Road": (1) The corporation were empowered to purchase all rights in or over the said road or street and all rights of levying tolls on the traffic thereon, and the interests of all persons in any tolls so levied; (2) for the purposes of such purchase the said rights and interests were to be deemed lands within the meaning of the Act and any Act incorporated therewith: (3) On the completion of such purchase all the rights and interests aforesaid were to be absolutely extinguished, the corporation were to remove all gates, etc, and thenceforth the said road or street was to be a street open to the public and subject to all provisions relative to the sewering, draining, and paving of streets not being highways repairable by the inhabitants at large: (4) The corporation's powers of compulsory purchase under this section were not to be exercised after the expiration of five years from the commencement of the Act, and (5) were not to extend to the soil of the said road or street.'

The result of the statute was that the owners of the land adjoining Shaw Road had had the benefit of the trustees' covenant to maintain the road, but the Corporation asserted that the road was not maintainable at public expense. So the plaintiff asserted that the Corporation, having acquired title to the road with notice of the covenant to keep it in repair, was liable on the covenant to a successor in title of the covenantee. Cotton and Lindley LLJ (both party to the decision in *Haywood*) were on the bench, with Fry LJ, to hear the appeal from the Vice-Chancellor of the County Palatine of Lancaster. Cotton LJ said (somewhat inaccurately) that he and Lindley LJ had, in *Haywood*, expressed their opinion against *Cooke v Chilcott*[2] being 'a correct development of the doctrine established by *Tulk v Moxhay*, or for which *Tulk v Moxhay* was an authority'. All three of the judges in the Court of Appeal decided that the covenant of the trustees of the road could not run with the land so as to bind the Corporation, despite the notice which the Corporation had had as the successor in title to the trustees of the existence of the obligation to maintain and repair the road.

1 (1885) 29 Ch D 750.
2 (1876) 3 Ch D 694.

IMPACT OF THE LAW OF PROPERTY ACT 1925

9.8 From the time of *Austerberry v Oldham Corporation*,[1] there were no further decisions of the courts of England and Wales directly on the question of the scope of *Tulk v Moxhay*. It was suggested from time to time that section 79 of the Law of Property Act 1925 had changed the law. That section provided that a covenant relating to land of a covenantor, or capable of being bound by him, was deemed to be made by the covenantor for himself and his successors in title, and persons deriving title from the covenantor or his successors, and was to have effect as if those persons were expressed. This language would seem to be designed to make a covenant 'run with the land', whether positive or negative. The point was raised (without a decision) in *Tophams Ltd v Earl of Sefton*,[2] where Lord Upjohn and Lord Wilberforce both considered that section 79 did not have the effect of making a covenant run with the land.

1 (1885) 29 Ch D 750.

2 [1967] 1 AC 50, HL.

EFFECT OF THE RESTRICTION OF *TULK V MOXHAY*

9.9 The effect of the restriction of *Tulk v Moxhay* economically was mainly to entrench the necessity for leasehold tenure where buildings were to be divided horizontally, since the upper apartments required the support of those below: the burden of a covenant to maintain the lower premises in existence and in good repair would not survive a transfer by the covenantor. Only a structure of covenants in favour of the reversioner whose burden passed with the assignment of the lease would answer. Prof H W R Wade pointed out the disadvantages resulting from the restriction of *Tulk v Moxhay*, and suggested that the narrow interpretation of the case had limited the law without purpose.[1]

Law Commission[2] recommended that positive covenants should be made binding on successors in title of the covenantor. One result would be that freehold titles to apartments and flats horizontally divided could be created and transferred.

In *Rhone v Stevens*[3] the question was raised directly for the first time. Counsel for the appellant (a future Lord Justice and chairman of the Law Commission) roundly submitted that *Haywood* and *Austerberry* were no more than assertions to the effect that *Tulk v Moxhay* could not be extended to the case of a positive covenant. It will be apparent from the narrative above that this argument has substantial support. Lord Templeman, who gave the only substantive speech, pointed out the difficulties of undoing the restrictions: a rule of equity would be converted into the simple application of notice, the rule against enforcement of positive covenants had stood for a century, the consequences of reversal of *Austerberry* would require detailed parliamentary consideration, and (most importantly) the relentless application of logic might well have very undesirable consequences. Lord Templeman pointed out that the running of the burden of covenants with long leases had led to massive repairing liabilities on the tenants for the time being of leasehold property at the expiry of the lease which Parliament had had to relieve (Leasehold Property (Repairs) Act 1938; Landlord and Tenant Act 1954).

1 Wade, HWR, 'Covenants – a "Broad and Reasonable View" ', *Cambridge Law Journal*, Vol 31, No 1, 1972(B): Jubilee Issue (Apr 1972), pp 157–175.

2 Law Commission Report No 127, on Transfer of Title to Land (1984).

3 [1994] 2 AC 310.

LEGISLATIVE REFORM

9.10 The legislative reform which the Law Commission recommended in 1984 has not been begun in England and Wales. In Australia, the State of Victoria passed a Strata Titles Act in 1967, and New South Wales followed in 1973. (All the States now have such legislation.) The strata titles enable the creation of a particular form of freehold, but the legislation is also concerned with the planning and administrative demands created by the erection of buildings divided into units horizontally.

In Hong Kong, all the land in the former colony was held on leasehold tenure, ultimately from the Crown (which, as is well known, was itself a lessee of the land in the colony lying on the mainland of China and outside the island of Hong Kong). The Conveyancing and Property Ordinance (cap 219) section 41 provides:

> '(3) Notwithstanding any rule of law or equity but subject to subsection (5), a covenant shall run with the land and, in addition to being enforceable between the parties, shall be enforceable against the occupiers of the land and the covenantor and his successors in title and persons deriving title under or through him or them by the covenantee and his successors in title and persons deriving title under or through him or them.
>
> (5) (A positive covenant shall not, by virtue only of this section, be enforceable against—
>
> (a) a lessee from the covenantor or from a successor in title of the covenantor or from any person deriving title under or through the covenantor or a successor in title of the covenantor; or
>
> (b) any person deriving title under or through such a lessee; or
>
> (c) any person merely because he is an occupier of land.

Subsection (5) deals simply and effectively with the objection that the burden of a covenant should not extend to an interest in the burdened land which is inferior to or derived out of the interest of the covenantor (the yearly tenant mentioned in *Haywood v Brunswick Building Society*[1]).

1 (1881) LR 8 QBD 403.

DID *TULK V MOXHAY* CHANGE THE WORLD?

9.11 In the very short term, the decision preserved Leicester Square from one developer, enabling the Tulk owners in short order to let in another, who was the forerunner of the providers of public entertainment surrounding the former gardens. Jack Judge's countrymen could spend their leisure time in its purlieus and heartily join in the chorus to 'Tipperary'.

In the long term, had the judges been prepared to impose positive obligations in equity, the market in urban land would have been quite different. Freeholds might have been sold more freely on the basis that positive covenants would be made enforceable in equity on the basis of notice. The enterprising frontagers of Shaw Road, Oldham might have seen their overall scheme come to fruition, instead of being frustrated. The judges, however, insisted that the common law must prevail, and that Lord Cottenham had not been entitled to release the transmissibility of positive obligations from the sphere of leasehold covenants where it had been confined since 1583.

10

A PROMISE IS A PROMISE

Central London Property Trust Ltd v High Trees House Ltd

Robert Pearce QC

INTRODUCTION

10.1 As every law student and practitioner knows, Denning J's decision in *Central London Property Trust Ltd v High Trees House Ltd*[1] ('*High Trees*') launched the modern development of the equitable doctrine of promissory estoppel.

1 [1947] KB 130.

THE FACTS

10.2 The facts of the case are simple. By a lease dated 24 September 1937 the claimant let a newly constructed block of flats to the defendant for a term of 99 years from 29 September 1937 at a ground rent of £2,500 a year. It was intended that the defendant would sub-let individual flats to occupational lessees. As a result of the outbreak of war, the flats proved to be hard to let. Consequently, an arrangement was made between the claimant and the defendant, which was recorded in a letter dated 3 January 1940 from the claimant to the defendant and in a board resolution of the claimant. The letter stated: 'we confirm the arrangement made between us by which the ground rent shall be reduced as from the commencement of the lease to £1,250 per annum'. The defendant paid the reduced rent from 1940 onwards. In 1941 the claimant went into receivership. By the beginning of 1945, war conditions having eased, all the flats were fully let.

By a letter dated 21 September 1945 (received on 24 September 1945), the claimant's receiver wrote to the defendant saying that rent must be paid at the full rate, and claiming arrears of £7,916. Subsequently, the claimant commenced proceedings claiming £625, the difference between the original and the reduced rent for the quarters ending 29 September 1945 and 25 December 1945.

The defendant raised three defences, namely (1) the letter of 3 January 1940 constituted an agreement that the rent should be £1,250 and applied for the whole duration of the lease, (2) alternatively the claimant was estopped from alleging that the rent exceeded £1,250 and (3), in the further alternative, by failing to demand rent in excess of £1,250 before its letter of 21 September 1945, the claimant had waived rent in excess of the reduced rent that had accrued prior to receipt of that letter.

The claimant replied to the defendant's first defence by arguing that, since the lease was under seal, it could only be varied by a deed.

THE DECISION

10.3 Dealing with the defendant's first defence, Denning J, applying *Berry v Berry*,[1] held that equity would give effect to an agreement evidenced in writing to vary a lease under seal. But he continued:

> 'That equitable doctrine, however, could hardly apply in the present case because the variation here might be said to have been made without consideration.'

Denning J rejected the defendant's second defence, of estoppel, on the ground that *Jorden v Money*[2] established that an estoppel by representation had to be of an existing fact, whereas a representation that payment of the rent would not be enforced at the full rate was a representation as to the future.

Denning J then proceeded to formulate the statement of principle for which the case is famous. He deduced from cases decided in the previous 50 years 'which, although they are said to be cases of estoppel, are not really such' a principle that:

> 'where a promise was made which was intended to create legal relations and which, to the knowledge of the person making the promise, was going to be acted on by the person to whom it was made, and which was in fact acted on . . . the courts have said that the promise must be honoured.'

Having accepted that 'under the old common law, it may be difficult to find any consideration for' the promises in the cases where courts had held such promises to be binding, Denning J said:

> 'The courts have not gone so far as to give a cause of action in damages for the breach of such a promise, but they have refused to allow the party making it to act inconsistently with it.'

He regarded the decisions as 'a natural result of the fusion of law and equity'.

Applying that principle, Denning J then proceeded to determine 'the scope of the promise in the present case'. He held that: 'the promise was understood by all parties only to apply under the conditions prevailing at the time it was made, namely, when the flats were only partially let', and that it 'ceased to apply' when in early 1945 the flats became fully let. He therefore held that the claimant was entitled to recover the sum claimed.

1 [1929] 2 KB 316.
2 (1854) 5 HL Cas 185.

AN UNLIKELY CASE FOR INNOVATION

10.4 Few landmark cases have been decided so economically. The case occupies only six and a half pages of the Law Reports. The entire hearing appears to have been completed within a day, and Denning J's judgment was unreserved. Despite 'a tidying up afterwards for the Law Reports',[1] the judgment retains the feel of the spoken word.

For several reasons, *High Trees* was an unlikely occasion for the development of the law.

First, it is surprising that the case was litigated at all. The commercial justification for the litigation is not obvious. Denning J described the action as 'friendly proceedings'. The lower the rent payable by the defendant to the claimant, the greater the defendant's profitability. But the defendant was a subsidiary of the claimant, and hence the defendant's increased profitability through payment of a lower rent would have been for the ultimate benefit of the claimant in its capacity as a shareholder in the defendant. Further, the claimant might have been able to exercise its rights as a shareholder in the defendant to procure that the defendant entered into a further agreement reinstating the full rent.

Second, the claimant's claim was only for the recovery of the rent for the quarters ending on 29 September 1945 and 25 December 1945. Denning J held as a question of fact that the promise on which the defendant relied did not extend to the period after early 1945. He could, therefore, easily have disposed of the claim by a short decision on the facts. As it is, his reasons why the claimant could not have recovered the full rent for the period covered by the promise, including his formulation of the doctrine of promissory estoppel, are not part of the ratio decidendi of the case and are obiter dicta.[2]

Third, even had it been necessary for Denning J to consider the recoverability of the full rent for the period before war conditions eased, there were other, more conventional methods, by which a less innovative judge could have arrived at the same result. One such method might have been to discover some consideration for the claimant's agreement to accept a lower rent. The defendant argued that 'The reduction in rent was made so that the defendant might be enabled to continue to run their business and that was sufficient to enable a court to hold the agreement binding on' the claimant. It may be that in other circumstances Denning J would have acceded to such an argument, since his treatment of it ('the variation here might be said to have been made without consideration') is not a clear rejection of it.

Similarly, although Denning J rejected the defendant's case on estoppel on the ground that estoppel required a representation of existing fact, it may be that in other circumstances he would have explored further the possibility of finding in the claimant's statements to the defendant an implied representation of an existing fact concerning the claimant's intention as to the duration of the rent concession, which might have allowed a more conventional estoppel argument to succeed.

1 Denning, *The Discipline of Law* (1979) OUP, p 203.

2 See the discussion between R E Megarry and JHC Morris at (1948) 64 LQR 28, 193, 454 and 463.

TWO LOOSE ENDS

10.5 Denning J's judgment could perhaps have been a little more explicit on two points. As already noted, he held that 'the scope of the promise' which the claimant made to accept a lower rent was limited to the period before early 1945. But it is not entirely clear whether this conclusion was reached as a matter of construction of the agreement between the parties or by taking a broader view of the extent to which it was unconscionable for the claimant to go back on its promise. The claimant's letter of 3 January 1940 did not by its express terms limit the reduced rent to the duration of wartime conditions. It seems doubtful whether, if that letter had contractual force, it could properly have been construed as being so limited. Denning J stated: 'the promise was understood by all parties only to apply under the conditions prevailing at the time it was made, namely, when the flats were only partially let'. This is arguably a finding that, notwithstanding the unqualified terms of the promise, it was not unconscionable for the landlord to revoke it after the conditions in which it was made had ceased to apply.

Second, Denning J did not deal expressly with the defendant's third defence, namely, that the claimant had waived rent that had accrued prior to the defendant's receipt of the claimant's letter dated 21 September 1945. Here, one may feel that the defendant was unlucky. Denning J found as a fact that the claimant's promise to accept a lesser rent had ceased to apply by early 1945. But he could have held, consistently with that finding, that the claimant had to give reasonable notice of its wish to restore payment of the full rent. The claimant wrote seeking payment of the higher rent on 21 September 1945. That does not seem to be reasonable notice in respect of the rent payable (apparently) on 29 September 1945. Furthermore, the rent seems to have been payable quarterly in arrears, so the claimant's letter was not written until almost the end of the period to be covered by the September instalment. But the claimant recovered the full quarter's rent for the quarter ending on 29 September 1945 as well as (unexceptionably) for the quarter ending on 25 December 1945.

THE SOURCE OF PROMISSORY ESTOPPEL

10.6 Although Denning J professed to derive the principle he formulated in *High Trees* primarily from 'a series of decisions over the last fifty years', these decisions can be explained on other grounds.[1] The true source of the principle was the decision of the House of Lords in *Hughes v Metropolitan Railway Co*[2] as interpreted by Bowen LJ in *Birmingham & District Land Co v London & North Western Railway Co.*[3] Denning J referred to these cases in *High Trees*, although they had not been cited to him. His use of them reflects a submission he himself had made four years earlier, with partial success, as counsel in the Court of Appeal in *Salisbury v Gilmore.*[4]

In *Hughes v Metropolitan Railway* a landlord forfeited a lease for breach of a covenant to repair on notice. The House of Lords upheld an order granting relief from forfeiture on the ground that correspondence between the parties during the currency of a notice to repair had the effect in equity of extending the period available to the tenant to comply with the notice.

In *Birmingham & District Land Co* building agreements made between a landowner and a builder allowed the builder to occupy land for the purpose of erecting buildings, and required him to vacate if the buildings were not completed by a specified date. The landowner subsequently requested the builder to suspend building, and the builder did so. A successor in title of the landowner took possession of the land shortly after the original specified date. The Court of Appeal held that the effect of the landowner's request that work be suspended was to extend the time available to the builder to complete the work, and that his interests under the agreements subsisted at the time the successor in title took possession.

Both of these cases concerned situations in which a landowner sought to enforce a provision in a contract entitling him to take possession of land following the default by a person in occupation in the performance of an obligation owed to the landowner. They can, on their facts, be understood as applications, or modest extensions, of equity's jurisdiction to relieve against forfeiture.

However, in *Birmingham & District Land Co*, Bowen LJ stated the principle to be derived from *Hughes v Metropolitan Railway Co* in wide terms. He stated that it:

> 'has nothing to do with forfeiture . . . It was applied in *Hughes v Metropolitan Railway Company* in a case in which equity could not relieve against forfeiture upon the mere ground that it was a forfeiture, but could interfere only because there had been something in the nature of acquiescence, or negotiations between the parties, which made it inequitable to allow the forfeiture to be enforced. The truth is that the proposition is wider than cases of forfeiture. It seems to me to amount to this, that if persons who have contractual rights against others induce by their conduct those against whom they have such rights to believe that such rights will either not be enforced or will be kept in suspense or abeyance for some particular time, those persons will not be allowed by a Court of Equity to enforce the rights until such time has elapsed, without at all events placing the parties in the same position as they were before.'

Denning J's achievement in *High Trees*, and in the subsequent cases in which he applied and extended its principle, was to show how Bowen LJ's re-statement of the equitable principle applied in *Hughes v Metropolitan Railway Co* offered an elegant, simple and flexible alternative to the difficult[5] common law rules concerning the variation of contractual obligations and alteration of the mode of their performance.

1 See DM Gordon QC, 'Creditors' promises to forego rights' [1963] CLJ 222.

2 (1877) 2 App Cas 439.

3 (1888) 40 Ch D 268.

4 [1912] 2 KB 38.

5 For a modern review of the common law rules, see Phipps, AJ, 'Resurrecting the doctrine of common law forbearance' (2007) 123 LQR 286.

CURRENT STATUS OF PROMISSORY ESTOPPEL

10.7 Denning J's statements of legal principle in *High Trees* itself are in somewhat discursive terms. Four years later, in *Combe v Combe*,[1] he sought to re-state definitively the principle he had identified in *High Trees*. In that case, a wife sued a husband on a written promise to pay maintenance on which she claimed to have relied by refraining from applying for maintenance to the court. The Court of Appeal allowed an appeal from a judgment in her favour. Denning J stated:

> 'The principle, as I understand it, is that where one party has, by his words or conduct, made to the other a promise or assurance which was intended to affect the legal relations between them and to be acted on accordingly, then, once the other party has taken him at his word and acted on it, the one who gave the promise or assurance cannot afterwards be allowed to revert to the previous legal relations as if no such promise or assurance had been made by him, but he must accept their legal relations subject to the qualification which he himself has so introduced, even though it is not supported in point of law by any consideration but only by his word.
>
> Seeing that the principle never stands alone as giving a cause of action in itself, it can never do away with the necessity of consideration when that is an essential part of the cause of action. The doctrine of consideration is too firmly fixed to be overthrown by a side-wind. Its ill-effects have been largely mitigated of late, but it still remains a cardinal necessity of the formation of a contract, though not of its modification or discharge.'

Subsequent decisions have further refined elements of the doctrine. For the doctrine to apply, a promise must be clear and unequivocal.[2] It must be inequitable for the promisor to go back on his promise and insist on his strict rights. The doctrine is not applied where it would be not be inequitable for the promisor to go back on his promise.[3] The promisee must have altered his position in reliance on the promise, but it is not necessary that he should have acted to his detriment.[4] The doctrine is capable of extinguishing, as well as suspending, rights.[5]

At the present stage in its development, promissory estoppel is generally seen as an equitable alternative to the rules of the common law relating to the variation of contractual obligations and alteration of the mode of their performance. It is not understood to be capable of giving a remedy to a promisee where the promisor is in breach of a promise, unsupported by consideration, to confer a right on the promisee in the future. The doctrine is recognised to have elements in common with other forms of estoppel, but it is also generally recognised to differ from the other forms of estoppel to such an extent that it is not possible to assimilate them all into a single formulation of a broad principle restraining unconscionable conduct. Nevertheless, unconscionability provides the link between them.[6]

The doctrine of promissory estoppel raises questions which have yet to be satisfactorily resolved. Two of these are the relationship between the doctrine and the rule in *Foakes v Beer*,[7] and the question whether the doctrine should be developed so as to be capable of being used to found a cause of action.

1 [1951] 2 KB 215.

2 *Woodhouse AC Israel Cocoa Ltd SA v Nigerian Produce Marketing Co Ltd* [1972] AC 741.

3 *D & C Builders v Rees* [1966] 2 QB 617.

4 *Société Italo-Belge pour le Commerce et L'Industrie SA v Palm & Vegetable Oils (Malaysia) Sdn Bhd* [1982] 1 All ER 19.

5 *Ajayi (t/a Colony Carrier Co) v RT Briscoe (Nigeria) Ltd* [1964] 1 WLR 1326, PC.

6 See *Johnson v Gore-Wood & Co (a firm)* [2002] 2 AC 1 at 41 (Lord Goff).

7 (1884) LR 9 App Cas 605.

FOAKES V BEER

10.8 In *Foakes v Beer*[1] the House of Lords affirmed the existence of a general rule that an agreement to pay a lesser sum is not of itself consideration for the release of an obligation to pay a greater sum. In that case, a written agreement between a judgment creditor and debtor provided that if the debtor paid the judgment debt and costs by instalments the creditor would not take proceedings on the judgment. The debtor paid all the instalments. The creditor then sued for the interest due on the judgment debt. The House of Lords upheld the creditor's claim, holding that the written agreement was unsupported by consideration and was unenforceable by the debtor.

In *High Trees*, Denning J envisaged that the principle in *Hughes v Metropolitan Railway Co*[2] would be applied to reverse the effect of *Foakes v Beer*. He stated:

> 'The logical consequence, no doubt, is that a promise to accept a smaller sum, if acted upon, is binding notwithstanding the absence of consideration: and if the fusion of law and equity leads to this result, so much the better. This aspect was not considered in *Foakes v Beer*.'

Whilst *Hughes v Metropolitan Railway Co* was not cited or referred to in *Foakes v Beer* it is unlikely, as Denning J might appear to imply, that this was due to oversight. As Professor Robert Bradgate has pointed out,[3] Lords Selborne and Blackburn were parties to both decisions. Both of their speeches in *Foakes v Beer* are sympathetic to criticisms of the rule that that case affirmed, and they would surely have drawn attention to any equitable ameliorations of it of which they were aware. It seems likely that when *Foakes v Beer* was decided the principle of *Hughes v Metropolitan Railway Co* was not understood to have the far-reaching scope that Bowen LJ's dictum subsequently gave it.

The criticism of *Foakes v Beer* which Denning J implicitly supported by his dictum in *High Trees* is that where the debtor's agreement to pay a lesser sum is in fact a benefit to the creditor, there would be no injustice in upholding such an agreement.

The converse position, where injustice would result from upholding such an agreement, was considered in *D & C Builders v Rees*.[4] There a debtor who had the means to pay the full amount of a debt put pressure on an impecunious creditor to agree to accept part payment in full satisfaction. The Court of Appeal dismissed an appeal from a finding as a preliminary issue that there was no consideration to support the agreement and that it was unenforceable. Winn LJ, applying *Foakes v Beer*, held that there was no consideration for the agreement, and did not consider promissory estoppel. Lord Denning MR (with whom Danckwerts LJ agreed) also held that the agreement was unsupported by consideration, but did not decide the appeal on that ground. He held that the principle of *Hughes v Metropolitan Railway Co* was applicable, but that it only barred the creditor from his legal rights where it would be inequitable for him to insist on them. He continued:

> 'Where there has been a true accord, under which the creditor voluntarily agrees to accept a lesser sum in satisfaction and the creditor accepts it, then it is inequitable for the creditor afterwards to insist on the balance. But he is not bound unless there has been truly an accord between them.'

He then held that the pressure applied by the debtor to the creditor to enter into the agreement prevented there being a true accord, and that creditor was not prevented by the agreement from recovering the full sum.

Although all three members of the Court of Appeal agreed in the result in that case, their decision did not leave the law in a stable condition, as it would seem that they would have arrived at differing conclusions had the debtor not applied pressure on the creditor to accept a lesser sum.

1 (1884) LR 9 App Cas 605.
2 (1877) 2 App Cas 439.
3 *The Law of Contract*, 3rd edn, LexisNexis Butterworths, para 2.122.
4 [1966] 2 QB 617.

10.9 The interaction between *Foakes v Beer*[1] and promissory estoppel was further considered by the Court of Appeal in *Collier v P & M J Wright Holdings Ltd*.[2] A debtor and two others were jointly liable to a creditor to pay a debt by instalments. The debtor alleged that he and the creditor agreed that, in return for the debtor accepting sole responsibility for a one-third share of the instalments, the creditor would not seek payment from him of the other two thirds. The debtor paid a one-third share of the instalments and the creditor then sought to pursue him for the balance. Arden and Longmore LLJ both held that by virtue of the rule in *Foakes v Beer* the alleged agreement was unenforceable as a contract for want of consideration. The debtor sought to rely alternatively on promissory estoppel. Arden LJ concluded from the judgment of Lord Denning MR in *D & C Builders v Rees*[3] that, if the creditor and the debtor voluntarily made the agreement alleged by the debtor, the agreement and the subsequent payment by the debtor of one-third of the instalments would make it inequitable for the creditor to pursue the debtor for the balance. She stated:

> 'The facts of this case demonstrate that, if (1) a debtor offers to pay part only of the amount he owes; (2) the creditor voluntarily accepts that offer, and (3) in reliance on the creditor's acceptance the debtor pays that part of the amount he owes in full, the creditor will, by virtue of the doctrine of promissory estoppel, be bound to accept that sum in full and final satisfaction of the whole debt. For him to resile will of itself be inequitable. In addition, in these circumstances, the promissory estoppel has the effect of extinguishing the creditor's right to the balance of the debt. This part of our law originated in the brilliant obiter dictum of Denning J in the *High Trees* case.'

Longmore LJ was not prepared to go so far. He accepted that on the facts alleged by the debtor it would be arguable that it would be inequitable for the creditor to resile from its promise but said: 'There might however be much to be said on the other side'.

The decision of the Court of Appeal in *D & C Builders v Rees* is authority for the proposition that, if there is no 'true accord' between the creditor and the debtor that the creditor will accept a lesser sum in satisfaction of a liability to pay a larger sum, the doctrine of promissory estoppel will not prevent the creditor seeking payment of the balance. But it is unclear whether the courts will follow the suggestions made in *High Trees* and *D & C Builders v Rees* and adopted by Arden LJ in *Collier v P & M J Wright Holdings Ltd* that, as a corollary, if there is a 'true accord', it will necessarily follow that it will be inequitable for the creditor to seek payment of the balance. That approach has the practical effect of reversing *Foakes v Beer*, and it is difficult to feel enthusiasm for so prescriptive a view of what is 'inequitable'. The next step in the development of this area of the law should surely be a re-consideration by the Supreme Court of *Foakes v Beer*.

1 (1884) 9 App Cas 605.
2 [2007] EWCA Civ 1329, [2008] 1 WLR 643.
3 [1966] 2 QB 617.

PROMISSORY ESTOPPEL AS A CAUSE OF ACTION?

10.10 In *High Trees* itself and in *Combe v Combe*,[1] Denning J stated that promissory estoppel did not give rise to a cause of action, and in *Baird Textile Holdings Ltd Marks and Spencer plc*[2] the Court of Appeal held that it was precluded by authority from holding that promissory estoppel may in general found a cause of action.

Nevertheless, there are attractive arguments for saying that this limitation on the scope of the principle should be removed. Proprietary estoppel (which Lord Scott has recently described as a 'sub-species' of promissory estoppel),[3] can found a cause of action, and it is arguably illogical that promissory estoppel should not be able to do so. It is arguable that there is no necessary inconsistency between consideration being an essential element of a contract and giving a cause of action to a promisee who has acted on a promise which, though unsupported by consideration, was intended to affect legal relations. It is further arguable that the importance of consideration can be respected by drawing a distinction between the remedies for breach of a contract (such remedies being intended to give the claimant the benefit of his bargain) and remedies for breach of a non-contractual promise (such remedies to be limited to compensating the claimant for the detriment he sustains as a result of unconscionable action by the defendant).

Arguments on these lines have been accepted in Australia. In *Waltons Stores (Interstate) v Maher*[4] a builder agreed, subject to contract with a chain of retailers, to construct a store on land owned by him and to let it to the retailers. His solicitors sent signed contractual documents to the retailers for signature and exchange. Acting in the belief that contracts would be exchanged, the builder carried out work to construct the store. Meanwhile, the retailers, without informing the builder, decided to 'go slow', failed to exchange contracts and eventually withdrew from the transaction. The High Court of Australia dismissed an appeal from an order that the retailer pay the builder damages in lieu of an order for specific performance of an agreement for lease. A majority of the High Court held that the basic purpose of promissory estoppel was not to enforce a promise but to make good detriment suffered by the promisee in consequence of an unconscionable departure by the promisee from the terms of the promise. The majority further concluded that there was no justification for confining the scope of promissory estoppel to cases where the promise related to the enforcement of existing rights, and further that it should be regarded as an instance of a more general principle that precludes the unconscionable departure by one party from an assumption on which another had acted to his detriment.

1 [1951] 2 KB 215.
2 [2001] EWCA Civ 274.
3 *Yeoman's Row Management Ltd v Cobbe* [2008] UKHL 55, [2008] 1 WLR 1752 at [14]. In *Thorner v Major* [2009] UKHL 18, [2009] 1 WLR 776 at [67] Lord Walker said he had 'some difficulty' with this observation.
4 (1988) 164 CLR 387.

THE FUTURE

10.11 Sixty years after Denning J's extempore judgment in *High Trees* launched the modern doctrine of promissory estoppel, the doctrine has yet to be reviewed by the House of Lords or the Supreme Court. The need for such a review has long been recognised.[1] When the opportunity arises, it is to be hoped that the Supreme Court will take full advantage of it.

1 See eg *Woodhouse AC Israel Cocoa Ltd SA v Nigerian Produce Marketing Co Ltd* [1972] AC 741 at 758 (Lord Hailsham).

III

CRIMINAL LAW

The cases in the first two chapters in this Part are classics of law students' tutorials – the moral dilemma of the shipwrecked sailors, and the legal as opposed to medical definition of 'insanity'.

One of the most striking aspects of the real-life tale of *R v Dudley and Stephens* is that one of the participating cannibalistic seamen was not so put off by the whole experience that he would not repeat the voyage. As related in the essay, Dudley subsequently emigrated to Australia (where he met a more banal end of dying of the plague). But the issue of necessity is not confined to exotic facts from nineteenth century voyages: more recently the issue arose in the context of the tragic Siamese twin litigation (*Re A (children) (conjoined twins: surgical separation)* [2000] 4 All ER 961) and indeed in the well-known plight of trapped mountaineers recorded in the book and film *Touching the Void* (where one severed the rope connecting him to another in order to save his own life, though in the event both survived) albeit in that instance no litigation ever followed.

M'Naghten's case too has facts that are quite extraordinary. One way or another the wood turner turned would-be assassin was in possession of a large sum of money, quite inconsistent with his legitimate occupation. Was he paid to undertake 'the hit'? If so, whoever made the payment did so before the attempt (or at least made a substantial down payment), and therefore had to have had considerable confidence not only in Mr M'Naghten's contract killer skills but also his propensity to keep to a legally unenforceable bargain.

In the third chapter in this Part, the case of *R v Morgan* also contains an interesting factual angle, in that a man who initially pleaded guilty eventually had his conviction quashed. The tragedy of a fatal train crash always gains the attention of the national press. Usually too the press demand recrimination and reform, although the task of apportioning liability is inevitably a complex and controversial legal task. As *Morgan* demonstrates, the knee-jerk reaction of blaming the 'front line operator' such as the train driver may obscure more serious failings of a corporate nature.

11

LEGAL INSANITY

The Enduring Legacy of Daniel M'Naghten's Case

Jeremy Dein QC and Jo Sidhu

INTRODUCTION

> 'Your noble son is mad: mad call I it; for to define true madness, what is't but to be nothing else but mad? . . . Mad let us grant him, then: and now remains that we find out the cause of this effect; or rather say, the cause of this defect, for this effective defective comes by cause: thus it remains, and the remainder thus.'

11.1 So says Polonius to Hamlet's mother not long before he is himself slain by the Prince. Over the 300 years following the play's publication readers and audiences have been fascinated by the descent into madness apparently suffered by Shakespeare's most famous protagonist. For the modern lawyer, however, the more intriguing question might be: what if this troubled young man had been tried for murder today? Would his disturbed and delusional thoughts have afforded him a defence based on insanity?

If Hamlet's mental state at the time he despatched the 'wretched, rash, intruding fool' might protect him from a conviction for murder in a court today it is largely because of the legacy of one of the most seminal trials in English legal history: *M'Naghten's Case*.[1] Though the case dates back to the mid-nineteenth century its influence on our jurisprudence over the years since is difficult to overstate. It created what became known as the M'Naghten Rules which have remained the legal basis for the defence of insanity in England and in many other jurisdictions around the world.

It has always been a fundamental presumption in English law that every defendant is sane and should be held accountable for his or her actions. Such a presumption is, of course, rebuttable where proof to the contrary is available.[2] Hence, even prior to *M'Naghten's Case*, it had long been established that individuals labouring under a defect of reason at the time of an alleged crime could mount a defence. As stated in *Hadfield*:[3]

> 'It is agreed by all jurists, and is established by the law of this and every other country that it is the reason of man which makes him accountable for his actions; and that the deprivation of reason acquits him of crime.'

The historical significance and unique contribution of the M'Naghten Rules was that they constituted the first formal legal test for the defence of insanity. That they have remained the principal basis for that defence is no doubt testament to their durability, but also to the general unwillingness of the law to adopt a more sophisticated definition of legal insanity that properly reflects the huge advances in society's understanding of mental illness in the course of the twentieth century. On one view, therefore, while the Rules created a clear legal framework to assist the courts where previously there was none, they have over time become so calcified that they now pose more of an inconvenient anachronism for lawyers, judges and psychiatrists alike.

It is no coincidence then that the inflexibility of the Rules has meant that the insanity defence is only ever taken up by a small number of defendants despite many being diagnosed with severe mental health disorders. At the same time, the problematic interpretation of the Rules by our courts has resulted in epileptics, diabetics and sleepwalkers all potentially qualifying as legally insane. Perhaps such difficulties are unsurprising when we remind ourselves that the Rules were conceived at a time when psychiatry was still very much in its infancy as a branch of medicine. But that being the case, the question on the lips of many criminal lawyers today is whether the M'Naghten Rules remain truly 'fit for purpose'.

1 (1843) 10 Clark & Finnelly, 200.

2 *R v Layton* (1849) 4 Cox CC 149.

3 *Hadfield's Case* (1800) 27 State Tr 1281 at 1309–1310 (citation as reported in the Scottish Law Commission Report on Insanity and Diminished Responsibility (July 2004)).

DANIEL M'NAGHTEN'S CASE

11.2 Daniel M'Naghten was a Scottish actor turned carpenter who lived in Glasgow for most of his life. He held radical political views and was a wealthy and well educated man. In 1840 he sold his wood-turning business and, in 1841, appears to have suffered some form of mental breakdown. He told his father and the Glasgow commissioner of police that he was being persecuted by the Tories and was being followed by their spies. It seems that nobody took much notice of these claims initially.

On a January afternoon in 1843, Edward Drummond (the Prime Minister's private secretary) was walking down Whitehall. He was approached from behind by M'Naghten and shot in the back at point-blank range. M'Naghten might have fired another shot from a second pistol he was holding, but was immediately tackled by the police. It was initially thought that Drummond would recover but the treatment he received was unsuccessful and he subsequently died.

M'Naghten appeared at Bow Street magistrates' court the day after the shooting and made the following statement:

> 'The Tories in my native city have compelled me to do this. They follow, persecute me wherever I go, and have entirely destroyed my peace of mind . . . It can be proved by evidence. That is all I have to say.'[1]

His trial was inevitably a high profile affair and took place on 3 and 4 March 1843 at the Central Criminal Court. The reported summary of the proceedings reads as follows:

> 'Evidence having been given of the fact of the shooting of Mr Drummond, and of his death in consequence thereof, witnesses were called on the part of the prisoner, to prove that he was not, at the time of committing the act, in a sound state of mind. The medical evidence was in substance this: That persons of otherwise sound mind, might be affected by morbid delusions: that the prisoner was in that condition: that a person so labouring under such a morbid delusion, might have a moral perception of right and wrong, but that in the case of the prisoner it was a delusion which carried him away beyond the power of his own control, and left him no such perception, and that he was not capable of exercising any control over acts which had connexion with his delusion: that it was of the nature of the disease with which the prisoner was affected, to go on gradually until it had reached a climax, when it burst forth with irresistible intensity: that a man might go on for years quietly, though at the same time under its influence, but would all at once break out into the most extravagant and violent paroxysms.'[2]

The prosecution did not dispute the medical evidence adduced by M'Naghten's defence and the trial judge therefore directed the jury in the following terms:

> 'The question to be determined is, whether at the time the act in question was committed, the prisoner had or had not the use of his understanding, so as to know that he was doing a wrong and wicked act. If the jurors should be of the opinion that the prisoner was not sensible, at the time he committed it, that he was violating the laws of both God and man, then he would be entitled to a verdict in his favour: but if, on the contrary, they were of the opinion that when he committed the act he was in a sound state of mind, then their verdict must be against him.'[3]

The jury, without retiring, returned a verdict of not guilty on the ground of insanity. The Criminal Lunatics Act 1800 (introduced in the wake of James Hadfield's acquittal) required the court to order M'Naghten to be detained indefinitely. Accordingly, he was sent to Bethlam Asylum, and spent the rest of his life in detention.

1 Moran, R, *Knowing Right from Wrong: the insanity defence of Daniel McNaughtan* [sic] (1981) The Free Press, New York (as cited by Tamas Pataki in *Forensic Psychiatry: Intention, Excuse, and Insanity* (2006) Humana Press, at p 77).

2 *M'Naghten's Case* (1843) 10 Clark & Finnelly, 200 at 201–202.

3 At 202.

THE M'NAGHTEN RULES

11.3 The verdict provoked much consternation both in the press and in Parliament. Queen Victoria was moved to write to the Prime Minister to express her concern and the House of Lords was prompted to put five questions regarding the defence of insanity to a panel of judges. The answers to the second and third of those questions formulated the standard legal test for insanity that continues to be applied today.

The relevant part of the Rules requires that the jury be directed that:

> ' . . . every man is to be presumed to be sane, and to possess a sufficient degree of reason to be responsible for his crimes until the contrary be proved to their satisfaction; and that to establish a defence on the ground of insanity, it must be clearly proved that, at the time of the committing of the act, the party accused was

> labouring under such a defect of reason, from disease of the mind, as not to know the nature and quality of the act he was doing; or, if he did know it, that he did not know what he was doing was wrong . . . If the accused was conscious that the act was one which he ought not to do, and if that act was at the same time contrary to the law of the land, he is punishable; and the usual course therefore has been to leave the question to the jury, whether the party accused had a sufficient degree of reason to know that he was doing an act that was wrong . . . '[1]

1 *M'Naghten's Case* (1843) 10 Clark & Finnelly, 200 at 210–211.

HOW THE RULES HAVE BEEN INTERPRETED AND APPLIED

11.4 The foregoing extract from the Rules makes clear that the burden of proof lies on the defendant to establish the defence of insanity; the standard of proof being later clarified as the balance of probabilities.

Where the insanity defence is raised it requires resolution by a jury; a plea of guilty on that basis cannot be accepted by the prosecution even where the evidence of insanity may be overwhelming and uncontested. The remarkable strictness of this procedure may be contrasted with the more pragmatic approach available in cases of murder where the prosecution is able to accept a plea to manslaughter on the ground of diminished responsibility without the need for a trial, subject to appropriate expert evidence being adduced by both parties.

The Rules have therefore spawned a statutory framework that imposes a procedural straitjacket on the parties. As such, the issue of insanity must be decided by way of a special verdict returned by a jury that has heard written or oral evidence from two or more registered medical practitioners at least one of whom is duly approved.[1] But the entire process remains governed by Victorian legislation that demands that such a jury must be sure that the defendant 'did the act or made the omission charged, but was insane as aforesaid at the time when he did or made the same'.[2] Thus, it is only once the jury has determined that the *actus reus* of the offence has been proved that they can acquit the defendant on the ground of insanity by way of a special verdict.

Where the primary facts are not in dispute and there is agreement between the parties as to the mental condition of the defendant at the relevant time, quite how this mandatory and antiquated procedure serves the interests of modern justice is more than merely an academic question. The application of the Rules by this method is not simply time consuming and costly, but is hardly calculated to protect the mental well being of a defendant for whom the trial process is likely to pose much more of a psychological ordeal than is borne by someone unburdened by his difficulties.

While the Rules continue to be implemented by a rather industrial and inflexible mechanism it is not because the latter is their natural corollary. There is nothing inherent in the original answers given by the panel of judges that demands the continued adoption of the special verdict system. In the contemporary era where Parliament has devised relatively sophisticated procedures and rules for dealing with many aspects of criminal litigation, it appears that the retention of the trial process for every case where the insanity defence is raised cannot easily be explained by legislative inertia or oversight. On any view, a re-consideration by Parliament of the utility and desirability of that system is seriously overdue.

But what of the Rules themselves? Have they really provided a safe and reliable guide to assessing the viability of the insanity defence? The following discussion suggests that the interpretation of the Rules by our courts thus far may have been unduly restrictive in dealing with definitions of the terms 'wrong' and 'defect of reason', but quite generous in so far as what may constitute a 'disease of the mind'.

1 Criminal Procedure (Insanity and Unfitness to Plead) Act 1991, s 1(1).
2 Trial of Lunatics Act 1883, s 2(1).

WHEN DOES WRONG MEAN 'WRONG'?

11.5 When referring to a 'wrong' act what may have seemed obvious to the Victorians is arguably anything but in the context of the moral, ethical and religious complexities of the world in the new millennium. Hence, in considering the continuing relevance and applicability of the Rules to an assessment of insanity today, a useful starting point is how restrictively to define the word 'wrong'. On this question there appears to be a broad consensus in both the English authorities and in legal commentaries that knowledge of illegality is the only relevant consideration for a court; that is to say, that only where a defendant does not recognise that his act is unlawful can he avail himself of the defence of insanity.

A stark example of the narrowness of this formulation arose in the case of *R v Windle*.[1] The defendant had given his wife a lethal dose of aspirin before telephoning the police and saying 'I suppose I'll hang for this'. Although Windle was clearly suffering from a mental illness, he was aware that his act was legally wrong, and accordingly his insanity defence failed with the result that his expectation came true. The Court of Criminal Appeal placed a strict construction on what was meant by the word 'wrong' in the M'Naghten Rules. The Lord Chief Justice stated:

> 'In the opinion of the court, there is no doubt that the word 'wrong' in the M'Naghten Rules means contrary to law and does not have some vague meaning which may vary according to the opinion of different persons whether a particular act might or might not be justified.'[2]

The more recent case of *R v Johnson*[3] re-stated the restrictive view. The court dismissed the appeal which had been brought on the basis that, even though the appellant understood that his actions were unlawful, in consequence of his paranoid schizophrenia he had felt morally justified in committing the violence for which he was later prosecuted. The statement of the law in *Windle* as quoted above was approved as 'unequivocal'.

For a less dogmatic interpretation of the M'Naghten Rules we must look to the High Court of Australia which took issue with the view in *Windle*. In the case of *Stapleton v R*[4] the High Court identified several of the problems and contradictions involved in applying the Rules and expressed the view that the mere fact that a defendant acknowledged his conduct to be contrary to the law was inconclusive; if he nonetheless believed that his act would be approved by reasonable men then he should be acquitted.

By this reasoning, had the Australian perspective on the M'Naghten Rules been adopted in the trial of Peter Sutcliffe he may well have been found not guilty of the murders of his victims given his moral claim to have received messages from God to kill prostitutes. But, on the basis of English law, only if he had been labouring under the illusion that God had repealed the criminal law so as to allow him to carry out the killings would the option of raising insanity as a defence have been open to him.[5]

In applying the Rules for the purpose of deciding whether the '*accused had a sufficient degree of reason to know that he was doing an act that was wrong*' it is evident that the English courts have sought assiduously to adhere to a literal interpretation. But, even in *Johnson*[6] the court recognised that the inelasticity of the Rules in accommodating a more sophisticated understanding of irrational behaviour might eventually limit their shelf life and that, as such, a further review was to be welcomed.

1 (1952) 36 Cr App Rep 85.
2 *R v Windle* (1952) 36 Cr App Rep 85 at p 90.
3 [2007] EWCA Crim 1978, [2008] Crim LR 132, CA.
4 (1952) 86 CLR 358, Aus HC.
5 See Professor Alan Norrie's analysis, *Crime, Reason and History*, pp 175 and 181–182 (2nd edn, 2001) Butterworths.
6 *R v Johnson* [2007] EWCA Crim 1978, [2008] Crim LR 132, CA at para 24.

DEFECT OF REASON

11.6 A 'defect of reason' applies to those whose ability to reason is compromised or defective; it does not include emotional illnesses such as depression which might also play a crucial and causative part in the commission of an offence. A defect of reason therefore requires a cognitive fault such that there is a failure in a defendant's capacity to reason. Mere forgetfulness would not suffice.[1]

The Rules prescribe a nominal legal distinction between different types of delusion. But in practise they have operated on the basis of a highly restrictive concept of defect of reason which, in turn, has produced arbitrary outcomes in case law. As Professor Norrie puts it:

> 'The judges could not see that a 'partial delusion' obliquely, or not at all, related to the crime could inform its commission just as much as a more total delusion about the nature and quality of the act.'[2]

1 See *R v Clarke* (1972) 56 Cr App Rep 225.
2 Professor Alan Norrie, *Crime, Reason and History*, p 181 (2nd edn, 2001) Butterworths.

DISEASE OF THE MIND

11.7 Whilst the legal concept of what constitutes a cognitive defect is relatively narrow, the courts have developed an extremely broad definition of what constitutes a disease of the mind. In *Bratty v A-G for Northern Ireland*[1] it was held that 'any mental disorder which has manifested itself in violence and is prone to recur is a disease of the mind'.[2] In *R v Burgess*[3] the defendant attacked a friend whilst sleepwalking. Since the defendant's sleepwalking was prompted by internal causes, this condition was also categorised as a disease of the mind.

In *R v Sullivan*[4] the defendant suffered a minor epileptic fit during which he injured a man. The House of Lords held that epilepsy could constitute a disease of the mind because the effect of the epilepsy was to impair the defendant's ability to reason. It mattered not that the impairment was transient, as long as it existed at the time of the commission of the act.

In *R v Hennessy*[5] the internal/external test was applied to a defendant charged with driving while disqualified. The defendant was a diabetic who had failed to take any insulin and was suffering from low blood sugar levels. The Court of Appeal held that the defendant's loss of awareness had not resulted from the operation of external factors upon his body, such as the injection of insulin, but instead had resulted from diabetes, an inherent physical defect. It was therefore correct for the trial judge to direct the jury only as to the defence of insanity rather than to automatism.

The arbitrariness of the internal/external distinction means that an unconscious state in an epileptic caused by an overdose of insulin would not be insane under the *Sullivan* test (the overdose being caused by an external element), whilst an unconscious state arising from a natural build up of blood sugar is classified as insane.[6] This distinction highlights the arguably illogical outcome of the way in which the courts have interpreted the M'Naghten Rules.

However, there is more to the law's failure to embrace a rational grounding in this vexed area than simple benign neglect on the part of the legislature and judiciary. The absence of a satisfactory formulation has operated to introduce an element of social protection and policy into the assessment of insanity.

As Professor Ashworth puts it:

> '. . . the policy of social protection has gained the upper hand . . . the judiciary has been prepared to overlook the gross unfairness of labelling these people as insane in order to ensure that the court has the power to take measures of social defence against them.'[7]

1 (1962) 46 Cr App Rep 1.
2 As per Lord Denning at 20.
3 (1991) 93 Cr App R 41.
4 (1983) 77 Cr App R 176.
5 (1989) 89 Cr App R 10.
6 See Professor Alan Norrie, *Crime, Reason and History* (2nd edn, 2001) Butterworths, at p 180.
7 Professor Andrew Ashworth, *Principles of Criminal Law* (5th edn, 2006) OUP at p 143.

PSYCHIATRY AND THE LAW – A DIFFICULT MARRIAGE

11.8 The introduction of the M'Naghten Rules coincided with the nascent emergence of psychiatry in England. By the end of the nineteenth century the study of mental illness had made considerable advances in both understanding and treating such conditions. By contrast, the law on insanity had remained comparatively static. Tensions between the disciplines were as unavoidable as they were inevitable as psychiatry began to uncover forms of insanity where no outward symptoms of illness were visible while the courts found themselves locked into a legal definition of insanity that appeared devoid of flexibility.

Psychiatrists understood that an individual might retain rational and cognitive functions but, as a result of an underlying mental illness, be unable to avoid committing a criminal act. It was the subsisting illness that rendered the person insane. But, as we have seen, the Rules simply did not allow for any such volitional disorder. In Professor Norrie's analysis:

> 'For the lawyers, a society of rational individuals with a propensity for evil was held in check by a firm penal code which punished the wrongdoer for purposes of deterrence and justice . . . for the psychiatric professional on the other hand, as it developed its own viewpoint on insane criminality, the conception of mental disease and its effects on conduct went much further than the law allowed.'[1]

Unsurprisingly, the Rules have in the intervening years attracted frequent criticism; never more so than while the death penalty was in operation. In 1953 The Royal Commission on Capital Punishment went so far as to report that 'The M'Naghten test is based on an entirely obsolete and misleading conception of the nature of insanity'.

1 Professor Alan Norrie, *Crime, Reason and History* (2nd edn, 2001) Butterworths, at p 178.

DEEMED INSANE – WHAT'S IN A LABEL?

11.9 The failure to update and modernise the Rules has also meant the retention of the nomenclature contained within them, most notably the use of the word 'insane' itself with all its associated pejorative connotations. In consequence, a defendant assessed under the relevant criteria could end up labelled as 'insane' when, in reality, his condition bore no resemblance to the common (and often inaccurate) understanding of that term. Hence, for epileptics, somnambulists and diabetics success under the Rules can result in lifelong stigmatisation.

In its report on the incidence of mental illness amongst the convicted the Butler Committee concluded that 'the continued use of the words "insanity" and "insane" in the criminal law long after their disappearance from psychiatry and mental health law has been a substantial source of difficulty, and we attach importance to the discontinuance of the use of these words in the criminal law'.[1]

Other jurisdictions have long since introduced terminology that attaches more neutral and medically accurate descriptions to defendants who labour under a mental disability. The outmoded language of the Rules as still deployed in English courts does little to justify their retention.

1 The Butler Committee on Mentally Abnormal Offenders (1975), para 18.18.

NEED FOR REFORM

11.10 It took more than a century before the corset could be loosened and it came with the passing of section 2(1) of the Homicide Act 1957, which offered some relief through partial reform. The Act established the mitigatory defence of diminished responsibility for murder. Under section 2(1) the defendant must prove that he was suffering from an 'abnormality of mind' which 'substantially impaired his mental responsibility for the killing'. 'Abnormality of mind' is construed much more broadly than 'defect of reason' under the Rules[1] and covers defendants who suffered from paranoid psychosis.[2]

For the vast majority of mentally ill defendants charged with murder, the inherent flexibility of the diminished responsibility formulation has unsurprisingly made it a much more popular defence than insanity. But, of course, for the greatest number of offences typically heard in our criminal courts the safety valve afforded by diminished responsibility is of no assistance at all to defendants. Indeed, between 1991 and 2001 there were, on average, just 11.6 findings a year of not guilty by reason of insanity in England.[3]

Such statistics should be read in the context of research that reveals that one in five inmates in the prison system suffer from four of the five major mental health disorders.[4] Plainly, not all of those mentally disordered prisoners would have been afforded the insanity defence even under a revised formula, but these statistics do suggest that a significant number of mentally ill individuals could benefit from a law offering a broader, more scientific conception of mental illness. Hence, the growing demand for a radical revision of the Rules to acknowledge types of cognitive impairment which cohere with established psychiatric diagnoses of mental illness.

1 See *R v Byrne* (1960) 44 Cr App R 246.

2 See *R v Sanderson* (1994) 98 Cr App R 325.

3 Mackay, RD, Mitchell, BJ, Howe, Leonie: 'Yet more facts about the insanity defence' (Crim LR 399).

4 Prison Reform Trust – 'Trouble Inside: Mental Health Care in Prison' (2005).

CONCLUSION

11.11 There can be no doubt that the case of Daniel M'Naghten instigated a profound and paradigmatic shift in the way our courts dealt with mentally ill defendants. The Rules created in the wake of his acquittal reflected a more structured and serious approach to resolving a social phenomenon that was becoming increasingly acute at the time of their inception. But while the panel of judges who formulated the Rules undoubtedly did their best to devise a set of criteria that could provide a coherent and consistent method to test the insanity defence, the exact prescriptions could only be as good as their understanding of the illness they sought to define.

By the mid-nineteenth century, psychiatry was no more than a fledgling science and still a long way from developing the many and varied taxonomies which are recorded in the vast canon of works it can boast of today. No wonder then that within a hundred years of its introduction their Lordships' formula for defining legal insanity was begging more questions than it could sensibly answer. The world had moved on and the Rules could be stretched only so far. Yet, for some reason, they continued to defy that broad principle that good laws survive the test of time if, and only if, they can demonstrate their continuing relevance in new and challenging conditions.

Opinion will differ on whether the apparent resilience of the Rules reflects their intrinsic virtue as a legal compass or, less impressively, an institutional diffidence on the part of successive Parliaments and our appellate courts to modify or overhaul them. For our part, it has become manifestly clear that with each new advance in our understanding of mental illness the call to instigate a wholesale review of the M'Naghten Rules is increasingly urgent. The disturbingly high proportion of prisoners afflicted with severe mental illness only reinforces the need for expedition. But to be effective, any such review would undoubtedly benefit from contributions from lawyers, judges and psychiatrists alike; a multilateral approach that was singularly absent when the Rules were originally debated. We would be wise too to learn from the experiences of similar jurisdictions elsewhere that have successfully incorporated pragmatic proposals for reform whilst maintaining a proper scope for criminal responsibility.

12

DEATH ON THE HIGH SEAS: THE CABIN BOY, THE CANNIBALS AND THE CRIMINAL LAW

R v Dudley and Stephens

David Perry QC

12.1 On 6 September 1884, three English sailors, Tom Dudley, Edwin Stephens and Edward Brooks, arrived in Falmouth abroad the German sailing barque *Moctezuma*. The three men had been rescued 38 days earlier, adrift in an open boat, in the South Atlantic. On their arrival in Falmouth they gave an account of shipwreck, deprivation, the most fearful suffering and candidly admitted that they had survived only by resort to cannibalism.

This frankness was to lead to one of the most well-known decisions in the common law world and which to this day stands as authority for the proposition that necessity is not a defence to murder.[1]

The first paragraph of the headnote is one of the most startling in the Law Reports:

> 'A man who, in order to escape death from hunger, kills another for the purpose of eating his flesh, is guilty of murder; although at the time of the act he is in such circumstances that he believes and has reasonable grounds for believing that it affords the only chance of preserving life.'

In his brilliant and fascinating book, *'Cannibalism and the Common Law'*, Professor AW Brian Simpson[2] provides the rich detail surrounding the legal proceedings and anyone interested in this strange case should read his account.

1 *R v Dudley and Stephens* (1884–85) 14 QBD 273.

2 (1984) Chicago University Press.

12.2 The story behind the case, reduced to its essentials, is as follows. On 5 May 1884, the yacht *Mignonette* left Tollesbury in Essex bound for Sydney, where she was to be delivered to her new owner, an Australian lawyer and politician. There were four crew members, Captain Tom Dudley, aged 31, Mate Edwin Stephens, aged 37, Able Seaman Edwards Brookes, aged 36, and

12.2 *Death on the High Seas*

Ordinary Seaman Richard Parker, aged 17.

Two months after leaving port, following a terrible storm on 5 July 1884, the yacht was lost and the four crew members found themselves in an open boat with only two one-pound tins of turnips and no water. They were many days from land and, as a result of the route chosen by Dudley, off the regular sea lanes used by sailing vessels. On 7 July the men caught a turtle which, by careful rationing, lasted over 7 days. By 20 July, the four men were in a pitiful condition and Richard Parker, the weakest of the four, drank a considerable quantity of seawater and became violently ill. It appeared to the other three that he would soon die and they would soon follow. On either 24 or 25 July, Richard Parker was killed. The act itself was carried out by Dudley, using a small penknife. On 29 July, as the three survivors were having 'breakfast', they saw the sails of the *Moctezuma* and were later rescued, 990 miles east of Rio de Janeiro. The three men were in a most terrible condition and Dudley's was made worse the following day as a chamber pot on which he was sitting shattered causing a wound to his buttocks.

On their return to England the men provoked a good deal of sympathy among the seafaring community of Falmouth (and elsewhere) but the authorities saw an opportunity to strike a blow for Victorian morality. At this point it is relevant to note that survival cannibalism was, and had long been, regarded as a custom of the sea. (This explains why Tom Dudley had so frankly admitted that he had killed Richard Parker on the 20th day of their ordeal and that his flesh and blood had sustained the men until their rescue.) So far as the authorities were concerned, the incident provided a perfect opportunity for the custom of the sea to be declared bad as a matter of law and for individual survival to take second place in the law's priorities to the sanctity of life.

12.3 Before 1884, the existence and scope of the doctrine of necessity had divided Victorian legal opinion. In 1839, the Commissioners on Criminal Law suggested that the principle of necessity might serve to justify or excuse the act of homicide. By 1846, Her Majesty's Commissioners for Revising and Consolidating the Criminal Law decided on policy grounds not to support a general defence of necessity. Having noted that the justification or not of a homicide of an unoffending party, committed in order to save the life of the accused, had been much discussed by ancient and modern jurists, they preferred the 'less inconvenient' course of leaving those who had acted under circumstances of sudden and extreme peril 'to the mercy of the Crown'. The Criminal Code Bill Commissioners (who reported in 1879) were 'unprepared to suggest that necessity should in no case be a defence' but left the question to be determined by 'applying the principles of law to the circumstances of the particular case'. The judges now had the 'particular case'.

Shortly after their arrival at Falmouth, the three men were (to their great surprise) arrested on suspicion of murder and, on 11 September 1884, they appeared before the local justices, when, with the active connivance of the prosecution, they were admitted to bail. At this stage the prosecution was entrusted to junior Treasury Counsel (William Danckwerts) who arranged for Brooks (considered to be the least culpable of the three) to be discharged and turned into a witness for the prosecution. Later in September, Dudley and Stephens were committed to stand trial at the next assizes before judge and jury.

12.4 The trial itself (a ticket-only affair) began on 3 November 1884 at Exeter

Castle (which continued to function as a criminal court until 2004). Leading Counsel for the prosecution was Arthur Charles QC leading Charles Matthews. The defence were represented by Arthur Collins QC (leader of the Western Circuit and later Chief Justice of Madras). As was often the case in the days before legal aid, the legal fees were paid by a defence fund, to which sympathetic members of the public contributed.

The trial judge was Baron Huddleston (1815–1890), the son of a Captain in the Merchant Service and married to the daughter of a Duke, described by Professor Simpson as 'a colourful if unattractive individual' and a 'snob'. Huddleston was Judge Advocate of the fleet from 1865 to 1875 when he was appointed a judge of the Court of Common Pleas (a court with jurisdiction over civil cases but inferior to the Court of King's Bench). Later that year he was transferred to the Court of Exchequer (a court with jurisdiction over all actions except real actions) and given the customary title of Baron. On the consolidation of the Exchequer with the Queen's Bench Division, Huddleston became a judge of that court, although he was fond of calling himself 'the last of the Barons'. According to the Dictionary of National Biography, 'It was thought by his contemporaries that he was greater as an advocate than as a judge'. In court, he was in the habit of wearing gloves, suiting their colour to the nature of the case in hand (lavender for breach of promise of marriage and black for murder).

12.5 There seems little doubt that Huddleston was sent to Exeter with the express purpose of ensuring that Dudley and Stephens were convicted of murder. However, as Professor Simpson explains, not everything went according to plan.

First, Huddleston had to neutralise or overcome the strong local sympathy for the accused. In order to avoid an acquittal, he suggested to the jury that they should find the facts of the case in the form of a 'special verdict'. Just to explain. In English criminal practice, the possible verdicts are guilty and not guilty. These are known as general verdicts, either for or against the accused and these general verdicts tell us nothing about the facts which sway the jury either one way or the other. By way of contrast, a special verdict involves the jury finding certain facts proved either as part of their general verdict or leaving to the court the application of the law to the facts as found. Huddleston produced a special verdict for the jury (it had obviously been prepared beforehand, thus suggesting some strategic planning on the judge's part) which included the following:

> 'That on the eighteenth day (after the shipwreck) when they had been seven days without food and five without water, the prisoners spoke to Brooks as to what should be done if no succour came, and suggested that some one should be sacrificed to save the rest, but Brooks dissented, and the boy, to whom they were understood to refer was not consulted. That on 24 July, the day before the act now in question, the prisoner Dudley proposed to Stephens and Brooks that lots should be cast who should be put to death to save the rest, but Brooks refused to consent, and it was not put to the boy, and in point of fact there was no drawing of lots. That on that day the prisoners spoke of their having families, and suggested that it would better to kill the boy that their lives should be saved, and Dudley proposed that if there was no vessel in sight by the morrow morning the boy should be killed. That next day, 25 July, no vessel appearing, Dudley told Brooks that he better go and have a sleep and made signs to Stephens and Brooks that the boy had better be killed. The prisoner Stephens agreed to the act, but Brooks dissented from it.

> That the boy was then lying at the bottom of the boat quite helpless, and extremely weakened by famine and by drinking sea water, and unable to make any resistance nor did he assent to being killed. The prisoner Dudley offered a prayer asking for forgiveness for them all if either of them should be tempted to commit a rash act, and that their souls might be saved. That Dudley, with the assent of Stephens, went to the boy and telling that his time was come, put a knife into his throat and killed him then and there; that the three men fed upon the body and blood of the boy for four days; that on the fourth day after the act had been committed the boat was picked up by a passing vessel, and the prisoners rescued, still alive, but in the lowest state of prostration . . . That if the men had not fed upon the body of the boy they would probably not have survived to be so picked up and rescued but would within the four days have died of famine. That the boy, being in a much weaker condition, was likely to have died before then. That at the time of the act in question there was no sail in sight nor any reasonable prospect of relief. That under the circumstances there appeared to the prisoners every probability that unless they then fed or very soon fed upon the boy or one of themselves they would die of starvation. That there was no appreciable chance of saving life except by killing one for the others to eat. That assuming any necessity for killing anybody, there was no greater necessity for killing the boy than any of the other three men.'

The official Law Report then records that 'whether upon the whole matter . . . the killing . . . be felony and murder the jurors are ignorant and pray the advice of the Court thereupon . . . '.

12.6 Thus Baron Huddleston had obtained what he had set out to achieve: a set of facts upon which the judges sitting in London could provide an authoritative ruling on the law. The case was then adjourned until 4 December when it was argued before five judges, sitting in the Royal Courts of Justice in the Strand. These five judges included Baron Huddleston. The other four judges were Lord Coleridge CJ, Grove and Denman JJ and Pollock B. At the time of the hearing there was no Court of Appeal (the Court of Criminal Appeal was first established in 1907), but there was a procedure which allowed a judge to reserve a point of law for consideration by the Court of Crown Cases Reserved (established in 1848). Curiously, the procedure adopted by Baron Huddleston was not to reserve a point of law but to adjourn the assize. This led to some confusion and required an explanatory note in the law reports ((1884–85) 14 QBD at p 560): 'the argument was heard by judges, not as commissioners of assize but as judges of the Queen's Bench Division of the High Court of Justice'. On what basis the court was exercising its jurisdiction remains unclear. It was this procedural tangle which provides another oddity: *Dudley and Stephens* is the only case in which a sentence of death has been passed in the Royal Courts of Justice. This arose because the jury were never asked to give a verdict, and it was left to the High court to pronounce the verdict and proceed to sentence.

At the hearing, the court was required to reconcile the instinct for self-preservation in appalling circumstances (expressed through survival cannibalism, long established as a custom of the sea) with the sanctity for human life. The outcome was a foregone conclusion. This was the case the judges had been waiting for. The judgment of the court was delivered on 9 December 1884 by Lord Coleridge CJ (1820–1894) (remembered more for his eloquence as a trial lawyer than for his abilities as a judge). His summary of the facts made his own feelings clear:

> '. . . the prisoners put to death a weak and unoffending boy upon the chance of preserving their own lives by feeding upon his flesh and blood after he was killed, and with the certainty of depriving him of any possible chance of survival.'

As to the question whether the killing was or was not murder: 'The conclusion that it could be anything else was, to the minds of us all, both new and strange'. (The apparent novelty of the point overlooks the work of successive Commissions into the criminal law.) The court rejected any suggestion that:

> '. . . in order to save your own life you may lawfully take away the life of another, when that other is neither attempting nor threatening yours, nor is guilty of any illegal act whatever towards you or any one else.'

12.7 As a piece of legal reasoning, the court's judgment is not regarded as a classic. Treatment of the arguments advanced on behalf of the defendants contains no great depth of analysis. The court found no support for a defence of necessity in the authoritative texts on the criminal law: Bracton, Hale, Foster and East. The case of a single judge of the island of St Kitts, which provided some support to the defence, was described as 'unsatisfactory as possible' (on the basis that the island was possessed partly by France at the time of the decision (1641)). An American case (*United States v Holmes*)[1] is not even referred to by name in the report. It was said to be an authority unsatisfactory to a court in this country (it had decided that sailors had no right to throw passengers overboard to save themselves, but on the somewhat strange ground that the proper mode of determining who was to be scarified was to vote upon the subject by ballot). Lord Bacon's assertion[2] that a drowning man commits no offence if, out of necessity, he fights for a plank to save his own life and by doing so casts another to certain death, was said to be derived from the canonists (the medieval scholars who devoted their attention to the study of the canon law of the Roman Church) and was 'not law at the present day'. In Lord Coleridge's view:

> 'To preserve one's own life is generally speaking a duty, but it may be the plainest and the highest duty to sacrifice it . . . The duty, in the case of shipwreck, of a captain to his crew, of the crew to the passengers, of soldiers to children, as in the noble case of the Birkenhead; these duties impose on men the moral necessity, not of the preservation but of the sacrifice of their lives for others, from which in no country, least of all it is to be hoped, in England, will men ever shrink, as indeed they have not shrunk.'

Contemporary observers would have understood the reference to *HMS Birkenhead*, one of the first iron-hulled ships built for the Royal Navy, which sank on the outskirts of Cape Town in 1852. There were not enough lifeboats for all the passengers and soldiers and sailors stood to attention while the ship went down as women and children made their way to safety. This tragedy led to what became known as the 'Birkenhead Drill' ('women and children first') and was the subject of Rudyard Kipling's poem *'Soldier an' Sailor Too'*.

1 (1842) 26 Fed Cas 360.
2 Francis Bacon, *Elements of the Common Lawes of England* (1630).

12.8 Lord Coleridge's judgment exemplifies an attitude of high Victorian morality recognising the dangers of yielding to temptation. Underlying it is a fear that any defence of necessity 'once admitted might be made the legal cloak for unbridled passion and atrocious crime'. (It was this fear which led Hale to conclude that stealing to avoid starvation should be punished by death. Blackstone supported Hale on this point but, with a characteristic belief in the superiority of his nation, supposed that in England it was impossible that the most needy stranger should ever be reduced to the necessity of theft.) Acknowledging the awful suffering undergone by the defendants, Lord Coleridge noted: 'We are often compelled to set up standards we cannot reach ourselves, and to lay down rules which we could not ourselves satisfy'.

Despite this, the court left it to the Sovereign to exercise the prerogative of mercy and the sentence of death was later commuted to six months' imprisonment. As many commentators have noted there is some illogicality in the court's approach. While speaking of the need for heroic self-sacrifice to secure the greater good, it hints at the desirability of mercy. According to Professor Simpson this inconsistency meant that the impact of the case in seafaring communities was to confirm that the custom of the sea was acceptable and survival cannibalism continued to be practised, albeit survivors became more guarded in explaining how their shipmates had come to meet their end. The key to this apparent inconsistency is Lord Coleridge's fear that the legal definition of the crime of murder would be changed by entertaining an excuse of necessity and that an acquittal would be perceived by the public as a vindication of the defendant's act. Better for the judges to stand firm and for the defendants to be excused indirectly.

12.9 Despite its shortcomings and inconsistencies (the failure to distinguish between justification and excuse, the expectation of super human standards, the superficial dismissal of authority), the decision in *Dudley and Stephens* continues to assert a powerful influence on the criminal law. In *R v Howe*,[1] Lord Hailsham of Marylebone LC approved of the decision and expressed profound dissent with his predecessor (Lord Bacon). He noted that where the choice is between the threat of death and deliberately taking an innocent life:

> 'a reasonable man might reflect that one innocent human life is as least as valuable as his own or that of his loved one. In such a case a man cannot claim he is choosing the lesser of two evils. Instead he is embracing the cognate but morally disreputable principle that the end justifies the means.'

In *Re A (Children) (Conjoined Twins: Surgical Separation)*[2] the Court of Appeal held that it was lawful to carry out separation surgery on conjoined twins even though the inevitable effect of the operation was that one of the twins would die. According to Ward LJ:

> 'the policy of the law is to prevent A being a judge in his own cause of the value of his life over B's life or his loved one C's life and then being executioner as well.'

In the unique circumstances of the case it was impossible to preserve the life of one twin without bringing about the death of the other, and the very existence of the other would have brought about the death of the one. *Dudley and Stephens* was distinguished. But these cases highlight the problem confronting the law. Few of us face the choices confronting shipwrecked sailors (with families to support) who face certain death. Nor does any one theory of justice (utilitarianism, liberalism, human rights) provide a clear and satisfactory answer to the dilemma. This is demonstrated by the well-known runaway train hypothetical (a variation on the facts of *Dudley and Stephens*). The driver of a runaway train sees a number of workers on the line. He cannot stop. There is a side-track with only one worker on it. The train driver can turn the train into the side-track and kill one person instead of five. What should he do? To many, sacrificing one life to save several seems the right thing to do. But what if the one person is a woman or a pregnant woman or a child? Suppose on the side-track are two children or three, still fewer in number than the workers. The moral issues are acute. The problem of choosing who had to die was the problem which Lord Coleridge found unanswerable. Some theorists suggest that the situation is different if the victim is already designated for death. This point was made by Professor John Smith in his Hamlyn Lectures ('Justification and Excuse in Criminal Law' (1989)). He illustrated his point by reference to evidence which emerged at the coroner's inquest into the loss of a ferry, the *Herald of Free Enterprise*, at Zeebrugge in 1987. An army corporal stated that he and dozens of others were prevented from reaching safety by a man on a rope ladder who was petrified by fear. The corporal gave instructions that the man should be pushed off the ladder, and he was never seen again. According to Professor Smith, this situation was distinguishable from *Dudley and Stephens*, because the man was preventing others from going where they had a right to go.

As Professor Simpson notes, the judgment in *Dudley and Stephens* (a textbook example of the killing of an innocent person that might have been excused on the grounds of necessity) is used to introduce students 'both to the peculiarities of legal reasoning and to the practical and ethical problems with which the law is ultimately concerned'. There is no leading case which is more widely known or discussed or which produces such differing views on the correctness of the conclusion reached by the court. According to Professor Alan Norrie[3] (*Crime, Reason and History* (2001)) the decision is a 'classic illustration of the interface between legal discourse and social reality', a political clash between the well-heeled judiciary able to cultivate and proselytise refined manners and morals and sea-faring folk: 'It was because men like Dudley and Stephens were to sea at great risk to themselves that men like Lord Coleridge could sit on the judgment on them when things went wrong'.

And what of the protagonists? Huddleston's health deteriorated and during the last ten years of his life he suffered a chronic and painful disease. He died at his home in South Kensington in 1890. Lord Coleridge died at his Paddington home in June 1894. Stephens died a poor man, aged 66, in 1914. Dudley emigrated to Australia with his wife, in 1885 and in 1900 fell victim to an outbreak of bubonic plague, which struck Sydney in that year. He was aged 46.

1 [1987] 1 AC 417.

2 [2001] 2 WLR 480.

3 Norrie A, *Crime, Reason and History: A Critical Introduction to Criminal Law (Law in Context)* (2nd edn, 2001) Cambridge University Press.

13

RED LIGHT SPELLS DANGER

R v Morgan

Gerard Forlin QC

INTRODUCTION

13.1 In 1989, Robert Morgan, an experienced train driver of over 23 years' service with an unblemished driving record, drove his passenger train through a red light just north of Purley Railway Station. The train derailed after colliding with the rear of another train. Five people died and 87 passengers and bystanders were injured.

Mr Morgan was charged with two counts of manslaughter. On 2 September 1990, he pleaded guilty to both counts. He was sentenced to 18 months' imprisonment. Six months was to be served, with the balance of a year to be suspended.

THE APPEAL

13.2 Mr Morgan appealed against that sentence and on 30 October 1990, the Court of Appeal reduced the sentence from six months to one of four months' imprisonment.

The Lord Chief Justice Lord Lane, sitting with Roch and Auld JJ, found that there were a series of special considerations in the case: namely, there was no alcohol involved, Mr Morgan had himself been injured in the crash, he had no recollection of the accident, and his good record and prompt admission of responsibility.

The sentencing editor of the Crown Court Review [1991] Crim LR 214 stated from the sentencing remarks of the Court of Appeal that:

> 'the tasks of a train driver might be monotonous and repetitive, but the risk of death from a disregard of a signalling system and safety devices was so high that the reckless disregard to which the appellant had pleaded guilty did appear to deserve punishment'.

TO 'RECONCILE THE IRRECONCILABLE'

13.3 The sentence in a case such as this, said the Court of Appeal, was to:

> 'reconcile the irreconcilable. On the one hand, criminal behaviour must be punished and the offender should expiate what he had done: public disapproval must be marked to prevent people taking the law into their own hands and wreaking their own vengeance. On the other hand, the view of many would be that to send such a person as the appellant to prison did no good to him and no good to society. He was unlikely to drive a train again: the crime was arguably a crime of omission rather than commission and the results would be on the appellant's conscience for the rest of his life. The Court had come to a conclusion that a short immediate sentence would more properly meet the situation than a wholly or partially suspended sentence'.

The Court of Appeal then reduced the sentence to an immediate term of four months' imprisonment, thus allowing Mr Morgan to be released immediately as he had already served time in prison.

THE APPEAL AGAINST THE CONVICTION

13.4 In 2007, some 17 years later, a fresh team (including the author), mostly acting pro-bono, appealed against the actual conviction. This was an uphill task as Mr Morgan had originally pleaded guilty. At the hearing for leave to appeal out of time in May 2007, the Court of Appeal decided on the basis of the law that leave to appeal should be granted, and that fresh evidence be allowed to be admitted.

In December 2007, the full Court of Appeal, including Latham LJ and Cooke and Cranston JJ, quashed the original convictions and the status of someone of previous good character was restored to Mr Morgan.[1]

Tragically, a very sad postscript to this is that a few months after this event, Mr Morgan died. At least his good name had been restored whilst he had been alive.

In the judgment in December 2007, Latham LJ in the Court of Appeal stated the following:

> 'The basis upon which the application was made in the first instance was the fact that there was, it was said, new evidence which shed light on the way in which the accident occurred and which could have affected, had that material been known, the plea that was tendered, and any possible verdict that might have resulted from the plea of not guilty. Further it is submitted that the basis upon which the appellant was advised to plead guilty was an understanding of the law at the time, which had now been overtaken by events. As a result, it is said that the true issue which was raised by these counts of manslaughter was ever properly considered, and certainly never resolved by the jury. The prosecution accept the validity of those submissions . . . and do not oppose the appeal against conviction as a result . . . .'

The court went on to say:

> ' . . . to put the story in some more detailed perspective . . . the signal in question the red signal, was signal number 168.

> The way in which signals operate means that if a red signal is showing, the signal before it will be a single yellow and the signal before that will be a double yellow. It follows that as the appellant approached Purley he would have passed, and this is accepted, a double yellow signal at 182, and then a single yellow signal at 178. At each of those signals there would have been an audible indication in the cab to the appellant of that fact that these were yellow signals and not green signals. He would have had to operate a cancelling mechanism in order to prevent the brakes of the train from automatically operating.
>
> The consequence it follows was that the appellant was clearly warned – and again this is accepted – of the fact that the relevant signal, 163, was showing red . . .
>
> After the accident, the appellant, who had been significantly injured, was unable to explain why he had gone through the red signal. It was in those circumstances that when it came to trial he pleaded guilty to the two counts of manslaughter.'

They continued in the judgment:

> ' . . . The history of signal 168 showed that there had been four previous SPADs[2] in the five years immediately preceding the accident. In other words, this was the fifth SPAD in five years. That of itself would have been a significant factor in any jury's evaluation of the extent to which the appellant's fault could be said to amount not merely to negligence – that is, a breach of duty, but the sort of breach of duty which justifies the imposition of criminal sanctions.
>
> After this accident it became clear there was a great concern about the fact that there have been a number of SPADs at this signal, a safety measure was put in place, called a signal regulator which was intended to give an additional warning of the fact that signal 168 was at red.
>
> Despite that, a year after the appellant's conviction there was another SPAD at this signal.
>
> This caused Mr Bell, who was by now the engineer responsible for signalling in the area, to consider rather more significant measures.
>
> That was patently necessary because there were no apparent explanations for the fact that drivers were making these mistakes; but making them they were.
>
> There have been a number of suggestions as to why; but none have been conclusively established. It may be because there was in fact the opportunity or ability of a driver approaching 168 to see signals further down the line. Of course, bearing in mind that this is a junction signal, then those signals would not necessarily be appropriate as indications to a driver that his path was the same one which was being affected or controlled by the signals down the line. There was another suggestion that for some reason, again which is not clear, signal 178 was misinterpreted when yellow or displaying a double yellow.'

The court then went on to make the point that since Mr Bell did the alteration work there had been no further SPADs at signal 168.

The court concluded:

> ' . . . clearly accordingly something about the infrastructure of this particular junction was causing mistakes to be made. Had a jury known that, it is, at the very least impossible for us to conclude that the jury would inevitably have nonetheless convicted the appellant of manslaughter. Those facts would have all been matters

which the jury would have taken into account when assessing the level of fault of Mr Morgan. As a result, there is no way that we can say this conviction is safe.'

1 *R v Morgan* [2007] EWCA Crim 3313.
2 Signals passed at danger.

WHY WAS THE CONVICTION QUASHED?

13.5 The main reason why this conviction was quashed was because of the advances in both technological and psychological sciences. The Public Inquiry led by Lord Cullen in 2000 in the aftermath of the terrible train accident at Ladbroke Grove in 1999 had led to a number of findings as to why train drivers passed red signals and why in the vast majority of cases, in the absence of alcohol or drugs, a prosecution for gross negligence could never be successfully achieved.

The Court of Appeal in *Morgan* distinguished the old common law strand of cases commencing with *R v Bateman*[1] culminating with the test based upon the speech of Lord Diplock in *R v Caldwell*[2] which had originally been the applicable test in reckless driving, but extended to manslaughter. See also *R v Boswell*[3] and *R v Holmes*[4] in relation to death by reckless driving.

In essence, as pointed out by Lord Justice Latham in the judgment, the appropriate test was:

> ' . . . whether or not the defendant could be shown to have caused an obvious and serious risk of either death or injury, and did so either because he had not thought of the consequences or because he thought about them and went on to take the risk'.

The learned judge continued:

> 'the law, however, was subsequently clarified by, in particular, the speech of Lord MacKay in the case of *Adomako*.[5] Lord MacKay said as follows at pages 187B:
>
> > "On this basis, in my opinion, the ordinary principles of the law of negligence apply to ascertain whether or not the defendant has been in breach of a duty of care towards the victim who has died. If such breach of duty is established, the next question is whether that breach of duty caused the death of the victim. If so, the jury must go on to consider whether that breach of duty should be characterised as gross negligence and therefore as a crime. This will depend upon the seriousness of the breach of duty committed by the defendant in all the circumstances in which the defendant was placed when it occurred. The jury will have to consider whether the extent to which the defendant's conduct departed from the proper standard of care incumbent on him, involving as it must have done a risk of death to the patient, was such that it should be judged criminal."
>
> Counsel submits that the question posed by Lord MacKay was never examined in this case. If it had been, then there were factors which were not considered at all in the course of the hearing before the judge which were of considerable significance.'

1 (1925) 19 Cr App R 8 CA.
2 [1981] 1 All ER 961.
3 (1984) 6 Cr App Rep (S) 25, CA.
4 (1990) 12 Cr App R(S) 32.
5 *R v Adomako* [1994] 3 WLR 288, HL.

A TURNING POINT

13.6 This decision by the Court of Appeal marks a turning point in the courts. For many years, in the aftermath of a rail (or other disaster) the front line operator such as the train driver or pilot had been blamed.

In the run up to the decision in *Morgan*, both the train drivers at the Watford and Southall train crashes had been prosecuted for manslaughter and acquitted. The driver, Mr Hodder, who was in the cab when his train passed signal SN109 at red near Paddington Station, and died in the crash, was heavily criticised during the Inquiry, despite the final report by Lord Cullen generally absolving him of any blame which he said was caused by systemic and infrastructure failure. This report to Ladbroke Grove, it is submitted, was the bedrock to the successful appeal of Mr Morgan, as it was able to show the Court of Appeal all the many developments that had taken place since 1989. We now know much more about why drivers pass signals at red, and, most importantly, why signals passed need to be very carefully risk assessed. After the conclusion of this Inquiry, Network Rail and Thames Trains pleaded guilty to offences under the Health & Safety at Work Act 1974, and were fined.

In recent years the law has greatly moved towards the management and corporation (or non-incorporated body) being held responsible and away from those lower down in the command chain.

The Corporate Manslaughter and Culpable Homicide Act 2007 has also made it easier for organisations to be prosecuted as it swept away the old common law provisions that a directing mind of an organisation had to be also found guilty of gross negligence manslaughter. Now the test is one as set out in section 1(1):

> 'An organisation [corporate or other relevant body] . . . is guilty of an offence [of corporate manslaughter] if the way in which its activities are managed or organised—
>
> (a) causes a person's death, and
> (b) amounts to a gross breach of a relevant duty of care owed by the organisation to the deceased.'

Section 1(3) states:

> 'An organisation is guilty of an offence only if the way in which its activities are managed or organised by the Senior Management is a substantial element of the breach referred to in subsection (1).'

It is felt by many commentators that the prosecution will have an easier task particularly against larger organisations than under the old common law.

Fines for individuals found guilty of manslaughter are increasing. In *R v Wacker*,[1] a Dutch lorry driver was sentenced to 14 years' imprisonment after 58 illegal immigrants suffocated in his lorry.

In the recent case of *R v Winter and Winter*[2] the Court of Appeal upheld a sentence of seven years and reduced another from five to four years after two directors (a father and son) were found guilty of manslaughter after a fire broke out at a farm that went on to set off fireworks which had been stored in a metal shipping container. Two employees of East Sussex Fire and Rescue Service were killed by the explosion.

In *Connolly and Kennet*,[3] two directors were sentenced after appeal to seven and two years' imprisonment. This case arose out of the Teebay disaster where four workers died when a rail carriage descended the bank at high speed. Mr Connolly was also convicted of perverting the course of justice.

In relation to other directors and managers, since 16 January 2009 individuals can be imprisoned for up to two years for health and safety offences. This came about by virtue of the Health and Safety (Offences) Act 2008.

In *R v P*[4] the Court of Appeal held a director could sometimes be guilty of neglect, even if he/she did not know of the unsafe practices of their company. Under the Act, a breach would carry a maximum term of two years' imprisonment. The test is what they ought to have known, rather than what they said they knew, as an objective not subjective test.

Penalties for companies are also increasing. Transco plc have been fined £15 million and Balfour Beatty £7.5 million and a number of companies were recently sentenced in the aftermath of the incident at Buncefield – Total was fined £3.6 million and asked to pay £2.6 million costs.

The Sentencing Guidelines Council stated in February 2010 in their publication 'Corporate Manslaughter and Health and Safety Offences Causing Death – A Definitive Guideline' at page 7:

> 'The offence of Corporate Manslaughter, because it requires gross breach at a senior level, will ordinarily involve a level of seriousness significantly greater than a health and safety offence. The appropriate fine will seldom be less than £500,000 and may be measured in millions of pounds.
>
> The range of seriousness involved in health and safety offences is greater than that for Corporate Manslaughter. However, where the offence is shown to have caused death, the appropriate fine will seldom be less than £100,000 and may be measured in hundreds of thousands of pounds or more . . . '

In terms of the general laws relating to health and safety, the cases of *R v Porter*,[5] *R v EGS Limited*,[6] *R v Chargot Ltd*[7] and *R v Upper Bay Ltd*[8] all show that successfully defending prosecutions pursuant to the Health and Safety at Work Act 1974 is increasingly becoming more difficult. For instance, in *R v EGS Limited* the Court of Appeal said:

> 'In other words it is helpful to ask whether a reasonable person appreciates and guards against that risk in deciding whether the risk is more than trivial or fanciful'.

Lord Dyson went on to say:

> 'The prosecution did not have to prove that the risk was appreciable or foreseeable. They had to prove that the risk was not fanciful and was more than trivial.'

The court went on to indicate that in many cases, the defence will be little more able than to call their evidence in rebuttal as soon as the prosecution has proved that the accident happened in a work context. Further, there has been a series of recent guidance documents aimed at Directors and Board Members, culminating with a document in 2008 entitled 'Leading Health and Safety At Work: Leadership Actions for Directors and Board Members'.[9] The Guidance, in ten bullet points, sets out three essential principles:

(a) strong and active leadership from the top;
(b) worker involvement; and
(c) assessment and review.

It is an important document, as it specifically states, that can be used in court to benchmark an organisation's attitude to health and safety and will be used by prosecutors.

1 [2003] 1 Cr App Rep (S) 487.
2 [2010] EWCA Crim 1474 (July 2010).
3 [2007] EWCA Crim 270.
4 [2007] All ER (D) 173 , [2008] ICR 96.
5 [2008] EWCA Crim 1271.
6 [2009] EWCA Crim 1942.
7 [2008] UKHL 73.
8 [2010] EWCA Crim 495, (2010) Times, 28 April, [2010] All ER (D) 270 (Mar).
9 Published jointly by the Health and Safety Executive and the Institute of Directors.

CONCLUSION

13.7 Much water has passed under the bridge since Mr Morgan originally pleaded guilty in 1990. Prosecutors and courts are generally much more focused on looking at organisational and management failure than breaches of individual frontline workers. This approach is set to intensify and accelerate.

The case of *Morgan* will continue to be cited in the future, showing that frontline workers should not be the only people prosecuted and, in certain instances, they too can be seen as the victims of corporate failure.

IV

CIVIL LAW

No collection of 'cases that changed our lives' could omit *Donoghue v Stevenson*, the most important single step in the law of negligence, something most people encounter almost every day in their relations with neighbours, physical and otherwise. *Caparo v Dickman* is just one of the many significant cases which followed: the law of negligence has never showed signs of slowing its development since the epoch began with *Donaghue*. The number of times both cases are cited in the law reports each year indicates as much.

Mareva, another of Lord Denning's famous decisions, today forms a substantial amount of the business of the Commercial Court. In practical terms, securing the disputed assets prior to trial is of equal importance to any substantive legal right, for the obvious reason that any substantive legal cause of action may be rendered illusory by an elusive defendant dissipating his or her assets.

Anything approximating a new cause of action will also keep practitioners, judges and legal editors busy, and the developing law of privacy is no exception, as illustrated by the *Campbell* case. Of course, it comes squarely into conflict with one of English law's proudest traditions, freedom of the press, and as that chapter relates, the particular newspaper involved was not shy about asserting that tradition. The litigation still has not been concluded at the time of publication of this book, and in the meantime many a famous claimant has sought to rely on a right to privacy when seeking to suppress details of colourful activities which have kept the tabloid press busy.

14

THE SNAIL IN THE BOTTLE

Donoghue v Stevenson

Paul Reed QC and Philippa Harris

INTRODUCTION

14.1 Who would have thought that a tenacious solicitor, a dead mouse and a partially decomposed snail in a ginger beer bottle would change the course of English legal history? But that is what happened one summer's evening in August 1928, when May Donoghue, who was a shop assistant, entered the Wellmeadow Cafe in Paisley, Scotland. May ordered a ginger beer and then, to her horror, a partially decomposed snail slid out of the bottle and into her glass. May Donoghue sued for nervous shock and there began her journey from the streets of East Glasgow to the highest court in the land, the House of Lords, where her case would become one of the most famous in English law and change the law of negligence forever.[1]

[1] *Donoghue v Stevenson* [1932] AC 562.

THE FACTS

14.2 Surprisingly perhaps, the facts supporting May Donoghue's claim were not the most important issue and were never tested in court. Seventy years later questions still remain unanswered as to what occurred that evening. What the courts had to decide was whether May had any right to claim in law for the negligence of the man who bottled the ginger beer and thus obtain recognition and recompense for her shocking experience.

To return to the facts as we understand them, on the evening of 26 August 1928, May Donoghue travelled from her home in Glasgow to Paisley. Upon arriving in Paisley, she met a friend and both went into the Wellmeadow Cafe, owned and run by an Italian called Mr Francis Minchella. Mrs Donoghue's friend proceeded to order and pay for a pear and ice drink and a 'ginger beer ice cream float'. When the order came, the owner poured half of the bottle of ginger beer over the ice cream to make the 'float'. Mrs Donoghue drank some of the 'ice cream float' and then her friend lifted the ginger beer bottle to pour the remainder into her glass to drink. It was at this point that Mrs

Donoghue said that a partially decomposed snail slowly slid out of the bottle and into her glass. Mrs Donoghue alleged that she had suffered from both shock and severe gastroenteritis as a result of seeing the snail and drinking the contaminated beverage.

The offending bottle of ginger beer with snail inside had been bottled by a family business not more than one mile from the Wellmeadow Cafe, owned and run by a Mr David Stevenson. It was believed the snail had got into the bottle before it was filled and sealed at Mr Stevenson's factory. On 9 April 1929, Mrs Donoghue sued Mr Stevenson in negligence, hoping to recover £500 in compensation for the shock and illness she had suffered.[1] In 1932 this was a substantial sum of money.

1 See: Chapman, M, *The Snail and the Ginger Beer – The Singular Case of Donoghue v Stevenson* (1st edn, 2009) Wildy, Simmonds & Hill, Ch 1; McBryde, WM, 'Donoghue v Stevenson: The Story of the 'Snail in the Bottle' in Gamble, AJ, *Obligations in Context* (1990) W Green; and Alan Rodger QC, 'Mrs Donoghue and Alfenus Varus'(1988) 41 CLP1 for detailed background to the case.

BEFORE THE SNAIL

14.3 It is important to understand the law relating to consumers and product liability as it stood in the 1920s before looking at the later House of Lords' decision in *Donoghue v Stevenson*. Prior to Mrs Donoghue's case the law relating to consumers was formulaic and focused primarily on contract law, which confined a duty of care being owed, only to the parties in a contractual relationship with each other. If you did not have a contractual relationship, tort law was able to impose a duty of care on one party for the benefit of another, but only if the relationship between the parties fell into one of two special categories. For example, if the product proved to be dangerous under certain circumstances and an injured party had relied on fraudulent misrepresentation that they were safe or if the product were in a category of articles that were acknowledged as dangerous, then a non-purchaser could sue the manufacturer if he or she was injured by a such a defective product.[1] It followed, that if one did not fall into any one of these special categories, there was no remedy available. The reason the courts were unwilling to extend liability in tort to third parties beyond the special categories referred to above, was because of concern that the common law doctrine of 'privity of contract' would be eroded. As a result, tort law was perceived as outdated, illogical and unfair.[2]

Other common law jurisdictions were further advanced in their approach to this issue, for example, across the Atlantic the Americans had been active in developing the law of tort. Judge Benjamin Cardozo in the case of *MacPherson v Buick Motor Company*[3] (where a car had collapsed whilst being driven), abolished the common law requirement of privity of contract and developed a general duty of care, which was to be the starting point in any negligence claim. Unfortunately, however, such developments were not of much assistance to Mrs Donoghue, but it shows that common law was evolving to meet the changing needs of modern society.

1 See *Langridge v Levy* (1837) 150 ER 863; *Dom National Gas Co v Collins* (1909) AC 640; *Heaven v Pender* (1883) 11 QBD 503 (CA).

2 See *Markesinis and Deakin's Tort Law* (6th edn, 2007) OUP, pp 114, 115.
3 [1916] 217 NY 382.

OVER BEFORE IT STARTED?

14.4 From the facts alleged, it is plain that May's case fell outside the scope of the current law relating to consumers and product liability. For instance, she could not bring a cause of action in contract against the cafe owner because there was no contractual relationship, having not ordered or paid for the ginger beer. Mrs Donoghue's friend technically had a contractual relationship with the cafe owner but it was she, not her friend, who had consumed the contaminated ginger beer. Furthermore, ginger beer was not classed as a dangerous product per se nor had the ginger beer been fraudulently misrepresented to her by the manufacturer. Her claim did not fall into one of the categories of special relationship that established a duty of care. Was the case of Mrs Donoghue, the ginger beer and the deceased snail to end here?

MR LEECHAM – THE TENACIOUS SOLICITOR

14.5 Mrs Donoghue came to be represented by Mr Walter Leecham of WG Leecham & Co. Mr Leecham appears to have had a keen interest in this issue having already brought before the Scottish courts the issue of floating creatures in ginger beer bottles, in the case of *Mullen v AG Barr & Company Limited.*[1] In *Mullen*, a dead mouse had been discovered in a bottle of ginger beer. Mr Leecham had brought a claim for damages and tried to establish liability against the manufacturer of the ginger beer. However, the Scottish Court of Session rejected the claim and ruled there was no authority or legal basis to establish a duty of care that made the manufacturer liable. Leaving to one side one's natural curiosity as to how a mouse managed to find its way into a bottle of ginger beer (dead or alive), the decision of the Scottish court was unhelpful for Mrs Donoghue's case. Nevertheless, by this stage, she had found an indomitable spirit in Mr Leecham, who agreed to continue with her case; no doubt hoping to have more success with a decomposed snail than with the dead mouse.[2]

A writ was issued in the Court of Session in April 1929. In the writ, May claimed that she had suffered from shock and severe gastroenteritis after drinking part of the contents of the ginger beer bottle and that the manufacturer, Mr Stevenson, owed her a duty of care and that he should have exercised reasonable care that the ginger beer he manufactured did not contain noxious substances, including snails, which would be likely to cause her injury. Unsurprisingly, Mr Stevenson denied any liability or that he owed her any such duty of care.[3]

1 [1929] SC 461.
2 Chapman, M, *The Snail and the Ginger Beer – The Singular Case of Donoghue v Stevenson* (1st edn, 2009) Wildy, Simmonds & Hill, pp 17–20.
3 Ibid, pp 20–25.

ENTER THE SNAIL

14.6 The first hearing took place on 30 June 1930 before the Lord Ordinary, Lord Moncrieff, sitting in the Court of Session. Matters went in Mrs Donoghue's favour when Lord Moncrieff ruled that there was in fact a case to answer. Lord Moncrieff compared the case to those who release from their control, or maintain in their control, instruments of danger, thus his judgment stayed within the recognised limits of special relationships that imposed a duty of care.[1]

Inevitably, Mr Stevenson appealed and the appeal hearing was heard in November 1930. On appeal to the Second Division of the Court of Session, the judges reversed the decision of Lord Moncrieff and granted Mr Stevenson the appeal, arguing that Mrs Donoghue had no legal basis to bring her claim, based on the case of *Mullen* where it was held that no duty of care was owed. One of the judges stated that the only difference between Mrs Donoghue's claim and *Mullen* was the intrusive creature – be it dead mouse or decomposed snail – and that in Scots law that actually meant no difference at all.[2]

Mrs Donoghue's claim appeared hopeless. The Court of Session had now ruled twice that there was no legal basis for her to bring a claim for damages against the manufacturer, Mr Stevenson, as no contract existed between them nor was the ginger beer dangerous or fraudulently represented. Yet May Donoghue continued to pursue her claim for negligence and her legal team agreed to work for nothing. May was declared a 'pauper' by the courts in order to protect her from payment of Mr Stevenson's legal costs. She appealed the ruling of the Scottish Court of Session and began the long journey from Glasgow to the House of Lords.

1 See Lewis N Klar, QC, *Tort Law* (4th edn, 2008) Carswell, p 166 and Linden, 'The Good Neighbour on Trial: A Fountain of Sparkling Wisdom' (1983) 17 UBCL Rev 32.

2 See Tort Law (as n 1 above), p 166 and Chapman, M, *The Snail and the Ginger Beer – The Singular Case of Donoghue v Stevenson* (1st edn, 2009) Wildy, Simmonds & Hill, p 29.

THE HOUSE OF LORDS

14.7 A year later, legal argument in respect of Mrs Donoghue's appeal was heard over a two-day period before Lord Buckmaster, Lord Atkin, Lord Tomlin, Lord Thankerton and Lord MacMillan. The question the House of Lords had to answer was: did Mr Stevenson owe Mrs Donoghue a duty of care to bottle his ginger beer without the inclusion of noxious items such as snails? If there was no duty of care, Mrs Donoghue's claim would fail. Mrs Donoghue's legal representatives argued that the protection provided to manufacturers by the common law principle of privity of contract should be removed. Of course, Mr Stevenson's legal representatives argued that the good judgment of the Scottish judges in *Mullen* should prevail.

On 26 May 1932, the House of Lords handed down their opinion and by a majority of three to two held that Mr Stevenson did, indeed, owe a duty of care to Mrs Donoghue. What led them to this view? The leading judgment was delivered by Lord Atkin which introduced the 'neighbour principle' derived from the Christian principle of 'loving your neighbour' which introduced a general concept of relations giving rise to a duty of care, as follows:

> '. . . in English law there must be, and is, some general conception of relations giving rise to a duty of care, which the particular cases found in the books are but instances. The liability for negligence, whether you style it such or treat it as in other systems as a species of "culpa", is no doubt based upon a general public sentiment of moral wrongdoing for which the offender must pay. But acts or omissions which any moral code would censure cannot in a practical world be treated so as to give a right to every person injured by them to demand relief. In this way the rules of law arise which limit the range of complainants and the extent of their remedy. The rule that you are to love your neighbour becomes in law, you must not injure your neighbour; and the lawyers question, Who is my neighbour? receives a restricted reply. *You must take reasonable care to avoid acts or omissions which you can reasonably foresee would be likely to injure your neighbour. Who then, in law is my neighbour? The answer seems to be persons who are so closely and directly affected in my act that I ought reasonably to have them in contemplation as being so affected when I am directing my mind to the acts or omissions which are called in question.*'[1]

So, who is your neighbour? Lord Atkin concludes that this question is in essence an issue of proximity. He did not go as far as to state that a duty of care is owed to the entire world but if a person is sufficiently close to our actions or inactions, it may be deemed that they have a right to be protected. Lord Atkin went on to state that:

> '. . . a manufacturer of products, which he sells in such a form as to show that he intends them to reach the ultimate consumer in the form in which they left him with no reasonable possibility of intermediate examination, and with knowledge that the absence of reasonable care in the preparation or putting up of products will result in injury to the consumers' life or property, owes a duty to the consumer to take that reasonable care'.

When these two principles are applied, Lord Atkin concluded that it was reasonably foreseeable that Mrs Donoghue would be injured if Mr Stevenson bottled his ginger beer, to put it crudely, with snails in it, and Mr Stevenson owed Mrs Donoghue a duty of care not to do so. Lord Atkin did, however, point out that his conclusion would have been different if the seller of the ginger beer bottled by the manufacturer had been able to detect any noxious items in the bottle (for example, if the bottle was clear), before the public were allowed to purchase it. In such a case, it would not have been foreseeable that Mrs Donoghue as a consumer would be injured because it could be expected that the seller would intercept any such bottles that did contain noxious items such as snails.[2]

Lord Atkin was supported by Lord Thankerton and Lord MacMillan but Lord Buckmaster and Lord Tomlin dissented on the basis that the precedents were solidly against her claim and that if a duty were imposed, it would only serve to open the floodgates on future litigation.

The case was then returned to the Court of Session to be determined on the facts and the evidence presented. A trial was listed but it never took place. Mr Stevenson passed away shortly after judgement had been delivered and the executors of his estate settled the claim out of court, apparently for less than the £500 claimed.[3]

1 [1932] AC 580 (emphasis added).

[2] See Bagshaw, RM, and McBride, NJ, *Tort Law* (3rd edn, 2008) Pearson Longman, p 73.
[3] See Linden, 'The Good Neighbour on Trial: A Fountain of Sparkling Wisdom' (1863) 17 UBCL Rev 67.

THE SIGNIFICANCE OF *DONOGHUE V STEVENSON*

14.8 By reversing the appellate court's decision and finding in favour of Mrs Donoghue, the House of Lords made a pivotal contribution to the development of the law of negligence. Perhaps, most importantly, it freed the law of negligence from the iron grip of the doctrine of privity of contract and provided a remedy to consumers where there was no privity of contract. Secondly, it established that a duty of care owed in negligent actions is not confined to only 'special relationships' but is flexible and governed by the concept of proximity which is capable of extension to all sorts of new situations.[1]

The decision reflected changes in society including the widespread sale of pre-packaged goods and the fact that at the beginning of the twentieth century, with the population of the United Kingdom increasing, one's neighbour was more likely to be physically proximate than ever before and as a result it was necessary to regulate this by the imposition of duties.

The 'neighbour principle', however, was not without controversy, primarily because the courts believed it was too wide a concept to be accepted as a general principle about who will owe a duty of care.[2] Although it still remains the starting point of any consideration of the duty of care in negligence law, the case law, since Mrs Donoghue's case, has sought to try and define and, in some instances confine, and limit its parameters.

[1] See Lewis N Klar, QC, *Tort Law* (4th edn, 2008) Carswell, p 167.
[2] See Bagshaw, RM, and McBride, NJ, *Tort Law* (3rd edn, 2008) Pearson Longman, p 73.

WHAT HAPPENED NEXT?

14.9 The courts were for some time hesitant about applying the 'neighbour principle' but in *Home Office v Dorset Yacht Co Ltd*[1] Lord Reid confirmed that the neighbour test was a statement of principle and should be applied unless there was some reason for excluding it. Following this, in *Anns v Merton London Borough Council*,[2] Lord Wilberforce tried to rationalise the law regarding the imposition of a duty of care by introducing a two-stage test. First, is there a sufficient relationship of proximity of neighbourhood between the offender and the person who has suffered damage such that, in the reasonable contemplation of the former, carelessness on their part may cause damage to the latter, in which case a prima facie duty of care arises? Second, are there any considerations which ought to negative or reduce or limit the scope of the duty or the class of persons for whom it is owed or the damage to which a breach of it may give rise?[3] Thus, in essence, *Donoghue* would apply unless there was a legal reason for it not to or that it should be modified because of policy reasons.

The courts used *Anns v Merton London Borough Council* to expand the area of duty of care and soon realised that it involved a number of complex considerations. For example, in *Junior Books v Veitchi*[4] the House of Lords held that liability could arise in respect of economic loss and in *McLoughlin v O'Brian*,[5] the House of Lords considered the scope of nervous shock. However, there was almost immediate reaction against these decisions and the courts began to retreat from *Anns* because of concerns about having a wide rule of recovery and the potential of exposing individuals to indeterminate liability and opening the floodgates to claims without merit.[6]

Anns was criticised by later cases in the House of Lords including *Murphy v Brentwood District Council*[7] and *Caparo Industries plc v Dickman*.[8] In these cases, the courts turned their back on the broad formulation of a duty of care and stated that in 'novel' cases the courts should not assume a prima facie duty is owed but develop the law 'incrementally' with reference to established categories in previous case law. The incremental approach as expounded by the House of Lords has, however, adopted a rigid form in English common law and the two-tier test introduced by *Anns* has now been replaced by a more complex three-tier test in *Caparo* when a duty of care will be imposed but only if:

(a) the loss is reasonably foreseeable;
(b) there is a relationship of proximity between the claimant and the defendant; and
(c) it is fair, just and reasonable to impose a duty of care.

The courts have essentially developed the imposition of a duty of care from a strictly legal question as to whether a duty of care exists in *Donoghue v Stevenson* to replacing the wide test in *Anns* with a narrower incremental test in *Caparo* by carrying out a factual analysis of whether to impose a duty of care with specific reference to proximity and what is fair, just, and reasonable in the circumstances.

1 [1970] AC 1004, HL.
2 [1978] AC 728, HL. See further **15.7**.
3 [1977] 2 All ER 492, 499.
4 [1983] 1 AC 520, HL.
5 [1982] 2 All ER 298, HL.
6 See David Green, *Torts Law* (5th edn), p 16.
7 [1990] 2 All ER 908, HL.
8 [1990] 1 All ER 568, HL. See further Chapter 15.

THE LEGACY OF *DONOGHUE V STEVENSON*

14.10 May Donoghue changed the modern law of negligence, not only in the United Kingdom but in other common law jurisdictions throughout the world, including Australia, Canada and New Zealand. It continues to be the starting point for any discussion concerning the existence of a duty of care. It remains the subject of much debate and discussion, even with the passage of time. The answer to the question 'who then is my neighbour' has continued to be developed throughout the twentieth century in cases such as *Holbeck Hall Hotel Ltd v Scarborough Borough Council*[1] which considered the extent of the measured duty of care owed between adjoining occupiers of land. An Englishman is not at liberty to treat his home as his castle if by so doing he affects his neighbours land.

14.10 *The Snail in the Bottle*

May Donoghue would be pleased to know that at the beginning of the twenty-first century, with increasing population and worldwide manufacturing, the common law is alive and well and capable of continuing to adapt to provide a remedy to those who are injured or who suffer loss.

[1] [2000] 2 All ER 705, HL.

15

LEGAL CELEBRITY OR JURISPRUDENTIAL SUBSTANCE?

Caparo v Dickman

*John Randall QC**

INTRODUCTION

15.1 The great case[1] of *Caparo Industries plc v Dickman and others*[2] remains one of the most frequently cited authorities in the all too crowded field of where English law will find – or some would say impose – a duty of care in the law of tort. When the speeches in this case were first handed down by the House of Lords, even the most casual of readers could hardly avoid discerning that this was to be, and was intended by the judges to be, a landmark case. The passage of 20 years since then (yes, it really has been 20 years) affords the opportunity to reflect, with at least some sense of perspective, on whether it has stood the test of time[3] and remains what it first promised to be, a true landmark case of real jurisprudential substance. Or did it flatter to deceive? Is it now to be exposed as no more than a legal celebrity, attracting huge attention when first launched on the legal world, but in truth adding nothing of substance?

1 So described by Lord Scott of Foscote in *Trent Strategic Health Authority v Jain* [2009] UKHL 4 at [27], [2009] 1 All ER 957 at 969a–b.

2 [1990] 1 All ER 568 (HL), [1990] 2 AC 605.

3 As Lord Walker observed in *Customs and Excise Commissioners v Barclays Bank plc* [2006] UKHL 28 at [69], [2006] 4 All ER 256 at 279e–g (in the course of a military metaphor), it 'has sometimes been only long after' a decision concerning the development of the tort of negligence that it 'has been possible to assess [its] true significance'.

THE FACTS

15.2 Fidelity plc was a manufacturer of consumer electrical goods such as televisions, hi-fis and cordless telephones, whose shares were listed on the London Stock Exchange. Its auditors were the well-known firm of Chartered Accountants, Touche Ross. Although a quoted public company, it was still to a considerable extent a family business. Over the period of the take-over which gave rise to the litigation, Fidelity's Chairman and Managing Director was Steven Dickman, and his brother Robert was its Technical Director. Their father had been its founder. As at March 1984, members of the Dickman family held, between them, 19.5% of Fidelity's shares.

In the early 1980s the company had a chequered financial history, with a reported profit in the year to 31 March 1980 of £827,000, followed by losses (after interest charges) of £2.757 million in 1981, and £245,000 in 1982. Its fortunes improved somewhat the following year, with the annual accounts to 31 March 1983 reporting a modest profit of £80,000, and in July 1983 its directors forecast, in a rights issue circular, that pre-tax profits for the following year would, 'in the absence of unforeseen circumstances . . . be not less than £2.2 million'. Their still more optimistic internal forecast was a profit of £3.085 million, and £300,000 higher if the rights issue were successful. The (unaudited) half-yearly accounts to 30 September 1983 showed a pre-tax profit of £766,000, and the accompanying announcement from the directors asserted that the company's performance was 'going according to plan'.

However, this rosier picture did not last, and by a press release issued on 12 March 1984 the directors warned that profits for that year were likely to fall significantly short of their earlier forecast. Predictably enough, there was an immediate drop in the value of Fidelity's shares, which fell from 143 pence (at 1 March) to 90 pence, and then somewhat further to 75 pence (by 2 April). In the event Fidelity's accounts to 31 March 1984, audited by Touche Ross and accompanied by an unqualified audit certificate, showed a profit of £1,300,000. This result was announced on 22 May, and by 1 June the shares had fallen further, to 63 pence. On 12 June 1984, Fidelity's annual accounts were sent out to shareholders with the notice of its forthcoming Annual General Meeting. The accompanying Chairman's Report explained the shortfall, as compared with the forecast given at the time of the rights issue, as having been caused by 'unforeseen technical and production difficulties' encountered with regard to colour televisions, and 'unexpected delays . . . with the tests specification for the cordless telephones', whilst going on to assert that 'These difficulties have now been overcome, and [their] production . . . is going according to plan'.

Caparo plc sensed the opportunity for a take-over, and, indeed, at least one stockbroker's circular issued at around this time referred to the possibility of a take-over bid. Caparo made an initial purchase of 100,000 Fidelity shares at 70 pence on 8 June 1984, although it had not been registered as a shareholder by 12 June 1984 and was therefore, contrary to its pleaded case, not one of those to whom the accounts were sent out with the notice of the AGM.[1] Caparo purchased a further 50,000 Fidelity shares at 73 pence on 12 June 1984, and on 14 or 15 June it obtained a copy of the annual accounts. Its shareholding had then reached 5%, and it gave the notification of this required by the City Code to the Stock Exchange and to Fidelity on 18 June (by which time Fidelity's shares were trading at 93 pence). On 6 July 1984, just after the AGM (which it had not attended), Caparo acquired a further 550,000 shares, taking its holding to 13.6%. It continued purchasing shares and by 30 July its holding reached 29.9%, which meant that, under the City Code, if it intended to acquire more shares Caparo was bound to make a bid for all Fidelity's remaining shares.

Further purchases at the beginning of September 1984 took Caparo's holding up to 32.4%, and on 4 September it made the required bid, at 120 pence. That bid was not recommended for acceptance by the directors, but when modestly increased to 125 pence on 24 September (which precipitated a brief suspension of Fidelity's listing) it was recommended, and subsequently went unconditional on 23 October 1984. Caparo then held 91.8% of Fidelity's shares, and used its resultant compulsory rights to buy in the remainder. Under its new ownership, Fidelity was renamed Intersound Consumer Electronics ('Intersound').

Any pleasure which Caparo felt at this 'success' was, however, short-lived. It claimed that all its purchases after 12 June 1984, including throughout the formal bid, had been made in reliance on the accounts to 31 March 1984. Yet those accounts had, it alleged, materially mis-reported Fidelity's true results and financial position. The stock was over-valued (due to the inclusion of non-existent stock, and under-provision for obsolescent stock), insufficient provision had been made for after-sales credits (on the return of goods after the year end), and the supposed profit of £1,300,000 had, in truth, been a loss of £400,000. Had Caparo known this true position, it would not have made the purchases and bid that it did (or, indeed, any). It learned of the problems with the stock values following a stock count on 11 January 1985. Later that year it commenced proceedings against Stephen and Robert Dickman for fraudulent misrepresentation, and against Touche Ross for alleged negligence in certifying, in its unqualified audit certificate, that Fidelity's accounts for the year ended 31 March 1984 showed a true and fair view of its financial position. Within a few years, at the end of 1988, Caparo had closed down Intersound's operations.[2]

1 See per Lord Bridge [1990] 1 All ER 568 (HL) at 572d–e, [1990] 2 AC 605 at 615G–H. Contrast per Sir Neil Lawson at first instance: [1988] BCLC 387 at 390d–e.

2 See official transcript of judgment of Webster J discussed at **15.3** below, at p 5 (of 37).

THE PROCEEDINGS

15.3 In support of its allegation that Touche Ross owed it a duty of care in respect of all its purchases of shares made after 12 June 1984, Caparo relied on its status both as a shareholder and as an actual or potential investor. It pleaded that:

> 'Touche Ross, as auditors of Fidelity carrying out their functions as auditors and certifiers of the accounts in April and May 1984, owed a duty of care to investors and potential investors, and in particular to Caparo, in respect of the audit and certification of the accounts. In support of that duty of care Caparo will rely upon the following matters: (1) Touche Ross knew or ought to have known (a) that in early March 1984 a press release had been issued stating that profits for the financial year would fall significantly short of £2.2m., (b) that Fidelity's share price fell from 143p per share on 1 March 1984 to 75p per share on 2 April 1984, (c) that Fidelity required financial assistance. (2) Touche Ross therefore ought to have foreseen that Fidelity was vulnerable to a take-over bid and that persons such as Caparo might well rely on the accounts for the purpose of deciding whether to take over Fidelity and might well suffer loss if the accounts were inaccurate.'

Some time after the commencement of proceedings by a writ specially indorsed with the Statement of Claim, Sir Neil Lawson directed the trial of a preliminary issue as to whether, on Caparo's pleaded case, Touche Ross owed it a duty of care.

While the matter proceeded by way of a preliminary issue, Caparo was entitled to have all contested issues of fact assumed in its favour. As Lord Oliver summarised the position:

> 'it [was] to be assumed against [Touche Ross] that they showed a lack of reasonable care in certifying that the accounts of Fidelity for the year ended 31 March 1984 gave a true and fair view of Fidelity's position. It [was] also to be assumed that, when they certified the accounts, Touche Ross knew or would, if they had thought about it, have known that Fidelity was vulnerable to take-over bids, that a potential bidder would be likely to rely upon the accuracy of the accounts in making his bid and that investors in the market generally, whether or not already members of Fidelity, would also be likely to or might well rely upon the accounts in deciding to purchase shares in that company.'

In December 1987 Touche Ross succeeded in obtaining a negative answer to the preliminary question before Sir Neil Lawson at first instance,[1] but the following July lost by a majority (O'Connor LJ dissenting) in the Court of Appeal, which found for Caparo in respect of its claim brought as a shareholder.[2] In February 1990 Touche Ross' appeal to the House of Lords was allowed unanimously, and the judge's finding of no duty of care was restored.[3] Even that, however, did not mark an end to litigation arising from this ill fated take-over.

Caparo continued with its claim for fraudulent misrepresentation against the Dickmans. It is noteworthy that, when the action came to trial, neither Steven nor Robert Dickman chose to give evidence, despite the seriousness of the allegations of deceit against them. On 18 January 1991 Webster J gave judgment for Caparo.[4] He found that the defendants, who despite their seniority had personally taken a very active part in the year-end stock count conducted over the weekend of 31 March/1 April 1984, had been directly involved in falsifying five stock sheets, thereby over-stating the amount of stock held by a total of £544,000,[5] and that these particular stock sheets had then been deliberately excluded from those made available to Touche Ross.[6] He further held that obsolescence of stock was underprovided for in the accounts by £323,000 plus a further but unquantified amount,[7] and that after-sales credits were underprovided for by no less than £593,000.[8] Webster J found that both Steven and Robert Dickman had dishonestly made false statements about all three matters, with the intention of deceiving potential purchasers of shares in Fidelity as to their value.[9] Caparo's claim against them succeeded in respect of losses suffered on shares acquired after 15 June 1984,[10] the practical effect of which was to reduce its total recoverable losses by just over 2.2%.[11]

Caparo also caused a further action to be commenced against Touche Ross for breach of contract, in the name of Intersound, but it seems that this action did not make any progress.[12]

1 [1988] BCLC 387.
2 [1989] 1 All ER 798, [1989] QB 653.
3 [1990] 1 All ER 568, [1990] 2 AC 605.
4 Official transcript (by H Counsell) available from LexisLibrary.
5 At pp 16, 18, 20, 22 and 26 (of 37).

6 At pp 27, 28 (of 37).

7 At p 32 (of 37).

8 At p 34 (of 37).

9 At p 36 (of 37).

10 The date on which it had obtained a copy of the accounts to 31 March 1984, and hence the earliest date from which it could establish reliance thereon.

11 Caparo had acquired 250,000 of Fidelity's 11,280,000 shares before 15 June 1984.

12 *Markesinis and Deakin's Tort Law* (6th edn, 2007) Clarendon Press, Oxford, at p 166.

THE TIMES

15.4 The case came at a time when the need for some retreat from the so-called two-part test formulated by Lord Wilberforce in *Anns v London Borough of Merton*,[1] with its dominant role for foreseeability of loss, was both recognised and underway,[2] and when there was some concern as to the potential extent of the exposure of auditors to claims for negligence.

On the other hand, when its proceedings were launched all had not been bleak for Caparo. It had a decision of the New Zealand Court of Appeal, *Scott Group v McFarlane*,[3] where the majority included Cooke J, and dicta in decisions from both England, *JEB Fasteners v Marks, Bloom & Co*,[4] and Scotland, *Twomax v Dickson, McFarlane & Robinson*,[5] in its favour. And it went to the House of Lords as respondent, with the support of favourable judgments from two future Lord Chief Justices (Bingham and Taylor LJJ) in the Court of Appeal.

1 [1977] 2 All ER 492 (HL), [1978] AC 728.

2 Though its culmination, in the over-ruling of *Anns* by a seven judge House of Lords in *Murphy v Brentwood District Council* [1990] 2 All ER 908, [1991] AC 398 (four of whom had sat on the *Caparo* appeal) was still six months away.

3 [1978] 1 NZLR 553, NZ CA.

4 [1981] 3 All ER 289, esp at 296h–297b.

5 [1982] SC 113.

A LANDMARK FORESEEN

15.5 There can be no doubt that the judges of the House of Lords, four of whom delivered substantive speeches,[1] recognised this as a landmark case in the making even while writing their speeches. Lord Bridge commenced his consideration of the authorities with a citation from Lord Atkin's 'seminal speech' in *Donoghue v Stevenson*,[2] identifying it as marking the introduction of the more modern approach (than finding the existence of a duty of care in different specific situations, each exhibiting its own particular characteristics), but immediately adding that:

> 'Yet Lord Atkin himself sound[ed] the appropriate note of caution by adding . . .
>
> "To seek a complete logical definition of the general principle is probably to go beyond the function of the judge, for the more general the definition the more likely it is to omit essentials or to introduce non-essentials." '[3]

He went on expressly to recognise that, whilst acknowledging the importance of the underlying general principles common to the whole field of negligence, the approach which he and his fellow judges adopted in that case was part of a move away from Lord Atkin's 'more modern' approach:

> 'in the direction of attaching greater significance to the more traditional categorisation of distinct and recognisable situations as guides to the existence, the scope and the limits of the varied duties of care which the law imposes.'[4]

Lord Roskill agreed that:

> 'it has now to be accepted that there is no simple formula or touchstone to which recourse can be had in order to provide in every case a ready answer to the questions whether, given certain facts, the law will or will not impose liability for negligence or in cases where such liability can be shown to exist, determine the extent of that liability. Phrases such as 'foreseeability,' 'proximity,' 'neighbourhood,' 'just and reasonable,' 'fairness,' 'voluntary acceptance of risk,' or 'voluntary assumption of responsibility' will be found used from time to time in the different cases. But, as your Lordships have said, such phrases are not precise definitions. At best they are but labels or phrases descriptive of the very different factual situations which can exist in particular cases and which must be carefully examined in each case before it can be pragmatically determined whether a duty of care exists and, if so, what is the scope and extent of that duty . . . I think [a return to the traditional categorisation of cases as pointing to the existence and scope of any duty of care] is infinitely preferable to recourse to somewhat wide generalisations which leave their practical application matters of difficulty and uncertainty.'[5]

Lord Oliver added:

> 'for my part, I think that it has to be recognised that to search for any single formula which will serve as a general test of liability is to pursue a will-o'-the wisp. The fact is that once one discards, as it is now clear that one must, the concept of foreseeability of harm as the single exclusive test – even a prima facie test – of the existence of the duty of care, the attempt to state some general principle which will determine liability in an infinite variety of circumstances serves not to clarify the law but merely to bedevil its development in a way which corresponds with practicality and common sense.' [6]

All this was in marked contrast to the confident assertion of Lord Wilberforce in *Anns v London Borough of Merton* that:

> 'Through the trilogy of cases in this House – *Donoghue v Stevenson*,[7] *Hedley Byrne & Co Ltd v Heller & Partners Ltd*,[8] and *Dorset Yacht Co Ltd v Home Office*,[9] the position has now been reached that in order to establish that a duty of care arises in a particular situation, it is not necessary to bring the facts of that situation within those of previous situations in which a duty of care has been held to exist'.[10]

So these were speeches which were, from the start, consciously intended to set the law on a new path, and to reduce for the future the significance of a speech which had stood for almost 60 years as the definitive statement of the 'general principle' theory of the modern law of negligence, that of Lord Atkin in *Donoghue v Stevenson*.[11] That said, however, it should immediately be noted that this new path is not one which has been universally welcomed. As *Markesinis and Deakin's Tort Law* laments:

> 'The days of confidence have . . . given way to retrenchment . . . [and this] retrenchment has also come with an enhanced zeal for casuistry at the expense of the search for any underlying principles'.[12]

1 Lords Bridge, Roskill, Oliver and Jauncey. Lord Ackner contented himself with agreeing with the reasons of all four of his brethren.
2 [1932] AC 562 at 580, [1932] All ER Rep 1 at 11.
3 [1990] 1 All ER 568 (HL) at 573b–c, [1990] 2 AC 605 at 616G–H.
4 At 574c, 618C–D.
5 At 581j–582b, 628C–E.
6 At 585j–586a, 633F–G.
7 See n 2 above.
8 [1963] 2 All ER 575 (HL), [1964] AC 465.
9 [1970] 2 All ER 294 (HL), [1970] AC 1004.
10 [1977] 2 All ER 492 (HL) at 498f–h, [1978] AC 728 at 751G–H.
11 See n 2 above.
12 *Markesinis and Deakin's Tort Law* (6th edn, 2007) Clarendon Press, Oxford, at p 96.

FOR WHAT IS THE CASE FAMOUS?

15.6 In the present author's view, there are at least six points of particular note to be found in the speeches of the House of Lords in *Caparo*.

(1) The 'threefold test' – foreseeability does not suffice to establish proximity

15.7 First, inevitably enough, must come the 'threefold test', for which *Caparo* is to this day so often cited. Lord Bridge expressed it thus:

> ' . . . in addition to the foreseeability of damage, necessary ingredients in any situation giving rise to a duty of care are that there should exist between the party owing the duty and the party to whom it is owed a relationship characterised by the law as one of 'proximity' or 'neighbourhood' and that the situation should be one in which the court considers it fair, just and reasonable that the law should impose a duty of a given scope upon the one party for the benefit of the other.'[1]

The comparison which is necessary in order to appreciate the significance of this threefold test is with the two-part enquiry which Lord Wilberforce had found to be required in *Anns*:

> ' . . . the question [of whether a duty of care arises in a particular situation] has to be approached in two stages. First one has to ask whether, as between the alleged wrongdoer and the person who has suffered damage there is a sufficient relationship of proximity or neighbourhood such that, in the reasonable contemplation of the former, carelessness on his part may be likely to cause damage to the latter – in which case a prima facie duty of care arises. Secondly, if the first question is answered affirmatively, it is necessary to consider whether there are any considerations which ought to negative, or to reduce or limit the scope of the duty or the class of person to whom it is owed or the damages to which a breach of it may give rise . . . '[2]

Given that the second of Lord Wilberforce's two areas of enquiry could be summarised as, in essence, policy considerations, it may, at least broadly, be equated to the third of Lord Bridge's tests, namely whether the imposition of a duty is fair, just and reasonable in all the circumstances. The most crucial difference between them is with regard to the other elements of their tests: Lord Wilberforce's first area of enquiry equated foreseeability of damage with a sufficient relationship of proximity or neighbourhood between the parties, or made it the test for such proximity, whereas the threefold test separated them out into cumulative requirements. In addition, a further difference of importance is that under Lord Wilberforce's two-stage enquiry, once the first (foreseeability of damage) was satisfied, there was a prima facie assumption that a duty of care would exist, subject to the possibility of this being negated by policy considerations at the second stage, whereas all three limbs of the threefold test, including in particular the third 'fair just and reasonable' limb, must be addressed before a duty can be found in the first place.[3] The decision of the House of Lords in *Customs and Excise Commissioners v Barclays Bank*[4] to reject the assertion that a bank, on whom a copy of a Freezing Order against one of its customers had been served, owed the claimant a duty to take reasonable care to comply with the same, is but one recent example of the importance of the need for a claimant to be able to satisfy the court that the 'fair just and reasonable' requirement is satisfied.[5]

The threefold test never was put forward by Lord Bridge as providing practical tests which enable the question of 'duty or no duty' to be answered in any given case. His speech expressly recognised that:

> ' . . . the concepts of proximity and fairness embodied in these additional ingredients are not susceptible of any such precise definition as would be necessary to give them utility as practical tests, but amount in effect to little more than convenient labels to attach to the features of different specific situations which, on a detailed examination of all the circumstances, the law recognises pragmatically as giving rise to a duty of care of a given scope.'[6]

Indeed, Lord Walker has since referred to the 'increasingly clear recognition' that it 'does not provide an easy answer to all our problems, but only a set of fairly blunt tools'.[7]

However, what the threefold test did provide is a framework or structure which facilitates a more rigorous consideration of whether a duty of care should be found to exist in any given case. It has been used as such in many subsequent cases by doubtless grateful first instance judges, and continues to be so to this day, albeit that it is now frequently applied alongside other tests. To illustrate the point by reference to just one recent example, in *Patchett v Swimming Pool & Allied Trades Association*[8] the claimants had selected a contractor to build a swimming pool for them by reference to the website of the defendant trade association (SPATA), to which the contractor belonged. The contractor became insolvent and ceased trading, leaving the claimants with an incomplete and unsatisfactorily constructed swimming pool in their garden. Absent an effective remedy against the insolvent contractor, they sought redress from the defendant, on the basis of a variety of statements on its website, such as that its members:

> ' . . . are fully vetted before being admitted to membership, with checks on their financial record, their experience in the trade and inspections of their work. They are required to comply fully with the **SPATA** construction standards and code of ethics, and their work is also subject to periodic re-inspections after joining. Only **SPATA** registered pool and spa installers belong to **SPATASHIELD, SPA-**

> TA's unique Bond and Warranty Scheme offering customers peace of mind that their installation will be completed fully to **SPATA** Standards – come what may!'

The county court judge identified the potentially relevant tests as the assumption of responsibility, the threefold test, and the incremental approach (itself adopted in *Caparo*, as is discussed below). On the facts, the incremental approach was of little assistance (save as to cause him to note that neither party had referred to any legal authority involving misstatements on a website). Hence, both before the judge and the Court of Appeal, the parties accepted that the existence or otherwise of a duty of care should be determined by reference to the other two tests. When applying the threefold test, His Honour Judge Worster held that there could be no issue about foreseeability on such facts, and therefore addressed the questions of proximity, and whether it would be fair, just and reasonable to impose a duty of care, citing passages from Lords Bridge and Oliver in *Caparo*. The Court of Appeal, in a judgment given by Lord Clarke of Stone-cum-Ebony MR[9] dismissing the appeal, endorsed both his identification of the relevant legal principles, and his application of the same to the facts (which led to a decision that no duty was owed).[10]

1 *Caparo Industries plc v Dickman and ors* [1990] 1 All ER 568 (HL) at 573j–574b, [1990] 2 AC 605 at 617H–618B.

2 *Anns v London Borough of Merton* [1977] 2 All ER 492 (HL) at 498g–j, [1978] AC 728 at 51H–752B.

3 See per Lord Hoffmann in *Stovin v Wise* [1996] 3 All ER 801 (HL) at 824b–f, [1996] AC 923 at 949A–E.

4 [2006] UKHL 28, [2006], 4 All ER 256.

5 At [100], 289f per Lord Mance, describing it as 'the key question' in that case.

6 *Caparo Industries plc v Dickman and ors* [1990] 1 All ER 568 (HL) at 574a–c, [1990] 2 AC 605 at 618B–C; cited with approval *in Customs and Excise Commissioners v Barclays Bank* [2006] UKHL 28 at [6], [2006] 4 All ER 256 at 262e–h per Lord Bingham.

7 *Customs and Excise Commissioners v Barclays Bank* [2006] UKHL 28 at [71], [2006], 4 All ER 256 at 279j–280a. He went on to cite (at [72], 280c–d) the passage from Lord Bridge quoted in the main text, as having recognised both the limitations of the threefold test, and that its elements are, ultimately, labels.

8 [2009] EWCA Civ 717.

9 Now a Justice of the Supreme Court of the United Kingdom.

10 *Patchett v Swimming Pool & Allied Trades Association* [2009] EWCA Civ 717, in particular at [11]–[24] and [29]–[40].

(2) The incremental approach

15.8 Second, the retreat from the 'general principle' theory of the duty of care discussed above under the heading 'a landmark foreseen' was accompanied by an endorsement[1] of a new, more conservative approach, to any expansion of the circumstances in which legal liability may be established, namely the now well-recognised 'incremental approach':

> 'It is preferable . . . that the law should develop novel categories of negligence incrementally and by analogy with established categories, rather than by a massive extension of a prima facie duty of care restrained only by indefinable 'considerations which ought to negative, or to reduce or limit the scope of the duty or the class of person to whom it is owed.'[2]

1 *Caparo Industries plc v Dickman and ors* [1990] 1 All ER 568 (HL),[1990] 2 AC 605 – by Lords Bridge at 574c–e, 618C–E, Roskill at 581j–582c, 628D–F, and Oliver at 586a–c, 633G–634B.

2 At 574d–e, 618D–E, being a citation of words of Brennan J (see **15.13** below).

(3) Importance of the purpose of the defendant's activity or statement

15.9 Third, *Caparo* emphasises the importance of closely analysing the exact purpose for which the defendant undertook the activity or made the statement complained of. Hence on its own facts, a consideration of the purposes for which Parliament had laid down the requirements for a so-called statutory audit, as part of the accounting requirements for public companies laid down in the Companies Acts, was required. A careful analysis of the same was conducted by Lords Oliver and Jauncey in particular,[1] who concluded that the legislation existed for the purpose of protecting companies themselves and facilitating their informed control by the body of shareholders as a whole, including questioning its past management, but not to protect individual shareholders in relation to present or future investment in the company, nor investors in the market, nor the public at large.[2]

The most helpful contrast is with the decisions on the conjoined appeals in *Smith v Eric S Bush* and *Harris v Wyre Forest District Council*.[3] In each of these cases the defendant surveyor and valuer had provided a report and valuation for a prospective mortgage lender. However, in each case the whole purpose had been, as was either known or should have been obvious to the defendants, to assist with the proposed acquisition of the particular property in question by a particular prospective purchaser and mortgagor, who had borne the cost of the defendant's fee. Hence the position was very different from that contended for by the respondents in *Caparo*, which was for liability to any potential investor in the market, or at least to any person who already held shares in the publicly quoted company in question. Lord Bridge made the point thus:

> 'The salient feature of all these cases is that the defendant giving advice or information was fully aware of the nature of the transaction which the plaintiff had in contemplation, knew that the advice or information would be communicated to him directly or indirectly and knew that it was very likely that the plaintiff would rely on that advice or information in deciding whether or not to engage in the transaction in contemplation. In these circumstances the defendant could clearly be expected, subject always to the effect of any disclaimer of responsibility, specifically to anticipate that the plaintiff would rely on the advice or information given by the defendant for the very purpose for which he did in the event rely on it.'[4]

Hence, whilst liability was justified in the *Smith v Eric S Bush* cases, it could not be justified in *Caparo*. Lord Jauncey put the position directly:

> 'Possibility of reliance on a statement for an unspecified purpose will not impose a duty of care on the maker to the addressee. More is required. In *Smith v Eric S Bush* . . . it was probable, if not highly probable, that the potential purchaser would rely on the valuer's report. This probable reliance was an essential ingredient in establishing proximity. Had it merely been a possibility that the purchaser would rely on the report I very much doubt whether this House would have decided that the valuer owed a duty of care to the purchaser.'[5]

[1] *Caparo Industries plc v Dickman and ors* [1990] 1 All ER 568 (HL), [1990] 2 AC 605 at 583a–584j, 629H–632C and 605b–606e, 658G–660E & 607d–f, 661G–662A respectively.

[2] At 584h–j, 632B–C and 607f–g, 662A–B respectively.

[3] [1989] 2 All ER 514 (HL), [1990] 1 AC 831.

[4] *Caparo Industries plc v Dickman and ors* [1990] 1 All ER 568 (HL) at 576c–e, [1990] 2 AC 605 at 620H–621B.

[5] At 607a–c, 661C–E.

(4) A duty of care does not exist in the abstract

15.10 Fourth, several of the judges in *Caparo* identified the important point that the question of whether a duty of care exists in any given factual circumstances should not be asked in the abstract, but asked in respect of protection from a particular type of loss and damage. Today, this point is generally made by reference to the speech of Lord Hoffmann in *South Australia Asset Management Corp v York Montague*,[1] yet Lord Hoffmann took the point from Lord Bridge's speech in *Caparo*:

> 'It is never sufficient to ask simply whether A owes B a duty of care. It is always necessary to determine the scope of the duty by reference to the kind of damage from which A must take care to save B harmless.'[2]

[1] [1996] 3 All ER 365 (HL) at 370d–f, [1997] AC 191 at 211G–212B. It should, however, be noted that in the *South Australia Asset Management* case Lord Hoffmann made the extent of the inquiry into the 'type' of loss and damage more particular than had previously been recognised as necessary or appropriate, and arguably trespassed into areas more traditionally addressed at the stage of considering remoteness of damage.

[2] *Caparo Industries plc v Dickman and ors* [1990] 1 All ER 568 (HL) at 581b–c, [1990] 2 AC 605 at 627D. The same point could have been taken from Lord Oliver at 599f–g, 651F or Lord Jauncey at 607b–c, 661D–E.

(5) Potential liability of professionals to non-clients for negligent misstatement

15.11 Further to the previous point at **15.10** above, as Lord Bridge had earlier observed, the 'damage which may be caused by the negligently spoken or written word will normally be confined to economic loss sustained by those who rely on the accuracy of the information or advice they receive as a basis for action'.[1] Against that background, *Caparo* examined the circumstances in which a professional person may be held liable to a non-client (and hence in tort, absent any contract between the defendant professional and the claimant who relied on his statement) for negligent misstatement, albeit that on the facts before the House of Lords no such liability was found. The speeches of Lords Bridge and Oliver in particular explore those circumstances specifically,[2] in addition to their consideration of the appropriate test for liability in negligence generally.

[1] *Caparo Industries plc v Dickman and ors* [1990] 1 All ER 568 (HL) at 574j, [1990] 2 AC 605 at 619B.

[2] At 574j–577b, 619B–623B and 587d–589g, 635E–638E respectively.

(6) The limitations of assumption of responsibility as a test

15.12 Sixth, the case identified the inherent weakness of the test of 'assumption of responsibility' which had found favour in the *Hedley Byrne* case. Lord Roskill confessed to finding:

> 'considerable difficulty in phrases such as "voluntary assumption of responsibility" unless they are to be explained as meaning no more than the existence of circumstances in which the law will impose a liability upon a person making the allegedly negligent statement to the person to whom that statement is made; in which case the phrase does not help to determine in what circumstances the law will impose that liability or indeed, its scope.'[1]

Lord Oliver did not find it any more helpful:

> 'This is a convenient phrase but it is clear that it was not intended to be a test for the existence of the duty for, on analysis, it means no more than that the act of the defendant in making the statement or tendering the advice was voluntary and that the law attributes to it an assumption of responsibility if the statement or advice is inaccurate and is acted upon. It tells us nothing about the circumstances from which such attribution arises.'[2]

Though the assumption of responsibility test has enjoyed something of a come back since the subsequent House of Lords decision in *Henderson v Merrett Syndicates*,[3] the reservations about it expressed in *Caparo*, and the limits of the concept more generally, remain matters of judicial comment and interest to this day.[4]

1 *Caparo Industries plc v Dickman and ors* [1990] 1 All ER 568 (HL) at 582b–d, [1990] 2 AC 605 at 628F–H.

2 At 589a-c, 637G-H.

3 [1994] 3 All ER 506 (HL), [1995] 2 AC 145. In *Customs and Excise Commissioners v Barclays Bank* [2006] UKHL 28, [2006] 4 All ER 256, it was described by Lord Mance (at [83], 283f-g) as being 'on any view a core area of liability for economic loss' (but see also the citation from later in his speech in n 4 below).

4 See, for example, the discussion of the same in *Patchett v Swimming Pool & Allied Trades Association* [2009] EWCA Civ 717 at paras [14]–[18]; and in *Customs and Excise Commissioners v Barclays Bank* [2006] UKHL 28, [2006] 4 All ER 256 at [4]–[5], 261f–262e per Lord Bingham and [87], 284g–h per Lord Mance.

WAS *CAPARO* NO MORE THAN A LEGAL CELEBRITY?

15.13 So why, with at least six such major points to be found within its speeches, and so many subsequent citations in judgments at all levels, might critics nevertheless dismiss *Caparo v Dickman* as no more than a legal celebrity, famous for being famous, but which has in truth added nothing of substance to English jurisprudence?

The case against *Caparo* is that it had all been said before. So far as concerns the emergence of the threefold test, to replace the two-part enquiry postulated in *Anns*, the need for proximity to be separately established in addition to foreseeability, rather than simply following from it, emerged from the judgments of Lord Keith of Kinkel in *Governors of the Peabody Fund v Sir Lindsay Parkinson*,[1] and *Yuen Kun-yeu v Attorney General of Hong Kong*,[2] and of

Lord Goff in *Davis v Radcliffe*.[3] Indeed, it is striking that in his judgment at first instance in *Caparo* itself, Sir Neil Lawson directly applied the threefold test as representing the general principles which applied from his understanding of the authorities.[4]

The incremental approach was not original, but adopted from the judgment of Sir Gerard Brennan in the High Court of Australia case of *Sutherland Shire Council v Heyman*.[5] Furthermore, it has subsequently been said to be of little value as a test in itself, and only helpful when used in combination with a test or principle which identifies the legally significant features of a situation.[6] Brennan J was also the source of the point that a duty of care does not exist in the abstract, but must be stated in reference to the kind of damage which the would-be claimant has suffered.[7]

The importance of the purpose of the defendant's activity or statement upon which liability is sought to be founded was already well recognised, as was the potential liability of professionals to non-clients. In the specific context of the potential liability of accountants, this featured in Denning LJ's celebrated dissenting judgment in *Candler v Crane Christmas & Co*,[8] which had long since been vindicated in the *Hedley Byrne* case. It is, however, noteworthy that whereas in *Hedley Byrne* this judgment was cited in support of an expansion of the then recognised scope of tortious liability, so as to extend it to negligent misstatements, in *Caparo* its 'masterly analysis' was particularly hailed as a statement of the limitations on the scope of such liability.[9]

As to the limitations of the assumption of responsibility test, these had already been discussed, in particular by Lord Griffiths in the *Smith v Eric S Bush* appeals.[10]

1 [1984] 3 All ER 529 (HL) at 534b–g, [1985] AC 210 at 240F–241C.

2 [1987] 2 All ER 705 (PC) at 710e–712j, [1988] AC 175 at 191E–194F.

3 [1990] 2 All ER 536 (PC) at 540g–541a, [1990] 1 WLR 821 at 826B–F.

4 [1988] BCLC 387 at 392b–f.

5 [1985] HCA 41 at [14], 157 CLR 424 at 481.

6 In *Customs and Excise Commissioners v Barclays Bank* [2006] UKHL 28 at [7], [2006] 4 All ER 256 at 263c–e; per Lord Bingham.

7 At [27], 487, citing his own earlier judgment in *John Pfeiffer Pty Ltd v Canny* [1981] HCA 52 at [11], 148 CLR 218 at 241–2; cited by Lord Oliver in *Caparo Industries plc v Dickman and ors* [1990] 1 All ER 568 (HL) at 599h–600b, [1990] 2 AC 605 at 651H–652C.

8 [1951] 1 All ER 426 (CA) at 433A–436F, [1951] 2 KB 164 at 179–185, extensively cited in *Caparo*.

9 *Caparo Industries plc v Dickman and ors* [1990] 1 All ER 568 (HL) at 576j–577, [1990] 2 AC 605 per Lord Bridge at, 621F–623B.

10 [1989] 2 All ER 514 (HL) at 534b–e, [1990] 1 AC 831 at 862B–F – see **15.9** above.

CONCLUSION

15.14 So was Lord Scott right to refer to *Caparo v Dickman* as a great case?[1] If the test of a great case is original thought and analysis, then perhaps not. But how many great cases derive their greatness from pulling together various thoughts and ideas already in circulation, and packaging them so as to indicate not just a nuanced change to the then fashionable language of judgments, but a new direction for the law?

1 See n 1 at **15.1** above.

15.14 *Legal Celebrity or Jurisprudential Substance?*

* *The author is grateful to Mr Martin Matthews and Miss Sarah Green for their comments on an earlier draft of this chapter. Responsibility for its accuracy remains, of course, his own.*

16

'AS IF BY A SIDE-WIND . . .'

The *Mareva*/Freezing Order Jurisdiction in England

Paul Lowenstein QC

AN UNSATISFACTORY STATE OF AFFAIRS

16.1 A client discovers that he is the victim of a fraud or serious wrong. He seeks urgent advice from his lawyers. Rapid decisions are made: who to go after, what to claim and – in almost every case – whether there is such a risk that the money or property out of which any judgment will be enforced will disappear that an emergency application should be made to court to freeze those assets where they stand.

The interlocutory Freezing Injunction (formerly the *Mareva* injunction) is now so much part of the primary attack of the commercial litigator that it is hard to imagine that only 35 years ago the remedy was not available. Until May 1975, the established view was that unless a claimant could show a proprietary right, the court would not protect or secure him by the grant of an injunction *before* judgment against the risk that the defendant might seek to frustrate an eventual money judgment by putting his assets beyond the reach of the claimant.

This state of affairs was widely viewed as unsatisfactory since it left the victim of the fraud or wrong exposed to the risk that he would sue to judgment only to find that the calculating wrongdoer had removed or hidden his assets, with the consequence that there would be nothing against which the victim could enforce his judgment or from which he could recover his costs. There was particular disquiet in international mercantile trade since the lack of an effective early remedy left the wronged victim open to the risk (in particular) that a foreign defendant would remove his assets from England before the victim could obtain and enforce a judgment.

THE PRACTICE CHANGES

16.2 Then, on 22 May 1975, Japanese shipowners made an *ex parte* application to Donaldson J in the Commercial Court in London for an injunction to prevent the charterers of three of their ships from removing out of the jurisdiction any of their assets which were within the jurisdiction. The shipowners' complaint was that the charterers had failed to pay the hire for three voyages and that their attempts to find the charterers had not succeeded. However, on the application, the shipowners told the court that they had identified in bank accounts in London money which they believed to belong to the charterers. They said that they feared that the money might be transmitted out of the jurisdiction if something were not done to retain it in England. However, no proprietary claim could be asserted in respect of the money and the judge refused the application.

The shipowners appealed to the Court of Appeal.[1] The judgment is remarkable for its brevity: it is less than one page long. The principal reasoning is that of Lord Denning MR, who started by saying that the court had been told that an injunction of the kind that the shipowners were asking for – ie one to restrain the removal of assets *before* judgment – had never previously been granted in England; although the practice was different on the Continent of Europe.

That said, Lord Denning went on to make the order. The operative part of his judgment reads as follows:

> 'It seems to me that the time has come when we should revise our practice. There is no reason why the High Court or this court should not make an order such as is asked for here. It is warranted by s 45 of the Supreme Court of Judicature (Consolidation) Act 1925 which says the High Court may grant a mandamus or injunction or appoint a receiver by an interlocutory order in all cases in which it appears to the court to be just or convenient so to do. It seems to me that this is just such a case. There is a strong prima facie case that the hire is owing and unpaid. If an injunction is not granted, these moneys may be removed out of the jurisdiction and the shipowners will have the greatest difficulty in recovering anything . . . '[2]

Browne LJ agreed; as did Geoffrey Lane LJ, who summarised the reason for having adopted the new principle in the following brief terms:

> 'In the circumstances which exist in this case there is no reason why the court should not assist a litigant who is in danger of losing money to which he is admittedly entitled. There is nothing in the rules, as far as we have been told, to prevent it. The circumstances demand that the injunction should be continued.'

So, in an afternoon's work on an *ex parte* application, the decision in *Nippon Yusen Kaisha* laid the ground for the development of the new protective jurisdiction since it signalled in the clearest terms that the court had determined to 'revise our practice'.

However, there were fears that the decision was defective in that the court had not been referred to *Lister & Co v Stubbs*,[3] an earlier decision of the Court of Appeal, in which Cotton LJ had said:[4]

> 'I know of no case where, because it was highly probable that if the action were brought to a hearing the plaintiff could establish that a debt was due to him from the defendant, the defendant has been ordered to give security until that has been established by the judgment or decree . . . '

In the same case, Lindley LJ said:[5]

'. . . we should be doing what I conceive to be very great mischief if we were to stretch a sound principle to the extent to which the Appellants ask us to stretch it, tempting as it is . . .'

1 *Nippon Yusen Kaisha v G and J Karageorgis* [1975] 2 Lloyd's Rep 137.

2 Section 45 of the Supreme Court of Judicature (Consolidation) Act 1925 has been replaced by section 37(1) of the Senior Courts Act 1981 (formerly the Supreme Court Act), which provides as follows: 'The High Court may by order (whether interlocutory or final) grant an injunction or appoint a receiver in all cases in which it appears to the court to be just and convenient to do so'. This provision continues to provide the basis for the modern Freezing Order jurisdiction.

3 (1890) 45 Ch D 1.

4 At p 13.

5 At p15.

THE *MAREVA* CASE

16.3 This apparent defect was put to the test when a month later, on the afternoon of 23 June 1975, a junior barrister[1] acting on behalf of another set of shipowners applied to the Court of Appeal to extend an injunction which had earlier that day been granted *ex parte* by Donaldson J in the Commercial Court restraining the defendants from removing or disposing out of the jurisdiction any of their assets within the jurisdiction. The judge at first instance had granted the injunction for the limited period of a few hours out of deference to the decision in the *Nippon Yusen Kaisha* case; but had refused to extend it because he 'felt some doubt because [the court in *Nippon Yusen Kaisha* was] not referred to *Lister v Stubbs*'.[2] He therefore allowed the claimants protection for just enough time to renew their application before the Court of Appeal.

What resulted confirmed in absolute terms the jurisdiction to freeze the assets of an alleged wrongdoer on an *ex parte* basis, at the very start of the action, long before any judgment is obtained against him.

The judgment of the Court of Appeal in *Mareva Compania Naviera SA v International Bulkcarriers SA*[3] is remarkable in many ways:

- First, once again, it is remarkable for its brevity: the three judgments run to barely three pages of the law report.
- Second, whilst the judgment records that the arguments were put 'very fairly both for and against continuing the injunction', the decision was handed down after an *ex parte* hearing of which the defendants had no notice, which they did not attend and to which they made no contribution or argument. Whilst they were given permission to apply to discharge the order, there is no record that any such application was ever made.
- Third, for the reason that it might fairly be said that the court side-stepped the difficulty thrown up by *Lister v Stubbs*, with two of the three appeal judges giving differing reasons for distinguishing that case, whilst the third (Ormrod LJ) simply ignored the issue.

The facts of the *Mareva* application were similar to those of the *Nippon Yusen Kaisha* case. The claimant shipowners let their ship 'Mareva' to charterers. One of the hire charges was not paid and an exchange of telexes between the shipowners and the charterers made it plain that the charterers were unable to pay. The shipowners treated the charterers conduct as repudiation and sued for the unpaid hire and damages for repudiation. They also applied *ex parte* for an injunction to restrain the charterers from removing or disposing of out of the jurisdiction certain money which the charterers then had in an English bank account, arguing that they believed there was a grave danger that the money would otherwise disappear.

As in the *Nippon Yusen Kaisha* case, the first judgment was given by Lord Denning MR who devoted most of his reasoning to the view of Donaldson J, the judge at first instance, that he had no power to grant an injunction because (1) he was bound by the decision in *Lister v Stubbs* and that (2) the decision of the Court of Appeal in the *Nippon Yusen Kaisha* case was defective in that it had not been referred to the *Lister* case.[4] Lord Denning circumvented this apparent difficulty by reconsidering *Lister v Stubbs* in the light of section 45 of the Supreme Court of Judicature (Consolidation) Act 1925 – the same statutory provision that had been the foundation of the *Nippon Yusen Kaisha* decision. The judgment on this point reads as follows:[5]

> 'Now [counsel for the shipowners] has been very helpful. He has drawn our attention not only to *Lister & Co v Stubbs* but also to s 45 of the Supreme Court of Judicature (Consolidation) Act 1925, which repeats s 25(8) of the Judicature Act 1873. It says:
>
> > "A mandamus or an injunction may be granted or a receiver appointed by an interlocutory Order of the Court in all cases in which it shall appear to the Court to be just or convenient . . . "
>
> In *Beddow v Beddow* (1878) 9 Ch D 89 at 93 Jessel MR gave a very wide interpretation to that section. He said: "I have unlimited power to grant an injunction in any case where it would be right or just to do so . . . "
>
> There is only one qualification to be made. The court will not grant an injunction to protect a person who has no legal or equitable right whatever . . . '

Lord Denning therefore decided that so long as the applicant could demonstrate a legal or equitable right, the statutory provision, taken in conjunction with the principle in *Beddow v Beddow*, allowed the court free rein to grant an injunction in any case where 'it would be right or just to do so'. This was notwithstanding that the Court of Appeal in *Lister v Stubbs* had apparently ruled out injunctions to provide pre-judgment protection. Furthermore, it was not explained how the court could assert this free jurisdiction given that *Lister* was decided some 17 years after section 25(8) of the Judicature Act 1873 came into force and 12 years after *Beddow*.[6] It is notable that Lord Denning did not expressly distinguish the *Lister* case, but instead said that the risk of the money being taken out of the country made it just and convenient for the court to grant the injunction. He said that if the defendants had any grievance about it they could apply to discharge it.

It seems that the court understood that there was a real commercial need for this sort of pre-judgment protection and that it was determined to establish the jurisdiction – as a matter of practice – regardless of any apparent or historic obstacles. Such developments may perhaps be seen as an affront to English notions of precedent, but they are sometimes essential to ensure that the law provides the flexible and effective pre-emptive remedies required by a modern liberal economy. Other examples are the Search Order jurisdiction (effectively invented in the *Anton Piller*[7] case) and the expansion and internationalisation of the *Norwich Pharmacal*[8] jurisdiction, under which the court compels non-parties to make disclosure to assist the victim of a wrong to identify the wrongdoer and/or to follow up the consequences of the wrongdoing.[9] Lord Denning himself was under no illusion as to the novelty of what the court had done or as to its importance: indeed, in his book, *The Due Process of Law*,[10] he described the *Mareva* jurisdiction as 'the greatest piece of judicial law reform in my time'.

The only other substantive judgment in the *Mareva* case itself was given by Roskill LJ, who dealt with the *Lister* point somewhat elliptically, as follows:

> 'If therefore this court does not interfere by injunction, it is apparent that the shipowners will suffer a grave injustice which this court has the power to help avoid . . .
>
> In my judgment it would be wrong to tolerate this if it can be avoided. If it is necessary to find a reason for distinguishing this case from *Lister & Co v Stubbs*, I would venture to suggest that it is at least arguable that the court should interfere to protect the shipowners' rights which arise under cl 18 of the time charter. The relevant part reads: "That the Owners shall have a lien upon all cargoes, and all sub-freights for any amounts due under this Charter, including General Average contributions".
>
> There is or may be a legal or perhaps equitable right which the shipowners may be entitled to have protected by the court. The full extent and nature of that right has long been a controversial matter which may have to be resolved hereafter and I therefore say no more about it.'

In summary, then, the *Mareva* case decided that whatever the previous practice may have been, it was now to change so that where a right could be asserted either at law or in equity, the court would be enabled by the statute[11] in a proper case to grant an injunction to protect that right. As Lord Denning put it in the *Mareva* case:

> 'In my opinion [the] principle applies to a creditor who has a right to be paid the debt owing to him, even before he has established his right by getting judgment for it. If it appears that the debt is due and owing, and there is a danger that the debtor may dispose of his assets so as to defeat it before judgment, the court has jurisdiction in a proper case to grant an interlocutory judgment so as to prevent him disposing of those assets.'[12]

Since 1981, there has been no doubt at all as to the statutory foundation of the *Mareva*/Freezing Order jurisdiction, since the Senior Courts Act 1981,[13] section 37(3) provides as follows:

> '(3) The power of the High Court under subsection (1) to grant an interlocutory injunction restraining a party to any proceedings from removing from the jurisdiction of the High Court, or otherwise dealing with, assets located within that jurisdiction shall be exercisable in cases where that party is, as well as in cases where he is not, domiciled, resident or present within that jurisdiction.'

1 Mr Bernard Rix, now Rix LJ.

2 *Mareva Compania Naviera SA v International Bulkcarriers SA* [1975] 2 Lloyd's Rep 509 at p 510, col 1, [1980] 1 All ER 213.

3 As n 2 above.
4 At p 510.
5 At p 510, col 2.
6 Repeated in terms in s 45 of the Supreme Court of Judicature (Consolidation) Act 1925.
7 *Anton Piller KG v Manufacturing Processes Ltd and ors* [1976] Ch 55.
8 *Norwich Pharmacal Co v Comrs of Customs and Excise* [1973] 2 All ER 943.
9 See eg *Ashworth Hospital Authority v MGN Ltd* [2002] UKHL 29, [2002] 4 All ER 193 and the recent case of *Lockton Companies International v Persons Unknown and Google Inc* [2009] EWHC 3423 (QB) where Eady J confirmed that it was in order for the claimant to have permission to serve a *Norwich Pharmacal* application out of the jurisdiction on a foreign defendant.
10 (1980) OUP, p 134.
11 In other common law jurisdictions, such as Australia, *Mareva* style relief is granted as part of the inherent jurisdiction of the court which acts to protect the integrity of its own process or in support of the due administration of justice: see eg *Cardile v LED Builders Pty Ltd* (1999) 198 CLR 381 at [41], citing with approval *Patrick Stevedores Operations No 2 Pty Ltd v Maritime Union of Australia [No 3]* [1998]153 ALR 643 at 656.
12 Per Lord Denning MR at p 510, col 2 to p 511, col 1.
13 Formerly the Supreme Court Act.

DEVELOPMENT OF *MAREVA* PRINCIPLES

16.4 The principles on which *Mareva* injunctions (later re-named Freezing Orders) are granted have developed over time and are quite separate from the ordinary rules governing the grant of interlocutory injunctions.[1] Instead, there is now an established body of case law which addresses and finesses such matters as:

(a) the development of the nature of the injunctive relief available, with an early expansion away from injunctions simply prohibiting the removal of assets from the jurisdiction to injunctions restraining the respondent from dealing with his assets within the jurisdiction as well as from exporting them;
(b) the clarification that *Mareva* applications can be made even before the issue of the Claim Form with, in very urgent cases, undertakings given as to the production and service of all the necessary court documents as well as the written evidence;
(c) the scope and effect of the prohibitions in the injunction;
(d) protections for the respondent such as the need to include provisions allowing him reasonable living expenses and/or reasonable business expenses as well as reasonable sums for legal representation;
(e) the position of and effect on non-parties such as banks;
(f) the duty of the applicant to make full and frank disclosure on the initial *ex parte* application – an obligation which in practice is very onerous indeed and which adds considerably to the cost and to the pressure placed upon the applicant's team;
(g) ancillary orders such as injunctions requiring immediate disclosure of information necessary to allow the applicant to trace and secure the disputed assets. Indeed, in one recent case the Court of Appeal has remarked that the assets disclosure orders are the 'teeth' of the Freezing Order.[2]

Furthermore, the introduction of the Civil Procedure Rules in England in the late 1990s allowed the formulation of specific procedural rules to be followed in Freezing Order cases: see CPR 25.1(f).[3] In addition, the English courts have in recent years adopted a standard form of Freezing Order with case law and practice rules discouraging the use of different words unless they are necessary and specifically drawn to the attention of, and approved by, the court.

Although there have been significant developments, the three fundamental elements to be considered on every application for a Freezing Order can be found in the short judgment of Lord Denning in the *Mareva* case itself. They are as follows.

(1) Does the applicant have a good arguable case as to the merits of the legal or equitable right of his substantive claims?
(2) Is there a real risk that without an injunction the respondent may put his assets beyond the reach of the applicant with the consequence that a judgment or arbitral award in favour of the applicant would remain unsatisfied?
(3) In all the circumstances of the case is it just and equitable for the court to exercise its discretion in favour of the grant of the injunction?

1 In particular, the principles in *American Cyanamid v Ethicon* [1975] AC 396 are of no relevance.

2 *Motorola Credit Corp v Uzan and ors* [2002] EWCA Civ 989, [2002] 2 All ER (Comm) 945.

3 As well as the associated Practice Direction.

WORLDWIDE FREEZING ORDERS

16.5 The development of the *Mareva*/Freezing Order jurisdiction may be seen to have been in three phases. The earliest cases concerned injunctions to prevent foreign defendants from removing assets from England. There then followed orders freezing assets *within* England and Wales. The third phase has seen the rapid development of the jurisdiction in response to the needs of cases with a fully international element: particularly where the respondent's assets are abroad. There are three areas of particular note:

(1) First, since 1990[1] it has been possible in an appropriate case to apply for a worldwide pre-judgment Freezing Order. These orders prohibit the respondent from disposing of, or dealing with, assets *anywhere in the world*. Such orders are more sparingly granted and have their own particular built-in safeguards. They are personal orders addressed to the respondent and remain subject to the close control of the English court.
(2) This gives rise directly to the second matter of interest, namely the requirement that Worldwide Freezing Orders contain a prohibition that the applicant will not, without the permission of the court, seek to enforce the order in any country outside England and Wales or seek an order of a similar nature including orders conferring a charge or other security against the respondent or the respondent's assets. In this way the court is able to ensure that its order is not used to intrude upon the jurisdiction of any other court, as a means of oppression by the commencement of enforcement proceedings in a multiplicity of jurisdictions or to offend against principles of judicial comity. Thus, the applicant who wishes to take steps abroad in support of or to enforce his English Worldwide Freezing Order must first apply to the English court.[2]

(3) Third, under statutory authority,[3] the English court has jurisdiction to grant injunctive (including Freezing Order) relief in cases where there is no substantive claim on the merits in England. Such injunctions are most commonly sought in support of substantive claims made in actions proceeding abroad.[4]

The development of its international reach means that the English Freezing Order jurisdiction now meshes effectively with the similar regimes available in other jurisdictions (eg the '*Saisie Conservatoire*' in France or the '*Ricorso per Sequestro Conservativo*' in Italy) to provide a highly effective network of interim conservatory remedies in cases where the wrong or its consequences cross borders.

1 See *Derby & Co Ltd v Weldon (No 1)* [1990] Ch 48, CA and *Republic of Haiti v Duvalier* [1990] 1 QB 202 (judgment delivered almost simultaneously with *Derby*) following *Babanaft International Co SA v Bassatne* [1990] Ch 13 where the court first made a post-judgment Worldwide Freezing Order.

2 *Dadourian Group International Inc v Simms (Practice Note)* [2006] EWCA Civ 399, [2006] 1 WLR 2499, CA, where the Court of Appeal stated that the court has a discretion to grant an applicant permission to enforce a Worldwide Freezing Order abroad whenever it considers it just so to do. The court said that there is a range of factors which it is likely to need to consider. it set out and explained eight guidelines to be applied where a party applies for such permission (the '*Dadourian* guidelines').

3 Civil Jurisdiction and Judgments Act 1982, s 25(1).

4 Until the enactment of s 25, it was not possible to obtain an injunction ancillary to a foreign action: see *Siskina (Cargo Owners) v Distos Cia Naviera SA, The Siskina* [1979] AC 210 (HL) at 256, which was effectively overruled by s 25.

FREEZING ORDERS IN PRACTICE

16.6 In practical terms, Freezing Orders are available only to the well-resourced litigant with a sufficiently large claim to warrant heavy early expenditure on collection and presentation of (affidavit) evidence, the preparation of a suite of fairly complex court application papers and the associated costs in terms of lawyers' preparation and advocacy time. There may also be the need to prepare an application for service out of the jurisdiction, which will add to the cost. In almost every case, there will be an *inter partes* hearing soon after the initial *ex parte* application at which time the court will review the order and consider any applications that the respondent may wish to make – eg to vary or to discharge. In a complex or controversial case there may even be urgent interlocutory appeals. Further time and cost will be spent on the process of monitoring compliance with the order and on the consideration of, and response to, the tracing disclosure which the respondent will ordinarily have been ordered to give. Each of these steps is likely to be expensive and can be time consuming. At each juncture, the wronged client will require detailed and urgent advice and will be required to assimilate much information before being asked to give pressing instructions. Everyone works under significant pressure of time; with a premium placed on accuracy and veracity, particularly at the *ex parte* stage.

The effect on a wrongdoer of the victim obtaining a freezing order cannot be understated. There was a time when it seemed almost compulsory for every commentary (and, indeed, examination question) on the *Mareva* jurisdiction to include the adjective 'draconian'[1] at least once. This was for very good reason since, although as the principles on which Freezing Orders are granted have been refined, the protections for the respondent have strengthened it is nonetheless fair to say that in the majority of cases it is very difficult indeed for a respondent to recover from the initial impact. Service will generally come out of the blue. The form of order itself is complicated and there will usually be several folders of supporting evidence, exhibits and other court papers. Most such respondents will have no experience of the injunction jurisdiction and will have to find and then consult a lawyer. A great amount of information will have to be rapidly assimilated and understood. The injunction will often require the provision of asset tracing information within a few hours or days. This alone will generally keep the respondent heavily engaged. The cost of simply taking advice about what the order means is often high – the cost of considering and then preparing for an application to vary or to set aside the injunction can run into the tens of thousands of pounds in a very short period of time. But, perhaps most important is the effect on the respondent of his bank accounts being frozen since, although there will be provisions for reasonable withdrawals, banks tend to be cautious before releasing funds.

There is also the question of the consequences of breach to be considered: in a recent case,[2] the defendant was accused of fraud and the administrators of the claimant company obtained a Worldwide Freezing Order against him. The defendant was found to have breached the order in several ways including failure to disclose assets, to preserve evidence and to deliver up his passport. The court further held that the defendant had acted deliberately to frustrate the administrators in their duties. The penalty imposed by the court for the defendant's breaches was an immediate 18-month custodial sentence.

Furthermore, in practical terms it is far from straightforward for a respondent to mount a successful application to significantly vary or to discharge a Freezing Order. This is first because the threshold for establishing the legal or equitable right is relatively low: the applicant need only demonstrate that he has a good arguable case. In practical terms, the proof required is significantly lower than that which is necessary to succeed on an application for summary judgment.[3] Second, judges are now very experienced at assessing the evidence as to the risk of dissipation of assets at the *ex parte* stage; and, indeed, it is right to say that most experienced commercial litigators will ensure that the evidence that they deploy initially will stand up to the necessary scrutiny. Accordingly, it is relatively rare for a respondent to mount such a sufficiently strong challenge at the interlocutory *inter partes* hearing to demonstrate that there is no significant risk of dissipation. Usually, the best that he will be able to do is to gainsay the evidence of the applicant, in which case the court is likely in its discretion to leave the injunction in place. For these reasons, it is more common to find the disaffected respondent seeking to undermine the injunction on grounds such as:

- that the applicant failed to make full and frank disclosure at the time of the *ex parte* hearing;
- that the sums allowed for reasonable living and legal expenses are insufficient; or
- that the applicant should be required to fortify its cross-undertaking in damages.

1 Deriving from Draco, an Athenian law scribe under whom small offences had heavy punishments.

[2] *Lexi Holdings v Luqman and ors* [2007] EWHC 1508 (Ch), [2007] All ER (D) 23 (Jul).
[3] *Rasu Maritima SA v Perusahaan Pertambangan* [1978] QB 644 at 661F–G, 664F.

CONCLUSION

16.7 The *Mareva* injunction appeared as if from nowhere. Now, 35 years later, it is undoubted that the availability of Freezing Orders (whether used alone or in conjunction with the Search Order and/or *Norwich Pharmacal* jurisdictions) has swung the balance of advantage away from the calculating or conniving wrongdoer in favour of protecting the victim of the fraud or other wrong by preserving the status quo. Whilst in the 1970s *Mareva* injunctions were only exceptionally available, they are now regularly obtained. Having initially been declared to be a revision of the practice of the courts, the *Mareva*/Freezing Order jurisdiction has developed, been refined and has bedded down to the extent that it is now an indispensable part of the commercial lawyer's attack on the serious fraudster or wrongdoer. Of course, the Freezing Order provides no proprietary rights, with the consequence that the holder of the injunction obtains no priority in the event of insolvency. However, what started as a side wind has now developed to the extent where a judge, in the hearing of this writer, recently told a fraudulent respondent who complained about the effect on him of the Freezing Order: 'if you stand up in front of a whirlwind, you can expect to be knocked down'.

17

FROM CATWALK TO COURTROOM: PUBLIC FIGURE, PRIVATE LIFE

Naomi Campbell v MGN Limited

*Heather Rogers QC**

ONCE UPON A TIME

17.1 They were both at the top of their games. She was a supermodel, stunningly beautiful, internationally famous. He was brash, bright and talented, made editor of a national British tabloid newspaper before he was 30. When they met across a crowded courtroom in February 2002, it was for a case that made headlines and legal history. This was *Naomi Campbell v MGN Limited.*[1]

It all began with a *Daily Mirror* article, published on 1 February 2001. The front page included a large headline 'Naomi: I am a drug addict' and a photograph of Ms Campbell captioned: 'Therapy: Naomi outside meeting'. The article, on the front page and inside pages, revealed that Ms Campbell was attending Narcotics Anonymous in a 'courageous bid to beat her addiction to drink and drugs'. The report included that she had been attending regular counselling for three months (sometimes twice a day) and photographs showed her, dressed-down in jeans and a baseball cap, outside a lunchtime group meeting.

Ms Campbell had been the subject of a great deal of publicity before this article. In addition to her modelling career, she had launched a perfume and range of clothes, had a novel published under her name, and engaged in charitable work. She had given many interviews and talked about her private life. She said she did not take illegal drugs, maintaining publicly that, although drug use in the modelling industry was notorious, she had managed to remain immune. An emergency admission to hospital in Gran Canaria in June 1997 was, she claimed, the result of an adverse reaction to antibiotics.

Imagine the reaction at the newspaper when it learned[2] that Ms Campbell was attending Narcotics Anonymous (NA) in Chelsea. It dispatched a photographer to take photographs in the street. It had the story cold. And this was not just a story about a major celebrity: it was a scoop with significant public interest. As the Editor, Piers Morgan, later explained in evidence, there were two main reasons to justify publication: the apparent commission of criminal offences of possession and use of a Class A drug and the serious misleading of the public.[3]

The Daily Mirror had two possible 'angles': a negative story, focusing on Ms Campbell's deception of the public, exposing her as a drug addict and lying hypocrite; or a positive one, praising the supermodel for admitting to her drug problem and committing seriously to treatment to conquer it. The Editor decided not to 'go for the jugular', but to write a sympathetic piece about Ms Campbell's bravery in seeking treatment.[4] That was the line taken in the article published on 1 February 2001.

If anyone hoped that this would avoid any legal problems, they were mistaken. Contacted the day before publication, Ms Campbell's agent told the Editor that it would be 'morally wrong' to publish. As Ms Campbell later said in evidence, she was distressed and upset when she saw the Daily Mirror. On the day of publication, her solicitors sent a letter complaining of a breach of confidentiality and invasion of privacy and enclosing proceedings that had been issued against MGN Limited (MGN). The legal case was on its way.

The reaction of the Daily Mirror was to publish further – less sympathetic – articles on 5 February 2001, including one headed 'pathetic', condemning Ms Campbell's 'whinges' about privacy after her long years of drug use and deception of the public. More articles followed. Battle lines were being drawn.

1 [2004] UKHL 22,[2004] 2 AC 457 (HL).

2 In a pre-trial ruling (21 December 2001, p 10), the judge held that the identity of the source, and whether the newspaper had paid for the story, were irrelevant to any issue at trial.

3 The PCC Code of Conduct, available on www.pcc.org.uk, attempts a definition of 'public interest'.

4 Piers Morgan, *The Insider: the private diaries of a scandalous decade* (2005) Ebury Press (entry for 30 January 2001).

ROUND 1: MORLAND J

17.2 At a pre-trial hearing in December 2001,[1] Ms Campbell's lawyers emphasised that she did not complain about the publication of the fact that she was suffering from drug addiction or of the fact (without details) that she was receiving treatment or therapy. The essence of the claim was the publication of information about who was giving the therapy, where and with what frequency; this undermined, they said, the very structure of the therapy.

As for the defendant's case, the trial judge, the very experienced Morland J, made clear that while cross-examination of Ms Campbell about information she had put into the public domain would be permitted, he would not tolerate a 'general trawl' into her private life. He would rely on counsel for both parties to focus on the essential issues.

The trial took place over a week in February 2002. Ms Campbell gave evidence over two days. According to Mr Morgan, the fragrant Ms Campbell made a positive impression on the judge, who even left his chair to help her find documents in the witness box.[2] Her claim at trial was on the basis of the established cause of action for breach of confidence, without pursuing a separate claim for infringement of privacy.[3] The judge had no difficulty in finding that the three required elements were fulfilled: judgment at [38]–[44]. First, the details of Ms Campbell's attendance at NA had the 'badge' of confidentiality (the fact that there were some errors of detail in the reporting was irrelevant). Second, the information must have been imparted in breach of an obligation of confidence: although the newspaper's source was undisclosed, it must have been someone who attended NA, or a member of Ms Campbell's entourage, who obviously owed a duty not to disclose it. Third, publication of the information was to Ms Campbell's detriment, being likely to affect adversely her attendance and participation in therapy meetings.

The judge acknowledged that the public had a 'need to know' that Ms Campbell had been misleading them. The *Daily Mirror* was 'fully entitled' to put the record straight, particularly as Ms Campbell was a 'self-appointed role model to young black women'. But, while 'balanced and positive journalism' demanded that the public be told that she was receiving therapy for drug addiction, the details should not have been published. The judge considered Articles 8 and 10 of the European Convention on Human Rights, which protect the right to respect for privacy and freedom of expression. Balancing those Convention rights, he concluded that the media should respect details of the private lives of celebrities unless there was an 'overriding public interest duty to publish': [72–73].

So how much was the claim worth? Morland J was satisfied that Ms Campbell had suffered a significant amount of distress by the publication of the details of her therapy, over and above any distress caused by the revelation that she was a drug addict seeking treatment (about which she could not complain). But he approached her evidence with caution, since she had lacked 'frankness and veracity with the media', been 'manipulative and selective' in what she had revealed and lied (including in court) about why she had been rushed to hospital in Gran Canaria. The right amount of compensation was £2,500, to which a further £1,000 was added as aggravated damages for the *Daily Mirror* articles which had belittled her claim and, to use her lawyers words, 'trashed her'.

Ms Campbell had won Round 1. The *Daily Mirror* was hardly magnanimous in defeat: 'JUDGE GIVES LYING DRUG ABUSER £3,500' took up most of the front page, with a sub-headline '(But shhh . . . don't tell anyone. You know how Naomi likes to keep these things private)'. Stories about the judgment and reaction to it covered pages 2 to 6 of that day's paper.[4]

1 Morland J, judgment of 21 December 2001.

2 Piers Morgan, *The Insider* (n 4 at **17.1** above) (entry for 11 February 2002). Mr Morgan, 'on a £50 bet', thought the better of asking the judge for similar assistance during his evidence (entry for 12 February 2002).

3 Morland J, judgment of 27 March 2002, [2002] EMLR 10, at [5].

4 The headline across pp 2 and 3 read 'She was misleading and manipulative . . . and she deliberately told lies under oath' (attributed to Morland J); p 4 included an indignant denial that the reference to Ms Campbell's involvement in the anti-fur-trade campaign as being 'about as effective as a chocolate soldier' was racist; the editorial (p 6) could not be described as understated.

ROUND 2: THE COURT OF APPEAL

17.3 The appeal was heard over three days in July 2002[1] and the Court of Appeal delivered a unanimous judgment in October 2002.[2] The approach of the three appeal judges was radically different from that of the judge. They considered that such details as were given in the article about Ms Campbell's treatment, and the photographs, were a 'legitimate, if not essential, part of the journalistic package' that exposed her deception of the public by denials of drug taking: [62]. Since it was legitimate for the newspaper to publish the fact that Ms Campbell was a drug addict and the fact that she was receiving treatment, there was no particular significance in adding that the treatment was through attending NA: [53]. Any details 'faded into insignificance' compared to disclosure of the central fact that she was receiving treatment for addiction: [57].

Little significance was attached to the photographs of Ms Campbell. She had been photographed (without her knowledge) while standing in the street, outside the NA meeting. But, the court said, she made no legal complaint about the taking of these 'covert photographs' (although she claimed their publication caused distress): [54]–[55].

MGN had won Round 2. 'WE WON' proclaimed the *Daily Mirror's* front page for 15 October 2002: 'SHE made a stand for lying, drug abusing, prima donna celebrities; WE made a stand for press freedom and the right to expose hypocrisy'. The 'historic verdict' was reported in more detail inside, over four pages.

1 It was heard together with an appeal in a separate claim brought by Ms Campbell (started before the MGN litigation) against a former personal assistant, whose contract had included a duty of confidentiality and who had sold a story about Ms Campbell to *The News of the World* for £25,000: *Campbell v Frisbee* [2003] ICR 141. The Court of Appeal, with some reluctance, set aside a summary judgment in Ms Campbell's favour; the case might become a 'valuable addition' to the developing privacy jurisprudence if it went to trial, but the costs were likely to be disproportionate to what was at stake: [35]. There was no trial: the claim was discontinued in 2009.

2 [2003] QB 633.

ROUND 3: THE HOUSE OF LORDS (THE FIRST TIME)

17.4 Another year (or two), another hearing. In February 2004, the House of Lords spent two days hearing an appeal. The landmark decision was given on 6 May 2004.[1]

The five judges broadly agreed on the approach to the law, but they disagreed about the facts. On law, they agreed that the claim did not fit easily into the established cause of action for breach of confidence. However, having regard to the values enshrined in Articles 8 and 10 of the Convention, they recognised a right of action in respect of the 'misuse of private information' (or 'unjustified publication of private information'). The essence of this new claim was the publication, without consent, of information in respect of which a person had a 'reasonable expectation of privacy': [21], [51], [134].

Where they differed was on the approach to the inclusion of the details in the article and, crucially as it turned out, the photographs. Two Law Lords agreed with the Court of Appeal: Lord Nicholls thought the photographs added nothing of an essentially private nature (and noted that Ms Campbell had expressly made no complaint about them being taken): [30]–[31]; Lord Hoffmann considered that individuals could not object to being photographed in the street (although a photograph showing the individual in a state of severe embarrassment or distress might infringe privacy): [74]–[75].

The majority view was that the publication of the photographs went too far. For Lord Hope, the photographs were not simply street scenes, in which Ms Campbell happened to appear, but had been taken deliberately, in secret and with a view to their publication with the article and, in that context, were a gross interference with her privacy: [123]–[124]. Baroness Hale considered that although the mere fact that a photograph was taken covertly did not make the information contained in it confidential (the activity photographed must be private), these were not photographs of Ms Campbell in the street, going about her ordinary daily business (showing no more than 'how she looks if and when she pops out to the shops for a bottle of milk') but, in the context of the article, the connection to her attendance at the NA meeting, meant that her privacy was invaded: [153]–[155]. Lord Carswell agreed with Lord Hope and Baroness Hale.

It is clear from Lord Hope's speech that if the photographs had not been published, he would have regarded the balance between Articles 8 and 10 rights as 'about even' and found for the newspaper: [121]. And, although the decision turned on the photographs, the compensation, and the injunction, awarded covered both photographs and text.

So, by the narrow margin of 3:2, Ms Campbell succeeded in the highest domestic court. The *Daily Mirror* made space for a photograph of Ms Campbell and 'Liar Wins' on its masthead on 7 May 2004, criticising the 'Flaw Lords' on an inside page for having 'dealt a body blow to press freedom'.

1 [2004] 2 AC 457 (HL).

WHY *NAOMI CAMPBELL V MGN* IS A LANDMARK CASE

17.5 Before this decision, it could be said there was no 'right to privacy' in the law of England and Wales. Gordon Kaye, the actor photographed by a tabloid newspaper in his hospital bed while recovering from major surgery, could claim only a limited injunction in malicious falsehood.[1] Publication of CCTV footage of Geoffrey Peck, filmed in Brentwood in a highly distressed state, did not give rise to a cause of action for breach of privacy.[2] Nor was there any right to claim damages for the strip search of visitors to prison in the Wainwright case.[3] There might be some vindication of Article 8 rights in Strasbourg – but that would take years.[4] Yet the claim recognised by the House of Lords – misuse of private information – was a new substantive privacy right.[5]

After *Campbell*, without full analysis and as if by magic, Articles 8 and 10 have been absorbed into this area of domestic law.[6] The Convention has 'horizontal effect', affecting the relations of private bodies and individuals between themselves, not merely 'vertical effect' (between private parties and the State).[7] Those who predicted that the passing of the Human Rights Act 1998 would result in greater rights of privacy for individuals against the media have been proved right.

The decision has been of crucial importance in determining the approach the court must adopt in a case when Articles 8 and 10 both apply. Now, the court has regard to four generally applicable propositions, derived from *Campbell*, handily summarised by Lord Steyn in *Re S (A Child)*:[8]

> 'First, neither article has *as such* precedence over the other. Secondly, where the values under the two articles are in conflict, an intense focus on the comparative importance of the specific rights being claimed in the individual case is necessary. Thirdly, the justifications for interfering with or restricting each right must be taken into account. Finally, the proportionality test must be applied to each. For convenience I will call this the ultimate balancing test.'

In short, privacy and freedom of expression are rights that have equal status; which will prevail depends on the facts of each case.

1 *Kaye v Robertson* [1991] FSR 62 (CA).
2 *R (Peck) v Brentwood Borough Council* [1997] EWHC Admin 1041, [1998] EWCA Civ 296.
3 *Wainwright v Home Office* [2004] 2 AC 406 (HL).
4 *Peck v UK* (2003) 36 EHRR 719; *Wainwright v UK* (2006) 44 EHRR 89.
5 It is commonly referred to as a 'tort', although the Court of Appeal in *Douglas v Hello! (No 3)* [2006] QB 125 at [96] concluded (with hesitation) the claim by Michael Douglas and Catherine Zeta-Jones for invasion of privacy, in respect of unauthorised photographs of their wedding, was not a tort, because it had been shoehorned into the traditional cause of action for breach of confidence.
6 See, for example, *McKennitt v Ash* [2008] QB 73 (CA) at [11]; *Douglas v Hello! Ltd (No 3)* [2006] QB 125 (CA) at [53].
7 See, for example, Thomas Bennett, Horizontality's new horizons – re-examining horizontal effect: privacy, defamation and the Human Rights Act' (2010) *Entertainment Law Review* 96.
8 [2005] 1 AC 593 (HL) at [17].

THE DEVELOPING RIGHT TO PRIVACY IN FREEDOM OF EXPRESSION CASES

17.6 It is now established, following *Campbell*, that there are two essential elements to the claim for 'misuse of private information': first, does the claimant have a 'reasonable expectation of privacy' in respect of the information in question and, if so, secondly, must their privacy interests (Article 8) give way to the publisher's right to freedom of expression (Article 10).[1]

The first question is an objective one, determined on the basis of what a 'reasonable person of ordinary sensibilities' would feel if put in the claimant's position.[2] It is a broad question, taking into account all the circumstances of the case.[3] In some cases, the answer will be obvious. There are, however, areas of real difficulty. What about, for example, photographs taken in the street? The judge struck out the claim in *Murray v Express Newspapers*[4] on the basis that the child of famous 'Harry Potter' author, JK Rowling, could have no 'reasonable expectation of privacy' in respect of photographs taken as he sat, apparently unconcerned, in his push-chair in an Edinburgh street. But the Court of Appeal thought the claim was arguable, taking into account the Strasbourg decision in *Von Hannover v Germany.*[5] *Von Hannover*, decided after the House of Lords decision in *Campbell*,[6] envisages far greater protection for private rights in relation to photographs taken in the street. The *Murray* case never got to trial (it settled after the House of Lords refused permission to appeal).

The second question – the balancing test – depends on the outcome of the application of an 'intense focus' to the facts of the case. The court carefully evaluates the nature of the two rights and, by reference to each item of information (including any photograph) determines the proportionality of allowing or preventing its publication.[7] The 'public interest' in publication (or its absence) is often an important factor. Max Mosley's claim against *The News of the World*, which gave extensive publicity to his private sexual activities, succeeded when the judge found that there was no public interest in the revelations.[8]

The basics of the cause of action are clear, but questions remain, for example, how the court will assess the public interest, how far the law might protect 'trivial' private information and the extent to which the cause of action can (unlike a breach of confidence claim) survive publication of the information.[9] Perhaps the most hotly contested questions concern the availability of interim injunctions to prevent publication[10] and the grant of 'superinjunctions'. Sadly, detailed consideration of these interesting questions falls outside the scope of this chapter.[11]

Finally, so far as damages are concerned, awards by the court have, so far, been modest, the largest to date being £60,000 awarded to Max Mosley.[12] The decision (in Mosley's case) that, as a matter of principle, exemplary damages are not available for this claim may well be reviewed in a future case. Although Mr Mosley did not appeal the decisions in his case in the domestic courts, he has complained to Strasbourg in an attempt to create a rule requiring the media to give prior notice before publishing any private information.

1 *McKennitt v Ash* [2008] QB 73 (CA) at [11]; and see *Campbell* at [21] (Lord Nicholls).

2 *Murray v Express Newspapers* [2009] Ch 481 at [35]; and *Campbell* at [99] (Lord Hope).

3 *Murray v Express Newspapers* [2009] Ch 481 at [36].

4 [2009] Ch 481.

5 (2005) 40 EHRR 1. The European Court of Human Rights is to consider two further cases involving privacy and photographs which may well be significant: a second *Von Hannover* (more Princess Caroline photographs) and a complaint by Axel Springer; both are against Germany.

6 In *McKennitt v Ash* [2008] QB 73 at [39] the Court of Appeal observed that the very extensive argument in *Campbell* about the photographs might have been much shorter if the House of Lords had 'had the benefit' of *Von Hannover*. See also *Elton John v Associated Newspapers* [2006] EMLR 772 (no injunction to restrain innocuous photograph) and *R (Wood) v Metropolitan Police Commissioner* [2010] 1 WLR 123 (CA) (a 'certain level of seriousness' is required before Article 8 will be 'engaged': [22], [44]).

7 This approach is illustrated by *Campbell*, as well as other leading cases: *McKennitt v Ash* [2008] QB 73 (CA) (famous Canadian folk singer sued former associate over book which included a mass of private information about the singer, her home and relationships); *HRH Prince of Wales v Associated Newspapers* [2008] Ch 57 (CA) (summary judgment for Prince Charles after newspaper published leaked extracts from private travel journals); *Browne v Associated Newspapers* [2008] QB 103 (CA) (attempt to prevent publication of information disclosed by former partner).

8 *Mosley v News Group Newspapers Limited* [2008] EMLR 679: the court (not the media) determines what the public interest required: [135]–[137]. As to potential relevance of the 'reasonable belief' of the media, see also *LNS v Persons Unknown* [2010] EWHC 119 (QB) at [70]–[73].

9 See, for example, *Douglas v Hello! (No 3)* [2006] QB 125 (CA) at [105] (further publication of an intrusive photograph could be restrained); an interim injunction was refused where information had been very widely published: *Mosley v News Group* [2008] EWHC 687 (QB).

10 It is much easier to obtain an injunction in 'privacy' than in defamation: *Greene v Associated Newspapers* [2005] QB 972 (CA). Under the Human Rights Act 1998, s 12, a privacy injunction should not be granted unless the claimant is 'likely' to win at trial: see s 12(3);

Cream Holdings v Bannerjee [2005] 1 AC 253 (HL). The court must have regard to the extent to which the information is in the public domain and the extent of the public interest in its publication, as well as any relevant privacy code: see s 12(4). The *John Terry* case (n 8 above) was widely publicised after his claim for an injunction failed.

11 For more information, see Part 1 of the Second Report of the Select Committee for Culture Media and Sport 'Press Standards, Privacy and Libel' (24 February 2010). A report is awaited from the Committee chaired by Master of the Rolls (Lord Neuberger), set up in April 2010 to consider 'superinjunctions'.

12 For a list of awards, see Duncan & Neill, *Defamation* (3rd edn,2009) LexisNexis, Appendix 7, Table 2.

ROUND 4: THE HOUSE OF LORDS (THE SECOND TIME)

17.7 In May 2005, the House of Lords heard a second appeal by MGN, this time on the question of costs. Having lost the case, it was presented with a bill by Ms Campbell's solicitors for legal costs of over £1 million.[1] Since Ms Campbell's lawyers had acted on the appeal to the House of Lords under a conditional fee agreement (CFA), the fees claimed for that appeal of £288,468 were almost doubled by the 'success fee' (£279.981.35). Although the costs had not yet been 'assessed',[2] the newspaper challenged the success fee, as a matter of principle. That challenge failed: in October 2005, the House held that to require MGN to pay the success fee did not violate its Article 10 rights: [28], [57]. Given the important role of CFAs in promoting access to justice, finding ways of moderating the impact of the increased costs on defendants in media cases (with a 'chilling', if not 'blackmail', effect) would require a 'legislative solution': [37], [57]. At the time of writing, the question of legislative reform remains under consideration.[3]

1 *Campbell v MGN Limited (No 2)* [2005] 1 WLR 3394 (HL). The costs claimed for the trial were £377,070.07; for the Court of Appeal £114,755.40; and for the House of Lords £594.470.00; a total of £1,086,295.47: see [3].

2 On assessment, a party will recover only costs which were 'proportionately and reasonably incurred' and 'proportionate and reasonable' in amount: CPR 44.4 and 44.5 (similar principles applied in the House of Lords). As Lord Hoffmann helpfully observed at [4], the amount payable by MGN 'may' be lower than the sum demanded.

3 A (Labour) Government attempt in March 2010 (shortly before the General Election) to limit the success fee to a maximum of 10% passed through the House of Lords, but was not taken to the House of Commons. Proposals for reform are part of Jackson LJ's 'Review of Civil Litigation Costs: Final Report' (December 2009). During debate on 9 July 2010, Lord McNally (Minister of State) told the House of Lords that the new Conservative/LibDem Coalition Government was assessing those recommendations 'urgently' (cols 476–477).

DON'T FORGET: THE DATA PROTECTION ACT 1998

17.8 *Campbell v MGN Limited* in the Court of Appeal is the most important case for the media in relation to the Data Protection Act 1998 (DPA 1998). The DPA gave effect to a European Directive on Data Protection,[1] giving extensive rights to 'data subjects' in relation to their personal information, including rights to have access to data, to correct inaccurate data and to claim compensation for breach of certain provisions of the DPA.[2] Anyone 'processing' personal data must comply with the 'data protection principles' and other conditions specified in the DPA.[3]

The processing of data for 'the purposes of journalism' (one of the 'special purposes' in DPA 1998, s 3) is exempt from key provisions of the DPA 1998 under s 32, providing the processing is undertaken with a view to the publication of journalistic material and the data controller reasonably believes (i) that, having regard in particular to the special importance of the public interest of freedom of expression, publication would be in the public interest[4] and (ii) that, in all the circumstances, compliance with that provision is incompatible with the special purposes. This section seeks to strike a balance between the protection of privacy and the right to freedom of expression.[5]

The unduly restrictive approach of Morland J to the s 32 exemption – which would have left the media without any real protection – was overturned by the Court of Appeal.[6] It confirmed, crucially, that the exemption applies both before *and* after publication of the information ([120]–[127]) and that the exemption covered the act of publication itself:[7] where data becomes exempt as a result of the reasonable belief of the journalist that publication 'will be' in the public interest, 'the data remains subject to that exemption thereafter': see [128]–[129].

On the facts, the Court of Appeal was satisfied that the s 32(1) conditions were all fulfilled, so that Ms Campbell had no rights under the DPA 1998 in respect of the publication. On this point, at least, MGN had won.

1 Council Directive 95/46/EC on the protection of individuals with regard to the processing of personal data and the free movement of such data (see http://eur-lex.europa.eu). The DPA 1998 is notoriously complex (being described as a 'thicket' by MGN's counsel).

2 See DPA 1998, ss 7, 10, 12, 12A, 13 and 14.

3 See DPA 1998, ss 4(4) and 27; the data protection principles are set out in Sch 1; the conditions relating to 'personal data' in Sch 2 and those relating to 'sensitive personal data' in Sch 3.

4 There is a difference between the test for this exemption (and the defence for the criminal offence: DPA 1998, s 55), which depends on the 'reasonable belief' of the defendant that there is a public interest, and the test in a privacy case, which depends on the court's conclusion about public interest (see *Mosley* and *LNS v Persons Unknown*, cited in n 8 at **17.6** above).

5 For the approach of the ECJ to the balance between the right to freedom of expression and the protection of privacy under the Directive, see *Tietosuojavaltuutettu v Markkinaporssi Oy* (C-73/07) ECJ, 16 December 2008.

6 [2003] QB 633. There was no appeal on the DPA 1998 point to the House of Lords: [2004] 2 AC 457 (that claim was mentioned in passing at [32] and [130]).

7 The DPA 1998 applies to publication of newspapers (as hard copies, as well as electronic publication); 'processing' includes 'obtaining the information' at one end of the process and 'using the information' at the other end; so that the 'entire set of operations' falls within the DPA 1998: see Court of Appeal at [103], [101]–[106].

THE FINAL ROUND: IT'S NOT OVER YET

17.9 Having reached the top of the court system in England and Wales (twice), the domestic litigation had to stop. But this was not the end of the legal story. MGN has applied to the European Court of Human Rights, complaining that the decisions on liability and on costs violate its rights under Article 10. Its complaints are under consideration in Strasbourg. But there is, as yet (July 2010), no date for a hearing. Perhaps there will be a result before the tenth anniversary of the article.

SO, IN BRIEF, WHERE ARE WE NOW?

17.10 Everyone, including celebrities and other public figures, has a right to protect their private information. Whether the media can publish private information about an identifiable individual, without their consent, will depend upon an 'intense' scrutiny of the facts. The court decides where the balance is to be struck between the competing rights, Articles 8 and 10, by considering each item of information (including any photograph) to determine whether its publication is 'proportionate'. Media organisations, making decisions every day about what to publish, in books, articles and television programmes, have to try to second-guess what a court might think about the inclusion of any private information, particularly when there is a risk of an injunction.

As *Campbell v MGN Limited* shows, one person's necessary detail to explain a story is another person's unwarranted intrusion. Overall, five judges were in favour of publication, with four judges against. But the inclusion of the photographs led to the newspaper's defeat in the House of Lords, with liability to pay modest compensation and a massive bill for costs. The judgment of Strasbourg on the case is awaited but, whatever it decides, there is no doubt that there are more developments to come in the law of privacy – and more cases.

AND WHERE ARE THEY NOW?

17.11 Ms Campbell has continued to work as a successful supermodel. Stunningly beautiful still, she regularly hits the headlines for her activities off the catwalk (not least, her widely publicised community service). She has increasingly used her celebrity to do valuable charitable work.

Mr Morgan left the *Daily Mirror* in May 2004, sacked unceremoniously after a row over another high-profile story. But this was only to lead to the start of a new brilliant (and lucrative) career on television, as panellist on 'Britain's Got Talent' (and its American counterpart) and celebrity interviewer. And, yes, he has interviewed Naomi Campbell. The two appear to be on amicable terms and, in February 2010, they walked arm in arm down a London catwalk at 'Fashion Relief for Haiti'.[1] Like lawyers after a case, it seems there are no hard feelings.

[1] A fund-raising event organised by Ms Campbell after the devastating earthquake: as she said, 'It's just about bringing people together for something positive'. The event was widely reported, with pictures (including Ms Campbell and Mr Morgan on the catwalk), for example, http://www.dailymail.co.uk/home/moslive/article-1258631/Naomi-Campbell-I-didnt-think-I-make-40-Im-proud-Ive-done.html.

** The author has acted for Naomi Campbell (in Campbell v Frisbee [2003] ICR 141) and for MGN Limited (in various cases including Elton John v MGN Limited [1997] QB 586), but was not involved in any stage of Campbell v MGN Limited.*

V

THE RIGHT TO LIFE

Once again the issue of citizen and the state arises in this Part, in this case with what may uncontroversially be called the most important issue of all. The ultimate legal resolution in the cases of all three individuals considered in the chapters in this Part also devolved from another theme explored in Part I – the constitutional arrangements of the United Kingdom and, in particular, its relationship with Europe. At the heart of their cases lay the obligations of the United Kingdom under the European Convention on Human Rights, and the decisions thereon of the Court in Strasbourg. Among other things, that court has developed the obligation of contracting states under the Convention to undertake an effective investigation into deaths in certain circumstances.

18

'HOW . . . THE DECEASED CAME BY HIS DEATH'

R (on the application of Middleton) v West Somerset Coroner

Dr Karen Widdicombe

MORE THAN HALF HIS LIFE IN CUSTODY

18.1 In January 1999 Colin Middleton was 30 years old. He was also in prison. He had been in custody since 1982 when he had been convicted of murdering his niece, aged 18 months. His career in prison had been uneven; periods of progress had been interrupted by setbacks, some of his own making and some attributable to the hostility of other prisoners. After trial periods in open prisons in 1993, 1994 and 1996 he was transferred to HM Prison Horfield. He was receiving medication for depression. In November 1998 he harmed himself seriously. This led to the prison service raising a 'self-harm at risk' form. The form was 'closed' a few days later. On 11 January in the following year he wrote to the wing governor of the prison, referring to his 'mental illness' and his unhappiness. He spoke of suicide to another prisoner, who may, or may not, have passed on the information to the prison authorities. Three days later he hanged himself in his cell.[1]

1 *R (on the application of Middleton) v West Somerset Coroner* [2004] UKHL 10, [2004] 2 All ER 465.

THE RIGHT TO LIFE

18.2 Article 2 of the European Convention for the Protection of Human Rights and Fundamental Freedoms 1950 says that 'Everyone's right to life shall be protected by law'. That article imposes two obligations on the state. The first is an obligation not intentionally to take life and to take reasonable preventive measures to protect an individual whose life is at risk from the criminal acts of others or from suicide. The second obligation is one which the European Court of Human Rights has decided has arisen from the first; it is an obligation to investigate deaths where arguably there has been a breach of the first obligation. The suicide of Colin Middleton brought into focus, in England and Wales, the extent to which there is a duty on the state to conduct an investigation into a person's death where the question arises whether the state, exercising reasonable care, could and should have prevented that death.

DEATH IN PRISON

18.3 The Coroners Act 1988 requires that an inquest be held where there is reasonable cause to suspect that a person has died in prison; and in those circumstances (or where there is reason to suspect that the death occurred in police custody, or resulted from an injury caused by a police officer in the purported execution of his duty), the inquest must be held with a jury. The coroner has to adduce evidence 'as to the facts of the death' and the jury are to 'give their verdict and certify it by an inquisition' setting out, among other things, 'how . . . the deceased came by his death'. The Coroners Rules 1984 (rule 42) specify that:

> 'No verdict shall be framed in such a way as to appear to determine any question of—
>
> (a) criminal liability on the part of a named person; or
> (b) civil liability.'

Rule 36 provides that the proceedings and evidence at an inquest:

> 'shall be directed solely to ascertaining . . .
>
> (a) who the deceased was;
> (b) how, when and where the deceased came by his death;
> (c) the particulars for the time being required by the Registration Acts to be registered concerning the death.'

It goes on: 'Neither the coroner nor the jury shall express any opinion on any other matters'. At the inquest into the death of Mr Middleton, after all the evidence had been given to the jury, the coroner ruled that the issue of neglect should not be left to the jury. But he told them that if they wished to do so they could give him a note about any specific areas of the evidence which caused them concern, and he would consider the note, which would not be published, when considering the exercise of his power under rule 43 of the 1984 Rules, under which a coroner who believed that action should be taken to prevent the recurrence of fatalities similar to that in respect of which a particular inquest was being held could announce at the inquest that he was reporting the matter to the authority who had the power to take such action.

There was no dispute that Mr Middleton had committed suicide; the jury found the cause of death to be hanging and returned a verdict that he had taken his own life when the balance of his mind was disturbed. The jury did give the coroner a note which communicated its opinion that the prison service had failed in its duty of care for Mr Middleton. Mr Middleton's family asked that the jury's note should be annexed to the coroner's inquisition but the coroner refused that request. The jury's note expressed concern that the 'self harm at risk' form had been closed by two prison officers who had had no prior knowledge of Mr Middleton and it expressed their belief that his letter of 11 January 1999 to the wing governor contained sufficient indication to warrant another 'self harm at risk' form being opened.

PREVENTION OF SIMILAR FATALITIES

18.4 Exercising his power under rule 43, the coroner wrote to the Chief Inspector of Prisons, drawing attention to the jury's concern about the 'self harm at risk' form and to the jury's noting of 'a failure in the prison's responsibilities towards [Mr] Middleton and a total lack of communication between all grades of prison staff'. The coroner pointed out that, on the day before his death, Mr Middleton had not left his cell, even for meals, and had placed a rug all day over the inspection window into his cell.

JUDICIAL REVIEW

18.5 Mr Middleton's mother, Jean Middleton, brought a claim for judicial review of the coroner's decision. She applied to the court for an order that the jury's findings, set out in their note, be publicly recorded and that that there should thus be a formal public determination of the responsibility of the Prison Service for Mr Middleton's death. Her claim for judicial review thus raised the issue of whether the regime for holding inquests in England and Wales met the requirements of Article 2 of the Human Rights Convention. In the High Court, Mr Justice Stanley Burnton ruled that where there had been neglect on the part of the state, and that neglect was a substantial contributory cause of the death, a formal and public finding of neglect on the part of the state was necessary in order to satisfy the requirements of Article 2 of the Human Rights Convention. He granted a declaration that by reason of the restriction on the verdict at the inquest into the death of Mr Middleton that inquest had been inadequate to meet the procedural obligation in Article 2 of the Human Rights Convention. The Home Secretary – the minister responsible for prisons – appealed.

THE APPEAL

18.6 The Court of Appeal (Lord Woolf (the Lord Chief Justice), Lord Justice Laws and Lord Justice Dyson)[1] partly allowed the Home Secretary's appeal. They found that a verdict of neglect had to be available in order to be able to comply with Article 2, but they distinguished between individual neglect and systemic neglect. They set aside the judge's declaration and instead declared that in a case where (a) a coroner knew that it was the inquest which was in practice the way the state was to fulfil the procedural obligation under Article 2 and (b) a finding of neglect by the jury at the inquest could serve to reduce the risk of repetition of the circumstances, rule 42 of the 1984 Rules should be construed as allowing such a finding, provided no individual was named. Mrs Middleton appealed.

1 [2002] EWCA Civ 390, [2002] 4 All ER 336.

DECISION OF THE HOUSE OF LORDS

18.7 Lord Bingham gave the only judgment.[1] He introduced the issue as one concerning not the conduct of the investigation but its culmination and said that the consideration of three questions was necessary:

(a) what the Human Rights Convention required, by way of verdict, judgment, findings or recommendations, of a properly conducted official investigation into a death involving or possibly involving a violation of article 2;
(b) whether the regime for holding inquests established by the Coroners Act 1988 and the Coroners Rules 1984 met those requirements; and
(c) if not, whether that regime could be revised to do so, and if so how?

[1] The House of Lords gave a single judgment in the form of a 'report': 'a single text is prepared in the form of a report of the Appellate Committee and the House gives effect to that. That has been done, for example, in criminal cases where the argument is said to be that there is advantage in a very clear and uncluttered formulation to be used by judges directing juries'. See Andrew Le Sueur, 'A Report on Six Seminars About the UK Supreme Court' (December 2008). Queen Mary School of Law Legal Studies, Research Paper No 1/2008, p 29.

PRISON SUICIDE STATISTICS

18.8 Lord Bingham referred to the grim reading which the statistics of prison suicides made. While the suicide rate among the population as a whole was falling, the rate among prisoners was rising. Between 1990 and 2003 there were 947 self-inflicted deaths in prison, 177 of which were of detainees aged 21 or under. Almost two people killed themselves in prison each week. Over a third had been convicted of no offence. One in five was female (a proportion far in excess of the female prison population). One in five deaths occurred in a prison hospital or segregation unit and 40% of self-inflicted deaths occurred within the first month of custody. Those statistics, he said, highlighted the need for an investigative regime which would not only expose any past violation of the state's substantive obligations under Article 2 of the convention, but would promote measures to prevent or minimise the risk of future violations.

WHAT THE HUMAN RIGHTS CONVENTION REQUIRED

18.9 Lord Bingham concluded that a systemic failure to protect human life might call for an investigation which could be no less important and perhaps even more complex than an investigation into the use of lethal force by agents of the state, and that it would not promote the objects of the Human Rights Convention if domestic law were to distinguish between cases where an agent of the state might have used lethal force without justification and cases in which a defective system operated by the state might have failed to afford adequate protection to human life. He said that in England and Wales an inquest was the means by which the state ordinarily discharged its obligation to investigate under Article 2 and that to meet the procedural requirement an inquest ought ordinarily to culminate in an expression, however brief, of the jury's conclusion on the disputed factual issues.

WAS THE REGIME OF THE CORONERS ACT 1988 AND THE CORONERS RULES 1984 ADEQUATE?

18.10 Cases in which the inquest verdict did not express the jury's factual conclusion on the events leading up to the death did not meet the requirements of the Human Rights Convention.

HOW WAS THE REGIME TO BE CHANGED?

18.11 The word 'how' in the 1988 Act and the 1984 Rules ('how . . . the deceased came by his death') should be interpreted in future as meaning not simply 'by what means' but 'by what means and in what circumstances'. The prohibition in rule 36 of the expression of opinion on 'any other matters' had to be read with reference to the broader interpretation of 'how' and so it did not preclude conclusions of fact as opposed to expressions of opinion. But however the jury's factual conclusion was conveyed, rule 42 should not be infringed: there could be no finding of criminal liability on the part of a named person or any determination of civil liability. Complying with the Human Rights Convention did not mean that the coroner's power to make a report to the appropriate authority ought to be exercisable by the jury, but the procedural obligation under Article 2 would be most effectively discharged if the coroner announced publicly not only his intention to report any matter, but also, 'neutrally expressed', the substance of that report.

PUBLISHED TO THE WORLD

18.12 Lord Bingham said that the jury had not been permitted to express its conclusion on the crucial facts of whether Mr Middleton should have been recognised as a suicide risk and whether appropriate precautions should have been taken to prevent him taking his own life. There had been a full and satisfactory investigation and Mrs Middleton was not seeking another inquest. The conclusions of the jury, which she had sought to publicise, 'have been published to the world'.

'SO I SAID WHAT GIVES THEM THE RIGHT TO HIT A 14 YEAR OLD CHILD IN THE NOSE AND DRAW BLOOD AND THEY SAID IT WAS A RESTRAINT'

18.13 The practical effect of *Middleton*'s case can be seen in another application for judicial review of the inquest into the death of a person who died in custody some five years later.[1] Jean Pounder, who brought the claim, was the mother of Adam Rickwood, 'who has the mournful distinction of being the youngest person to die in a British penal establishment, at least in modern times'. Adam was found in his bedroom cell at Hassockfield Secure Training Centre on 8 August 2004, shortly before midnight. He had strangled himself with a shoe lace. He was 14 years old. He had a history of offending, self-harm, substance abuse and absconding from care. He had been remanded to the secure training centre on a charge of wounding with a knife and burglary. It was his first experience of custody. In his cell were found two documents; a farewell letter to his family and a statement complaining of his treatment at the secure training centre some six hours earlier. The evidence at the inquest revealed that in the early evening Adam and another inmate had been in their free association period outside their bedroom cells. A third inmate passed a note under his cell door to Adam. As a result of disobeying an order to hand it over, Adam was ordered to go to his own cell. He refused; he sat down and resisted requests to move. The training officer called a more senior officer whose attempts to persuade Adam to move were also unsuccessful. He made a 'first response' call for emergency assistance. Four more training officers arrived and Adam was physically removed. He was lifted off the ground and moved face downwards to his cell where he was placed on the floor. During that manoeuvre the officer holding Adam's head applied a 'nose distraction' technique: a 'short sharp movement applying force by fingers under the nostril against the counter-force of the other hand holding the back of the head'. It made Adam angry and upset and caused his nose to bleed. After he had calmed down he was allowed out of his cell again. He spoke to his solicitor. He was seen by a nurse who did not consider hospital treatment was needed. Later he went to bed and was last checked at around 9.30 pm when he seemed to be calm.

There were controversial questions at the inquest about whether the use of any physical restraint to enforce a staff order had been lawful, and whether any member of staff had been entitled to use a pain-compliant nose distraction technique on a child of Adam's age in the circumstances of his case. The rules of the secure training centre allowed physical force only to prevent a trainee from escaping, from harming himself or others, from damaging property, or from inciting another trainee to harm himself or others or damage property. They stated: 'Physical force will not be used for any other reason or simply to obtain compliance with staff instructions, it will be a measure of last resort'. Some of the staff apparently considered that the statute, which provided that they had the duty to ensure good order and discipline with the power to use reasonable force where necessary, took priority over the rules.

The coroner decided, at the end of the evidence, and before delivering his instructions to the jury, that it was unnecessary and undesirable for him to rule on the legality of the restraint used on Adam; all that mattered were the primary facts including the question whether any staff using physical restraint honestly thought they had the power to do so. Adam's mother, Carol Pounder, applied for judicial review of the inquest. The judge concluded that a proper inquiry into factors that might have contributed to Adam's death and formed a material circumstance as to 'how he came by his death', required consideration of whether the force used on him had been legitimate and whether the staff at the secure training centre had been operating in accordance with the law in their use of force on the children assigned to their care. A fresh inquest was ordered.

1 *R (on the application of Pounder) v HM Coroner for the North and South Districts of Durham and Darlington)* [2009] EWHC 76 (Admin), [2009] 3 All ER 150.

BY WHAT MEANS AND IN WHAT CIRCUMSTANCES

18.14 The addition of those four words, 'and in what circumstances' has had an abiding effect. *Middleton*'s case has been applied[1] and considered in many other inquest cases. Together with the developing law on the relation of independent public investigations and inquests in the context of Article 2 of the Human Rights Convention exemplified by *R (on the application of Amin) v Secretary of State for the Home Department*,[2] which was heard at the Court of Appeal stage together with *Middleton*'s case, the opening up of the coroner's inquiry has changed the public expectations about inquests involving the responsibility of the state. The Coroners and Justice Act 2009, in provisions to come into effect in April 2012, adopts the ruling in *Middleton*'s case about the proper scope of an inquest, and makes a coroner's report, and an official response to it, mandatory, where in the coroner's opinion action should be taken to prevent the occurrence or continuation of circumstances creating a risk of other deaths. And so Article 2 adds another stitch to the fabric of our national life.

1 See *R (on the application of Sacker) v West Yorkshire Coroner* [2004] UKHL 11, [2004] 2 All ER 487; *Re Jordan's Applications for Judicial Review* [2004] NICA 29, [2005] NI 144; *R (on the application of Pekkelo) v Central and South East Kent Coroner* [2006] EWHC 1265 (Admin), [2006] All ER (D) 472 (Jul); *R (on the application of Cash) v County of Northamptonshire Coroner* [2007] EWHC 1354 (Admin), [2007] 4 All ER 903; *R (on the application of Warren) v Northamptonshire Assistant Deputy Coroner* [2008] EWHC 966 (Admin), [2008] All ER (D) 393 (Apr); *R (on the application of Smith) v Secretary of State for Defence* [2009] EWCA Civ 441, [2009] 4 All ER 985; *R (on the application of P) v Coroner for the District of Avon* [2009] EWCA Civ 1367, 112 BMLR 77.

2 [2003] UKHL 51, [2003] 4 All ER 1264.

19

HOW THE LAW LORDS MADE WAY FOR A COMPASSIONATE CLARIFICATION OF THE LAW ON ASSISTING SUICIDE

R (on the application of Purdy) v Director of Public Prosecutions

*Lynne Townley**

INTRODUCTION

19.1

> 'Society has changed massively since the Suicide Act became law in 1961. Back then, abortion was illegal, and so was homosexuality. Man hadn't landed on the Moon. Martin Luther King hadn't had his dream. There hadn't been any heart transplants. Barack Obama hadn't been born, and there were many states in the US where a white mother wouldn't have been able to sit down to dinner in a restaurant with his black father. It's a different world now. Medical advances are keeping us alive longer than ever, but not necessarily with an acceptable quality of life. Dying is a fundamental part of being human, and it's time that we revisited a law that informs the way we spend the end of our lives. I'm not ever sure exactly what the law should say. With the arrogance of youth, I used to be convinced I knew all the answers and I was certain about what an assisted dying law should include. The more I've met people with real concerns, though, the more my approach has softened. It's not a black and white situation.'[1]

This chapter charts extraordinary developments in the law on assisted suicide as a result of legal actions instigated by two courageous women, Diane Pretty and Debbie Purdy. Both women had been diagnosed as having deteriorative and presently incurable diseases. Distressed by the suffering that their diseases might cause them to endure in future, they both wished to control how and when they died. Motivated by a concern that those who might assist them to end their life in accordance with their wishes (chiefly their loved ones), faced possible prosecution under the English law for assisting another to commit suicide, they sought clarification from the courts on whether a prosecution in the circumstances of their particular cases was likely.

1 Debbie Purdy, *It's Not Because I Want to Die* (2010) HarperCollins, pp 276–277.

BACKGROUND: THE LAW ON ASSISTING OR ENCOURAGING SUICIDE

19.2 The criminal offence of committing or attempting to commit suicide was abolished by section 1 of the Suicide Act 1961. Section 2(1) of that Act, however, provides for an offence of complicity in suicide. A person commits an offence under that section if he or she does an act capable of encouraging or assisting the suicide or attempted suicide of another person, and that act was intended to encourage or assist suicide or an attempt at suicide. The consent of the Director of Public Prosecutions (DPP) is required before an individual may be prosecuted. The offence of encouraging or assisting suicide carries a maximum penalty of 14 years' imprisonment.

DIANE PRETTY'S CASE (2001)

19.3 In 2001, the issue of the liability for complicity in assisting the suicide of another sparked mass-media interest when Diane Pretty's case came before the House of Lords. Diane suffered from motor neurone disease (an incurable, degenerative disease associated with muscle weakness affecting the voluntary muscles of the body). While her condition was at an advanced stage and her life expectancy was poor, her capacity to make decisions was not impaired. Diane indicated that she was frightened and distressed at the suffering and indignity that she would endure if the disease ran its course and she stated a strong wish to be able to control how and when she died so that she would be spared suffering and indignity. Bearing in mind that it was a crime under English law to assist another to commit suicide, Diane, through her solicitor, sought an undertaking from the DPP not to prosecute her husband, Brian, should he assist her to commit suicide in accordance with her wishes. The DPP refused and Diane sought to challenge that decision by way of judicial review, arguing that a blanket ban on assisted suicide interfered with her rights under the Convention for the Protection of Human Rights and Fundamental Freedoms 1950 ('the Convention'). On her behalf, it was argued that such a blanket ban breached, amongst other things, her right to life under Article 2, the prohibition on 'inhuman or degrading treatment' (Art 3), and the right to private and family life (Art 8).

The Divisional court, in refusing her application for judicial review, held that the DPP did not have power to give the undertaking not to prosecute and that the statutory prohibition on assisted suicide was not incompatible with the Convention. At the time of this judgment, Diane was paralysed from the neck down, her speech had become slurred, and her condition was deteriorating fast. Nevertheless, she had the courage to appear on television, describing how her greatest fear was that of eventually dying of suffocation. She went on to describe how she had suffered choking fits on a couple of occasions as a result of her illness and how she found them to be utterly terrifying. Her condition notwithstanding, Diane did not hesitate to announce that she and her husband intended to appeal.

19.4 In the event, the House of Lords upheld the judgment of the Divisional Court and concluded that there had been no violation of Diane's Convention rights in the particular case. Delivering the leading judgment in the case, Lord Bingham of Cornhill observed that 'no one of ordinary sensitivity could be unmoved by the frightening ordeal which faces Mrs Diane Pretty, the appellant'. His Lordship went on to outline the complexities of the wider issues surrounding the case and, most particularly, the limited role of the Appellate Committee of the House of Lords on the issue in hand (*R (on the application of Pretty) v DPP*):[1]

> ' . . . It is accepted by her counsel that under the common law of England she could not have hoped to succeed.
>
> In discharging the functions of the House, the Appellate Committee has the duty of resolving issues of law properly brought before it, as the issues in this case have been. The committee is not a legislative body. Nor is it entitled or fitted to act as a moral or ethical arbiter. It is important to emphasise the nature and limits of the committee's role since the wider issue raised by this appeal are now the subject of profound and fully justified concern to many people. The question whether the terminally ill, or others, should be free to seek assistance in taking their own lives, and if so in what circumstances and subject to what safeguards, are of great social, ethical and religious significance and are questions on which widely differing beliefs and views are held, often strongly. Materials laid before the committee (with its leave) express some of those views; many others have been expressed in the news media, professional journals and elsewhere. The task of this committee in this appeal is not to weigh or evaluate or reflect those beliefs or views or give effect to its own but to ascertain and apply the law of the land as it is understood to be.'

Diane and Brian Pretty thereafter complained to the European Court of Human Rights. The case was heard by the court in March 2002. By that time Diane's condition had deteriorated to such an extent that she had to travel to Strasbourg in a private ambulance, accompanied by paramedics and an intensive care nurse for the duration of the twelve-hour journey. By this stage, she could also only speak with the aid of an artificial voice synthesiser. The tragic issues in the case were put into context by Diane's husband, Brian. When he was interviewed by journalists outside the court, he remarked, 'It's very poignant that our very first trip abroad is to come here to argue for Diane's right to die'.

Diane was to be disappointed, however, when that court concurred with the judgment of the House of Lords, holding that that there had been no violation of her Convention rights, including those under Articles 2, 3 and 8 of the Convention. The court ruled that the right to life guaranteed under Article 2 could not be interpreted as conferring a diametrically opposite right, namely a right to die, and, that no positive obligation could be derived from Article 3 requiring the state to sanction actions intended to terminate life. In relation to Article 8, the court considered that, while Article 8 was engaged (because the applicant was prevented by law from exercising her choice to avoid an undignified and distressing end to her life which potentially constituted an interference with her right to respect for private life), the blanket nature of the ban on assisted suicide was not disproportionate and the interference with that right could be justified in a democratic society for the purposes of Article 8(2).

Diane, who had broken down and was in tears when she left the court, told waiting journalists that 'The law has taken away all my rights'. Sadly, Diane died in a hospice two weeks after that judgment was pronounced. Tragically, she had died in the way that she had most feared – having suffered breathing difficulties, she had choked and struggled for breath for a number of days before falling into a coma for a few days prior to her eventual death.

1 [2001] UKHL 61 at [1], [2].

19.5 When the European Court of Human Rights announced its judgments in Diane's case, scores of concerned individuals were watching with interest. One of them was the then 37-year-old Debbie Purdy, who had been diagnosed with primary progressive multiple sclerosis six years before. Debbie has admitted to being 'stunned' when she heard about Diane Pretty's case. She commented:

> 'I was watching the news when it was announced that someone called Diane Pretty, who was terminally ill with motor neurone disease, was taking a case to court asking the Director of Public Prosecutions to give her husband immunity from prosecution if he should ever help her to commit suicide. I was stunned. Couldn't people do that already? If not, why not? A whole new kind of worry entered my head.'

Horrified by the potential ramifications that the judgment in the Diane Pretty case could have on her own life, Debbie began to conduct research on the internet about what possible options were open to her, should her condition deteriorate to such an extent that she would seek to choose to end her own life. Initially, she came across The Voluntary Euthanasia Society (now called Dignity in Dying), but became frustrated when that organisation explained that it would be illegal for them to give her any practical information or assistance on the subject of assisted suicide.

Debbie was also dismayed when she made inquiries at the Dutch Embassy. While she had discovered that voluntary euthanasia was legal in Holland, it soon became apparent that this was not an easy option because there were strict residency requirements and voluntary euthanasia was only permitted in certain limited circumstances and open to patients who were registered with a Dutch doctor. Not to be put off, however, she continued to search for a solution. Debbie, who had a background in journalism and marketing, was eventually to become a board member of Dignity in Dying and she became heavily involved in the work of the organisation. However, it was to be another seven years before she was to make, what she refers to as her 'own little piece of history', when her own test case was to bring the issue of assisted suicide before the Appellate Committee of the House of Lords once again.

LEGISLATIVE INTERVENTIONS AND OTHER DEVELOPMENTS ON THE LAW ON ASSISTING OR ENCOURAGING SUICIDE (2003–2009)

19.6 In the intervening years after Diane Pretty's case and before Debbie Purdy's case came before the House of Lords in 2009, a number of other high-profile assisted suicide cases had resulted in growing public concern in respect of the law in that area. In 2003, the mass media first reported on the activities of 'Dignitas', a clinic based in Zurich, Switzerland, after a British man suffering from motor neurone disease, Reg Crew, had been helped to die there. In Switzerland assisting in the suicide of someone who is suffering and wants help to die is not illegal, provided that the assister's motivations are selfless. All patients are examined by a doctor to make sure that they have the medical condition they claim and to ensure that they are of sound mind in making the decision. If the doctor is satisfied on both aspects, the patient is supplied with a lethal dose of barbiturates, either as a drink or a drip (to be self-administered if possible).

Between 2003 and 2010, some 150 people from the United Kingdom had visited the Dignitas clinic for an assisted suicide. Some cases were high profile and caused particular public concern. One such case was that of Daniel James, a 23–year-old man who was accompanied by his parents in September 2008 to the Dignitas clinic to die. Dan was not terminally ill, but he had been left paralysed from the chest down following an injury sustained during rugby training a year earlier. Dan had tried to commit suicide unsuccessfully on three occasions before his parents reluctantly agreed to assist him to go the Dignitas clinic to be administered with a lethal dose of drugs. A member of the public made a report to the police about the actions of Dan's parents and, following an inquest, the case was referred to the DPP to consider a possible prosecution.

There had also been a number of reports in the media about horrific failed suicide attempts by terminally ill people. On the other hand, the Government was also facing increased pressure for a relaxation of the law on assisting suicide in the context of the terminally ill. In the United States assisted suicide had been legal in the state of Oregon since 1997, and more recently, in the state of Washington. Luxembourg had also recently introduced laws. In the United Kingdom, Lord Joffe had attempted to introduce a series of private member's Bills in Parliament on assisted dying for the terminally ill.

The Government's focus on the suicide law was to change somewhat, with attention being drawn to another aspect of the debate, which did not involve the terminally ill but which was equally concerning. The Government had commissioned Professor Tanya Byron to conduct research on internet safety, following a spate of suicides amongst young people where there was a concern about a possible link to suicide websites.

19.7 In March 2008, following the findings of the Byron Review ('Safer Children in a Digital World', published on 27 March 2008) which called for the law around internet suicide sites to be clarified, the Government expressed concern over whether the current suicide law was adequate to deal with the growing number of suicides amongst people where suicide websites may have been a factor. The findings of the Byron Review were echoed in a report by the Culture, Media and Sport Committee of the House of Commons.[1] A study in the British Medical Journal (published on 11 April 2008) also suggested that suicidal people searching the internet were more likely to find sites encouraging them to commit suicide than sites offering support. The Government then went on to announce that it would review whether the law in that area could be strengthened or clarified.

While the Government recognised that a fine balance had to be struck between policy pressures which appeared to be pulling in different directions, in September 2008 it announced its intention to simplify and modify the statutory language of section 2 of the Suicide Act 1961.[2] Thereafter the proposed draft amendments, contained in clause 41 of the Coroners and

Justice Bill were debated by Parliament.

Notably both the Rt Hon Patricia Hewitt and Lord Falconer tabled amendments to the Bill in order to provoke debate on the subject of assisted dying in the case of the terminally ill. Lord Falconer's amendment, in particular, aimed to add safeguards to the currently unregulated practice of people travelling abroad to be assisted to die by organisations such as Dignitas. While the amendments were defeated in the House of Lords, it was notable that more Peers voted on the issue than ever before and the amendment was defeated by a very small margin – a majority of just 8% of the vote.

Whilst the Coroners and Justice Bill was progressing through Parliament, the Royal College of Nurses (RCN) had taken the opportunity to consult its members on the issue of assisted dying, with a view to reviewing its policy position. The RCN had previously changed its stance from one of neutrality in 2004, to one of opposition. This decision was reversed as a result of the consultation. Over 1,200 responses were received – the majority of individuals supported assisted suicide (49%), however there was also substantial opposition (40%). The remaining submissions were either neutral on the issue (9%) or failed to record a position (1%). This stance was welcomed by groups such as Dignity in Dying and those campaigning for choice on the issue.

With effect from 31 January 2010, section 59(4) of the Coroners and Justice Act 2009 added section 2A into the Suicide Act 1961. The effect of this provision was threefold. It provides that a person may encourage or assist the suicide of another person in the following circumstances:

(a) they arrange for someone else to do an act capable of so encouraging;
(b) they encourage or assist another person even where it is impossible for the actual act undertaken by the suspect to provide encourage or assistance; or
(c) they threaten or put pressure on the victim.

These amendments to section 2A of the Suicide Act, which were designed to modernise the language of the statute and to make it clear that section 2 also applied to an act undertaken via a website in exactly the same way as it did to any other act, were welcomed by those lobbying for greater controls over websites promoting suicide and suicide methods. It would, however, fall to the courts to provide the same level of comfort to those lobbying for greater clarity on the law on assisting the suicide of a terminally ill person.

1 10th Report of 2007 – 8 session, published on 31 July 2008.
2 Written Ministerial Statement of the Parliamentary Under Secretary of State for Justice, Maria Eagle, 17 September 2008, Hansard Column 142 WS.

DEBBIE PURDY'S CASE (2008–2009)

19.8 Following the defeat of Lord Joffe's final Bill in Parliament, Dignity in Dying decided to support legal cases in order to test the law on end-of-life choices. The organisation first supported the case of Kelly Taylor, a seriously ill Bristol woman. When Kelly decided to withdraw her case in order to consider other medical options that might be available to her, Debbie Purdy's case first came under consideration. At the time, Debbie was a member of the board of Dignity in Dying. She gave her position much thought before agreeing to step down from the Board in order to be the subject of the test case. In the end she was persuaded by her concern that she did not want to end her life before she was ready just so that she could protect her loved ones. Debbie was also concerned that if she waited until her disease progressed to the stage where she was not capable of travelling to Dignitas by herself that her beloved husband, the acclaimed musician Omar Puente, may face criminal prosecution if he assisted her to travel there.

In April 2008, Debbie's lawyers issued judicial review proceedings against the DPP. Debbie's case was couched in different terms to Diane Pretty's case. While Diane had sought immunity from prosecution for her husband if he helped her to die, Debbie sought to review the failure of the DPP to promulgate a specific policy, in addition to the Code for Crown Prosecutors (issued under the Prosecution of Offences Act 1985 giving guidance on general principles to be applied, amongst other things, in determining in any case whether proceedings for an offence should be instituted) as to the factors to be taken into account when deciding whether a prosecution would be brought under section 2 of the Suicide Act 1961. On Debbie's behalf, it was argued that, in the absence of such a policy, the prohibition against assisted suicide interfered with her right to respect for private and family life under Article 8 of the Convention.

At the time, Debbie made the following telling observations about the large numbers of people upon which any judgment in her case could profoundly affect:

> 'By the time our case first came to court, on 11 June 2008, almost 800 UK residents had signed up as members of Dignitas. (You have to become a member before you can avail yourself of their services.) If all 800 of those people chose to die in the Zurich clinic, and each was accompanied there by two relatives, that could be 2,400 people who needed to know how decisions on prosecutions were made. Surely they had the right to know their position?'

Debbie has said that she was 'devastated' when her claim for judicial review was dismissed.[1] Debbie was granted leave to appeal to the Court of Appeal. In dismissing the appeal, that court considered that it was bound by the decision of the House of Lords in the Diane Pretty case to the effect that Article 8 was not engaged in such circumstances. The court, however, accepted that that decision was inconsistent with the later judgment given by the European Court of Human Rights in Diane's case. The court further ruled that if there had been an interference with Debbie's rights under Article 8, then it had been justified as being in accordance with the law. Debbie appealed and the case was set down to be heard by the House of Lords in June 2009.

In the interim, the DPP published a full list of the reasons as to why he did not consider that it would serve the public interest by prosecuting Daniel James' parents. The DPP stated that while there was sufficient evidence to mount a prosecution under the Suicide Act, it was not in the public interest to do so for a number of reasons. Dan had repeatedly said that he wanted to die and he had written a letter in which he had made his intentions very clear. It was also obvious that his parents had tried to change his mind on a number of occasions. The DPP also reasoned that, had the case gone to court, it was unlikely that a custodial sentence would have been imposed. Debbie Purdy viewed this as a sign of how out of step the Suicide Act was with public opinion, especially if, as she argued, the DPP was declining to use the legislation.

Debbie was sitting in the front row on the day that the House of Lords handed down its judgment in her case on 30 July 2009. The world media also watched as Lord Hope of Craighead delivered the leading judgment in the case. In allowing Debbie's appeal, the House of Lords held that the right to respect for private life under Article 8 of the Convention was engaged and that the DPP would be required to promulgate an offence-specific policy identifying the facts and circumstances which he would take into account in deciding in a case such as the instance case, whether or not to consent to a prosecution. Debbie and her supporters were delighted with the decision and they immediately took Debbie to a wine bar where they ordered a bottle of champagne to celebrate. Debbie told waiting journalists 'I've been given back control over my own life'.

The DPP immediately announced that it was his intention to issue an interim offence-specific policy identifying the facts and circumstances which he would take into account in deciding whether or not to consent to a prosecution under section 2(1) of the Suicide Act 1961 by the end of September. A consultation exercise would also be launched. Once the DPP had considered all the responses, he stated that he would decide whether, and if so, how to amend the policy. The CPS launched an 'Interim Policy for Prosecutors in respect of Cases of Assisted Suicide' and announced a public consultation on the same day on 23 September 2009.

The consultation document noted that the CPS had never prosecuted any individual for assisting a suicide in relation to suicides committed abroad, including the Dignitas clinic in Switzerland. It noted that it had considered eight cases in the ten years to September 2008 where the parties travelled or intended to travel abroad in order to commit suicide. It also made clear that the DPP did not have any authority to change the law but did have discretion to decide, in cases where there is sufficient evidence, whether a prosecution is in the public interest or not. All cases of suspected assisted suicide were, and would be, referred to a central CPS team, the Special Crime Division, which employed some of the most experienced prosecutors within the CPS.

The consultation, which remained open for a three-month period, received a substantial number of responses – over 5,000 in total. This was perhaps a measure of the level of public concern over the issue. Having taken into account the public responses received during the consultation, the DPP issued a revised Policy for Prosecutors on 25 February 2010. The Policy, in addition to confirming handling arrangements for such cases within the CPS in order to ensure uniformity throughout the country, listed the public interest factors tending in favour of and against prosecution in cases where there was sufficient evidence to support a charge of encouraging or assisting suicide.

Factors tending in favour of a prosecution included those where the victim was under 18 years of age, the victim lacked the capacity (as defined by the Mental Capacity Act 2005) to reach an informed decision to commit suicide, and where the suspect was not wholly motivated by compassion (eg where the suspect was motivated by the prospect that he or she or a person closely connected to him or her stood to gain in some way from the death of the victim). Factors tending against prosecution included those where the victim had reached a voluntary, clear, settled and informed decision to commit suicide and the suspect was wholly motivated by compassion. Debbie Purdy welcomed the revised guidance stating that:

> 'Clearly he [the DPP] had taken notice of the contributions to his public consultation and the new guidelines concentrated more on the motivation of the assistant, rather than the physical situation of the assisted'.

The debate, however, continues. While Debbie Purdy finds comfort from the CPS policy guidance and hopes for a cure for her illness one day, she says that she wishes that she could chose, if it came to it, to end her life at home rather than having to travel to Switzerland to do so. On 4 February 2010, the author, Sir Terry Pratchett, who suffers from Alzheimer's disease, gave the 2010 annual Richard Dimbleby Lecture which was broadcast on the BBC. His lecture, entitled 'Shaking Hands with Death', called for a pre-assisted suicide tribunal, whereby a group of appropriately qualified people would assess the physical condition, mental capacity and any external factors of someone wanting to choose an assisted death. Sir Terry even volunteered to be the test case for such a body.

1 *R (on the application of Debbie Purdy v Director of Public Prosecutions* [2008] EWHC 2565.

CONCLUSION

19.9 In the final analysis it was a judicial decision, rather than any legislative intervention, that would serve to provide those individuals and groups lobbying for a choice of death for the terminally ill with clarity and peace of mind. Ironically, the judiciary had found a way to do so without changing the law or interfering with the function of the legislature, about which Lord Bingham had expressed so much concern when delivering his judgment in Diane Pretty's case. The change in the scope of the case argued by Debbie Purdy's lawyers had made such a decision possible. The case stands as an example of the role of the courts in providing clarity, short of legislative intervention, on an issue of immense concern both to the litigants and to the public in general.

* *Lynne Townley is a barrister practising criminal law. Any views expressed in this chapter are entirely the author's own.*

VI

THE STATE AND TERRORISM

English law has occasionally had to deal with individuals whose potential or perceived threat greatly exceeds that of 'ordinary criminals', and perhaps inevitably its responses (seen, for example, in *Liversidge v Anderson* during the Second World War and the Diplock courts in Northern Ireland during the 1970s) have elicited much controversy.

In the twenty-first century, the issues are perhaps more complex than ever before, for at least two reasons. The first is the somewhat nebulous nature of the contemporary enemy which is modern international terrorism: strictly identifying Al Qaeda and its members is a formidable task for the authorities in the present day, arguably more so than other enemies of the British state in the past. The second reason concerns the international obligations the United Kingdom now owes, most notably in the form of the European Convention on Human Rights.

Relations with other nations is a further complicating factor as acutely demonstrated by the *Corner House* decision, where the somewhat less than seaworthy vessel of English bribery law foundered on the rocks of an allied state's objections to a criminal investigation.

20

THE COURTS AND COUNTER-TERRORISM: ASSERTING THE RULE OF LAW?

A v Secretary of State for the Home Department

Alexander Horne

> 'In this country, amid the clash of arms, the laws are not silent. They may be changed, but they speak the same language in war as in peace.'
>
> *Liversidge v Anderson* [1942] AC 206, 244, per Lord Atkins

INTRODUCTION

20.1 National security cases have habitually presented the courts with difficulties. In the past, it has frequently been suggested that the courts have been too reluctant to intervene when the Government has argued that the security of the nation is threatened.[1] Lord Atkins' oft quoted passage in *Liversidge v Anderson* was a striking statement, upholding the rule of law. Moreover, it is so famous that its timeless nature is regularly remarked upon.[2] Nevertheless, it is worth noting at the outset that his judgment was a lone dissent.

In reality, the case was one in which the House of Lords considered the interpretation of the wartime power conferred on the Home Secretary to intern certain persons[3] if he had reasonable cause to believe that they had hostile associations. As Francis Bennion put it, 'the question was whether or not the existence or non-existence of such reasonable cause was a question of fact into which the court could inquire in the usual way'.[4] By four to one, the House of Lords held that the crucial words should be construed as meaning, in effect, if the *Secretary of State* thinks *he* has reasonable cause to believe (leaving the judgment of whether there was a reasonable suspicion entirely for the Home Secretary). Viscount Maugham stated that:

> 'if there is a reasonable doubt as to the meaning of the words used, we should prefer a construction which will carry into effect the plain intention of those responsible for the Order in Council rather than one which will defeat that intention.'[5]

Subsequent deportation cases, such as *R v Home Secretary, ex p Hosenball*,[6] *R v Home Secretary, ex p Cheblak*[7] and *Secretary of State for the Home Department v Rehman*,[8] have demonstrated the courts' continuing reluctance to intervene in cases where the Government has claimed that its decisions were based on national security considerations.

In order to understand fully the context of the House of Lords decision in *A v Secretary of State for the Home Department*, it is first important to consider the impact of an earlier judgment of the European Court of Human Rights, in what was effectively an immigration case. In *Chahal v UK*,[9] the Strasbourg court considered the attempted deportation to India of Mr Chahal (an Indian national and Sikh separatist) on national security grounds. *Chahal* confirmed, in clear terms, the previous decision of *Soering v UK*[10] that it was unlawful, under the European Convention on Human Rights ('the Convention'), for a state to deport an individual to another state where they might be subjected to torture or inhuman and degrading treatment. In *Chahal*, the majority of the court affirmed the absolute nature of the prohibition on torture and inhuman and degrading treatment as applying irrespective of public emergency or terrorist threat and held, inter alia, that:

> 'The prohibition provided by Article 3 [of the Convention] against ill-treatment is equally absolute in expulsion cases. Whenever substantial grounds have been shown for believing that an individual would face a real risk of being subjected to treatment contrary to Article 3 if removed to another State, the responsibility of the Contracting State to safeguard him or her against such treatment is engaged in the event of expulsion. In these circumstances, the activities of the individual in question, however undesirable or dangerous, cannot be a material consideration.'[11]

This judgment, the ratio of which was recently upheld by the Grand Chamber of the European Court of Human Rights in the case of *Saadi v Italy*,[12] was to cause signatory states particular difficulties in the post-9/11 environment, where many suspected terrorists came from unstable or authoritarian regimes with dubious human rights records and therefore could not be deported to their country of origin with any assurance of safety.

Notwithstanding this decision, the UK Government's view appeared to be that the first priority of any Government was to ensure the security and safety of the nation and members of the public. Prior to the House of Lords decision in *A v Secretary of State for the Home Department* (hereafter 'the *Belmarsh* case'),[13] the then Home Secretary, Rt Hon David Blunkett MP, wrote an article in *The Independent* newspaper, entitled 'Freedom from terrorist attack is also a human right' arguing:

> 'What am I to do with those that the [security services] have indentified as a risk to national security? Ask the same security service to spend day and night actually tracking them, in the hope they will be able to stop them before a major tragedy occurs? I'm not going to gamble with people's lives.'[14]

The answer, at least according to the Government, was to be the indefinite detention of those suspected international foreign terrorists that it was unable to prosecute or deport. Blunkett stated that:

> '[I]t seems to us that when a third country cannot be found, holding such people – with proper rights of appeal and the opportunity for a return to their case – is

preferable to sending them back to certain death when their guilt has not been ascertained.'[15]

1 See, for example, Kavanagh, A, 'Judging the Judges under the Human Rights Act: Deference, Disillusionment and the "War on Terror" ' [2009] Public Law 287.

2 See, for example, the Australian case, *George v Rockett* (1990) 170 CLR 104 at 112, where it was described as 'famous, and now orthodox'. See also: Barak, A, *The Judge in a Democracy*(2008) Princeton University Press, p 287, where the author refuted Cicero's famous maxim 'Silent enim leges inter arma' (often popularly translated as ''in times of war, the law falls silent'), arguing that the statement was 'regrettable' and that he hoped that it did not 'reflect our democracies today'.

3 Under the Defence (General) Regulations 1939 (SI 1939/927), reg 18B.

4 Bennion, F, 'The Terrorists Should not be Allowed to Win' (2004) 13 *Commonwealth Lawyer* 36 at 37. See also Simpson, AWB, *In the Highest Degree Odious: detention without trial in wartime Britain* (1992) Clarendon Press, Oxford.

5 The judgment of the majority in *Liversidge* was recently criticised by Lord Bingham of Cornhill, a former Senior Law Lord, as one of which the country could not be proud. Bingham, T, 'The Rule of Law – The Sixth Sir David Williams Lecture', Cambridge, 16 November 2006 in Neate, F (Ed), *Rule of Law: Perspectives from Around the Globe* (2009) LexisNexis.

6 [1977] 3 All ER 452.

7 [1991] 2 All ER 319.

8 [2001] UKHL 47, [2003] 1 AC 153.

9 (1996) 23 EHRR 413.

10 (1989) 11 EHRR 439.

11 *Chahal v UK* (1997) 23 EHRR 413, para 80.

12 *Saadi v Italy*, Application No 37201/06,(2008) 49 EHRR 730, [2008] Crim LR 898.

13 [2004] UKHL 56, [2005] AC 68 (HL).

14 Blunkett, D, 'Freedom from terrorist attack is also a human right', *The Independent*, 12 August 2004.

15 House of Commons Debate, 15 October 2001, cols 927–28.

THE ANTI-TERRORISM, CRIME AND SECURITY ACT 2001

20.2 The Anti-Terrorism, Crime and Security Act 2001 (ATCSA 2001), described as 'one of the most dramatic and contentious measures introduced immediately after 9/11'[1] introduced a power to detain suspected international terrorists indefinitely, without trial, if their removal from the UK was prevented by legal obligations arising under international law (particularly of the type described above).

While the Home Secretary had said that he did not envisage withdrawing from the European Convention on Human Rights, in order to introduce the measures, contained in Part IV of the Act, the Government had to derogate from Article 5 of the Convention (the right to liberty), pursuant to section 14 of the Human Rights Act 1998. Article 15 of the Convention allowed states to derogate 'in time of war or other public emergency threatening the life of the nation', although any such derogation could only be to the 'extent strictly required by the exigencies of the situation' and 'provided that such measures are not inconsistent with its other obligations under international law'. This derogation followed under the Human Rights Act 1998 (Designated Derogation Order) 2001[2] in November 2001.

Detention under section 23 of the 2001 Act could be authorised in circumstances where the Home Secretary issued a certificate against a person on the grounds that he had a reasonable belief that the person's presence in the UK was a risk to national security and that he had a reasonable suspicion that the person was a terrorist, concerned in the commission, preparation or instigation of acts of international terrorism.[3] The regime[4] applied only to foreign nationals and the Act came into force in December 2001, only a few months after the Bill had been first introduced into Parliament. Vernon Bogdanor, Professor of Government at Oxford University, recorded that the Bill 'was debated for just 16 hours in the House of Commons, and for an even shorter time in the House of Lords' which he clearly considered 'insufficient time . . . for the proper scrutiny of legislation bearing so closely on human rights and personal liberties'.[5] Commentators argued that Part IV of the 2001 Act created 'the possibility of internment' since it provided for the indefinite detention without trial of non-British nationals subject to specified immigration controls and falling within section 21, if the Home Secretary decided to certify them.[6] Accordingly, it has been suggested that the 2001 Act was 'the most draconian legislation Parliament has passed in peacetime in over a century'.[7]

Appeals against certification were taken to the Special Immigration Appeals Commission (SIAC). SIAC had been established some time earlier, under the Special Immigration Appeal Commission Act 1997, following the aforementioned case of *Chahal*,[8] in order to hear cases where the Secretary of State had determined that persons should be deported on the grounds that it was conducive to the public good.

SIAC's rules of procedure allowed for special 'closed' hearings that would take place without the presence of the accused or his or her legal representative. Instead, a security cleared 'special advocate' would be appointed to represent the detainee's interests. Many of the procedures in the detention cases were modelled on this system. Concerns were expressed about this practice, not only due to the reliability (or otherwise) of the secret evidence, which the detainee would not have been entitled to see, but also as that evidence may 'have contained information or evidence supplied by foreign intelligence services extracted under torture'.[9]

The House of Commons Constitutional Affairs Committee observed that:

> 'The Special Advocate procedure was introduced as a response to the European Convention on Human Rights *Chahal* judgment . . . It introduced a measure of due process into the system of immigration decisions leading to deportation which had previously not been appropriately adjudicated upon. This process was severely tested when it was used for the detention of individuals under Part 4 of the Anti-Terrorism, Crime and Security Act 2001. It has been subject to a large number of legitimate criticisms, both from the Special Advocates themselves and human rights bodies.'[10]

Following the entering into force of the Act, eight men were detained and removed to high security prisons. A further nine individuals were subsequently taken, and the majority were held at the Belmarsh high security prison (some were later detained at Broadmoor Hospital, a high security psychiatric facility). Many of the individuals remained anonymous, referred to only by initials, however, it emerged that one of the suspects was Abu Qatada (frequently referred to in the press as 'Al Qaeda's spiritual ambassador in Europe'). Other suspects came from Algeria, Egypt, Tunisia and Libya. The legislation allowed for certification to be cancelled where the detainee wished to leave the UK and two of the suspects did depart, one to Morocco and the other to France.

Conditions in detention were criticised by non-governmental organisations (NGOs), despite the fact that there was a ministerial promise that, whilst in prison, the detainees would be treated as if on remand.[11] Particular complaints were made about prolonged solitary detention and access to family visits or telephone calls.[12]

Use of detention without trial was considered to be 'particularly emotive, because of the parallel incarceration of foreign nationals (including British nationals and British residents) by the United States at Guantanamo Bay'.[13] While this was a comparison that was strongly rejected by the Government,[14] it is said that, in February 2005, the Zimbabwean Ambassador remarked to Chris Mullin MP, a former Parliamentary Under-Secretary at the Foreign Office, that: 'we have the rule of law in Zimbabwe. We don't lock up people for years without trial, as you do in Belmarsh'.[15]

The legislation was reviewed by a series of Parliamentary Committees, including the Joint Committee on Human Rights and the Newton Committee. The latter, a committee of Privy Counsellors, reported in 2003. It observed that Part IV of the 2001 Act was ineffective, since it failed to deal with threats from British nationals with similar terrorist links. The Committee noted that it had 'been told that, of the people of interest to the authorities because of their suspected involvement in international terrorism, nearly half are British nationals'.[16]

1 Ewing, KD and Tham, J-C, 'The Continuing Futility of the Human Rights Act' [2008] Public Law 668 at 668.

2 SI 2001/3644.

3 ATCSA 2001, s 21.

4 For a fuller description of the system, see, for example, Walker, C, 'Prisoners of War All the Time', EHRLR 2005, 1, 50–74 at 54.

5 Bogdanor, V, *The New British Constitution* (2009) Hart Publishing, Oxford, p 56.

6 Fenwick, H, 'Detention without Trial under ATCSA', in Freedman, L (Ed), *Superterrorism – Policy Responses* (2002) Blackwell Publishing, p 91.

7 Tomkins, A, 'Legislating Against Terror: The Anti-terrorism, Crime and Security Act 2001' [2002] Public Law 205 at 205.

8 See n 11 at **20.1** above.

9 See, for example, Ewing, KD, *Bonfire of the Liberties* (2010) OUP, p 230 and Grief, N, 'The Exclusion of Foreign Torture Evidence: A Qualified Victory for the Rule of Law', EHRLR 2006, 2, 201–216. Such evidence is not meant to be admissible (*A v Secretary of State for the Home Department (No 2)* [2005] UKHL 71, [2006] 2 AC 221), however, question marks remain over how far the Government can (or is willing to) go to investigate whether material supplied by foreign security services was obtained by torture.

10 Constitutional Affairs Committee, 'The operation of the Special Immigration Appeals Commission (SIAC) and the use of Special Advocates', HC 323–I, Seventh Report of Session 2004–05, para 110.

11 Walker, C, 'Prisoners of War All the Time', EHRLR 2005, 1, 50–74 at 59.

12 Ewing, KD, *Bonfire of the Liberties* (2010) OUP, p 229.

13 Ewing, KD and Tham, J-C, 'The Continuing Futility of the Human Rights Act' [2008] Public Law 668 at 669.

14 Blunkett, D, 'Freedom from terrorist attack is also a human right', *The Independent*, 12 August 2004.

15 Mullin, C, *A View from the Foothills* (2009) Profile Books, London, p 537.

16 Privy Counsellor Review Committee, 'Anti-terrorism, Crime and Security Act 2001 Review', HC 100, 2003–04.

THE *BELMARSH* CASE

20.3 The detainees brought proceedings challenging the powers under the 2001 Act and the derogation order. The case was initially heard by the Special Immigration Appeals Commission, which accepted that there was a state of emergency (for the purposes of Article 15 of the Convention) but concluded the relevant provisions of the ATCSA 2001 were discriminatory (and in violation of Article 14 of the Convention) as they only applied to foreign nationals. That decision was subsequently overturned by the Court of Appeal.

Eventually, what was to become known as the 'Belmarsh case' (presumably due to the profusion of alphabetised case names in the counter-terrorism field, used in order to protect the suspects' anonymity) reached what was then the UK's highest court, the House of Lords, in October 2004. While the majority of the Law Lords accepted that there was a public emergency, by a majority of eight to one, they quashed the order allowing the derogation and declared the detention provision in section 23 of the 2001 Act to be incompatible with Article 5 of the Convention. The House of Lords ruled, in short, that the measures had not been strictly required by the exigencies of the situation, the interference with the suspects' Article 5 rights had been disproportionate and that the powers granted under section 23 of the 2001 Act were discriminatory.[1]

The case has been described as 'extraordinary',[2] not only because it was determined by a panel of nine Law Lords, but also as it is an extremely rare example of the courts interfering in a case where the Government sought to rely on national security considerations.[3] Lord Bingham (who gave the leading judgment) considered submissions by the Attorney General that:

> '37 . . . It was for Parliament and the executive to assess the threat facing the nation, so it was for these bodies and not the courts to judge the response necessary to protect the security of the public. These were matters of a political character calling for an exercise of political and not judicial judgment. Just as the European Court allowed a generous margin of appreciation to member states, recognising that they were better placed to understand and address local problems, so should national courts recognise, for the same reason, that matters of the kind in issue here fall within the discretionary area of judgment properly belonging to the democratic organs of the state. It was not for the courts to usurp authority properly belonging elsewhere.'

He rejected this argument, concluding that:

> '42 . . . The function of independent judges charged to interpret and apply the law is universally recognised as a cardinal function of the modern democratic state, a cornerstone of the rule of law itself. The Attorney General is fully entitled to insist on the proper limits of judicial authority, but he is wrong to stigmatise judicial decision-making as in some way undemocratic. . . . The 1998 Act [The Human Rights Act] gives the courts a very specific, wholly democratic mandate. As Professor Jowell has put it "The courts are charged by Parliament with delineating the boundaries of a rights-based democracy".'

Only Lord Hoffmann did not accept the Government's submission that there was a public emergency potentially justifying derogation. He competed with Lord Atkin in the rhetorical stakes stating that:

> '96. This is a nation which has been tested in adversity, which has survived physical destruction and catastrophic loss of life. I do not underestimate the ability of fanatical groups of terrorists to kill and destroy, but they do not threaten the life of the nation. Whether we would survive Hitler hung in the

> balance, but there is no doubt that we shall survive Al-Qaeda. The Spanish people have not said that what happened in Madrid, hideous crime as it was, threatened the life of their nation. Their legendary pride would not allow it. Terrorist violence, serious as it is, does not threaten our institutions of government or our existence as a civil community.
>
> 97. For these reasons I think that the Special Immigration Appeals Commission made an error of law and that the appeal ought to be allowed. Others of your Lordships who are also in favour of allowing the appeal would do so, not because there is no emergency threatening the life of the nation, but on the ground that a power of detention confined to foreigners is irrational and discriminatory. I would prefer not to express a view on this point. I said that the power of detention is at present confined to foreigners and I would not like to give the impression that all that was necessary was to extend the power to United Kingdom citizens as well. In my opinion, such a power in any form is not compatible with our constitution. The real threat to the life of the nation, in the sense of a people living in accordance with its traditional laws and political values, comes not from terrorism but from laws such as these. That is the true measure of what terrorism may achieve. It is for Parliament to decide whether to give the terrorists such a victory.'

This was clearly seen by some as an 'about face' from the position which he took in the previously mentioned case of *Rehman*,[4] where Lord Hoffmann reasoned, on separation of powers grounds, that the question of what constitutes the interests of national security is a matter for the executive, not the courts.[5]

The judgment of the majority was more nuanced. First, they determined that (applying, inter alia, the jurisprudence of the European Court of Human Rights) the Government had been entitled to conclude that there was a public emergency. This was treated as being almost a 'political question' and the court did not view the closed material which had been relied upon by the Government.

However, they decided that the derogation from Article 5 of the Convention was unlawful, as the measures taken to deal with it did not satisfy the 'strictly required' condition in Article 15. In particular, the court focused on the proportionality of the measures adopted.

The Law Lords observed that, while the Government accepted that the threat of international terrorism was not limited to the activities of non-nationals, the detention power was, noting that the appellants' argument on this point permitted 'little elaboration':[6]

> 'If the threat presented to the security of the United Kingdom by UK nationals suspected of being Al-Queda terrorists or their supporters could be addressed without infringing their right to personal liberty, it is not shown why similar measures could not adequately address the threat presented by foreign nationals.'[7]

They also considered that since the detainees were free under the Part IV scheme to accept deportation and to travel to third countries, such as France or Algeria, where they might further terrorist plots, it was difficult to discern that their detention was strictly required, since this form of detention equated to a 'prison with three walls'.

Lord Hope of Craigshead stated, in his judgment, that:

> '[I]t is an essential safeguard, if individual rights and freedoms are to be protected in a democratic society which respects the principle, that minorities, however unpopular, have the same rights as the majority.'[8]

This issue was also picked up by Baroness Hale[9] and Lord Bingham returned to it again in his book *The Rule of Law* (which he wrote following his retirement as senior Law Lord). He observed that the discrimination inherent in Part IV of the 2001 Act was 'a deliberate political decision'[10] noting that the Government had considered that it would be 'a very grave step' to detain British citizens in a similar way.[11] He echoed the famous observation of the American Supreme Court judge, Justice Jackson, that 'there is no more practical guaranty against arbitrary an unreasonable government than to require that the principles of law which officials would impose upon a minority must be imposed generally'.

The conclusions of the majority were, perhaps, validated only a few months later, when it emerged that the terrorist attacks on London on 7 July 2005 had been carried out by British nationals.

1 For a helpful summary of the reasoning and key points, see: Walker, C, 'Prisoners of War All the Time', EHRLR 2005, 1, 50–74 at 64–66.
2 Tomkins, A, 'Readings of A v Secretary of State for the Home Department' [2005] Public Law 259 at 259.
3 As n 2 above.
4 *Secretary of State for the Home Department v Rehman* [2003] 1 AC 153, paras 53–55.
5 For an interesting assessment of Lord Hoffman's judgment, criticising it on constitutional grounds, see: Dyzenhaus, D, 'An Unfortunate Outburst of Anglo-Saxon Parochialism in Cases: A v Secretary of State for the Home Department' (2005) 68 (4) MLR 654–680, at 673.
6 *A v Secretary of State for the Home Department* [2004] UKHL 56, [2005] AC 68 (HL), para 35.
7 Ibid, para 31.
8 Ibid, para 108.
9 Ibid, para 238.
10 Bingham, T, *The Rule of Law* (2010) Allen Lane, p 145.
11 Ibid, p 58.

THE AFTERMATH

20.4 Following the judgment, the Government did not immediately release the detainees (although they were released from detention within a few months). It did accept the Law Lords' declaration of incompatibility and swiftly repealed the relevant provisions. They were replaced with a new system of 'control orders' under the Prevention of Terrorism Act 2005. Hence, while the detainees were initially released on conditional bail, once their certification as 'international terrorists' had been lifted, they were subsequently placed under control orders. The representatives of some of the detainees described the process as 'chaotic' and demonstrating 'a complete lack of humanity'.[1]

The control order system addressed some of the concerns in the *Belmarsh* judgment, as it applied both to nationals and non-nationals alike. Described by critics as akin to 'house arrest', the regime initially allowed for extended periods of home curfew and a series of other restrictions, such as restrictions on association, communication, movement and occupation.

The new regime resulted in substantial further litigation, too extensive to be described here.[2] A certain irony, however, is that the legitimacy of the new control order regime was dealt a resounding blow by further consideration (by the Grand Chamber of the European Court of Human Rights) of the *Belmarsh* case. Shortly after the House of Lords decision, 11 of the detainees brought proceedings before the European Court of Human Rights, on the grounds that their circumstances had not changed (at that stage, eight remained in detention, while two had chosen to leave the UK and one had been released on bail conditions amounting to house arrest).

Before the Strasbourg court, the applicants sought declarations that:

> '[T]hey had been unlawfully detained, in breach of Articles 3, 5 § 1 and 14 of the Convention and that they had not had adequate remedies at their disposal, in breach of Articles 5 § 4 and 13.'[3]

The Grand Chamber ruled that the operation of the Part IV regime had resulted in breaches of Article 5 of the Convention and awarded the applicants some modest compensation (substantially lower than it had made in other case of unlawful detention – to take account of the fact that the scheme had been devised 'in good faith' in a situation where both the domestic and Strasbourg courts accepted that there was 'a public emergency threatening the life of the nation').[4]

In reaching its conclusion, the court considered (and approved) many aspects of the House of Lords decision.[5] During the course of the proceedings, the applicants raised the issue of the unfairness of the special advocate process (which had been directly transposed into the new control order regime). They argued that they were not told the case against them, and the special advocates were not permitted to communicate with them, once they had seen the secret evidence.

The court held that the evidence on which the state had relied to support the principal allegations made against some of the individuals had largely been found in the closed material and that the special advocates could not fulfil their function of safeguarding the detainees' interests in any useful way, unless the detainee was provided with sufficient information about the allegations against him to give effective instructions to the advocate.

The result of this was that in a subsequent case, *Secretary of State for the Home Department v AF (No 3)*,[6] the House of Lords felt obliged to follow the decision of the European Court of Human Rights in the control order litigation, by ruling that the use of evidence that was kept from a suspect could be unfair and in breach of human rights legislation, where it left the suspect unaware of even the gist of the accusations against him and he could not give effective instructions to his lawyers. The judgment appeared to leave this aspect of the Government's counter-terrorism strategy in disarray.[7]

It has been suggested that any forthcoming reform of the control order system should ensure that a strict time limit is placed on the use of any future control orders (for instance, 12 months without renewal) to ensure that the orders are not used for 'the warehousing of suspects'.[8] Instead, for example, Professor Clive Walker has proposed a period of investigation, with the aim of compiling a dossier, beyond which any restraint on the suspect should be based on criminal charges.

1 Ewing, KD, *Bonfire of the Liberties* (2010) OUP, p 239.

2 For a recent description, see: Walker, C, 'The Threat of terrorism and the fate of control orders' [2010] Public Law 4.

3 *A and ors v UK*, Application No 3455/05, (2009) 49 EHRR 625, (2009) Times, 20 February.

4 Ibid, para 252.
5 For a useful analysis, see: Shah, S, 'From Westminster to Strasbourg: A and others v United Kingdom' (2009) HRLR 9:3, 473–488.
6 [2009] UKHL 28.
7 See: Horne, A, 'Control Orders: Where Do We Go From Here', *World Defence Systems* (2009), Vol 1, p 172.
8 Walker, C, 'The Threat of terrorism and the fate of control orders' [2010] Public Law 4 at 16.

CONCLUSION

20.5 The tensions between the view that *salus populi suprema est lex*[1] and Benjamin Franklin's observation that 'he who would put security before liberty deserves neither', lie at the heart of the debate about terrorism legislation and the rule of law. The *Belmarsh* case did not settle this dispute, nor did it immediately provide a remedy for those detained. Keith Ewing has cited the Government's response to the case as demonstrating the 'continuing futility' of the UK's Human Rights Act. The repeal of Part IV of the 2001 Act resulted in the implementation of the controversial control order regime and a flood of further litigation. Furthermore, the end of the detention provisions appeared to coincide with an expansion of the use of secret evidence well beyond the anti-terrorism sphere.[2]

In those circumstances, when it could be said that the *Belmarsh* judgment was just the first of a series of skirmishes between the Government and the courts over counter-terrorism laws, why has it been described as 'one of the most constitutionally significant ever decided by the House of Lords'?[3]

First, it is important to recognise that, while this short essay has focused on the practical significance of the case, and its impact on the Government's counter-terrorism legislation, the judgment itself was complex and multi-faceted. As the *Modern Law Review* recognised, 'the ruling . . . illustrates the extent to which British constitutional discourse has become more nuanced and more complicated following the enactment of the Human Rights Act'.[4]

The *Belmarsh* judgment considered the relationship between the role of the Government, the legislature and the judiciary and contains, what Tom Hickman has described as an 'elucidation of the separation of powers' which he welcomed as 'an important statement of constitutional principle that properly affirms a commitment to the rule of law as understood in modern liberal democracies'.[5]

The decision of the House of Lords certainly has its critics, as some believe that it did not go far enough,[6] or that the court approved a too deferential approach to the issue of derogation.[7] None the less, as Bogdanor has observed, the judgment was very much in accord with the words of Winston Churchill on preventative detention, when he said that:

> 'The power of the executive to cast a man into prison without formulating any charge known to the law, and particularly to deny him the judgment of his peers, is in the highest degree odious and the foundation of all totalitarian government, whether Nazi or Communist.'[8]

This leaves us with a terrible challenge, since it is likely to remain the case that suspected terrorists, who cannot be deported or prosecuted will remain a threat, particularly in this new age of mass casualty terrorism. The UK Government has sought memoranda of understanding and diplomatic assurances with a number of regimes, with the aim of removing suspect foreign nationals, but this strategy is also under legal challenge[9] and has been criticised by human rights NGOs and others.

To end, in the language of another famous Englishman, William Shakespeare, we may all wish for a time in which we might claim:

> ' . . . Let us be clear'd
>
> Of being tyrannous, since we so openly
>
> Proceed in justice, which shall have due course . . . '[10]

For when a senior appeal court judge feels able to rewrite Kafka's *The Trial* to take account of the phenomenon of special advocates[11] one may fear the direction of travel.

1 The safety of the people is the supreme law.

2 See, for example, JUSTICE, Secret Evidence, June 2009 (available at: http://www.justice.org.uk).

3 Editorial, *Modern Law Review*, 'Cases: A v Secretary of State for the Home Department' (2005) 68 (4) MLR 654–680 at 654.

4 Ibid.

5 Hickman, T, 'Between Human Rights and the Rule of Law: Indefinite Detention and the Derogation Model of Constitutionalism', in 'Cases: A v Secretary of State for the Home Department' (2005) 68 (4) MLR 654–680 at 664–665.

6 Or at least that the Government's response to the case demonstrates that the courts are more of an irritant rather than an obstacle: see Ewing, KD and Tham, J-C, 'The Continuing Futility of the Human Rights Act' [2008] Public Law 668 at 691. See, also, Ewing, KD, *Bonfire of the Liberties* (2010) OUP, p 238.

7 Hickman, T, 'Between Human Rights and the Rule of Law: Indefinite Detention and the Derogation Model of Constitutionalism', in 'Cases: A v Secretary of State for the Home Department' (2005) 68 (4) MLR 654–680 at 663, 666–668.

8 Cited in Bogdanor, V, *The New British Constitution* (2009) Hart Publishing, Oxford, p 72.

9 *RB and OO v Secretary of State for the Home Department* [2009] UKHL 10, [2009] 2 WLR 512 and *Othman v United Kingdom* Application Number 8139/09, ECHR (judgment still pending at the time of writing).

10 Shakespeare, W, *The Winter's Tale*, Act III, Scene II.

11 Rozenberg, J, 'Judge Speaks up for Human Rights', Standpoint Blog, 22 October 2009.

21

THE DAY WE SOLD THE RULE OF LAW

R (on the application of Corner House Research) v Director of the Serious Fraud Office

*John Cooper QC**

INTRODUCTION

21.1 The laws in relation to bribery in the United Kingdom had been chronically neglected. So inadequate were they, the Organisation for Economic Co-operation and Development (OECD) Working Group,[1] were highly critical of the Government's attitude to the subject. The OECD Working Group on bribery is responsible for monitoring the implementation and enforcement of the OECD anti bribery convention, which establishes legally binding standards to criminalise the bribery of foreign public officials in International Business Transactions. In 2008, the Working Group was particularly damning of the United Kingdom in its failure to bring its anti-bribery laws into line with international obligations and began to put pressure on the United Kingdom to introduce new legislation. The Working Group also highlighted systemic deficiencies that emphasised the need to safeguard the independence of the Serious Fraud Office and simplify the procedure for potential prosecution.

This was not the first time the OECD had focused upon the United Kingdom's apparent disinterest in strengthening and clarifying the law relating to bribery. Since 2003 the OECD had been recommending that the United Kingdom enact new foreign bribery legislation at the earliest possible date. The criticisms were particularly acute, given the elevated position that the UK Government had placed itself in relation to the integrity and transparency of international relations.

It was perceived that there was more than a little hypocrisy upon display when administrations in certain African countries are condemned for the inadequacy of their response to fraud and corruption when one of the elite G7 Nations faced such graphic criticism over its own approach to bribery.

[1] OECD Working Group on Bribery in International Business Transactions, Report on the application of the Convention of combating bribery of foreign officials in International Business Transactions and the 1997 recommendations on combating bribery in International Business Transactions (16 October 2008).

CRIMINAL LAW REFORM

21.2 At a time when the previous Government was not reticent in creating new laws, it was perplexing why the law of bribery was so neglected. Putting the raft of statutory instruments to one side, creating a wealth of regulations ranging from nuclear reactors to the size of potatoes, the last Government was responsible for a prodigious amount of primary criminal legislation, some of it, to this day, yet to come into force.

Fundamental reforms to the law of hearsay, bad character, double jeopardy, disclosure and a wealth of procedural and evidential changes to the criminal courts have made the criminal law, over the last decade or so, the most dynamic discipline of all the legal specialisations.

In tandem with their root and branch reforms in the general criminal law, there have been complex and far-reaching reforms to the law relating to the proceeds of crime, hate crime, harassment and a completely new subject created under terrorism law. Yet amongst all this activity, bribery was left completely unreformed and in such a state which drew the sort of criticism articulated by the OECD. One could only speculate why this was so.

THE LAW OF BRIBERY

21.3 There is no doubt that from a political, public perception point of view, the significant change to the way children and vulnerable witnesses were dealt with in court and the strengthening of the law to protect society from paedophiles would be more popular than the rather dusty law relating to bribery. Of course, politicians are only reflections of the society that they serve and the lack of interest in considering the law of bribery as ripe for reform may lead back to the fact that, in the calendar of legal offences, the public do not feel that bribery was the most heinous of crimes. It is considered by many right-minded members of the community to be a victimless crime and, more particularly, one which did not involve violence.

For instance, supporters of a football team become significantly exercised over what players their team sign, but there is little reaction to the allegations that are sometimes heard regarding the behind the scenes payment to those involved in the transaction, or 'bungs' as they are called, which actually brings the players to the clubs. On a simplistic level, 'slipping' an individual a financial or other incentive to do, or not to do, something was just not considered to be that serious.

That, perhaps, is the reason, or one of the reasons, why legislatures have not been driven to change the law in this discipline. But bribery is more insidious than the above homely example. At an individual level, the victim of bribery can be placed in significant fear and suffer immense intimidation. The victims are often vulnerable and impressionable people. Bribery of low level officials and decision makers can result in worthwhile and valuable initiatives being halted or decisions being made which could devalue the quality of life of normal people in their community, such as inappropriate planning developments where they are not suited to be. Bribery at higher levels of government and in the international arena has proportionately even greater impact.

In the foreword to the Draft Bribery Bill, the Secretary of State for Justice, Jack Straw, continued to express apparent satisfaction in the general state of the law:

> 'Our current statutory criminal law of bribery is functional: cases are prosecuted successfully. However, it is old and anachronistic – dating back to around the turn of the twentieth century – and it has never been consolidated. Consequently, there are inconsistencies of language and concepts between the various provisions and a small number of potentially significant gaps in the law . . . the result is a bribery law which is difficult to understand for the public and difficult to apply for prosecutors and the courts.'[1]

In her paper entitled, 'Bribery: Corporate Liability under the Draft Bill 2009', Professor Celia Wells[2] observed that, 'it is hard to think that laws that are rarely invoked are functional'.[3] Strikingly, Professor Wells writes that the United Kingdom brought no cases of foreign bribery in 2007 while the United States managed 69 cases and Germany 43 cases. She adds that Transparency International notes that the United Kingdom is one of three G7 countries with 'little or no enforcement . . . showing lack of sufficient commitment to date'.[4]

The snapshot of these statistics reflects poorly upon a country which signed the convention on combating bribery of public officials in international business transactions as far back as 17 December 1997. It was into this vacuum of disinterest on behalf of both the legislature and law enforcement agencies and their disinclination to enforce the law of bribery that the circumstances of the Saudi Al Yamamah arms sale came into play.[5]

1 Ministry of Justice, Bribery: Draft Legislation 2009, Cm 7570.
2 *Criminal Law Review*, Issue 7 (2009) p 479.
3 At p 480.
4 Transparency International Progress Report on Enforcement of OECD Convention 2008.
5 *R (on the application of Corner House Research) v Director of the Serious Fraud Office* [2008] UKHL 60, [2008] EWHC 246 (Admin).

THE AL YAMAMAH ARMS SALE

21.4 The Al Yamamah contract was a valuable arms contract between Her Majesty's Government and the Kingdom of Saudi Arabia for which BAE Systems was the main contractor. Within the contract was a confidentiality clause which bound both UK and Saudi governments. The close relationship between the United Kingdom and Saudi regimes was, and continues to be, well documented and one can only imagine the sensitivity and delicacy that needed to be exercised in the drafting of this important contract; importance which spread beyond the commercial into the political lives of both nations. It was certainly not the sort of document that either party intended to be examined on a public platform, let alone in a court of law.

A critical part of the contract provided for the supply of Typhoon aircraft and between 2004–2006 was the subject of complex negotiation. During this time the Serious Fraud Office[1] were investigating allegations of corrupt payments, allegedly made by BAE in connection with the contract.

By virtue of the Criminal Justice Act 1987, the Serious Fraud Office may investigate any suspected offence, which appears to them on reasonable grounds to involve serious or complex fraud.[2] The Director of the Serious Fraud Office may, if he thinks fit, conduct any such investigations in conjunction either with the police or any other person who is, in the opinion of the Director, a proper person to be concerned in it.[3] This investigation not only included lawyers from the Serious Fraud Office, but also aligned a formidable team of accountants, financial investigators and police officers.

On 14 October 2005, the investigation team required BAE to disclose details of payments to agents and consultants in connection with the Al Yamamah contract. In less than a month BAE had written to the Attorney General, Lord Goldsmith QC, in a communication marked 'Strictly Private and Confidential'. The essence of this document was soon to be anything but private and confidential. BAE asserted that disclosure of the required information would adversely effect relations between the United Kingdom and Saudi Arabia and jeopardise the Al Yamamah contract because the Saudis would regard it as a serious breach of confidentiality by BAE and the United Kingdom Government.

The position taken by BAE was, in the view of the Serious Fraud Office, in breach of Article 5 of the OECD Convention on Bribery which states:

> 'Investigation and prosecution of the bribery of a foreign public official shall be subject to the applicable rules and principles of each Party. They shall not be influenced by considerations of national economic interest, the potential effect upon relations with another State or the identity of the natural or legal person involved.'

By mid-November 2005, the Permanent Under Secretary of State at the Ministry of Defence, Sir Kevin Tebbit, had contacted the Director of the Serious Fraud Office to inform him that, in his view, the Serious Fraud Office investigation into alleged bribery created a serious risk of damage to important aspects of the United Kingdom's relationship with Saudi Arabia. It was at this stage that the advice of the Attorney General was sought. Lord Goldsmith, with the agreement of the Director of the Serious Fraud Office, invited the views of other government ministers as to whether it would be contrary to the public interest for the investigations into the contract to proceed. The importance of this step should not be underestimated; effectively the Attorney General and the Director were eliciting advice as to whether or not it was in the public interest to prosecute a case where in the normal course of events there was sufficient evidence to do so, usually assessed as a 50/50 chance of success.[4]

One of the vital issues raised during this exercise was the importance of the commercial relationship between the United Kingdom and Saudi Arabia and also the significance of that relationship in the context of national security, counter terrorism and the search for stability in the Middle East. Interestingly, Saudi Arabia was described as 'a key partner in the fight against Islamic terrorism'.[5]

It was here that the battle lines were drawn. On the one side of the argument was the view championed by the Serious Fraud Office with the root of its argument embedded in Article 5 of the OECD Convention. The Serious Fraud Office and its investigative partners had a reasonable belief that a crime had been committed and felt obliged to investigate all reasonable lines of enquiry both in accordance with domestic law and international obligations. The position of the law enforcement authorities was that Article 5 of the Convention envisaged an independent role for law enforcement outside of economic or political considerations. Fundamentally, there was a public interest in the rule of law, which must be balanced against economic and political consequences. For the law enforcement authorities, the stakes were high. At risk, was the integrity of the rule of law and the importance of criminal investigation where there was proper suspicion that offences may have been committed. But it went further than this for the Serious Fraud Office and their partners. At stake here, was the very independence of the law enforcement agencies.

On the other side of the argument were those who genuinely held the belief that not only would commercial relationships with the Saudis be damaged but also, and perhaps more critically, that the important axis of co-operation between the UK and Saudi Arabia in the so-called war on terror would be severely compromised.

In early January 2006, the Attorney General concluded that it was in the public interest for the investigation to continue. The next phase of that investigation involved an examination of bank accounts in Switzerland to ascertain whether payments had been made to an agent or public official of Saudi Arabia. Having failed to influence the decision towards the end of 2005, the Saudi authorities reacted directly. They threatened that if the Al Yamamah investigation were continued, Saudi Arabia would:

- withdraw from the existing bi-lateral counter-terrorism co-operation arrangements with the United Kingdom;
- withdraw co-operation with the United Kingdom in relation to its strategic objectives in the Middle East; and
- end the negotiations then in train for the procurement of Typhoon aircraft.

This was a signal to the UK Government which bolstered the explicit threats being made by the Saudi regime. The United Kingdom Prime Minister, Tony Blair, concluded that the recent developments had given rise to a real and immediate risk of a collapse in UK/Saudi security, intelligence and diplomatic co-operation which was likely to have seriously negative consequences for the UK public interest in terms of their national security and the United Kingdom's highest priority foreign policy objectives in the Middle East.

Although expressing strong support for the OECD Convention, the Prime Minister was clearly putting this secondary to national interest. The ratchet was significantly tightened when the United Kingdom's Ambassador to Saudi Arabia confirmed that, should the investigation into the Al Yamamah contract continue, then British lives would be at risk.

In a direct conflict between the effectiveness of the rule of law and commercial and political considerations focused around national security, with the so-called war of terror reaching its peak, there was always, and only ever going to be, one winner.

21.4 *The Day We Sold the Rule of Law*

For many the perceived threat by the Saudis had finally achieved its objectives, supported by the United Kingdom's Ambassador to Saudi Arabia and by influential figures in the Cabinet including the Prime Minister, the pressure seemed to tell upon the Director of the Serious Fraud Office. Lord Goldsmith, the Attorney General, changed his position and began to doubt the overall strength of the prosecution case and ultimately the investigation into the Al Yamamah contract was halted.

1 Established by the Criminal Justice Act 1987, s 1(1).
2 See Criminal Justice Act 1987, s 1(3).
3 See Criminal Justice Act 1987, s 1(4).
4 This exercise is known as the Shawcross exercise, based on a statement by Sir Hartley Shawcross QC, the Attorney General in the House of Commons on 29 January 1951.
5 Cabinet Secretary's note to the Attorney General (16 December 2005).

IMPACT OF THE CLOSURE OF THE INVESTIGATION

21.5 In many quarters the integrity of the criminal justice system had been severely impugned. The inherent constitutional principle of separation of powers giving the courts absolute integrity from the executive had been challenged and, on the face of it, the executive had prevailed. Had the same actions been taken by an individual, then that person,would have been liable to prosecution for attempting to pervert the course of justice.[1]

The Constitutional Reform Act 2005 observed that the rule of law amounted to nothing if it failed to constrain overweening power. For many, there could be no better example of the rule of law being so usurped than the power and influence of the Saudi government forcing a statutory investigative authority in the United Kingdom to halt a bona fide investigation. In surrendering to the threat from the Saudis, it would be argued that the Director of the Serious Fraud Office, although exercising independent judgement, had completely capitulated to the perceived intimidation.

1 See *R v Selvage and Morgan* [1982] QB 372, 73, where it was held that in order to lay a charge of attempting or conspiring to pervert the course of public justice, a course of justice must have been embarked upon in the sense that proceedings of some kind are in being or imminent or investigations which could or might bring proceedings about are in progress. Even if an investigation establishes in due course that no offence has been committed, the enquiry is still part of the administration of justice.

CORNER HOUSE RESEARCH

21.6 It was not until November 2007 that the courts were seized of this controversial issue, in a case which was to decide between the constitutional requirements of the rule of law and commercial and political imperatives. For some, the issue was more blunt: could a foreign regime bribe or attempt to bribe an independent law enforcement authority in the United Kingdom so as to discontinue a sustainable prosecution?

The action, in the form of a judicial review, was brought by Corner House Research.[1] Founded in 1997, The Corner House has supported democratic and community movements for environmental and social justice in campaigns ranging from disputes over land or water rights, damaging mining, dam or forestry projects or struggles against racial discrimination. The organisation is a not for profit company limited by guarantee under the United Kingdom law. It presented its outline skeleton arguments to the High Court on 9 November 2007.[2]

The Divisional Court ruled that there could be no integrity in the role of the court to protect the rule of law if they abdicated responsibility as a result of a threat from a foreign power.[3] The court was also of the opinion that further steps could have been reasonably taken, to divert the threat.[4] In short, there had been no sufficient appreciation of the damage to the rule of law caused by submission to the Saudi threat, which had been directed squarely at the administration of justice in the United Kingdom. Lord Justice Moses was driven to the conclusion that the Director's submission to the threat was unlawful.[5]

So it was that the case found itself before the House of Lords. Immediately the court stressed that the Director of the Serious Fraud Office is entrusted with discretionary powers to investigate suspected offences which reasonably appear to him to involve serious or complex fraud and to prosecute in such cases. The court made the analogy with the position of the Director of Public Prosecutions. This analogy brought with it the recognition by the House of Lords that although both individuals were not immune from review, discretionary decisions made by them would only be overturned in highly exceptional cases.[6] In essence, the issue before the House of Lords was not whether the Director's decision was right or wrong, nor whether the Divisional Court or the House of Lords agreed with it, but whether it was a decision which the Director was lawfully entitled to make.

Indeed, at para 41 of the House of Lords' judgment, the court accepted that the threat from the Saudis was 'an ugly and obviously unwelcome threat.' But this, in the view of a strong tribunal in the House of Lords, was not to the point. They were of the view that the Director's decision was one which he was entitled to make. They went on to say that they doubted whether a reasonable decision maker could, on the facts before the Director, have decided otherwise.[7]

The decision in the House of Lords was firmly based upon judicial review principles. The law relating to judicial review is closely defined and governed by the *Wednesbury* reasonableness principles.[8] Put another way, although the tribunal may not agree with the decision, it is the process undertaken by the decision maker, which will be subject to scrutiny and if that process cannot be considered unreasonable to the high threshold contained within judicial review law, then the decision will stand. Effectively, a judge can say, 'It may not be the decision I would have made, but it cannot be impugned'.

An analysis of the *Corner House Research* case is not complete without a consideration of its approach to Article 5 of the OECD Convention. It was common ground in the House of Lords that the Director had ignored Article 5 and the court considered the status of an unincorporated treaty provision which did not stand in domestic law.[9]

Their Lordships did not decide the question as to whether when an individual, such as the Director in this case, purported to act consistently with an unincorporated treaty, the court can then review the compatibility of the decision with the treaty.[10]

1 *R (on the application of Corner House Research and another) v Director of Serious Fraud Office (BAE Systems plc, interested party)* [2008] 4 All ER 927.

2 The skeleton addressed the reasons given by a High Court Judge in May 2007 in refusing to grant a Judicial Review.

3 See para 76 of the Divisional Court Judgment.

4 See paras 86–88 of the Divisional Court Judgment.

5 See para 102 of the Divisional Court Judgment.

6 See para 30 of the House of Lords Judgment.

7 Para 42 of the House of Lords Judgment.

8 *Associated Provincial Picture Houses v Wednesbury Corporation* [1948] 1 KB 223 – see further, Chapter 3.

9 Despite this the Director, in argument and publicly, claimed to be acting in accordance with Article 5.

10 See *R v Secretary of State for the Home Department, ex p Launder* [1997] 1 WLR 839 (HL) and *R v Director of Public Prosecutions, ex parte Kebiline* [2000] 2 AC 326.

THE IMPACT OF CORNER HOUSE ON UK BRIBERY LAW

21.7 There can be little doubt that upon proper legal construction, the decision in *Corner House* was correct. The Director had acted perfectly properly in accordance with his discretion. However, the efficacy of the United Kingdom's bribery laws did not come out so well.

The problem was perhaps flagged by Baroness Hale of Richmond in the House of Lords' judgment.[1] She stated that:

> 'I confess that I would have liked to be able to uphold the decision (if not every aspect of the reasoning) of the Divisional Court. It is extremely distasteful that an independent public official should feel himself obliged to give way to threats of any sort. The Director clearly felt the same when he resisted the extreme pressure under which he was put for as long as he could. The great British public may still believe that it was the risk to British commercial interests which caused him to give way, but the evidence is quite clear that this was not so. He only gave way when he was convinced that the threat of withdrawal of Saudi security co-operation was real and that the consequences would be an equally real risk to "British lives on British streets". The only question is whether it was lawful for him to take this into account.'

That ruling was given in the House of Lords on 20 July 2008. On 20 November of that year the Law Commission published its Final Report on bribery. Their recommendations included replacing the existing law with two general offences of bribery and one specific offence of bribing a foreign public official. The Law Commission described the law of bribery as 'riddled with uncertainty and in need of rationalisation'.[2]

The new Act replaces common law and statutory offences dating back to 1889 with the two general offences and an additional offence of bribing a foreign public official. The new general offences encompass active and passive bribery. Active bribery occurs where a person offers, promises or gives financial or other advantage to another intending to induce a person to act improperly in relation to a public or business activity or knowing or believing that the acceptance would constitute improper performance. Passive bribery is where the person requests, agrees to receive or accepts a financial advantage intending that an activity will be improperly performed by him or any other person or knows or believes that the acceptance would constitute improper performance.

The bribery of foreign public officials occurs where an individual bribes a foreign public official with the intention of influencing that individual in their capacity as such an official with the bribery intending to obtain or retain a business advantage.

Whilst the pressure for reform of the United Kingdom's bribery laws was well in train before the Al Yamamah saga, the unfolding facts of the case before the Divisional Court, and then ultimately the House of Lords, could not but have provided extra initiative in legislative circles for the significant rationalisation and upheaval of our bribery laws which now appear in the new Bribery Act.

1 See para 52 of the House of Lords' Judgment.

2 Law Commission Reforming Bribery, No 313, November 2008, para 1.1.

CONCLUSION

21.8 The *Corner House* case will be viewed from various perspectives. Initially, and in its high season, it was the battleground between the rule of law and the challenge of the executive to the courts. The independence of power, a staple lesson for any first-year law student and dating back to the Act of Settlement, was at the heart of that conflict.[1]

The case also became synonymous with the height of the 'war on terror' hysteria both in government, media and public circles and should be seen in context with the draconian and, at times, illegal legislation being passed by the Government.

But more reflectively, the *Corner House* case illustrated the poor performance of the United Kingdom in the prosecution of foreign bribery cases and its conflict with OECD Convention parameters.

It is hoped that the next *Corner House*, if there is one, will be in the context of modern and effective United Kingdom bribery law legislation.

1 See Sir Ivor Jennings, *The Law and the Constitution* (1976) Hodder and Stoughton, p 18.

* *The author is a barrister at 25 Bedford Row London.*

VII

FAMILY LAW

The first two chapters in this Part concern the division of property between married or co-habiting couples. Obviously the law in this area involves rather more than simply the allocation of money and property; it reflects, occasionally belatedly, changes in social attitudes. In the late 1970s, Basil Fawlty* was apoplectic at the thought of an unmarried couple staying in the same room in his hotel. Even if some of the humour of the episode was directed at Basil for his old fashioned views, it would never have worked had it not been plausible for 1970s viewers that someone might openly share Mr Fawlty's values. It is fairly safe to assume, therefore, that Mr Fawlty would not have approved of unmarried couples seeking legal enforcement of property rights as in *Stack v Dowden*. Indeed, the law regarding married couples' rights itself has undergone significant transformation over the years, in line with changing social attitudes, as reflected in cases such as *White v White*.

Occasionally litigants' names become part of legal parlance for precisely the opposite reason to that which they intended. The unfortunate claimant husband in *Scott v Scott* [1911–13] All ER Rep 1 went to court hoping to keep his marital issues quiet; instead, his failed appeal to the House of Lords remains the leading statement on the common law principle of open justice almost a century later. A similarly ironic fate was shared by Mrs Gillick, the (unsuccessful) claimant in the final chapter in this Part. Objecting to doctors treating her teenage daughter without her consent, the phrase *Gillick*-competence has become standard legal shorthand for the test for whether a child is competent to give consent to medical treatment independently of his or her parents.

* *A reference to one of the most popular television programmes in English history*

22

IS IT THAT SIMPLE?

Stack v Dowden and Buying a House Together

His Honour Judge Stephen Wildblood QC

INTRODUCTION

22.1 What are the property rights of people who live together but do not marry (or engage in a civil partnership)? Many countries have a statutory scheme that deals with this issue. For instance, in New Zealand such issues are generally dealt with under the Property (Relationships) Act 1976, as amended. In England and Wales there is no such statutory code and so separating cohabitees have to rely on the vagaries of the law of trusts. This leads to immense difficulties and uncertainty. It can also lead to very expensive litigation. However, the attempts that have been made to introduce a statutory code have foundered; for instance a Cohabitation Bill has got stuck on 30 April 2009 when it reached the committee stage in the House of Lords.

As a result, the House of Lords (now replaced by the Supreme Court) has given a number of lengthy and conceptualised judgments. *Pettitt v Pettitt*,[1] *Gissing v Gissing*[2] and *Lloyds Bank v Rosset*[3] were the first three. However, the cherry on the cake has now been provided by *Stack v Dowden*.[4]

Before the case was decided two important issues needed to be resolved. First, in order to succeed in claiming a share in a house where there is no express declaration of trust, what does the person claiming the share in it have to prove? Once a person has provided that he or she has an interest in a property, how should the court assess the size of that interest?

The answer of the majority in the House of Lords is that a claim to a share in a house should be based primarily on the common intention of the parties. Thus a person may claim a share in a house (where there is no declaration of trust) if the parties intended that they should both have an interest in it. Progressively, the House of Lords held that the necessary common intention could be found to exist not only on the basis of express evidence or inference from conduct, but also by the court imputing to the parties the intention that they should have formed.

In deciding upon the size of the shares of the parties' interests, the House of Lords said that the court should take a holistic view and should carry out a survey of the whole course of dealing between the parties. Thus the importance of the case is that it sets down the tests that a court must apply when considering upon the property rights of people who have been involved together in a property and have not defined their property rights in formal legal documents. This will apply to many people who live together outside marriage or civil partnership. Although the case clarifies the law as it must be applied, the reliance that it is placed upon the common intention of the parties does very little to achieve certainty for those who are trying to sort out their rights at the time of a relationship breakdown. The one point that does create some greater certainty is that the House of Lords stated that the starting point is that the interests in a property will follow the legal title (eg joint legal title = joint ownership) unless the person making the claim proves otherwise.

1 [1969] 2 All ER 385.
2 [1970] 2 All ER 780.
3 [1990] 1 All ER 1111.
4 [2007] UKHL 17, [2007] 2 All ER 929.

THE FACTS

22.2 Barry Stack (aged 50) and Dehra Dowden (aged 48) met as teenagers and began living together in their mid-20s in 1983. They had four children. They separated in 2002. The house concerned in the litigation was in Chatsworth Road, London NW2. It had been bought in joint names in 1993. It was sold in November 2005 for £746,245. The 1993 transfer contained no words of trust and there had been no discussion, at the time of purchase, as to the respective shares in of the property. However, it contained a declaration by the purchasers that the survivor of them was entitled to give a valid receipt for capital money (the declaration).

Before Chatsworth Road they had lived in one other property, Purves Road, London NW10. Purves Road had been in the sole name of Ms Dowden. The mortgage on Purves Road had been in Ms Dowden's sole name. She worked hard for the London Electricity board and had paid all of the bills on the house, including the mortgage. Mr Stack was a self-employed builder of limited income (he did not make tax returns). The Court of Appeal concluded (correctly, said the House of Lords) that Mr Stack had no beneficial interest in Purves Road. The net proceeds of sale of Purves Rd (£66,613) were paid to Ms Dowden.

Chatsworth Road cost £190,000. £128,813 came from Ms Dowden's Halifax account (which held the proceeds of Purves Rd). The balance of the purchase price came from a Barclay's mortgage in joint names. By the time of the sale, Mr Stack had paid £27,000 towards the reduction of the mortgage capital; Ms Dowden had repaid £38,345. Mr Stack paid the mortgage interest and the premiums on the joint endowment policy (which together totalled £33,747). Ms Dowden paid the utility bills. The parties kept their finances separate.

The judge at first instance (HHJ Levy QC, sitting at the Inner London county court) held that the beneficial interests were held equally. The Court of Appeal allowed the appeal by Ms Dowden and held that the beneficial interests were held 65%/35% in her favour. The House of Lords unanimously dismissed Mr Stack's appeal.

BASIS FOR THE DECISION

22.3 The basis for the decision was that there was no express declaration of trust. The property was in joint names and, therefore, it was for Ms Dowden to show that the common intention was that they should hold the property other than as beneficial joint tenants. She could easily do so as a result of their unequal contributions to the property. Having regard to their contributions to the purchase and mortgage, the most that Mr Stack might claim was about 35%. They did not pool their resources. Ms Dowden paid for all regular commitments, other than the mortgage interest and endowment premium. The assumption would be that the beneficial interests follow the legal title unless the contrary is proved; joint legal owners will be assumed to hold as beneficial joint tenants and sole legal owners will be assumed to hold the beneficial interest unless the contrary is proved. The contrary is proved by having regard to the parties' express, inferred or imputed intentions. The court should not conclude that the beneficial interests do not follow the legal title lightly but, also, should not confine itself strictly to the contributions that the parties have made to the property. Baroness Hale gave a list of factors that might be relevant in the seminal para 69 of the judgment. The main majority speech is that of Baroness Hale.

Lord Neuberger (now Master of the Rolls) gave a dissenting judgment, which has been much respected by commentators. However, his speech is the minority view and therefore does not represent the law. He agreed that the legal title of a property would determine the beneficial interests in it, absent other evidence. Unequal contributions to purchase would create unequal shares in the absence of contrary intention, express or inferred. Thus, he said, consider title, resulting trust (who paid what) and then constructive trust (what did the parties intend). The majority view was: (i) consider the documents of title and then (ii) consider constructive trusts.

THE LAW SHOULD BE SIMPLE

22.4 In a judgment that ran to 158 paragraphs the judges all agreed that, if there was an express declaration of trust within the documents of title that would be conclusive of the parties' shares in the property (unless there was a valid claim for the express declaration to be rectified or rescinded on contractual grounds). Further, they made the well-known point that the nature of the relationship would not determine the shares of the parties in the property (how could it?). There are two questions to be asked, of course. First, has the claimant shown that he has a beneficial interest in the property? Second, (and if so), what share does the claimant have?

The starting point, therefore, is the document of title. Baroness Hale said:

> '. . . just as the starting point where there is sole legal ownership is sole beneficial ownership, the starting point where there is joint legal ownership is joint beneficial ownership. The onus is upon the person seeking to show that the beneficial ownership is different from the legal ownership. So in sole ownership cases it is upon the non-owner to show that he has any interest at all. In joint ownership cases, it is upon the joint owner who claims to have other than a joint beneficial interest . . . at least in the domestic consumer context, a conveyance into joint names indicates both legal and beneficial joint tenancy, unless and until the contrary is proved.'

At the time that the property at Chatsworth Road was bought the standard form of property transfer (known as Form 19 JP) only required the purchasers to state whether the survivor of joint proprietors was able to give a valid receipt for the capital moneys received on sale. Each of the judges stated that that wording of the transfer could be taken neither as a declaration of trust nor as a basis for inferring an intention to share the ownership of the property.

Departing from that starting point led to the main division between the majority view and the dissenting speech of Lord Neuberger. The central passages of the main majority speech of Baroness Hale[1] are as follows:

> 'The search is to ascertain the parties' shared intentions, actual, inferred or imputed, with respect to the property in the light of their whole course of conduct in relation to it.'
>
> . . .
>
> 'The burden will therefore be on the person seeking to show that the parties did intend their beneficial interests to be different from their legal interests, and in what way. This is not a task to be lightly embarked upon. In family disputes, strong feelings are aroused when couples split up. These often lead the parties, honestly but mistakenly, to reinterpret the past in self-exculpatory or vengeful terms. They also lead people to spend far more on the legal battle than is warranted by the sums actually at stake. A full examination of the facts is likely to involve disproportionate costs. In joint names cases it is also unlikely to lead to a different result unless the facts are very unusual. Nor may disputes be confined to the parties themselves. People with an interest in the deceased's estate may well wish to assert that he had a beneficial tenancy in common. It cannot be the case that all the hundreds of thousands, if not millions, of transfers into joint names using the old forms are vulnerable to challenge in the courts simply because it is likely that the owners contributed unequally to their purchase.
>
> In law, "context is everything" and the domestic context is very different from the commercial world. Each case will turn on its own facts. Many more factors than financial contributions may be relevant to divining the parties' true intentions. These include: any advice or discussions at the time of the transfer which cast light upon their intentions then; the reasons why the home was acquired in their joint names; the reasons why (if it be the case) the survivor was authorised to give a receipt for the capital moneys; the purpose for which the home was acquired; the nature of the parties' relationship; whether they had children for whom they both had responsibility to provide a home; how the purchase was financed, both initially and subsequently; how the parties arranged their finances, whether separately or together or a bit of both; how they discharged the outgoings on the property and their other household expenses. When a couple are joint owners of the home and jointly liable for the mortgage, the inferences to be drawn from who pays for what may be very different from the inferences to be drawn when only one is owner of the home. The arithmetical calculation of how much was paid by each is also likely to be less important. It will be easier to draw the inference that they intended that each should contribute as much to the household as they reasonably could and that they would share the eventual benefit or burden equally. The parties' individual characters and personalities may also be a factor in deciding where their true intentions lay. In the cohabitation context, mercenary considerations may be more to the fore than they would be in marriage, but it should not be assumed that they always take pride of place over natural love and affection. At the end of the day,

having taken all this into account, cases in which the joint legal owners are to be taken to have intended that their beneficial interests should be different from their legal interests will be very unusual.

This [ie the above] is not, of course, an exhaustive list. There may also be reason to conclude that, whatever the parties' intentions at the outset, these have now changed. An example might be where one party has financed (or constructed himself) an extension or substantial improvement to the property, so that what they have now is significantly different from what they had then.'

1 [2007] UKHL 17 (HL) per Baroness Hale at 68 and 69.

IMPUTING A BENEFICIAL INTEREST

22.5 The majority held that a court should ascertain the parties' shared intentions, actual, inferred or imputed, in relation to the property. The introduction of the word 'imputed' into this court activity is innovative and met with firm disapproval from the dissenting Lord Neuberger. To impute a common intention means that a court decides what the parties should have intended, in the light of their whole course of conduct in relation to the property. Lord Neuberger's opinion was that the court should limit itself to ascertaining the express or inferred intention.

INDIRECT CONTRIBUTIONS

22.6 From the case law prior to this decision there was some disagreement about whether indirect contributions to a property's value (ie contributions other than paying the initial purchase price or paying the mortgage) might justify an inference that a constructive trust exists. The speeches of Baroness Hale, Lord Hope and Lord Walker all suggest that such contributions may justify the inference or imputation that such a trust exists.

As Lord Hope said:

'I think that indirect contributions, such as making improvements which added significant value to the property, or a complete pooling of resources in both time and money so that it did not matter who paid for what during their relationship, ought to be taken into account as well as financial contributions made directly towards the purchase of the property.'

Lord Walker said:

' . . . the Court should in my opinion take a broad view of what contributions are to be taken into account . . . The law should recognise that by taking a wide view of what is capable of counting as a contribution towards the acquisition of a residence, while remaining sceptical of the value of alleged improvements that are really insignificant, or elaborate arguments (suggestive of creative accounting) as to how the family finances were arranged . . . For reasons already mentioned, I would include contributions in kind by way of manual labour, provided that they are significant.'

QUANTIFYING THE SHARES

22.7 The House of Lords said that, when quantifying a beneficial interest where a constructive trust has arisen, there should be a 'holistic approach' to quantification. The court should undertake a survey of the whole course of dealing between the parties and should take account of all conduct which throws light on the question what shares were intended. Although this may be music to the litigators' ears, it does leave the parties vulnerable to costly litigation.

PROPRIETARY ESTOPPEL

22.8 Prior to this decision had been suggestions that the principles relating to constructive trusts and those relating to proprietary estoppel should be married together and become the same. The House of Lords in Stack v Dowden stood back from this marriage and stated that the principles should remain distinct. Lord Walker said as follows:

> 'I have to say that I am now rather less enthusiastic about the notion that proprietary estoppel and "common interest" constructive trusts can or should be completely assimilated. Proprietary estoppel typically consists of asserting an equitable claim against the conscience of the "true" owner. The claim is a "mere equity". It is to be satisfied by the minimum award necessary to do justice (*Crabb v Arun District Council* [1976] Ch 179, 198), which may sometimes lead to no more than a monetary award. A "common intention" constructive trust, by contrast, is identifying the true beneficial owner or owners, and the size of their beneficial interests.'

COMMERCIAL PROPERTIES

22.9 Commercial properties may well not be governed by this decision. The majority speeches make it plain that they are considering the law relating to domestic properties. Lord Neuberger, in his dissenting speech, states that the same principles should apply to commercial and domestic properties. Lord Walker added a qualification to his support for the majority view by saying that where people engage in an emotional and commercial partnership (eg they agree to 'do up' an old cottage on the basis that they will share the profit), the resulting trust may still be a useful tool. In the subsequent case of *Laskar v Laskar*,[1] the Court of Appeal applied resulting trust principles to a claim between a mother and daughter-in-law relating to an investment property, holding that the approach of Baroness Hale in *Stack v Dowden* was not applicable.

1 [2008] EWCA Civ 347.

COHABITATION

22.10 Cohabitation outside marriage (or civil partnership) is an everyday feature of our society. Baroness Hale[1] said in her speech:

> 'People embarking on their first serious relationship more commonly cohabit than marry. Many of these relationships may be quite short lived and childless. But most

people these days cohabit before marriage – in 2003, 78.7% of spouses gave identical addresses before marriage, and the figures are even higher for second marriages. So many couples are cohabiting with a view to marriage at some later date – as long ago as 1998 the British Household Panel Survey found that 75% of current cohabitants expected to marry, although only a third had firm plans (see J Ermisch *Personal Relationships and Marriage Expectations: Evidence from the 1998 British Household Panel* (2000) Working Papers of the Institute of Social and Economic Research: Paper 2000–27). . . . Cohabitation is much more likely to end in separation than is marriage, and cohabitations which end in separation tend to last for a shorter time than marriages which end in divorce. But increasing numbers of couples cohabit for long periods without marrying and their reasons for doing so vary from conscious rejection of marriage as a legal institution to regarding themselves 'as good as married' anyway (see Law Com Consultation Paper no 179, Pt 2, p 39 (para 2.45)). There is evidence of a wide-spread myth of the 'common law marriage' in which unmarried couples acquire the same rights as married after a period of cohabitation (see A Barlow et al 'Just a Piece of Paper? Marriage and Cohabitation', in A Park et al *British Social Attitudes: Public policy, social ties. The 18th Report* (2001), pp 29–57). There is also evidence that "the legal implications of marriage are a long way down the list of most couples' considerations when deciding whether to marry" (see Law Com Consultation Paper no 179, Pt 5, p 96 (para 5.10))'.

1 [2007] UKHL 17 (HL) at 45.

HOW HAS THIS CASE CHANGED OUR LIVES?

22.11 This case is now the leading authority on the property rights between people who have not married. Thus it plays a very important role in social regulation. It leaves us with a legacy that does little to confer certainty for those who need to rely on it to resolve their rights when relationships end. Of particular difficulty has been the decision that the court can 'impute' a common intention, since it introduces a new level of argument about what the parties should have intended.

It was hoped that this case would be no more than a stop gap until legislation could provide a statutory code to deal with this complex area. However, it seems likely that *Stack v Dowden* is here to stay for the foreseeable future. The moral of the tale (for those who can bear it) is to sort out property rights at the start of the relationship and not the end of it.

23

AN ORDINARY TALE OF FARMING FOLK?

White v White and its Legacy

Janet Bazley QC and Stephen Jarmain

INTRODUCTION

23.1 In 1973, around the time Parliament was enacting legislation to reform the way in which the court approached financial provision for families following relationship breakdown, the then Master of the Rolls, Lord Denning, in dealing with the ancillary relief case of *Wachtel v Wachtel*, stated:[1]

> 'If we were only concerned with the capital assets of the family . . . It would be tempting to divide them half and half . . . that would be fair enough if the wife afterwards went her own way, making no further demands on the husband. It would simply be a division of the assets of the partnership. That may come in the future.'

Lord Denning was right, but it took over a quarter of a century for his prophecy to be fulfilled in the shape of the House of Lords decision in *White v White*.[2]

1 [1973] Fam 72 at para 95.
2 [2000] 2 FLR 981.

WHITE AND WHITE

23.2 *White* was a landmark case in the history of family law. Previously, the widely accepted practice had been for courts to provide divorcing wives with enough to cover their 'reasonable requirements', but no more. This approach was disapproved in *White* as a judicially developed concept which provided an impermissible gloss on the provisions of section 25 of the Matrimonial Causes Act 1973 (MCA 1973). Those provisions required the court to give careful consideration to a number of important criteria, including the length of the marriage, each party's financial resources, their financial needs and obligations and their contributions to the marriage. It was the approach of the House of

Lords to this last aspect – 'contribution' – for which *White* is best remembered.

THE FACTS

23.3 Mr and Mrs White were hardworking farmers from farming families. Their marriage had lasted for over 30 years and had produced three children. Throughout their married lives Mr and Mrs White had run a dairy farming business in a partnership which had originally consisted of one farm, owned jointly and purchased with the aid of an interest free loan from Mr White's father. Later in the marriage, Mr White had inherited a farm from his father and, although this was held in Mr White's sole name, the farming business was thereafter run from both farms.

At the time of the ancillary relief proceedings in 1996, the parties' overall net assets were assessed at £4.6 million, comprised of jointly owned property worth £2.67 million, Mrs White's property worth £190,000, and Mr White's property worth £1.78 million. At first instance Mr Justice Holman, applying the 'reasonable requirements' approach, assessed the wife's needs at £980,000 and awarded her just £800,000 from the joint assets in addition to her own property.

Mrs White felt this was unfair and appealed to the Court of Appeal. Given her contribution not only to the farming business but also to the upkeep of the home and care of the children, she felt she deserved more than 21% of the overall assets. The Court of Appeal agreed with Mrs White that the first instance decision was unfair, and that she should receive more. Her award from the joint assets was increased from £800,000 to £1.5 million, giving Mrs White about 40% of the overall assets. The Court of Appeal considered that this fairly reflected Mrs White's contributions both to the business and the marriage as a whole.

However, neither party was satisfied with the decision in the Court of Appeal and both appealed to the House of Lords. The appeals were dismissed, but the speeches of the House of Lords have been of huge importance in the development of family law ever since.

THE JUDGMENT

23.4 Lord Nicholls gave the lead judgment in the case. He considered the factors in section 25 and reinforced the central importance of a 'fair' outcome when considering such cases, which should be influenced by the fact that the traditional division of labour in a marriage, whereby the husband goes out and earns the money and the wife runs the home and cares for the children, was no longer routinely the case. Crucially, when considering fairness, Lord Nicholls stated that there must be 'no bias in favour of the money-earner and against the home-maker and child carer'.

This new, non-discriminatory approach to the differing roles taken by the parties to a marriage introduced a fresh measure of fairness, referred to by Lord Nicholls as the 'yardstick of equality of division', against which a judge considering an application for ancillary relief would be 'well advised to check his tentative views'. Further, in most cases:

'. . . equality should be departed from only if, and to the extent that, there is good reason for doing so. The need to consider and articulate reasons for departing from equality would help the parties and the court to focus on the need to ensure the absence of discrimination.'

An approach limited to a wife's 'reasonable requirements' was not, therefore, appropriate. Lord Nicholls was, however, careful not to introduce a presumption of equality, pointing out that standards of fairness in a field such as family law change and develop over time.

Although the introduction of the concept of equal division was the main thrust of *White*, it should be remembered that the outcome of the case was not an equal share of the assets as the House of Lords upheld the Court of Appeal's decision awarding Mrs White just 40%. In circumstances in which Mrs White not only brought up the children and ran the home, but was a 'hands on' farmer throughout the marriage, one might have thought that her contribution merited an equal or very nearly equal division, despite the husband's inheritance. It is clear that some of their lordships felt that the Court of Appeal's award to Mrs White was on the low side, and Lord Cooke, in particular, seemed to favour an equal division, indicating that the £1.5 million award was 'probably about the minimum that could have been awarded to Mrs White without exposing the award to further increase on further appeal'. However, the departure from equality was said to be justified as a result of the fact that Mr White had inherited one of the farms and a significant proportion of the overall assets from his father. It was further pointed out that, on the breakdown of marriage, certain types of property – such as that acquired before the marriage or inherited during the marriage – came from a source 'wholly external to the marriage' and should not necessarily be treated in the same way as what might loosely be termed 'matrimonial property'.

In summary, therefore, the points or general application which arose from *White* are as follows:

(a) the objective implicit in the provisions of MCA 1973, s 25 was to achieve a fair outcome, giving first consideration, where relevant, to the welfare of children;

(b) fairness required the court to take into account all the circumstances of the case but also required that the division of labour of husband and wife should not prejudice either when considering their respective contributions to the welfare of the family. A judge should check his tentative views against the yardstick of equality and only depart from it if, and to the extent that, there was a good reason for so doing, such reasons to be articulated;

(c) section 25 did not rank the matters listed in any hierarchy; other matters might also be relevant and the importance and weight to be attached to them depended upon the facts of the particular case. When considering MCA 1973, s 25(2)(b), 'confusion would be avoided if the courts ceased to use the expression "reasonable requirements" ';

(d) Duxbury calculations,[1] leading to the provision of a lump sum on the basis that it was to be fully extinguished in order to meet the wife's reasonable needs during her expected lifetime (according to actuarial tables), would be of much less importance;

(e) a parent's wish to leave something to the children (one of Mrs White's arguments) would not normally be treated as a financial need but, where resources exceeded needs, that wish could be included as a relevant factor and given appropriate weight;

(f) the fact that property was inherited was one of the circumstances of the case to be given appropriate weight;
(g) the section 25 exercise did not require a detailed investigation of proprietorial interests of the parties;
(h) the judge had been wrong to regard reasonable requirements as the determinant factor.

1 A Duxbury calculation is an assessment of what level of lump sum a person will need in order to spend the rest of their life at a certain amount of expenditure each year.

POST *WHITE V WHITE*: ACCEPTANCE AND DEVELOPMENT

23.5 There is no doubt whatsoever that the decision in *White* created a sea change in family law and revolutionised the approach taken by courts to the fair division of assets after divorce. The case has been cited in over 100 reported cases since 2000 and many commentators consider that the decision has resulted in a significant change in public perception of divorce. Most family law practitioners consider that *White* has dramatically improved the fairness of divorce provision for wives; in fact, the Court of Appeal in *Charman*[1] noted that (certainly in cases where the assets were considerable) the '*White* factor' had more than doubled the awards to wives. Other commentators have cited the central role of *White* in England being seen as the 'divorce capital of the world' for wives, while others would blame the case – fairly or unfairly – for the steady decline in the marriage rate since 2000.

Whatever has been said of *White*, and despite the many judicial interpretations, the principles enunciated in the case remain little altered. In fact, the House of Lords more recently[2] had an opportunity to move the law on but declined to do so. As a result of *White*, it is clear that the goal of financial provision is fairness. This does not always mean equality but does mean that there must be no discrimination between spouses as a result of their different roles in the marriage. The husband who has gone out to work or run a successful business whilst his wife ran the home and looked after the children have each made equally valid contributions to the family and that must be reflected in the outcome.

Equally, the *White* approach to inherited assets has held good. The principles were applied by Mr Justice Munby, as he then was, in the case of *P v P (Inherited Property)*,[3] another farming case where the marriage had lasted ten years and there were two children with special needs. The husband had inherited the family farm, a business in which both parties had worked hard during the marriage. It was found that in this particular case the husband's life was inexorably linked to the farm, and there had been an intention to retain the farm intact for future generations. The wife had agreed that the husband should receive more as a result of his inheritance, and offered him 60% of the assets, although this would have meant a sale of the farm. She was awarded just 25% in view of the inheritance and the intention behind it. This decision may seem hard to reconcile with *White*, although it was cited with approval by the House of Lords in *Miller* and *McFarlane* (see **23.6** below).[4]

Issues of inheritance and the question of which assets should be susceptible to the *White* yardstick of equality have vexed the courts in a number of cases since *White*. This has developed into a debate as to which assets are either 'matrimonial' – and therefore subject to the yardstick of equality – or 'non-matrimonial' – and therefore less so. This issue came before the Lords in the conjoined appeals of *Miller v Miller* and *McFarlane v McFarlane* in which the House of Lords further interpreted the concept of fairness derived from *White*.

1 *Charman v Charman (No 4)* [2007] EWCA Civ 503.

2 In *Miller v Miller; McFarlane v McFarlane* [2006] UKHL 24 – see **23.6** below.

3 [2005] 1 FLR 576.

4 *Miller v Miller; McFarlane v McFarlane* [2006] UKHL 24.

MILLER/MCFARLANE: THE FACTS

23.6 The cases of Alan and Melissa Miller and Kenneth and Julia McFarlane attracted considerable media attention in 2005 and 2006. The Millers had been married for less than three years and had no children. The assets stood at some £32 million at the date of trial and had been almost entirely generated by Mr Miller before and during the marriage. It was agreed that Mrs Miller would receive no maintenance but the question for the court was how much of the capital, generated by Mr Miller, she should receive. The High Court Judge considered that even after such a short marriage, £5 million was appropriate. That decision was upheld in both the Court of Appeal and the House of Lords.

The McFarlane's situation was quite different. They had been married for 16 years and had three children. The husband was an accountant, earning some £750,000 net per annum at the date of the ancillary relief hearing. The wife had been a solicitor, earning as much as the husband but had, by agreement between the parties, given up her career to care for the children. There was no dispute as to what should happen to the capital, which had been divided by agreement. The issue was the quantum and term of Mrs McFarlane's periodical payments. At first instance the District Judge had made a 'joint lives' order at the level of £250,000 per annum (some one-third of the husband's income) saying that the order 'reflects the wife's needs, obligations and the contribution that she has made over the years of the marriage'. The District Judge was clear that, as part of the contribution for which the wife was to be compensated was her role in enabling the husband to concentrate on his career, resulting in him reaching the height of his earning capacity at or after the end of the marriage. This echoed the sentiments expressed by Lord Nicholls in *White* in relation to the weight to be given to the domestic contribution.

Mr McFarlane was not content with this outcome and issued the first of three appeals in the case. Mr Justice Bennett in the High Court allowed the appeal, reducing the annual periodical payments to £180,000, again on a joint lives basis. He held that that the award was 'way above' the wife's needs and that her ability to save and accumulate capital out of the award would subvert the principle that periodical payments are for maintenance, a capital award being made only once.

Mrs McFarlane then appealed to the Court of Appeal, seeking to reinstate the District Judge's order. Thorpe, Latham and Wall LJJ heard the appeal, together with the appeal from the judgment of Mr Justice Bennett in the case of the footballer, Ray Parlour.[1] The court held that, in exceptional cases, periodical payments orders may properly be used as a means to enable the payee to accumulate capital. The order was restored to £250,000 per annum. However, a term of five years (without a bar) was imposed, the court being concerned that a joint lives order would not give due effect to the 'clean break' principle.

The wife appealed to the House of Lords, again seeking to reinstate the District Judge's order, and was successful.

1 *McFarlane v McFarlane; Parlour v Parlour* [2004] EWCA Civ 872, [2004] 2 FLR 893.

MILLER/MCFARLANE: THE JUDGMENT

23.7 It was against the very different facts of these two cases that the House of Lords again came to consider the issue of financial provision following divorce and, in particular, the interpretation of the earlier decision of *White*.

White was considered a number of times in the speeches in *Miller/McFarlane* and its reasoning and principles upheld and restated. For example, Baroness Hale – who had joined the House since *White* – referred to the decision as a 'great leap forward' for fairness of approach in deciding ancillary relief cases, describing the previous 'reasonable requirements' approach as 'deeply discriminatory'. She also felt – with the admitted benefit of hindsight – that *White* should have been a simple case where the solution might have been to give one farm to each party so that they could farm independently.

In *Miller/McFarlane*, particularly close consideration was given to the *White* concept of 'fairness', which was broken down by the House of Lords in *Miller/McFarlane* into strands:

- needs (generously interpreted);
- compensation; and
- sharing.

The themes of equality and non-discrimination from *White* were echoed in the description of these strands: for example, the meeting of needs was considered to be fair, particularly where that need arose from the relationship of mutual interdependence. Compensation would arise from any prospective economic disparity as a result of the way the parties ran their marriage,[1] for example, by the wife surrendering her career, particularly a lucrative and successful career as Mrs McFarlane had, in order to bring up the family. Baroness Hale spoke of this as 'relationship-generated disadvantage' and pointed out that the economic disadvantage generated by the relationship might go beyond needs 'however generously interpreted'.

The influence of *White* could perhaps most clearly be seen in the third strand: *sharing* of 'the fruits of the matrimonial partnership'. Whilst pointing out that this did not necessarily dictate an equal division of the assets on divorce, Baroness Hale spoke of 'a widespread perception that marriage is a partnership of equals'.[2]

Lord Nicholls was of a similar view and indeed used similar language:

> 'Marriage, it is often said, is a partnership of equals . . . This is now recognised widely, if not universally. The parties commit themselves to sharing their lives. They live and work together. When their partnership ends each is entitled to a share of the assets of the partnership, unless there is good reason to the contrary. Fairness requires no less.'[3]

The foundations of such a perception can fairly be said to have been laid by the principles of *White* and it is demonstrably clear that those principles, at least in the eyes of the House of Lords, remain good.

1 Lord Nicholls at para 13; Baroness Hale at para 140.
2 Paragraph 41.
3 Paragraph 16.

THE FUTURE: EQUAL SHARING OF INCOME?

23.8 Despite the far-reaching influence of *White* in encouraging judges and practitioners to recognise the fairness of sharing marital assets equally, the courts have so far stopped short of applying the same approach to the other important source of financial support for a family: the income earned by the parties. It is almost never the case that, on the breakdown of a marriage, both the husband and the wife will have identical earning capacities or incomes. Is it also fair, then, for each party to have an equal share of the income on the breakdown of a marriage, by way of the higher earning party making regular balancing payments to the other party? On the basis of the *White* approach it might be tempting to answer that question in the affirmative, particularly in a case where one party has sacrificed their ability to earn in order to bring up the family and allow the other party to concentrate on their career.

The courts have, however, rejected that approach. In *Rossi v Rossi*,[1] Nicholas Mostyn QC, sitting then as a Deputy High Court Judge, considered which assets were to be regarded as 'matrimonial' and therefore, normally, for equal division, and which assets qualified to be treated differently, as non-matrimonial assets. It was his view that post-separation assets of an income nature (including a bonus) should qualify as *non-matrimonial* if accrued more than 12 months post separation. That approach to post-separation income was adopted by Singer J in *S v S (Ancilliary Relief after lengthy Separation)*.[2]

Charles J in *H v H (Financial Provision)*[3] took a different view, rejecting what he described as an 'arbitrary' approach in *Rossi*. In that case, the marriage had lasted some 20 years and produced four children. There were assets of £24.6 million and, in addition, the husband had accrued substantial bonuses post-separation. The wife was awarded half the assets at the date of separation and declining percentages of the husband's next three bonuses. Charles J said:

> 'In my view, the concept of the matrimonial property to which the yardstick of equality applies readily and with force is based on the concept of an equal and voluntary partnership providing mutual emotional, economic and general support and matching contributions to it of different kinds.'

He made clear his view that the point for defining matrimonial property is when the mutual support ends and, therefore, that there should not be equal sharing of income into the future.

There was a suggestion in the speech of Baroness Hale in *Miller/MacFarlane* that the court's may, in the future, consider earning capacity to be an 'asset' of the marriage and therefore susceptible to sharing. However, Baroness Hale accepted, that, in general:

> '. . . it can be assumed that the marital partnership does not stay alive for the purpose of sharing future resources unless this is justified by need or compensation.'[4]

The courts have adopted this approach since *Miller/MacFarlane* and have refused to give both parties an equal share of ongoing income, even bonuses, where not strictly necessary to meet the reasonable needs of the other party. In a well-known Court of Appeal case, *Vaughan v Vaughan*,[5] Lord Justice Wilson expounded the principle very clearly:

> '. . . there is no foundation in law for the proposition that, after divorce, a wife is entitled to any award that brings her up to one-half of the joint net incomes.'[6]

The yardstick – or presumption – of equality does not therefore currently extend to the parties income. Some might argue that it is still possible for unfairness to be worked against the homemaker in a relationship, who get only half of the assets and an extremely limited earning capacity when compared with their former spouse, who can combine his share of the capital with a healthy income, which in turn can be used to build even more capital and pension into the future. There is scope, it therefore seems, for the highest court in the land to look again at the concept of equality in the future and decide whether in fact the application of the yardstick should be extended yet further.

1 [2007] 1 FLR 790.
2 [2007] 1 FLR 2120.
3 [2009] 2 FLR 795.
4 [2009] 2 FLR 795 at para 144.
5 [2008] 1 FLR 1108.
6 [2008] 1 FLR 1108 at para 42.

CONCLUSION

23.9 It is hard to think of another case in the last quarter-century which has so radically changed the law in the area of financial provision. *White* has played a defining role in not only shaping the courts' approach to fairness for divorcing couples, but also to the public's perception of marriage and the equal but different roles played by the parties to it. It is now not unusual for pensions to be split on the basis of equalising the income in payment. The future may even see the effects of *White* spread still further to equalise the incomes of divorcing couples, particularly after long marriages or in situations like that of Mrs MacFarlane, who gave up an equivalent career to her husband's in order to bring up the children and look after the home. If this is to be the way forward, the court will have to revisit section 25A(1) of the MCA 1973 which places it under a duty, when making financial provision orders, to consider whether it is appropriate to make orders to terminate each party's financial obligation to the other as is 'just and reasonable'.

Whatever the future holds for the yardstick of equality, it is without doubt that *White* will continue to influence the approach of judges and practitioners to the question of financial fairness for many years to come.

24

GILLICK AND THE DWINDLING RIGHT OF PARENTAL AUTHORITY

Gillick v West Norfolk and Wisbech Area Health Authority

Janet Bazley QC and Stephen Jarmain

> 'You know your children are growing up when they stop asking you where they came from and refuse to tell you where they're going.'
>
> PJ O'Rourke

INTRODUCTION

24.1 In 1977, as part of wider reform of the National Health Service, Parliament enacted an apparently innocuous statutory provision[1] requiring the Secretary of State to arrange the provision of contraceptive advice, medical examination and treatment, including the supply of contraceptive substances and appliances, within England and Wales. No age limit was prescribed and the extent of the duty to provide such services to children received apparently scant consideration.

Three years later, a memorandum of guidance, issued by the former Department of Health and Social Security (DHSS), was amended to address the approach to be taken to those under the age of 16. In essence, the guidance discouraged the provision of such services to children, urging physicians to take special care not to undermine parental authority and expressing the hope that a doctor or other professional would always seek to persuade the child to involve her parents; in fact, it should be 'most unusual' to provide advice about, or prescribe, contraception without parental consent. A caveat within the guidance did, however, acknowledge that consultations between doctors and patients (including children) were confidential, and that some parents would be unconcerned, unresponsive or even disturbed by knowledge of such issues. In such exceptional cases, the decision whether to provide contraception would fall to the doctor in the exercise of his or her clinical judgment.

It was not long before the guidance came under the critical scrutiny of Victoria Gillick, a mother of ten, including five daughters aged one to thirteen. None of her daughters had sought any advice on contraception or abortion, but Mrs

24.1 *Gillick and the Dwindling Right of Parental Authority*

Gillick was concerned at the prospect of her parental authority being disturbed without her knowledge. She therefore wrote to her local health authority seeking confirmation that no advice on contraceptive or abortive treatment would be given to her daughters without her express knowledge and consent. The authority, however, bound as it was by the guidance, did not consider itself able to offer such a guarantee. Undeterred, Mrs Gillick responded in strong terms, forbidding the local authority from giving such advice or treatment to any of her daughters without her consent and – when this did not prompt the requisite change of attitude from the health authority – took the matter further. Mrs Gillick began a nationwide petition against the DHSS before taking her case to court.[2]

1 National Health Service Act 1977, s 5(1)(b).
2 [1986] 1 FLR 224.

THE CASE

24.2 Mrs Gillick brought her application in the High Court, seeking declarations that the guidance offered by the DHSS had no legal authority, was unlawful and adversely affected her parental rights and duties and that no doctor, or other health professional employed by the local health authority, could give any advice or treatment relating to contraception or abortion to any of her children without her consent. Her purpose was really to establish the extent of parental rights and duties in respect of children under the age of 16.

The case first came before Mr Justice Woolf for hearing.[1] He held that the DHSS was entitled to assume that its employees would follow its advice in a lawful manner and accordingly that, as Mrs Gillick could not establish that in following the DHSS advice a health professional would be committing a criminal offence or otherwise be guilty of unlawful conduct, she was not entitled to the declarations she sought. Importantly, however, the court decided that, depending on her maturity and understanding of the nature of the treatment, a girl under the age of16 could be capable of consenting to medical treatment.

Mrs Gillick was not satisfied with the decision and appealed.[2] The Court of Appeal agreed with her view and held that, except by order of a competent court or in an emergency, it was never lawful for a doctor to give contraceptive advice or treatment to a girl under 16 without her parent's consent because:

(a) a girl under 16 did not have the legal capacity to give valid consent to matters concerning her custody and upbringing (including contraceptive advice and treatment); and
(b) the giving of such advice or treatment without the consent of a parent or guardian infringed the rights of a parent or guardian which, with certain exceptions, could neither be abandoned nor transferred.

The judgment was a strong one, and only the DHSS (and not the local health authority) was brave enough to appeal the matter to the House of Lords.[3] The case came on for hearing in the summer of 1986 and was widely reported.

The House of Lords did not find the case an easy one to dispose of. In fact, the decision to allow the appeal was made only by a majority of one. That majority, Lords Fraser, Scarman and Bridge, held that the guidance was, in fact, lawful and while it would (and should) be 'most unusual' for a doctor to give contraceptive advice and treatment to a child under 16 without the knowledge and consent of her parents, who were usually best placed to decide what is best for a child, the parental right to determine whether or not a child under 16 would have medical treatment terminated if and when the child achieved sufficient understanding and intelligence to enable him or her to understand fully what was proposed.

This was a significant development of the existing law, under which the force of parental rights had been strongly respected. Although the House of Lords did not deny the existence of such rights, it held that they are derived from parental duty and essentially, therefore, exist for the protection of the child, whose welfare would always be paramount. Parental rights did not include the right to completely control a child throughout their minority; rather, once the child reached a sufficient understanding and intelligence to be capable of making an informed decision, parental control yielded to the child's right to make decisions in her own interests. To that extent, parental authority was 'a dwindling right', the duration of which was not found by reference to a particular age but depended upon a judgment as to what was best for the particular child.

The House of Lords also noted that the duty of a health authority to provide services and treatment in relation to contraception had no lower age limit and therefore to provide such services to under-16s could not be considered unlawful. It therefore followed that the memorandum of guidance was not unlawful, nor contrary to public policy, and could be followed by health professionals without any infringement of parental rights.

The court also considered the lawfulness of a physician's actions in prescribing contraceptive treatment to a girl under 16, as it was argued that to do so might constitute aiding and abetting the offence of unlawful underage sex. The court rejected that argument. Lord Fraser felt it unlikely that a doctor honestly intending to act in the best interests of the child would be committing a criminal offence. Lord Scarman went further, and was clear in his judgment that the bona fide exercise by a doctor of his clinical judgment as to what was necessary for the physical, mental and emotional health of his patient completely negated the guilty mind necessary for the commission of the offence of aiding and abetting unlawful sexual intercourse. The intention of the doctor was, therefore, the important issue.

1 [1984] FLR 249.
2 [1985] FLR 736.
3 *Gillick v West Norfolk and Wisbech Area Health Authority and anor* [1986] 1 FLR 224.

THE *GILLICK* TEST AND *GILLICK* COMPETENCY

24.3 Although Mrs Gillick failed in her application, her case was a landmark decision and has had far-reaching implications, not only within the law but also for social, educational and health services across the commonwealth. The most famous consequence of the case was 'the *Gillick* test', set down by Lord Scarman, which is now widely used for determining whether a child under the age of 16 could consent to medical advice:

> 'Once the child is of sufficient intelligence and understanding to have legal capacity to give consent to treatment, this terminates the parental right to determine whether or not such advice or treatment.'

However – importantly – this does not mean that such advice or treatment should normally be given without parental knowledge or consent. This should only happen in exceptional circumstances. As Lord Fraser put it:[1]

> 'In the overwhelming majority of cases, the best judges of a child's welfare are his or her parents . . . any important medical treatment of a child under 16 would normally only be carried out with the parents' approval . . . it would and should be "most unusual" for a doctor to advise a child without the knowledge and consent of the parents on contraceptive matters . . . [the physician should] always seek to persuade [the girl] to tell her parents that she is seeking contraceptive advice, and the nature of the advice she receives.'

In fact, Lord Fraser went further and set down guidelines (sometimes referred to as the 'Fraser Rules') for doctors to follow before they could proceed without parental guidance or knowledge:

> 'there may well be cases, and I think there will be some cases, where the girl refuses either to tell the parents herself or to permit the doctor to do so and in such cases, the doctor will, in my opinion, be justified in proceedings without the parents' consent or even knowledge provided he is satisfied on the following matters:
> (1) that the girl (although under 16 years of age) will understand his advice;
> (2) that he cannot persuade her to inform her parents or to allow him to inform the parents that she is seeking contraceptive advice;
> (3) that she is very likely to begin or to continue having sexual inter-course with or without contraceptive treatment;
> (4) that unless she receives contraceptive advice or treatment her physical or mental health or both are likely to suffer;
> (5) that her best interest require him to give her contraceptive advice, treatment or both without the parental consent.'

Lord Fraser issued a stern warning to medical professionals that the failure to follow these guidelines would, in his opinion, be a matter for disciplinary action.

1 [1986] 1 FLR 224 at 238–239.

SINCE *GILLICK*

24.4 The House of Lords judgment in *Gillick* was considered to be a clear, unequivocal and well-respected statement of the law which has been followed and applied consistently since being handed down. However, the effects of the judgment were not initially universally welcomed; for example, in *Re W (A Minor) (Consent to medical treatment)*,[1] a case concerning the issue of blood and organ donation, the court felt that it was 'highly improbable' as a matter of law that a child of 16 would be *Gillick* competent to consent to the procedure, and that in any event it would, as a matter of medical ethics, be 'inconceivable' for such an operation to proceed.

1 [1993] 1 FLR 1.

PARENTAL RESPONSIBILITY

24.5 The effects of *Gillick* on the approach of the courts to issues of parental responsibility was, however, more swiftly ascertainable. Historically, and before *Gillick*, the concept of parental responsibility had been defined largely as a matter of a parent's right of control over a child. After *Gillick*, the emphasis shifted and some ten years later the approach of the courts to parental responsibility was defined by the Court of Appeal as seeming 'to move away from rights and concentrate on responsibilities'.[1] This is consistent with the view of the court in *Gillick* that parental rights exist solely, or at least primarily, for the benefit of the child and are justified only in so far as they enable a parent to perform his or her duties towards a child.

1 Per Ward LJ in *Re S (Parental Responsibility)* [1995] 2 FLR 648; see also *Re K (A Minor) (Custody)* [1990] 2 FLR 64.

REFUSAL OF TREATMENT

24.6 Since *Gillick* the court has also had to consider the competence of a child to refuse medical treatment. *Re R (A minor) (wardship: medical treatment)*[1] concerned a 15-year-old girl with a history of disturbed behaviour. Her mental state fluctuated and, as it deteriorated, she began to suffer hallucinations and express suicidal thoughts. A consultant psychiatrist diagnosed a psychotic state and sought permission from the local authority (in whose care the child was) to administer anti-psychotic medication. The local authority took wardship proceedings, joining the girl and her parents as defendants. The permission of the court was sought to administer such medication as was necessary without the girl's consent. At first instance, the judge, applying *Gillick*, held that, where a child had legal capacity to give a valid consent (or refusal), it was not for the court to substitute its own view. However, he held that in this case the minor did not have capacity; accordingly, he granted the local authority's application. The Official Solicitor appealed, seeking guidance as to:

(a) whether the child was *Gillick* competent;
(b) if so, whether the parent had the power to override the minor's decision to refuse treatment;
(c) whether the court in wardship had power to override the child's decision.

The Court of Appeal's judgment cast a slightly different light on *Gillick*. The court held that, for a child's capacity to refuse medication to meet the criteria in *Gillick*, there had to be a *full understanding on a lasting basis* of the consequences of the treatment and of its withdrawal. No child with fluctuating mental health who only had a sufficient degree of understanding on a good day could pass the test and, accordingly, the judge's decision that the girl lacked capacity had been right. The court could authorise medication. Further, whether or not the child was *Gillick* competent, the wardship court (whose powers were wider than those of the parents and derived from the delegated performance of the duties of the Crown to protect its subjects, particularly children) had power, in the interest of the child's welfare, to override her decision to refuse medical treatment. On that basis also, leave to administer treatment was given.

Lord Donaldson MR expressed the further view that the judge had been in error in treating *Gillick* as deciding that a *Gillick*-competent child acquired a right to refuse treatment, which terminated the parents' rights to consent to it. The right of the *Gillick*-competent child was concurrent with that of a parent or guardian and only failure to, or refusal of, consent by all having that power could create a veto. The consent of either the parent or the child enabled treatment to be undertaken lawfully.

In *Re L (Medical Treatment: Gillick Competency)*[2] the court was considering the case of a 14-year-old girl with a life-threatening condition. She required treatment which would be likely to involve blood transfusions but refused to consent on the basis that blood transfusion was against her religious beliefs (as a Jehovah's Witness). The hospital authority sought the permission of the High Court to administer blood transfusions in the course of operative treatment, the issue being whether the girl was competent within the rule in *Gillick* to decide whether or not to agree to the proposed medical intervention.

The then President of the Family Division, Sir Stephen Brown, heard the case. He made an order that the treatment should take place without the girl's consent on the basis that she was not *Gillick*-competent and the treatment was necessary to give her a good chance of survival.

The reasons the President gave for determining that the girl was not *Gillick*-competent demonstrated the depth of inquiry necessary when considering the issue of competency. He held that there was a distinction between the child's sincerely and strongly held beliefs which were, in her mind, not subject to discussion, as compared with the constructive formulation of an opinion which occurred with adult experience. The girl had led a sheltered life, largely influenced by the Jehovah's Witness congregation to which she belonged. This necessarily limited her understanding of matters which were grave and meant that she did not have all the information which it would be right for her to have in mind when deciding whether or not to consent to treatment. The President further expressed the opinion that it would have been appropriate to authorise treatment without the girl's consent even if she had been *Gillick*-competent because this was an extreme case where she was in a grave situation.

Some lawyers and academics have argued that these and similar decisions on the refusal of treatment implicitly set a higher test for refusing a medical procedure or treatment than for consenting to one. Certain medical ethicists have commented that there appears to be a 'Catch 22' situation where a child whose competence is in doubt will be found rational if he accepts medical advice but not if he rejects it. Whilst one can see that the court might override the decision of the *Gillick*-competent child on welfare grounds, it is more difficult to understand the approach which says that, where a *Gillick*-competent child refuses consent, either of his parents may grant it and thereby override the decision of the child.

1 [1992] 1 FLR 190.

2 [1998] 2 FLR 810.

REPRESENTATION OF CHILDREN IN LEGAL PROCEEDINGS

24.7 *Gillick* and the subsequent development of the law in the area of the legal capacity of children has also had a direct impact on how children are able to participate in legal proceedings. The *Gillick* test was effectively incorporated into the Children Act 1989 and the Family Proceedings Rules 1991 that went with it. It is utilised where the court is determining whether a child is of 'sufficient understanding'[1] to be able to participate in proceedings concerning his welfare without having an adult to represent her. Although the court is the final arbiter of whether the child is of sufficient understanding, solicitors asked to represent children in proceedings concerning their welfare must make the initial judgment and, in practice, the test applied is the *Gillick* test and a child of sufficient understanding is referred to as '*Gillick*-competent'.

The Court of Appeal considered the state of the law in this area in *Mabon v Mabon*,[2] where three children (aged 17, 15 and 13) sought leave to instruct a solicitor to represent them without a guardian. Lord Justice Thorpe pointed out that:

> 'The direction set by Rule 9.2A(6) is a mandatory grant of the application provided that the court considers "that the minor concerned has sufficient understanding to participate as a party in the proceedings concerned". Thus the focus is on the sufficiency of the child's understanding in the context of the . . . proceedings.'

The court gave the clear indication that articulate, educated, mature teenagers will generally be permitted to participate directly in proceedings concerning their welfare, considering it:

> ' . . . simply unthinkable to exclude young men from knowledge of and participation in legal proceedings that affected them so fundamentally.'

In fact, the court was clear that due weight must be given to children's wishes and feelings when making decisions about the welfare. The development in the law since *Gillick* was perhaps best summarised by Lord Justice Thorpe:

> 'in the twenty-first century, there is a keener appreciation of the autonomy of the child and the child's consequential right to participate in decision making processes that fundamentally affect his family life . . . unless we in this jurisdiction are to fall out of step with similar societies . . . we must, in the case of articulate teenagers, accept that the right to freedom of expression and participation outweighs the paternalistic judgment of welfare.'[3]

Effectively, then, and primarily as a result of *Gillick*, the position under English law has developed to the extent that parents' decision-making rights over a child effectively disappear, or go into abeyance, once a child has sufficient understanding and intelligence to enable him or her to fully understand what is proposed in any course of action.

1 Within the meaning of r 9.2A(6) of the Family Proceedings Rules 1991.

2 [2005] 2 FLR 1011.

3 *Mabon v Mabon* [2005] 2 FLR 1011 at 1017.

AXON

24.8 That development was perhaps most closely considered in the judgment of Mr Justice Silber in the case of *Axon*,[1] heard in the High Court in 2006. The applicant in the case was Sue Axon, a mother of five children, including two teenaged girls aged 13 and 16. Mrs Axon had herself undergone a termination at the age of 30 which she deeply regretted and was concerned that one of her two teenage daughters might opt for an abortion without her being able to offer support or advice. Mrs Axon did not seek to go as far as Mrs Gillick; she did not deny the right of the health authority to give advice on matters of contraception or abortion, but rather challenged guidance issued by the Department of Health in 2004 that encouraged health professionals to keep sensitive advice given to under-16s confidential if the child involved did not want their parents to be involved. Mrs Axon argued that there should be no such policy; on the contrary, she asserted, physicians should be required to consult parents unless to do so would be likely to be inimical to the child's physical or mental health. It seemed incongruous to Mrs Axon that her daughters required parental consent to have her navel pierced, but could have an abortion without any parental knowledge at all.

Mr Justice Silber dismissed Mrs Axon's applications and held that the guidance was, in fact, lawful. He considered that *Gillick* was still good law, and indeed 'it would be ironic and indeed not acceptable now to retreat from the approach adopted in *Gillick*'.[2] Mr Justice Silber further relied upon the developments in the law of human rights, particularly the UN Convention on the Rights of the Child (which came into force in November 1989, post-dating *Gillick*), which he considered had strengthened children's rights to self-determination. As in *Gillick*, the court defined parental rights to refuse consent as 'dwindling':[3] as a matter of law, as the parental right of determination lessens and effectively ceases when the child becomes legally competent to give their own consent,[4] regardless of the child's chronological age. Indeed, Mr Justice Silber felt that the *Gillick* approach should apply more generally to all forms of medical advice and treatment.[5] Indeed, in his view:

> 'there does not appear to be any reason why that approach should not also apply to other proposed treatment and advice as the litmus test for determining if any such treatment and advice can be given without parental knowledge.'[6]

The court rejected any argument based on the right to family life enshrined in Article 8 the European Convention for the Protection of Human Rights and Fundamental Freedoms 1950, relying on the well-known authority of *Yousef v Netherlands*[7] to the effect that where parental rights clashed with those of children, the latter would be paramount. Mr Justice Silber in fact went further by suggesting that it was doubtful that there was a right to family life where a child was competent to decide for themselves to the contrary, although this approach has been much criticised. Silber J felt that a child's motivation for not discussing matters with a parent was largely irrelevant; confidentiality would apply whether the reason was 'hostility to their parents, a wish for privacy or even plain embarrassment'. It was argued on behalf of Mrs Axon that secrecy was inimical to the welfare of family; while Mr Justice Silber accepted this argument as powerful and cogent, it did not override the duty of confidentiality.[8]

The outcome of the *Axon* case was regarded by the media as a heavy defeat for Mrs Axon, and perhaps that was her initial reaction as well, albeit she did not seek leave to appeal the judgment. On a closer reading of *Axon*, however, there were positives to be drawn for Mrs Axon from the judgment. For example, Mr

Justice Silber was very careful to point out that the question of a child's competence is issue-specific: that is, the seriousness of the procedure would be relevant to the child's ability to consent. In the case of abortion, for example, the requisite understanding:

> '. . . would constitute a high threshold and many young girls would be unable to satisfy the medical professional that they fully understood all the implications of the options open to them.'[9]

The court also took pains to point out, as had the court in *Gillick*, that parents are, in the overwhelming majority of cases, the best judges of a young person's welfare.[10] Perhaps most importantly for Mrs Axon, Mr Justice Silber went on to remind the medical world that:

> '. . . it remains the initial and significant duty of the medical professional to try to persuade the young person to inform his or her parents or to allow the medical professional to inform his or her parents'[11]

before going on to effectively restate Lord Fraser's test, sending out a staunch warning to medical professionals that they are only entitled to provide medical advice and treatment on sexual matters without parental knowledge or consent where:

> '(1) the child under 16 understood all aspects of the advice;
> (2) that the child could not be persuaded to inform her parents or allow the medical professional to do so;
> (3) that where contraceptive treatment is concerned, the child is highly likely to enter into a sexual relationship without contraception;
> (4) that without the advice or treatment, the child's physical and/or mental health is likely to suffer; and
> (5) proceeding is in the child's best interests.'[12]

1 *R (Axon) v The Secretary of State for Health and the Family Planning Association* [2006] 2 FLR 206.
2 At para 80.
3 Taking inspiration from Denning MR in *Hewer v Bryant* [1970] 1 QB 357, at 369.
4 *R (Axon) v The Secretary of State for Health and the Family Planning Association* [2006] 2 FLR 206, at 253
5 See para 86.
6 At para 87.
7 [2003] 1 FLR 210.
8 *R (Axon) v The Secretary of State for Health and the Family Planning Association* [2006] 2 FLR 206, at para 64.
9 At para 240.
10 See para 2.
11 At para 101.
12 At 154.

CONCLUSION

24.9 In the twenty-first century, in a society which is increasingly less paternalistic, there are strong arguments for showing greater respect for children's autonomy and permitting teenagers to make their own decisions as to matters such as contraception, informed by advice which they can access freely, without recourse to their parents. Unsurprisingly, those that oppose this development often cite the teenage pregnancy figures for England and Wales which, over many years, have been the highest in Europe. Whether the influence of the *Gillick* judgment on the rights of children to self-determination should be considered positive or negative is a matter of considerable moral debate; the authors will leave it to their readers to make up their own minds.

Index

A v Secretary of State for the Home Department **(UK)**
- conclusion, 20.5
- decision, 20.3
- effect, 20.4
- facts, 20.3
- introduction, 20.1
- legislative background, 20.2

Assisting suicide
- background, 19.2
- conclusion, 19.9
- *Debbie Purdy's* case (2008), 19.8
- *Dianne Pretty's* case (2001), 19.3—19.5
- introduction, 19.2
- legal framework, 19.2
- post-*Pretty* legal interventions and developments, 19.6—19.7

Associated Provincial Picture Houses v Wednesbury Corporation **(UK)**
- generally, 3.1—3.6

Australia
- freedom of speech
  - *Australia Capital Television Pty Ltd v The Commonwealth*, 5.3
  - conclusion, 5.8
  - introduction, 5.1
  - *Lange v Australian Broadcasting Corporation*, 5.6
  - *Nationwide News Pty Ltd v Wills*, 5.2
  - *Stephens v West Australian Newspapers Ltd*, 5.5
  - subsequent cases, 5.7
  - *Theophanous v The Herald and Weekly Times Ltd*, 5.4
- *Mabo v The State of Queensland* (Aus)
  - conclusion, 8.7
  - contemporaneous reactions, 8.5
  - facts, 8.3
  - introduction, 8.1—8.2
  - reasoning, 8.4
  - subsequent developments, 8.6
- native title, 8.1—8.7
- terra nullius, 8.1—8.7

Belmarsh **case (UK)**
- conclusion, 20.5
- decision, 20.3
- effect, 20.4

Belmarsh **case (UK)** – *cont.*
- facts, 20.3
- introduction, 20.1
- legislative background, 20.2

Bribery
- conclusion, 21.8
- *Corner House Research*
  - decision, 21.6—21.7
- El Yammah Arms sale, 21.4
- general law, 21.3
- impact of closure of investigation, 21.5
- introduction, 21.1
- law reform, 21.2

Cannibalism
- necessity, 12.1—12.9

Caparo v Dickman
- assumption of responsibility, 15.12
- conclusion, 15.14
- effect, 15.6—15.12
- facts, 15.2
- foreseeability, 15.7
- generally, 15.5
- incremental approach, 15.8
- introduction, 15.1
- 'legal celebrity', as, 15.6—15.13
- liability of professionals to non-clients, 15.11
- nature of duty of care, 15.10
- proceedings, 15.3
- proximity, 15.7
- purpose of defendant's activity or statement, 15.9
- relevant case law, 15.4
- 'threefold test', 15.7

Causes of action
- promissory estoppel, and, 10.10

Central London Property Trust Ltd v High Trees House Ltd **(UK)**
- decision, 10.3
- effect, 10.4—10.7
- facts, 10.2
- introduction, 10.1

Children
- *Gillick v West Norfolk and Wisbech AHA*
  - background, 24.2
  - effect, 24.3

Children – *cont.*
Gillick v West Norfolk and Wisbech AHA – *cont.*
generally, 24.3
subsequent developments, 24.4
medical treatment
Axon decision, 24.8
conclusion, 24.9
Gillick v West Norfolk and Wisbech AHA, 24.2—24.3
introduction, 24.1
parental responsibility, 24.5
post-*Gillick* developments, 24.4
refusal of treatment, 24.6
representation of children in proceedings, 24.7
Civil law
Caparo v Dickman
assumption of responsibility, 15.12
conclusion, 15.14
effect, 15.6—15.12
facts, 15.2
foreseeability, 15.7
generally, 15.5
incremental approach, 15.8
introduction, 15.1
'legal celebrity', as, 15.6—15.13
liability of professionals to non-clients, 15.11
nature of duty of care, 15.10
proceedings, 15.3
proximity, 15.7
purpose of defendant's activity or statement, 15.9
relevant case law, 15.4
'threefold test', 15.7
Donoghue v Stevenson
Court of Session decision, 14.6
effect, 14.10
facts, 14.2
House of Lords decision, 14.7
introduction, 14.1
legacy, 14.10
neighbour principle, 14.7
relevant product liability law, 14.3—14.4
role of *Mullen v AG Barr & Co*, 14.5
significance, 14.8
subsequent developments, 14.9
duty of care
Caparo v Dickman, 15.1—15.14
Donoghue v Stevenson, 14.1—14.10
freezing orders
background, 16.2
commercial need, 16.3
conclusion, 16.7
Civil law – *cont.*
freezing orders – *cont.*
development of principles, 16.4
introduction, 16.1
Mareva decision, 16.3
practice, in, 16.6
worldwide orders, 16.5
introduction, 14
Mareva Compania Naviera SA v International Bulkcarriers SA
background, 16.2
facts, 16.3
introduction, 16.1
subsequent developments, 16.4
Naomi Campbell v MGN Limited
background, 17.1
Court of Appeal decision, 17.3
data protection point, 17.8
European Court of Human Rights, and, 17.9
High Court decision, 17.2
House of Lords decisions, 17.4—17.7
negligence
Caparo v Dickman, 15.1—15.14
Donoghue v Stevenson, 14.1—14.10
product liability, 14.1—14.10
professional negligence, 15.1—15.14
Cohabitation
division of property, 22.1—22.11
Coke, Sir Edward
See also **Dr Bonham's case**
career and character, 1.2
Common Fisheries Policy
Factortame Ltd v Secretary of State for Transport, 4.1—4.4
Contraception
parental authority
Axon decision, 24.8
conclusion, 24.9
Gillick v West Norfolk and Wisbech AHA, 24.2—24.3
introduction, 24.1
parental responsibility, 24.5
post-*Gillick* developments, 24.4
refusal of treatment, 24.6
representation of children in proceedings, 24.7
Control orders
A v Secretary of State for the Home Department
aftermath, 20.4
generally, 20.3
conclusion, 20.5
introduction, 20.1
legislative basis, 20.2
introduction, 20

***Corner House Research* decision (UK)**
bribery, 21.6—21.7
Coroners' inquests
R (on the application of Middleton) v West Somerset Coroner
background, 18.1
coroner's inquest, 18.3
Court of Appeal decision, 18.6
facts, 18.1
House of Lords decision, 18.7
judicial review decision, 18.5
nature of right, 18.2
rule 43 letter, 18.4
Covenants over land
Cooke v Chilcott, 9.4
effect of LPA 1925, 9.8
Formby v Barker, 9.6
Haywood v Brunswick Permanent Benefit Building Society, 9.5
introduction, 9.1
Tulk v Moxhay, 9.2—9.3
Criminal law
bribery
conclusion, 21.8
Corner House Research decision, 21.6—21.7
El Yammah Arms sale, 21.4
general law, 21.3
impact of closure of investigation, 21.5
introduction, 21.1
law reform, 21.2
cannibalism, 12.1—12.9
control orders
A v Secretary of State for the Home Department, 20.3
aftermath of *A*, 20.4
conclusion, 20.5
introduction, 20.1
legislative basis, 20.2
introduction, 11
legal insanity
conclusion, 11.10
defect of reason, 11.6
disease of the mind, 11.7
introduction, 11.1
M'Naghten Rules, 11.3—11.4
M'Naghten's case, 11.2
problems with terminology, 11.9
psychiatry, and, 11.8
reforms, 11.10
'wrong', 11.5
manslaughter, 13.1—13.7
M'Naghten Rules
application, 11.4
background, 11.2
generally, 11.3
Criminal law – *cont.*
M'Naghten Rules – *cont.*
interpretation, 11.4
introduction, 11.1
necessity, 12.1—12.9
R v Dudley and Stephens, 12.1—12.9
R v Morgan
appeal against conviction, 13.4—13.5
appeal against sentence, 13.2
conclusion, 13.7
facts, 13.1
'reconciling the irreconcilable', 13.3
sentencing, 13.2
turning point, as, 13.6
Customs of the sea
survival cannibalism, 12.1—12.9
Data protection
privacy cases, and, 17.8
Defamation
Australia, in
qualified privilege, 5.1—5.8
Defect of reason
legal insanity, and, 11.6
Disease of the mind
legal insanity, and, 11.7
Division of property
Stack v Dowden
basis for decision, 22.3
cohabitation, and, 22.10
commercial properties, and, 22.9
effect, 22.11
facts, 22.2
imputing beneficial interest, 22.5
indirect contributions, 22.6
introduction, 22.1
need for simplicity, 22.4
proprietary estoppel, 22.8
quantifying shares, 22.7
Donoghue v Stevenson
Court of Session decision, 14.6
effect, 14.10
facts, 14.2
House of Lords decision, 14.7
introduction, 14.1
legacy, 14.10
neighbour principle, 14.7
relevant product liability law, 14.3—14.4
role of *Mullen v AG Barr & Co*, 14.5
significance, 14.8
subsequent developments, 14.9
***Dr Bonham's* case (UK)**
context, 1.4
effect in England and the Commonwealth, 1.5
facts, 1.3
future in England, 1.6

***Dr Bonham's* case (UK)** – *cont.*
influence in US, 1.5
introduction, 1.1
Sir Edward Coke, 1.2
***Dr Sacheverell's* trial (UK)**
generally, 6.1—6.11
Duty of care
Caparo v Dickman
assumption of responsibility, 15.12
conclusion, 15.14
effect, 15.6—15.12
facts, 15.2
foreseeability, 15.7
generally, 15.5
incremental approach, 15.8
introduction, 15.1
'legal celebrity', as, 15.6—15.13
liability of professionals to non-clients, 15.11
nature of duty of care, 15.10
proceedings, 15.3
proximity, 15.7
purpose of defendant's activity or statement, 15.9
relevant case law, 15.4
'threefold test', 15.7
Donoghue v Stevenson
Court of Session decision, 14.6
effect, 14.10
facts, 14.2
House of Lrds decision, 14.7
introduction, 14.1
legacy, 14.10
neighbour principle, 14.7
relevant product liability law, 14.3—14.4
role of *Mullen v AG Barr & Co*, 14.5
significance, 14.8
subsequent developments, 14.9
El Yammah Arms sale case
bribery, 21.4
Exercise of power
Associated Provincial Picture Houses v Wednesbury Corporation, 3.1—3.6
***Factortame Ltd v Secretary of State for Transport* (UK)**
background, 4.2
effect, 4.4
general, 4.3
introduction, 4.1
Family law
division of property
unmarried cohabitees, 22.1—22.11
financial provision
conclusion, 23.9
Family law – *cont.*
financial provision – *cont.*
contributions to the marriage, 23.2—23.7
equal sharing of income, and, 23.8
introduction, 23.1
McFarlane v McFarlane, 23.6—23.7
Miller v Miller, 23.6—23.7
White v White, 23.2—23.5
Gillick v West Norfolk and Wisbech AHA, 24.2—24.3
introduction, 22
McFarlane v McFarlane
facts, 23.6
judgment, 23.7
Miller v Miller
facts, 23.6
judgment, 23.7
parental authority
Axon decision, 24.8
conclusion, 24.9
Gillick v West Norfolk and Wisbech AHA, 24.2—24.3
introduction, 24.1
parental responsibility, 24.5
post-*Gillick* developments, 24.4
refusal of treatment, 24.6
representation of children in proceedings, 24.7
Stack v Dowden
basis for decision, 22.3
cohabitation, and, 22.10
commercial properties, and, 22.9
effect, 22.11
facts, 22.2
imputing beneficial interest, 22.5
indirect contributions, 22.6
introduction, 22.1
need for simplicity, 22.4
proprietary estoppel, 22.8
quantifying shares, 22.7
White v White
effect, 23.5
facts, 23.3
introduction, 23.2
judgment, 23.4
Financial provision on divorce
conclusion, 23.9
contributions to the marriage, 23.2—23.7
equal sharing of income, and, 23.8
introduction, 23.1
McFarlane v McFarlane
facts, 23.6
judgment, 23.7
Miller v Miller
facts, 23.6

Financial provision on divorce – *cont.*
Miller v Miller – *cont.*
judgment, 23.7
White v White
effect, 23.5
facts, 23.3
introduction, 23.2
judgment, 23.4
Freedom of speech or expression
Australia, in
Australia Capital Television Pty Ltd v The Commonwealth, 5.3
conclusion, 5.8
introduction, 5.1
Lange v Australian Broadcasting Corporation, 5.6
Nationwide News Pty Ltd v Wills, 5.2
Stephens v West Australian Newspapers Ltd, 5.5
subsequent cases, 5.7
Theophanous v The Herald and Weekly Times Ltd, 5.4
Naomi Campbell v MGN Limited
background, 17.1
Court of Appeal decision, 17.3
data protection point, 17.8
European Court of Human Rights, and, 17.9
High Court decision, 17.2
House of Lords decisions, 17.4—17.7
Freezing orders
background, 16.2
commercial need, 16.3
conclusion, 16.7
development of principles, 16.4
introduction, 16.1
Mareva decision, 16.3
practice, in, 16.6
worldwide orders, 16.5
***Gillick v West Norfolk and Wisbech AHA* (UK)**
background, 24.2
effect, 24.3
generally, 24.3
subsequent developments, 24.4
***High Trees* decision (UK)**
decision, 10.3
effect, 10.4—10.7
facts, 10.2
introduction, 10.1
Human rights
Associated Provincial Picture Houses v Wednesbury Corporation, and, 3.6
freedom of speech in Australia
Australia Capital Television Pty Ltd v The Commonwealth, 5.3
Human rights – *cont.*
freedom of speech in Australia – *cont.*
conclusion, 5.8
introduction, 5.1
Lange v Australian Broadcasting Corporation, 5.6
Nationwide News Pty Ltd v Wills, 5.2
Stephens v West Australian Newspapers Ltd, 5.5
subsequent cases, 5.7
Theophanous v The Herald and Weekly Times Ltd, 5.4
Naomi Campbell v MGN Limited
background, 17.1
Court of Appeal decision, 17.3
data protection point, 17.8
European Court of Human Rights, and, 17.9
High Court decision, 17.2
House of Lords decisions, 17.4—17.7
privacy
data protection, and, 17.8
development of right in freedom of expression cases, 17.6
Naomi Campbell v MGN Limited, 17.1—17.11
Insanity
conclusion, 11.10
defect of reason, 11.6
disease of the mind, 11.7
introduction, 11.1
M'Naghten Rules
application, 11.4
background, 11.2
generally, 11.3
interpretation, 11.4
introduction, 11.1
M'Naghten's case, 11.2
problems with terminology, 11.9
psychiatry, and, 11.8
reforms, 11.10
'wrong', 11.5
Interim relief against primary legislation
Factortame Ltd v Secretary of State for Transport, 4.1—4.4
Land law
Central London Property Trust Ltd v High Trees House Ltd
decision, 10.3
effect, 10.4—10.7
facts, 10.2
introduction, 10.1
effect of restriction of *Tulk v Moxhay*, 9.9
Foakes v Beer, 10.8—10.9
High Trees decision
decision, 10.3

Land law – *cont.*
High Trees decision – *cont.*
effect, 10.4—10.7
facts, 10.2
introduction, 10.1
introduction, 9
Law of Property Act 1925, 9.8
legislative reform, 9.10
positive obligations
Austerberry v Oldham Corporation, 9.7
effect of LPA 1925, 9.8
promissory estoppel
cause of action, as, 10.10
current status, 10.7
Foakes v Beer, 10.8—10.9
future review, 10.11
High Trees, 10.2—10.5
introduction, 10.1
source, 10.6
proprietary estoppel, 10.10
restrictive covenants
Cooke v Chilcott, 9.4
effect of LPA 1925, 9.8
Formby v Barker, 9.6
Haywood v Brunswick Permanent Benefit Building Society, 9.5
introduction, 9.1
Tulk v Moxhay, 9.2—9.3
Tulk v Moxhay
development of principle, 9.3
effect, 9.11
facts, 9.2
introduction, 9.1
subsequent developments, 9.4—9.10
Legal insanity
conclusion, 11.10
defect of reason, 11.6
disease of the mind, 11.7
introduction, 11.1
M'Naghten Rules
application, 11.4
background, 11.2
generally, 11.3
interpretation, 11.4
introduction, 11.1
M'Naghten's case, 11.2
problems with terminology, 11.9
psychiatry, and, 11.8
reforms, 11.10
'wrong', 11.5
Mabo v The State of Queensland **(Aus)**
conclusion, 8.7
contemporaneous reactions, 8.5
facts, 8.3
introduction, 8.1—8.2
reasoning, 8.4
Mabo v The State of Queensland **(Aus)** – *cont.*
subsequent developments, 8.6
Manslaughter
R v Morgan
appeal against conviction, 13.4—13.5
appeal against sentence, 13.2
conclusion, 13.7
facts, 13.1
'reconciling the irreconcilable', 13.3
sentencing, 13.2
turning point, as, 13.6
Marbury v Madison **(US)**
background, 2.2
introduction, 2.1
judges, 2.3
opinion, 2.4
Mareva Compania Naviera SA v International Bulkcarriers SA **(UK)**
background, 16.2
facts, 16.3
introduction, 16.1
subsequent developments, 16.4
Mareva injunctions
background, 16.2
commercial need, 16.3
conclusion, 16.7
development of principles, 16.4
introduction, 16.1
Mareva decision, 16.3
practice, in, 16.6
worldwide orders, 16.5
McFarlane v McFarlane **(UK)**
facts, 23.6
judgment, 23.7
Medical treatment
Gillick v West Norfolk and Wisbech AHA
background, 24.2
effect, 24.3
generally, 24.3
subsequent developments, 24.4
parental authority
Axon decision, 24.8
conclusion, 24.9
Gillick v West Norfolk and Wisbech AHA, 24.2—24.3
introduction, 24.1
parental responsibility, 24.5
post-*Gillick* developments, 24.4
refusal of treatment, 24.6
representation of children in proceedings, 24.7
Miller v Miller **(UK)**
facts, 23.6
judgment, 23.7

Misuse of private information
Naomi Campbell v MGN Limited
background, 17.1
Court of Appeal decision, 17.3
data protection point, 17.8
European Court of Human Rights, and, 17.9
High Court decision, 17.2
House of Lords decisions, 17.4—17.7
M'Naghten Rules
application, 11.4
background, 11.2
generally, 11.3
interpretation, 11.4
introduction, 11.1
Murder
necessity, 12.1—12.9
***Naomi Campbell v MGN Limited* (UK)**
background, 17.1
Court of Appeal decision, 17.3
data protection point, 17.8
European Court of Human Rights, and, 17.9
High Court decision, 17.2
House of Lords decisions, 17.4—17.7
National security
A v Secretary of State for the Home Department
conclusion, 20.5
decision, 20.3
effect, 20.4
facts, 20.3
introduction, 20.1
legislative background, 20.2
bribery
conclusion, 21.8
Corner House Research decision, 21.6—21.7
El Yammah Arms sale, 21.4
general law, 21.3
impact of closure of investigation, 21.5
introduction, 21.1
law reform, 21.2
control orders
A v Secretary of State for the Home Department, 20.3
aftermath of *A*, 20.4
conclusion, 20.5
introduction, 20.1
legislative basis, 20.2
introduction, 20
Native title
Mabo v The State of Queensland (Aus)
conclusion, 8.7
contemporaneous reactions, 8.5
facts, 8.3
Native title – *cont.*
Mabo v The State of Queensland (Aus) – *cont.*
introduction, 8.1—8.2
reasoning, 8.4
subsequent developments, 8.6
Necessity
survival cannibalism, 12.1—12.9
Negligence
Caparo v Dickman
assumption of responsibility, 15.12
conclusion, 15.14
effect, 15.6—15.12
facts, 15.2
foreseeability, 15.7
generally, 15.5
incremental approach, 15.8
introduction, 15.1
'legal celebrity', as, 15.6—15.13
liability of professionals to non-clients, 15.11
nature of duty of care, 15.10
proceedings, 15.3
proximity, 15.7
purpose of defendant's activity or statement, 15.9
relevant case law, 15.4
'threefold test', 15.7
Donoghue v Stevenson
Court of Session decision, 14.6
effect, 14.10
facts, 14.2
House of Lrds decision, 14.7
introduction, 14.1
legacy, 14.10
neighbour principle, 14.7
relevant product liability law, 14.3—14.4
role of *Mullen v AG Barr & Co*, 14.5
significance, 14.8
subsequent developments, 14.9
'Neighbour' principle
Donoghue v Stevenson, and, 14.7—14.9
Norwich Pharmacal orders
freezing orders, and, 16.7
Obedience to lawful authority
Dr Sacheverell's trial, 6.1—6.11
Parental authority
Gillick v West Norfolk and Wisbech AHA
background, 24.2
effect, 24.3
generally, 24.3
subsequent developments, 24.4
medical treatment for children
Axon decision, 24.8
conclusion, 24.9

Parental authority – *cont.*
medical treatment for children – *cont.*
Gillick v West Norfolk and Wisbech AHA, 24.2—24.3
introduction, 24.1
parental responsibility, 24.5
post-*Gillick* developments, 24.4
refusal of treatment, 24.6
representation of children in proceedings, 24.7
Positive obligations
Austerberry v Oldham Corporation, 9.7
effect of LPA 1925, 9.8
Prison suicides
Coroners Act regime, 18.10—18.14
ECHR requirement, 18.9
R (on the application of Middleton) v West Somerset Coroner
background, 18.1
coroner's inquest, 18.3
Court of Appeal decision, 18.6
facts, 18.1
House of Lords decision, 18.7
judicial review decision, 18.5
nature of right, 18.2
rule 43 letter, 18.4
statistics, 18.8
Privacy
data protection, and, 17.8
Naomi Campbell v MGN Limited
background, 17.1
Court of Appeal decision, 17.3
European Court of Human Rights, and, 17.9
High Court decision, 17.2
House of Lords decisions, 17.4—17.7
Privity of contract
negligence, and, 14.1—14.10
Product liability
Donoghue v Stevenson
Court of Session decision, 14.6
effect, 14.10
facts, 14.2
House of Lords decision, 14.7
introduction, 14.1
legacy, 14.10
neighbour principle, 14.7
relevant product liability law, 14.3—14.4
role of *Mullen v AG Barr & Co*, 14.5
significance, 14.8
subsequent developments, 14.9
Professional negligence
Caparo v Dickman
assumption of responsibility, 15.12
conclusion, 15.14
Professional negligence – *cont.*
Caparo v Dickman – *cont.*
effect, 15.6—15.12
facts, 15.2
foreseeability, 15.7
generally, 15.5
incremental approach, 15.8
introduction, 15.1
'legal celebrity', as, 15.6—15.13
liability of professionals to non-clients, 15.11
nature of duty of care, 15.10
proceedings, 15.3
proximity, 15.7
purpose of defendant's activity or statement, 15.9
relevant case law, 15.4
'threefold test', 15.7
Promissory estoppel
cause of action, as, 10.10
current status, 10.7
Foakes v Beer, 10.8—10.9
future review, 10.11
High Trees decision
decision, 10.3
effect, 10.4—10.7
facts, 10.2
introduction, 10.1
introduction, 10.1
source, 10.6
Proprietary estoppel
cause of action, as, 10.10
Psychiatry
legal insanity, and, 11.8
Public law
Associated Provincial Picture Houses v Wednesbury Corporation, 3.1—3.6
changing perspectives on constitution and courts, 1.1—1.6
Dr Bonham's case
context, 1.4
effect in England and the Commonwealth, 1.5
facts, 1.3
future in England, 1.6
influence in US, 1.5
introduction, 1.1
Sir Edward Coke, 1.2
Dr Sacheverell's trial, 6.1—6.11
Factortame Ltd v Secretary of State for Transport
background, 4.2
effect, 4.4
general, 4.3
introduction, 4.1

Public law – *cont.*
freedom of speech in Australia
Australia Capital Television Pty Ltd v The Commonwealth, 5.3
conclusion, 5.8
introduction, 5.1
Lange v Australian Broadcasting Corporation, 5.6
Nationwide News Pty Ltd v Wills, 5.2
Stephens v West Australian Newspapers Ltd, 5.5
subsequent cases, 5.7
Theophanous v The Herald and Weekly Times Ltd, 5.4
interim relief against primary legislation, 4.1—4.4
introduction, 1
Mabo v The State of Queensland (Aus)
conclusion, 8.7
contemporaneous reactions, 8.5
facts, 8.3
introduction, 8.1—8.2
reasoning, 8.4
subsequent developments, 8.6
Marbury v Madison (US)
background, 2.2
introduction, 2.1
judges, 2.3
opinion, 2.4
native title, 8.1—8.7
obedience to lawful authority, 6.1—6.11
Plessy v Ferguson (US)
background, 7.2
epilogue, 7.6
introduction, 7.1
judges, 7.3
majority opinion, 7.4
minority dissent, 7.5
racial segregation
Brown v Board of Education (US), 7.6
Plessy v Ferguson (US), 7.1—7.5
right to resist, 6.1—6.11
supremacy of the US constitution, 2.1—2.4
suspension of primary legislation by court, 4.1—4.4
terra nullius, 8.1—8.7
Qualified privilege
defamation actions, in Australia, 5.1—5.8
'Quota-hopping'
Factortame Ltd v Secretary of State for Transport, 4.2
***R v Dudley and Stephens* (UK)**
necessity, 12.1—12.9
***R v Morgan* (UK)**
appeal against conviction, 13.4—13.5
appeal against sentence, 13.2
conclusion, 13.7
facts, 13.1
'reconciling the irreconcilable', 13.3
sentencing, 13.2
turning point, as, 13.6
***R (on the application of Middleton) v West Somerset Coroner* (UK)**
background, 18.1
coroner's inquest, 18.3
Court of Appeal decision, 18.6
facts, 18.1
House of Lords decision, 18.7
judicial review decision, 18.5
nature of right, 18.2
rule 43 letter, 18.4
***R (on the application of Purdy) v DPP* (UK)**
assisting suicide, 19.8
Racial segregation
Brown v Board of Education (US), 7.6
Plessy v Ferguson (US), 7.1—7.5
Railway accidents
manslaughter, 13.1—13.7
Reasonableness
Associated Provincial Picture Houses v Wednesbury Corporation, 3.1—3.6
Restrictive covenants
Cooke v Chilcott, 9.4
effect of LPA 1925, 9.8
Formby v Barker, 9.6
Haywood v Brunswick Permanent Benefit Building Society, 9.5
introduction, 9.1
Tulk v Moxhay, 9.2—9.3
Right to life
assisting suicide
background, 19.2
concl;usion, 19.9
Debbie Purdy's case (2008), 19.8
Dianne Pretty's case (2001), 19.3—19.5
introduction, 19.2
legal framework, 19.2
post-*Pretty* legal interventions and developments, 19.6—19.7
introduction, 18
prison suicides
Coroners Act regime, 18.10—18.14
ECHR requirement, 18.9
R (on the application of Middleton) v West Somerset Coroner, 18.1—18.7
statistics, 18.8
R (on the application of Middleton) v West Somerset Coroner

Right to life – *cont.*
R (on the application of Middleton) v West Somerset Coroner – *cont.*
background, 18.1
coroner's inquest, 18.3
Court of Appeal decision, 18.6
facts, 18.1
House of Lords decision, 18.7
judicial review decision, 18.5
nature of right, 18.2
rule 43 letter, 18.4
R (on the application of Purdy) v DPP, 19.8
Right to resist authority
Dr Sacheverell's trial, 6.1—6.11
Rule of law
A v Secretary of State for the Home Department
conclusion, 20.5
decision, 20.3
effect, 20.4
facts, 20.3
introduction, 20.1
legislative background, 20.2
Search orders
freezing orders, and, 16.7
Sir Edward Coke
See also **Dr Bonham's case**
career and character, 1.2
Stack v Dowden **(UK)**
basis for decision, 22.3
cohabitation, and, 22.10
commercial properties, and, 22.9
effect, 22.11
facts, 22.2
imputing beneficial interest, 22.5
indirect contributions, 22.6
introduction, 22.1
need for simplicity, 22.4
proprietary estoppel, 22.8
quantifying shares, 22.7
Supremacy of the US constitution
Marbury v Madison, 2.1—2.4
Survival cannibalism
necessity, 12.1—12.9
Suspension of primary legislation by court
Factortame Ltd v Secretary of State for Transport, 4.1—4.4
Terra nullius
Mabo v The State of Queensland (Aus)
conclusion, 8.7
contemporaneous reactions, 8.5
facts, 8.3
Terra nullius – *cont.*
Mabo v The State of Queensland (Aus) – *cont.*
introduction, 8.1—8.2
reasoning, 8.4
subsequent developments, 8.6
Terrorism
A v Secretary of State for the Home Department
conclusion, 20.5
decision, 20.3
effect, 20.4
facts, 20.3
introduction, 20.1
legislative background, 20.2
control orders
A v Secretary of State for the Home Department, 20.3
aftermath of *A*, 20.4
conclusion, 20.5
introduction, 20.1
legislative basis, 20.2
introduction, 20
Train accidents
manslaughter, 13.1—13.7
Tulk v Moxhay **(UK)**
development of principle, 9.3
effect, 9.11
facts, 9.2
introduction, 9.1
subsequent developments, 9.4—9.10
US case law
Marbury v Madison
background, 2.2
introduction, 2.1
judges, 2.3
opinion, 2.4
Plessy v Ferguson
background, 7.2
epilogue, 7.6
introduction, 7.1
judges, 7.3
majority opinion, 7.4
minority dissent, 7.5
racial segregation, 7.1—7.6
supremacy of the US constitution, 2.1—2.4
White v White **(UK)**
effect, 23.5
facts, 23.3
introduction, 23.2
judgment, 23.4